Time and Money

The Making of Consumer Culture

Gary Cross

London and New York

£000214485 9001

First published in 1993
by Routledge
11 New Fetter Lane, London EC4P 4EE

Simultaneously published in the USA and Canada
by Routledge
29 West 35th Street, New York, NY 10001

© 1993 Gary Cross

Phototypeset by Intype, London
Printed in Great Britain by Clays Ltd, St Ives plc

British Library Cataloguing in Publication Data
Cross, Gary S.
  Time and Money: Making of Consumerist
  Modernity
  I. Title
  306.3

Library of Congress Cataloging in Publication Data
Cross, Gary S.
    Time and money : the making of consumer culture / Gary Cross.
      p. cm.
    Includes bibliographical references and index.
      1. Consumption (Economics)—History—Cross-cultural studies.
    2. Leisure—History—Cross-cultural studies.   3. Hours of labor—
    History—Cross-cultural studies.   I. Title.
    HC79.C6C76   1993
    339.4'7'09—dc20   92–28020

ISBN 0–415–07002–3   0–415–08855–0 (pbk)

Time and Money:
The Making of Consumer Culture

Gary Cross tackles one of the great conundrums of modern society: why, despite quantum leaps in technology and production methods, do we never have either enough money or enough time? He argues that in the 1920s and 1930s, advanced western societies opted for consumerism (rather than for more leisure, and a different approach to culture), creating insatiable needs which oblige us to work more than industrialism requires. In this wide-ranging analysis, he explains how consumerism prevailed over alternative uses of economic growth.

To many observers in 1920, mass production implied not endless consumption but increased time free from work. But within one generation, both dreams and fears of a leisure society had faded in a powerful cultural and institutional bias towards an ethic of work-and-spend. By charting the complex intellectual and political conflicts over the right to, and meaning of, free time, Gary Cross reveals lost options and explains why they failed. His analysis of the changing attitudes of working families towards leisure and goods offers a new way of understanding popular consumerism. In the light of recent trends, he concludes with an assessment of possible changes in the balance between consumption and free time.

Encompassing both the American and European experience, this book reveals a history neglected by both optimists and pessimists of popular culture. By linking mass consumption to changing meanings of free time, Gary Cross offers a fresh context for understanding the dilemmas of modern consumerism.

Gary Cross is Professor of History at Pennsylvania State University. He is the author of *A Quest for Time: The Reduction of Work in Britain and France, 1840–1940* and *Worktowners at Blackpool: Mass-Observation and Popular Leisure in the 1930s*.

Contents

Preface   vii

1 Modern dilemmas of time and money   1

2 The modern moral economy of needs   15

3 Barriers and bridges: cultural elites and the democratisation
   of time and money   46

4 Time becomes money: the politics of distribution and
   recovery   76

5 Democratic leisure and the failure of cultural politics   99

6 Traumas of time and money in prosperity and depression   128

7 The consumer's comfort and dream   154

8 Consumerist modernity: an end of history?   184

Notes   213
Index   287

Preface

Those who submit to the rigours of industrial work are promised time and money. These are the central scarcities of life with which we create leisure and buy things. Even if equity in sacrifice and reward are often flawed, necessity and freedom appear to be dynamically balanced. This is surely a key to what makes us modern. But time and money are unequal pleasures. Industrialism is biased toward producing goods rather than leisure: this is what usually happens when investments are made in 'labour-and-time-saving' technology. The accumulation of material wealth has reduced time to money; potential leisure is often sacrificed to work in order to earn the wherewithal to pile up still more goods. This consumerist bias has been acquired in a long historical process; but it reached its modern extreme only recently. Consumerism is not an inevitable stage in industrial development. Rather it has been a choice made within complex cultural, political, and social contexts.

This book will explore that choice and those contexts in three countries in this century. This is not a work of measurement or economic logic. Others have done this far better than I could. I attempt instead to cut across disciplines to explain consumer culture as a social decision. In order to make my case, I borrow from students of high and popular culture, economic theory, work and labour history, and mass consumption. I see the phenomenon of consumerist modernity as essentially transnational, which simultaneously, if unevenly, emerged where productivity and mass distribution were relatively advanced. The United States, Britain, and France in the years between the World Wars seemed to offer the richest evidence of the origins of the consumerist choice, even if its full implications would emerge only after World War II. I do not attempt a systematic comparison; rather I draw upon evidence from the three countries and offer analysis of similarities and contrasts when useful. Necessarily much was omitted that would have been included if this was a work that focused on a single country. This book covers much ground. It therefore must distil complex issues into simple ones in order not to lose the thread of the argument. Hopefully it does not oversimplify. This volume is a work of history, even academic history. But it is also an essay of social criticism and engagement that is continually focused on the present.

I approach this topic as if it were a foreign country in much the way that, as an American, I study European history. Like most privileged academics, free time and money for me are not exclusively compensation for the pains and sacrifice of work. They are in some degree incidental to the pleasures of the intellectual life. For this reason, it is difficult for the academic to understand the dilemmas of 'real life'. I do not even particularly enjoy leisure time and I positively hate to shop (as my family would confirm). Like many who were children in the 1950s and early 1960s, the golden age of American consumerism, I was fascinated and frustrated by the social imperatives of goods. The fact that my family was one of the less affluent on the block, and thus less able to participate in the consumer society, only heightened my interest in the phenomenon. And from my mother, Shirley Cross Tupper, an artist and teacher, I absorbed a critical awareness of that consumer culture. While, at times, I surely was tempted to join those who simply condemned mass consumption, neither my family nor my experiences in late 1960s allowed me to do so. I emerged from those 'troubled' times as an unrepentant, if critical, populist. My training as a labour historian led me to reject unqualified attacks on the 'masses' and their culture. But it made me also think about the impact of work on that culture and how women and men coped. Responsibility for what modern society has made of its affluence is shared by intellectuals, not merely the working 'masses' and the merchandisers. In this way of thinking, I suspect that I share much with those who are now reassessing the history and meaning of popular culture and mass consumerism.

However, I come at the topic from the back door, so to speak. In the 1980s, I was absorbed with understanding labour's struggle for freedom from work and how this quest related to complex political and economic changes. But I found that I could comprehend the limits and meaning of free time and leisure only if I looked at their twins and sometimes alternatives, money and consumption. Most of those nineteenth- and early twentieth century reformers who dreamed of a progressive liberation from work did not expect a consumer society. Its emergence and the failure of a culture less dependent upon goods and work cannot be taken for granted. If we do, we deny ourselves the possibility of choice and the liberty of contemporary history. In this period when ideological choice has been so dramatically narrowed with the collapse of state economies, it may be fruitful to reassess historic alternatives within the market system. A central choice has been and is between cultures of free time and money.

A project like this would have been impossible without the assistance of people with widely different interests and area specialties. Conversations with John Walton, John Lowerson, Dan LeMahieu, and Steven Gelber have helped me through knotty problems in the history of leisure and popular culture. In different ways sociologists of leisure Stanley Parker, Geoffrey Godbey, Robert Stebbins, Richard Butsch, and Alan Tomlinson have led me to sources and ideas. Ellen Furlough and James Obelkovich have lent aid with their expertise as historians of consumption in France and Britain. Historians Herrick Chapman, Lizabeth Cohen, Michael Miller, James Cronin, Michael Seidman, and Robert Frost have also provided information and sources. Benjamin Hunnicutt, Ronald Edsforth, and Juliet Schor shared their promising research in the labour history and economic analysis of worktime. Their comments on chapters were much appreciated as were the readings of Ellen Furlough, Victoria de Grazia, Dan LeMahieu, Nancy Love, Alan Sica, Greg Whitwell, and Robert Proctor. Victoria de Grazia and her seminar on comparative consumer history at the Center for Historical Analysis at Rutgers University provided valuable criticism of this project. Cultural historian Anson Rabinbach has been especially encouraging. And, I greatly value those long telephone conversations with Benjamin Hunnicutt, during which we shared our common interest in the history of free time. I wish to thank also Charles Ameringer and Gary Gallagher who greased the administrative gears to give me the time and money to complete this project. Thanks are due to the editor of *Journal of Contemporary History* (London) for permission to reproduce part of chapter 5 which appeared in earlier form as: 'Vacations for All: The Leisure Question in the Era of the Popular Front', *Journal of Contemporary History*, 24 (1989): 599–621. Finally, this project was supported by a generous grant from the German Marshall Fund of the United States.

And, as always, my thanks go to Maru Cross for everything else.

1 Modern dilemmas of time and money

Time and money are the great scarcities of modern life. Most of us complain that we have not enough of one and perhaps of either. Despite the 'time is money' culture of modern production, few of us experience either a sufficiency or comfortable balance of the two. American and European families continue to feel this scarcity despite the fact that many in the middle class may possess cluttered two-car garages or enjoy multiple vacations per year. The dilemma of the less affluent is expressed recently by an American working mother: 'time is my biggest problem right now. Before I went back to work, money was. So you have time or money. Those are the two choices in life.'[1] For the frustrated middle class, at least, an industry of experts in time and personal-goods management stands ready to offer help in coping with hurry and clutter.

But how do we account for this ironic sense of scarcity in the midst of plenty? The well-known dynamics of social emulation explain our discomfort when we find that our possessions often pale in comparison with those of others.[2] But goods also create scarcities of time: prosperity has intensified the problem of 'budgeting' the day, not only in the 'making' of money, but in its spending in so far as goods and their use saturate our 'free time'. We have become both a 'harried' leisure and working class, frustrated by the demands of consumption on our time and obliged to labour more than we would like to earn the means to consume. Time has become money in both work and 'after hours'. We experience a scarcity of both goods and leisure. But ultimately the problem is that we lack time free from working and spending.[3]

There is much evidence of this. Economist Juliet Schor has recently showed that Americans work an average of a month more per year in 1987 than they did in 1969.[4] Many two-income couples, especially those unable to purchase personal services, have experienced a 'domestic speedup' when the traditional realms of personal life – family care and leisure – are crammed into shorter periods of the week. Naturally, people adapt to this change by a vast array of shortcuts – eating out far more, a return to catalogue shopping, greater tolerance of messy houses, daycare centres for fewer children, and or even rejection of family life altogether.[5]

Yet we seldom notice the irony in that productivity has led to increased consumption but not to a parallel growth of free time. While some commentators (even politicians) have regretted the time famine which has spread with the two-income family, few make the obvious linkage between worktime and the dominant culture of consumption. An effective solution to the problem of balancing time and money may well require collective action. But contemporary policy and cultural languages offer few tools to articulate this need. Central to the contemporary frustration of scarcity in prosperity is the loss of these languages.[6]

Paralleling these contradictions of everyday life is the apparent narrowing of social and political options. By the late 1980s, the industrial world seemed to face a poverty of choice between capitalist consumerism and socialist scarcity. The collapse of communism is a surprising conclusion to a century which began with widespread doubts about the ability of capitalism to manufacture or distribute goods. With the advent of mass-production capitalism in the early decades of the twentieth century, the western world turned toward two increasingly integrated trajectories: 'Fordist' mass-consumption and an arms race accelerated twice by general war and, since 1945, by cold war. Both unquestioningly assumed that technological innovation produced endless growth and more work. Other options, based on a balance of material security and social enrichment – and centred on the progressive liberation of time from obligation – have repeatedly been dismissed. In a world of international competition and consensus in favour of limitless economic expansion, these alternatives appeared to be naive or even elitist. The final demise of European communism appears to have produced an unqualified victory for Fordism – market-generated mass production. The West did not win so much with its guns as with its butter. Nevertheless the traditional threat of economic competition continues to lash nations to the wheel of work in a 'post-Fordist' world economy. At the same time, the promise of limitless goods seems to shape ideas of freedom and equality almost everywhere.

Still, some of us are sceptical about predictions that we have reached the 'end of history,' remembering similar proclamations of an 'end of ideology' in the past.[7] And, beneath the surface smugness of capitalist triumphalism is an uneasiness about the apparent lack of real alternatives. This feeling is deepened by the awareness that Americans especially have not planned for a demilitarised economy and may have no way out of a political economy of debt-driven consumption with disastrous moral, economic, and ecological effects. Nor has this victorious socio-economic order produced a satisfying balance of money and time.

The decline of political and ideological alternatives parallel personal frustration at the absorption of life with work and consumption. What is clearly missing is an understanding of the possibilities of the democratisation of leisure. By this, I mean two things: a balance of work with time free from economic obligation and forms of leisure that provide the widest possible choice, access, and participation. I do not suggest that time totally liberated from work is either possible or desirable; nor do I argue that leisure completely beyond the market is even conceivable in an efficient economy (even though public, as opposed to commercial, forms of leisure have an untested democratic potential). The essential irrationality that I am exploring is the relative insignificance of non-economic, self-initiated activities in a society that is laudably productive.

In the generation after World War I, these possibilities were widely discussed and, in limited ways, even practised. In the interwar years, people from every rank and persuasion believed that industrial productivity, symbolised by Ford's assembly lines and the munitions factories of World War I, was about to realise an historic dream – the satiation of human physical needs. This, in turn, would necessarily lead to greater time free from work and create new opportunities for organising public leisure. Advocates of reduced worktime claimed a share of productivity in successful movements for an eight-hour workday and paid holiday leaves as rights of industrial citizenship; some went on to propose a progressive disengagement from the pains of work for a society built around personal autonomy and renewed social solidarities in leisure. Of course, this was not the only option for distributing affluence. Others counselled an industrial policy of 'high wages', mass marketing, and state-sanctioned income redistribution, in hopes of creating a popular consumer's sovereignty. Without doubt, cultural and economic conservatives abhorred the democratisation of both time and money. But the idea of time partially free from work had an influence that has largely disappeared today.

This book is about how and why these democratic ideas about

time failed by mid-century, how that defeat is related to the emergence of mass-consumer society in the US and western Europe, and
how that history has affected trends since 1945 and current prospects for a new balance of time and money. In sum, this book
seeks to throw light on why we experience scarcities of time (and
money) in the midst of plenty.

This is not a simple story. I insist that the contemporary distribution of time and money is not a *natural* allocation of work, rest,
and material need: there is no physiological or psychological optimal
workday and workyear, which once reached, need not be further
reduced. Nor is there necessarily an unlimited demand for goods,
which, once the optimum worktime is achieved, is free to be
expressed to the boundaries of productivity. This division is not
simply a market response to the demand for maximising leisure and
wages as is assumed by many economists. It is not even a 'Fordist
compromise' between capital and labour to the crisis of early
twentieth-century capitalism. Ford's concession of a 'high wage'/
40-hour workweek may have helped to balance mass-production
work with mass consumption. It may have won wage-earners to
steady work to pay for their constantly expanding consumer needs,
thus providing capitalists with disciplined workers and reliable markets. But none of this was inevitable, universal, or permanent. The
way in which we allocate growth between time and money was a
product of a more complex and contingent historical process.

I also resist the temptation to blame the 'failure' of the free-time
option (or the victory of mass consumerism) on a collective fall
from grace or a betrayal of ideals. Clearly modern consumer culture
cannot be understood as merely the 'enemy' that murdered 'time'
by creating 'false' needs through modern manipulative advertising.
Indeed, origins of the consumer society have been found in quite
different contexts over a long period – from the Dutch 'embarrassment of riches' in the seventeenth century to the American 'Gospel
of Abundance' in the twentieth century.[8] Recent histories of the
'consumer revolution' have illuminated changing attitudes toward
goods, especially as they affected the middle and upper classes.
They correct the still common belief that consumer culture is merely
the product of twentieth-century merchandisers.

Nevertheless it is still difficult to discard an underlying corollary
– that there was a time when the 'people' were free from the 'social
control' of improvers or impresarios of pleasure who produced
consumer culture.[9] But as historian G. Stedman Jones notes, the
'authentic' popular culture of one period is the commercialism of

an earlier era.[10] I too am sceptical that there were ever any 'good old days'. Even if powerful conservative and privileged classes stood in the way of alternatives to consumer society, I do not assume a conspiracy. In fact, this transformation was very complex, influenced as much by conflicts and ambiguities among the advocates of free time as by the power and persuasion of their opponents.

The scholarly study of the interactions between producers and users of goods has produced valuable insights into the consumer society.[11] But I take a very different road. I stress how the consumer society was linked to uses and meanings of time. The triumph of consumerism meant a rejection of the progressive reduction of worktime and of 'democratic leisure'. It realised instead the dominance of a work-and-spend culture.[12] This culture was the culmination of historic choices made within, but also outside, the market in the complexities of intellectual, political and social life. And consumer culture had as much to do with work as with spending. To explain the linkages between consumerism and the modern allocation of work and free time is to understand our 'Fordist-consumer' society as more than a logical solution to the problem of distribution in a mass-production economy or even the remaking of the worker into a reliable consumer. Rather, out of a multi-layered history consumer culture emerged in the often unacknowledged social decision to direct industrial innovation toward producing unlimited quantities of goods rather than leisure. This 'decision' meant a culture of work and spend. And time was transformed into money on and off the job.

Obviously we must begin with definitions: both 'time' and 'money' have many meanings even as equivalents of leisure and spending. Nuances in their usage play a major role in this book. Indeed these two concepts converge in commercial entertainment. But it is helpful to define the 'frontier' meanings of this couplet: 'time' as 'leisure' can be understood as duration free from both income-producing work and from consumption. 'Money' as 'consumerism' may be defined as the quest for 'non-essential' goods which requires time at work that is relatively undiminished by increased productivity and which reduces time available for non-market activities. These meanings have the great advantage of relating 'time' to 'money'. Still there are many problems with such definitions: the 'non-economic time' of women homemakers remains unrecognised; the problem of how to define 'essentials' is left unanswered; and the possibility of social life unmediated by goods is assumed, but not demonstrated. But these meanings frame the terms of the debate over time and money in the interwar years, and thus cannot be avoided in this essentially historical work. They help clarify the centrality of conflict between leisure and consumption in the interwar years. Even more important, because these meanings of time and money were part of the thinking of advocates of democratic leisure, they help explain why these movements had such a disappointing history. They help explain why the opposition of time and money has largely collapsed into an identity in consumer culture.

My intention is not to offer a historical phenomenology of the diverse meanings of time and money in the twentieth century. I make no *systematic* effort to explain their significance across the boundaries of class, gender, or nationality. Instead I focus on the *waged* worker who has been directly affected by increased productivity and the politics of its distribution. In this century, waged work has increasingly become a more common status. But, between the World Wars, the period of my central concern, work for pay was a lifelong experience *primarily* of male providers, even though many single women held jobs and during and after World War II married women would begin to enter the workforce in large numbers. This, of course, did not mean that the waged workers' understanding of the dilemmas of time and money were not affected by those largely outside the labour market. In my period of analysis especially, they were dependent upon the domestic and consumption work of women. Wage-earners' decisions were also shaped by the economic decisions and consumer behaviour of capitalists and their families. And, of course, intellectual and political elites played major roles in framing and frustrating workers' expectations. In later chapters, gender will enter more centrally into my argument about modern allocations of work and leisure. This book focuses on wage-earners but it cannot ignore other groups.

An appropriate place to analyse the potential and fate of these options is in the capitalist democracies between the World Wars. This book will be drawn from the experience of Britain, France, and the United States. I will make no attempt at systematically comparing these three countries; but I will refer to their experiences when sources allow and as appropriate for the advance of my argument. I selected these countries because they shared much with, but also differed greatly from, each other. I stress the interaction and simultaneous development of ideas, movements, and social trends on both sides of the Atlantic. While the precocious productivity of the US obviously played an important and even predominant role, the American experience was neither unique, nor an all-powerful influence or model. The 'Americanisation' of Europe is sometimes a misleading notion because the British and French took their own paths toward the consumer society. Moreover, different patterns of economic performance, class stratification, intellectual tradition, and political mobilisation produced contrasting responses to the problems of time and money in these countries. In the 1930s, for example, France was embroiled in bitter political conflict over the reduction of worktime, the US found a commercial Keynesian solution to the 'threat of leisure', and Britain was mired in stalemate over the same issue. These political and cultural differences have contributed to noticeably distinct solutions to the problems of democratising free time today. There is little doubt that the culture of work and spend is more dominant in the U.S. in the early 1990s than it is in western Europe. My task is to offer both an international and comparative history, not as an intellectual exercise, but in order to elucidate a complex argument about how work- and free time relate to the origins of mass-consumer culture.

TIME AND MONEY: FROM OPPOSITION TO CONVERGENCE

Early in this century, mass-production technology seemed to promise endless quantities of goods. Average purchasing power of Americans rose 40 per cent between 1910 and 1929; even more important, increasingly larger shares of it were devoted to new consumer durables, especially automobiles.[13] Advertisers helped to create new needs and the instalment plan made luxuries accessible at least to white-collar and skilled workers. Europeans looked enviously upon the American 'people of plenty'. But, in many ways, British and even French shared in the dream, and sometimes even the reality, of this new age of consumerism.[14] It is hardly surprising that mass production seemed to offer the possibilities of mass distribution. This promise suggested that economic equilibrium depended upon high wages that rose with productivity.

What is less well understood today was the common assumption in 1920 that free time, not the endless increase of consumption, was the inevitable consequence of growth. This, many believed, would create a mass leisure society – even as it undermined the work ethic. Indeed participants in this discussion were divided between those who favoured this future and those who feared it. Still most assumed limited needs, and thus a progressive reduction of worktime. The practically universal demand for the eight-hour day (i.e., 48 hour workweek) immediately after World War I seemed to prove the argument. Not only consumer goods but free time were to flow from increased productivity.

Both economists and productivity-minded reformers expected that growth brought expanded free time. This assumption became the rationale for the demand of trade unionists and socialists that more intense and productive work justified shorter durations of labour. In 1932, American trade unions seriously advocated a 30-hour workweek while their European counterparts pushed for a 40-hour standard. Indeed, when the Depression in the 1930s brought unemployment, organised labour's explanation was that increased productivity in the 1920s had not been balanced by reduced worktime. Thus, instead of waged leisure, many workers experienced impoverished idleness. At the heart of these movements for a shorter workweek lay the assumption of limited needs.

At the same time, faith that growth would continue to liberate time from work provided the essential rationale for 'democratic leisure': these were efforts to organise public culture and recreation outside the manipulative environments of the market and partisan politics. A disparate group of liberals and social democrats on both sides of the Atlantic attempted to create, for example, a voluntary and decentralised system of holiday camps, discussion groups, and sports clubs. A central concern was to regain in free time the social integration lost in urban mass-production society. Even more, advocates conceived of democratic leisure as an extension of social citizenship – an expansion of the right to time free from work and an opportunity for personal participation outside the compulsion of the market and hierarchy of productive enterprise. In western Europe, at least, the holiday with pay became a symbol of a social solidarity to be realised in leisure beyond the control of the market and the state. Productivity in both prosperity and depression seemed logically to require the reduction of worktime and a democratic organisation of leisure.

Although it is far more difficult to document, there is also evidence that the rank and file shared this perspective on leisure. Working people's interest in free time (as opposed to merely higher wages) was intermittent and almost always intertwined with concerns for job security and income. But, in the interwar years, the bias toward money was usually defensive rather than animated by the lure of consumer goods – even if there were important exceptions. The phenomenon of 'moonlighting' came later and, I believe, has been misunderstood by many observers. Rather, in the interwar years, the whip of job and wage insecurity and the absence of a viable organised alternative seems to have dampened a longing for free time. Part of the proof is in the enthusiasm with which working people embraced additional leisure time when it became available in 1919 with the coming of the eight-hour day.

These ideas, movements, and social trends, however, suffered nearly total defeat mid-century. It is hardly a coincidence that this failure corresponded to the full flowering of mass-consumer culture and the collapse of time into money. Why did this occur? An obvious explanation is that, while economic growth appeared to liberate free time, that same productivity created an affluence that proved to lash wage-earners to jobs and the income that work provided. But it is essential to recognise that this occurred only within the contingencies and conflicts of early twentieth-century industrial democracies.

In the 1920s, elites were positively disturbed by the idea of liberating more time from work. The commitment of intellectuals to the democratisation of free time was ambiguous at best. Both social scientists and humanists (who often differed on the benefits of industrialism) were uneasy about the social implications of mass production: the assembly line undermined work incentives by reducing the necessity of long hours to meet basic needs; it also eroded cultural standards by potentially giving the 'masses' time and access to cultural goods.

In the interwar years, many orthodox social scientists found a solution to their anxiety in the discovery that economic growth could discipline labour; mass productivity need not subordinate consumption to leisure. Rather, if growth was linked to higher wages, the resulting increased demand for goods could unlock the limit on needs. This, in turn, would chain the wage-earner to a steady, even greater, duration of work necessary in order to earn the income to purchase those new goods. The key was the realisation that psychological needs were not finite as were most physiological needs. During the Depression, many social scientists saw growth in output as the progressive alternative to the 'stagnation' of reduced workdays and the demoralisation of the idle. The tapping of new and unlimited needs (through Keynesianism especially) not only overcame the threat to the work ethic but guaranteed growth. This new thinking had a profound impact on public policy that continues to the present.

For most humanists, there were no such satisfactory solutions to the problem of 'democratic time'. Mass culture led the protectors of high culture either to self-imposed isolation or to the difficult task of 'uplifting' mass taste. Even among populist intellectuals, the gap between elite and popular tastes made impossible a positive discourse of democratic free time. The result has been the cultural jeremiad that continues to underlie much thinking about consumer culture. Most intellectuals attempted to separate the ideas and practices of 'true' leisure from consumerism; but these efforts may well have only contributed to the convergence of free time and spending in mass culture. The wall between high and popular culture was raised higher and the practical possibilities of a broadly based cultural alternative to the market nearly disappeared. After the war, the only effective alternative to the jeremiahs against mass culture were the apologists of economic growth; and, especially in the U.S., the dream of a democratic leisure beyond the limits of consumer sovereignty largely dropped from public discourse.

Indeed, by 1950, the literature on consumerism had largely split into the non-debate between 'practical' optimists of modernisation and 'humanistic' pessimists of modernity. Growth in consumption became the measure of progress to economists and politicians, while the content of this democracy of goods was usually condemned by cultural critics. What both groups shared was a new belief that growth meant endless expansion of consumption but not a parallel extension of free time. As a result, the historical 'balance' of time and money – a fixed eight-hour day and seemingly endless growth of consumption – was embedded in the 'two cultures' as natural or inevitable.[15] The result has been the inability of contemporary people to think concretely about the balance of labour and leisure.

But the victory of the culture of work and spend goes far beyond the failure of intellectual leadership. Economic and political constraints also shaped the legitimation of mass consumerism. The quest for time was dominant in collective consciousness across the industrial world (and beyond) in 1919 with the coming of the eight-hour day. Yet it depended on the extraordinary confluence of national and international political pressures to overcome the normal bias against free time. Even though capital resisted both a reduction of worktime and higher wages, it had special reasons for rejecting free time. When employers lost access to unlimited hours of their employees, they felt deprived of a 'right' to flexible production. Reduced hours threatening to place a limit on output, growth, and profit. And competition increased employer resistance.[16] Moreover, wage-earners usually shared this bias against time. Especially between 1920 and 1950, inflation, global competition, and job insecurity increased work discipline and acceptance of overtime. A job, no matter the conditions and hours, was the difference between self-respect and humiliation. The Depression and the post-1945 effort to catch up with deferred consumption further tilted the worker toward money.

Short-hour movements in the Depression were widespread and powerful. But their objectives were not only to share work (and leisure) but to increase spending. Reduced worktime was to encourage mass consumption by raising wages and to offer weekend and holiday 'packages' of time available for spending. American workers accepted the New Deal's public works and the idea of 'full-time' work as a practical alternative to the revolutionary idea of a six-hour day. Public works and other forms of government spending created jobs. Around this goal of 'full employment' and 'full consumption' a shaky American political consensus was built. Moreover, international competition (and the destruction of the German labour movement) made inevitable the failure of the French experiment with the 40-hour week in the late 1930s. The reduction of worktime, like many improvements in the labour standard, required international cooperation. Worktime reformism in 'one country' has worked no better than has communism in a global market economy. These defeats signalled the end of the ideology of the progressive reduction of worktime and the emergence of a political consensus around a democracy of goods. This did not end the dream of weekend leisure or the holiday with pay. But these periods of time free from work were increasingly devoted to consumption and thus were constrained by demands for income-producing work.

Movements for 'democratic leisure' suffered a similar defeat. Their advocates, of course, lacked the resources of their commercial and totalitarian rivals; but, even more important, they were frustrated by an abiding misunderstanding about what time and money meant to working people: movements for democratic leisure surely underestimated the strength and flexibility of consumer capitalism. By mid-century, a consumerism that brought, not commitment and purpose, but private pleasure, dominated free time.

Well-meaning advocates of a more democratic public culture often ignored the appeals of popular consumerism and were hampered by a utopian understanding of free time. They did not fully recognise that, for wage-earners, money was a compensation for increasing degradation of work. On this point, business leaders were sometimes more insightful. Ford understood this principle when he nearly doubled the wages of production workers in the 'Five-Dollar Day' of 1914. But during the crisis of the Depression, when the deprivation of the jobless paralleled the affluence of others, the psychological need for consumer goods grew in intensity. As historian Thomas Hine points out, the 'excess' of post-1945 mass consumption in the US becomes intelligible as a social-psychological response to the intense experience of *relative* scarcity of the 1930s and war years.[17] Domestic consumption was part of a complex, largely female, culture of respectability. And the ability to participate in a fraternity of casual consumption with fellow workmates was part of the male's identity. Poverty in the Depression meant denial of access to the 'guest table' of consumer ritual. In this context, the real community was not in work or politics, but the promenade of consumer pleasure.[18] At the same time, joblessness during the Depression diminished the value of what many (mostly male) providers experienced as 'empty' time. Unemployment also reinforced the ideology of work as the organising principle of personality and society. Gender roles were similarly reconfirmed (at least for another generation) in the male ideal as provider and the female status as domestic consumer.

Advocates of democratic leisure did not understand that the consumer culture met real needs of social identity and individual distinction in a society where primary groups had largely disappeared. The utopian idea of a culture of free time beyond the market could not satisfy those needs nearly as effectively as could the consumer culture. Spending on the home and for commercial holidays provided nearly ideal ways of both conforming and being distinctive. And they were far less threatening than were intellectuals' pleas that working people join study groups or holiday fellowships. Domestic spending during weekends and tourist consumption during annual vacations would combine spending and leisure. Even if this was the experience of relatively few working people in the 1930s, these patterns formed the cultural groundwork for the reconciliation of money and time. The consumer comforts of weekends at home and the dreamlike affluence of holiday-making would eventually create a fullness of time realised in the fullness of spending.

Whatever may have been the motivation of merchandisers, we are not obliged to posit a conspiratorial theory of social control to understand the subversion of the 'real needs' of the masses. The consumerist bias was constructed within the specific constraints of the early twentieth century. The result was not only that workers were lashed to the wheel of work but that the broader society became biased toward market pleasure rather than the politics of leisure. My point is not that a consensus around mass consumerism was inevitable. It was not simply the culmination of the anti-democratic biases of the intelligentsia, the political power of capital, or the social and cultural subordination of workers. Such deterministic approaches have dominated thinking about mass society especially since the 1940s.[19] This literature, I believe, lets us all off too easily by blaming human nature, technology, hegemonic capitalism, or the 'masses' for the disappointing cultural results of post-scarcity.

I share much with anthropological approaches that seek to understand consumerism as a social and psychological construct rather than to posit theories of elite 'social control'. But I am wary of the tendency of this literature to neglect difficult historical questions about what conditioned those popular choices.[20] Instead my objective is to understand how this specific consumer culture emerged by mid-century. It is to uncover the complexity of the origins of that culture in the contingency of ideas, decisions, and behaviours. It is to insert consumerism into the context of the debate over time and money and of an emerging culture of work and spend.

As important, I am not convinced that the reduction of time to money is a *fait accompli* or is irreversible. As I argue in the final chapter, the history of leisure and consumer culture since 1945 does not point simply to an unambiguous victory of a work and spend ethic. Rather a postwar generation of triumphant consumerism has yielded to more ambivalent attitudes toward time and money since about 1970. Europeans, at least, have succeeded in distributing some of their productivity to free time and even the aspirations of the earlier advocates of democratic leisure have not vanished. Indeed there are some signs of their revival. Despite the enormous intellectual, political, and social pressures bolstering a work/consume culture, alternative ideas and actions presented in this book may possibly have a future as well as a history.

The past points not merely to 'lost possibilities' but to the historical contingency of our lived world and thus the freedom to change. This history reveals the need for a fresh understanding of the appeals of consumption, beyond both the condemnations of the cultural jeremiah and the tunnel vision of the output-driven economist. The alternatives over how to use the benefits of productivity were more clear in the formative years of the mass-consumer culture – even if the conditions for making such choices were not fortuitous. This is not to pose a radical split between time and money. In fact, during the interwar years, one could have been both an advocate of economic progress and also have been a supporter of a community free from the *dominance* of commodities. Indeed the two ideas were inextricably linked in the minds of many. What has declined is a sense of balance between the two and the idea that free time is the fruit of growth.

Most important, this history suggests the difficulties inherent in reaching a new balance of time and money. The last decade of this century may be a period for new choices, especially for alternatives long submerged by the Cold War. Early in the century, the advent of mass production created major debates about the future of democracy and the possibility of a 'cultural society'[21] based on those 'naive' notions of social balance and demilitarisation. At the core of these ideas was the belief that the solution to the historic problem of scarcity was at hand and that mechanised societies could begin a progressive democratic disengagement from the pain of work and create an unprecedented leisure society. Underlying various proposals was a belief in the possibility of economic efficiency without economic dominance, of life-fulfilling leisure without unchecked hedonism, and of distributive justice grounded not only in high wages but in choice in the use of free time. These notions were surely utopian – and that was part of their failure; but they pointed also to possibilities neglected after 1945. Their failure was less due to the machinations of advertisers or the cultural degradation resulting from the deskilling of work no matter how important these factors were. Rather the key problem was essentially political – the extremely difficult struggle to define democracy in everyday life and the problems of forming an alternative to capitalist consumption or socialist austerity as the social meaning of that democracy.

The only way we can effectively explore the history of this struggle is to reject the assumption of the 'end of history', be it expressed either as free market triumphalism or the cultural jeremiad. Most of all, we must direct ourselves to the historian's 'prophetic' function of drawing new meaning out of the past and new possibilities for the present. In that history, we may find some of our lost options, how and why they declined, and perhaps in what forms they may be recovered.

2 The modern moral economy of needs

One week after the armistice ending World War I, David Lloyd George admitted: 'it is not a question of whether the men can stand the strain of a longer day, but that the working class is entitled to the same sort of leisure as the middle class'. World War I, added John Maynard Keynes in 1919, 'has disclosed the possibility of consumption to all and the vanity of abstinence to many'. Clearly, the new productivity challenged the nineteenth century's bleak prediction that the working classes were forever enslaved to long hours of work and the 'iron law of wages'. And the traditional discipline of hunger and fear, noted R. H. Tawney in 1920, no longer sufficed to ensure efficiency. The democratisation of time and money seemed an imperative of social peace, economic stability, and even growth.[1]

In the interwar period, the mass-production economy promised both time and money. In the US, at least, the 1920s produced a 'people of plenty' (if we ignore the unskilled labouring classes) with an ever widening access to automobiles and other consumer durables. And Europeans looked longingly upon that land which held the 'secret of high wages'.[2] But, according to the Briton John Hammond (1933), mass production was also producing an era of 'Common Enjoyment'. Soon leisure rather than work would be the core of personal experience for all.[3]

But to many observers, mass productivity seemed to threaten work discipline and growth with its promise of 'high wages' and free time. To cultural conservatives, high wages undermined cultural standards with the invasion of the mass market. To most employers, prosperity meant an erosion of the incentive to work, with the attendant disruptions of absenteeism, high turnover rates, and demands for shorter working hours and vacations. In 1926,

American John Edgerton, president of the National Association of Manufacturers, expresses these fears very clearly:

> it is time for America to awake from its dream that an eternal holiday is a natural fruit of material prosperity. . . . I am for everything that will make work happier but against everything that will further subordinate its importance . . . the emphasis should be put on work – more work and better work, instead of upon leisure.[4]

What is striking about this debate is that both optimists like Hammond and pessimists like Edgerton shared a common perspective: the new productivity meant sated needs and thus a reduced willingness of wage-earners to commit time to wage labour. The demand for leisure was unlimited while the quest for goods was relatively finite (even if prone to false wants). And, for most intellectuals in the interwar years, this prospect was greeted more with fear and loathing rather than with hope for the democratisation of time and money.

What is even more impressive is how completely wrong these assumptions proved to be. That which emerged was not an age of leisure (either to the good or bad), but a culture of work and spend. This chapter will explore how social scientists and policy makers gradually abandoned these theories and discovered the possibilities of limitless work and consumption. Chapter 3 will consider the largely negative response of humanists to the democratisation of time and money and how this ultimately retarded the emergence of an alternative to work-and-spend in a democratic leisure culture.

LEGACY OF POLITICAL ECONOMY: TIME AND NEEDS IN DYNAMIC SOCIETY

For social scientists and policy makers in the interwar years, mass productivity produced the economic and moral dilemmas of leisure and consumer need. Free time and mass access to goods were problematic because of an ideological legacy that had roots that went back at least to the beginnings of industrialisation in the eighteenth century. That intellectual heritage retarded the emergence of the modern doctrines of unlimited consumer need and the normalcy of 'full-time' work. We need to explore these ideas with some care to make sense of the ambiguities of early twentieth-century intellectuals toward mass consumption and leisure.

A dream of the Enlightenment was to liberate time from the

necessity of work and to force the physical world to meet consumer needs. But many eighteenth-century political economists also worried that prosperity would reduce the willingness of labourers to sacrifice time for work. Authors, like Arthur Young and Nicholas Edmund Restif de la Bretonne, assumed that the motivation to work declined with higher wages; the demand for leisure would increase with the meeting of basic needs.[5] As often noted, other eighteenth-century economists rejected this classical notion of 'natural needs' when they argued that emulative desire, made possible with increased luxury, would spur additional effort. Still influential, however, was the stoic distinction between natural needs and those unnatural wants which seemed to undermine community and rational use of free time. Thus, to most Enlightenment thinkers, general affluence and extensive freedom from work were as much moral problems as they were economic benefits. For some, prosperity undermined work effort and created the anarchy of undisciplined time; for others, it multiplied need and produced a work-driven society based on 'false needs'.[6]

Rousseau provided one solution to these dilemmas in his critique of the multiplication of needs. Misery, he claimed, came not from deprivation but from the need for things. His 'republic' was an alternative to the endless expansion of the market; he offered a timeless community of self-sufficiency and self-imposed simplicity. David Hume suggested a second solution: he justified emulation as the only means of assuring economic progress. But his antidote to unrestrained vanity was the traditional stoic hero of self-control and fulfilment. The difficulty, of course, was that, while the Republic distorted life by repressing need, few individuals could, with Hume, combine hedonism and self-control.[7] The conflict between emulation and personal integrity could be overcome with the bourgeois ideal of early retirement from business (of which Benjamin Franklin is an exemplar), a strategy that divided time for money-making from a retirement of 'true leisure'. But this hardly guaranteed a life of contemplation or even disinterested service.[8]

The mid-nineteenth century offered a third broad solution to the problem of the linkage between free time and needs satiation and creation. An alternative to collectivist stoicism and individualist moderation was the progressive surmounting of scarcity and a shift toward a democratic culture in leisure. This perspective rejected both earlier assumptions, that prosperity either undermined work discipline or led to false needs. While classical economists despaired at the prospect of 'diminishing returns', J. S. Mill looked hopefully to a 'stationary state' where economic growth and ceaseless economic striving would end with the realisation of abundance. Universal participation in work and population constraint would allow a new leisure society where a learned class of educators could counteract the egoistic commercial spirit. Instead, time could be devoted to non-economic pursuits and social solidarity. This affluence would allow greater autonomy and participation of workers in cultural and political life; it would foster the growth of cooperatives; and it would lead to the decline of personal service. Affluence led to democratic leisure.[9]

Marx, like Mill, rejected the utopian primitivism of Rousseau and dreamed of a society of abundance created by capitalist productivity. Marx also expected prosperity to be coupled with the reduction of worktime for the self-discovery of authentic needs. The end of capitalism would eliminate the profit-driven creation of false needs and assure the realisation of sufficiency with the minimum of effort. Apparently Marx required no educator for the people to find their authentic culture. Still Marx shared with Mill's liberalism a dream of a society of limited and fulfilled needs.[10]

This differs little from the perspective of the American Edward Bellamy. In the utopia, *Looking Backward, 2000–1887*, mechanisation and equitable distribution would not only reduce worktime but elevate desire for non-economic pursuits. Work would become merely a 'necessary duty to be discharged before we can fully devote ourselves to the higher exercise of our faculties, the intellectual and spiritual enjoyments and pursuits which alone mean life'.[11]

A fourth solution to the problem of time and money was presented by John Ruskin. He rejected the striving for abundance for the presentist motto of 'there is no wealth but life'. The socialist Paul Lafargue agreed when he denounced, in his *The Right to be Lazy* (1880), 'the right to work'. A fixation on jobs produced unnatural material waste for the rich and dependency and oppression for the labourer. The right to life beyond work was the only solution to the Promethean drive for compressing time and accumulating goods.[12]

All four of these approaches were only theoretical responses to the possibilities of abundance. Significantly, their advocates often assumed the social predominance of a bourgeoisie that practised self-constraint. The long debate over material needs and leisure in industrial society are largely encompassed by these four alternatives. But the beginnings of a mass market in the last quarter of the nineteenth century raised the dilemmas of affluence to a new level.

The democratisation of goods seemed to swamp high culture with the untrained taste of the crowd. It also promised to intensify both competition and conformism in the pursuit of luxury.

Theory about consumer needs turned on familiar themes. The modern fear of unleashed mass appetites may have dated from the sumptuary laws of the fifteenth century. But it survived in the writings of the turn-of-the-century French economist Anatole Leroy-Beaulieu, the philosopher Louis Weber, and the sociologist Emile Durkheim. Their antidotes to mass consumption were social controls on luxury, exemplary asceticism, and social religion. In England, the social investigations of Booth and Rowntree shared a similar perspective on the pathologies of wasteful consumption of the urban underclass.[13]

By contrast, the American economist, Thorstein Veblen (1857–1929) in his classic of 1899, *The Theory of the Leisure Class*, rejected the double standard that condemned the excessive spending of the poor, but justified it in the rich as a stimulus to economic growth. Instead, he rooted waste in the 'leisure class' who set the standards for those below: 'members of each stratum accept as their ideal of decency the scheme of life in vogue in the next higher stratum'. This led the poor to squander their meagre resources. But these standards ultimately emanated from the desire of the few to display pecuniary prowess through their ability to avoid work and to consume in a conspicuous manner. The resulting excessive consumption, Veblen noted later, always threatened to absorb any surplus created by the ethic of 'workmanship'. The act of spending became increasingly more arduous in so far as society became more mobile and more urban: enhanced social interaction guaranteed greater opportunity of imitation and 'invidious comparison'. Mass consumption, Veblen suggested, led not to an egalitarian community of goods-holders but to a new intensity of competition and social isolation. Higher culture was reduced to an 'insignia of honor', reserved for the wealthy. Veblen confronted an old American concern: the conflict between the work ethic and the fruits of prosperity. And Veblen sided with the work ethic; he reduced consumption to a cultural contradiction – a threat to, rather than the fulfilment of, work.[14]

Waste in elite consumption was a pervasive theme of late nineteenth-century thinkers. Paul Lafargue favoured reducing working hours in order to eliminate the servant class and conspicuous consumers. The American feminist Charlotte Perkins Gilman made a similar point in her critique of the wastefulness of housewifery: she insisted that domestic functions be socialised and that women enter the labour force.[15] Both perspectives reflected a traditional critique of 'false' consumption.

Other writers, following the tradition of J. S. Mill, offered more positive assessments of the emerging mass age of plenty even if they continued to recognise a distinction between natural needs and unnatural wants. In 1907, the American economist Simon Patten held that working-class drunkenness, gluttony, and other forms of dysfunctional consumption were merely a cultural hangover: this behaviour conformed to an earlier period of scarcity and industrial disorder.[16] These pathologies, Patten argued, could be overcome if society adjusted to the emerging abundance. Essential to this change was a broader access to a variety of goods, consumer education, and social services (supported by progressive taxes). Patten rejected the traditional moralising of the wealthy against the improvident poor. 'Vice', he argued, 'must first be fought by welfare, not by restraint.' This thinking was similar to new approaches to alcoholism in Europe: the solution to drunkenness was access to 'higher' pleasures, not prohibition. And, like many of his generation, Patten despaired that work, increasingly rationalised by management and mechanisation, could be the principle organiser of personality. Instead, the excitement of vaudeville or the playground were to release the latent vitality of the working classes, too long repressed in unfulfilling work. This vitality would allow the people to seek higher cultural aspirations (even share with the middle class in the joys of a 'return to nature'). It would provide new powers of self-constraint. Moreover, 'the satiety of primitive desires which follows increased income, urges men to displace crude individual gratifications with grouped pleasures' of church, home, and community.[17] Patten was not defending consumerism as a vehicle of growth for its own sake or for job creation (as would become common in the twentieth century). Rather affluence for him was a means of raising cultural standards.

We should not be surprised that Americans were precocious in the positive discovery of abundance. But French and British theorists shared in this thinking. The French economist Charles Gide (1847–1932) agreed that abundance brought cultural refinement. But he also stressed the need for consumer education and cooperative control over distribution. Consumption, he argued, was not automatically regulated by the competition of producers seeking to satisfy individual buyers, but required social and political regulation. In stages, he hoped, consumer cooperatives could gain control over national production.[18] Still, Gide's objective was not to establish a rigid distinction between needs and luxury; he recognised that the latter became the former with economic growth. Beyond obvious rejection of consumption detrimental to health, Gide established a utilitarian guideline by asking 'whether the amount of wealth and labour that is devoted to [a luxury] is not likely to reduce the amount that should be reserved for other more immediate wants' of society as a whole.[19] Like Patten, Gide defended affluence without embracing unlimited consumerism.

The heterodox French sociologist, Jean Gabriel Tarde (1843–1904), went further: he rejected the preaching of either rational consumption (Gide) or constraint (Durkheim and Weber). Instead Tarde argued that a mass-goods society arose from the inevitable 'imitation' by the urbanised masses of the 'models' of a creative class of 'inventors'. Consumerist modernity meant the shift from a 'diversity of space for the diversity of time': instead of custom and the local fulfilment of periodic needs (e.g., in festivals), the modern economy was producing a national market which regularly met needs that frequently changed. Tarde agreed with Veblen that mass consumption originated, not in utility, but in common envy and the desire to buy the life-style of a trend-setting urban elite. But, unlike Veblen, Tarde claimed that this process led to a widening of the 'magic circle' of 'invention' through 'reciprocal imitation'. The trickle down of fashion could be reversed in a trickle up. While mechanisation might lead to the 'disassociation of men' (as Durkheim insisted), for Tarde this was not troubling because work no longer was the basis of social harmony. Rather these bonds depended on the interaction of consumers – the 'further exchange of examples'. This exchange not only universalised consumption styles, but created a cultural democracy constructed around the interaction of the elite and the masses. Moreover, 'after a period of capricious changes . . . usages might become fixed' as the masses learned to discriminate between consumer goods (with the help of education and 'moral inventors'). Tarde confidently predicted that people would seek the 'interior luxury' of spiritual goods when their physical needs were sated and when they discovered that the desires of ambition and emulation were frustrating, and thus, unworthy of pursuit. Tarde's optimism was boundless: in an incomplete utopian novel, he envisaged a future generation which would be forced to abandon material goods (because of a new ice age) and to live underground in a nearly goods-free world of sociability. There finally the society based on an 'exchange of services' would be replaced by a perfect society based on the 'exchange of reflections'. Ironically, the materialism of mass consumption would lead to its opposite – intellectual 'salons more beautiful than those of Versailles'. The ideal was the democratisation of the glorified social practice of the French elite.[20]

Out of a very different tradition of English utilitarianism, John Hobson (1858–1940) reached similar conclusions. Progressive taxation would reduce conspicuous leisure and the 'illth' of consumption stimulated by profit rather than utility. He even proposed that routine work be shared by all so that 'prestige' would be 'undermined' and thus a natural or 'rational standard' of consumption would be encouraged. Despite his optimism, Hobson had to admit the difficulty of defining utility in consumption: the chance for 'errors' and waste grew in so far as organic or biological needs were met and new desires and fads increasingly competed for the consumer's pocketbook. Nevertheless, he persisted in advocating regulation of 'harmful' consumption, consumer education, and faith in ordinary people.[21]

Even the orthodox economist, Alfred Marshall (1842–1924), shared this optimistic, if ambiguous, perspective. His *Principles of Economics* rejected as a 'half truth' Veblen's stress on 'cravings for distinction as driving demand beyond necessaries'. Instead, when basic needs were met, Marshall insisted, people would desire higher mental and physical activities. Prosperity would produce 'a growing desire for those amusements, such as athletic games and travelling, which develop activities rather than indulge any sensuous cravings'. Early twentieth-century decreases in liquor consumption, argued Marshall, were proof of 'more care and judgement in expenditures and to an avoidance of food and drink that gratify the appetite but afford no strength'. The lower classes would imitate, not only the inferior desire for 'distinction' so characteristic of the rich, but also the superior goal of 'excellence'. The educator, assumed to come from the upper class, became the guarantor of this optimistic appraisal of affluence.[22]

The debate over the democratisation of free time largely paralleled the discussion about consumption. Of course, the traditional identification of workers' leisure with opportunity for improvident spending and an erosion of the work ethic survived into the twentieth century.[23] In his *Theory of the Leisure Class*, Veblen equated free time with social waste and habits of inefficiency. Leisure was not the surplus of time (and money) to be enjoyed after biological needs had been satisfied (as implied by Mill). Rather for Veblen, leisure was mostly the wasteful display of social status which undermined efficient production. Leisure divided people rather than unified them. While free time might allow communion with nature and charity, the isolation of the leisure class (especially women) from production led only to a waste of resources. Later Veblen, following Rousseau, concluded that the only antidote to the frustration and decadence of status seeking in leisure was the 'simple life'.[24] Veblen's romantic invocation of austerity may have been an influential antidote to the irrationalities of the late nineteenth century leisure class, but it discounted the social potential of recreation. Because Veblen identified leisure with primitive displays of prowess, he could offer little guidance for leisure in a productive society. Veblen's thought obscured any positive linkage between production and free time and thereby privileged the values of work.[25]

Veblen's impact was very clearly seen in Lorine Pruette's *Women and Leisure. A Study of Social Waste* (1924). She found no solution to the problem of housewives becoming free from time-consuming domestic work other than a new devotion to work. The problem of gender inequality could be overcome if 'women had more work like men'. 'Useless leisure' of the housewife was part of an archaic system of 'planned waste associated with artificially instituted changes in fashion'. Pruette advocated the shift of women from the semi-skilled and inefficient work of homemaking where 'women . . . work for nothing' to paid employment outside the home. Pruette's contemporary, the conservative domestic economist Christine Frederick, also advocated domestic efficiency; but she did not seek the 'freeing' of women from unpaid housework. Still her proscription for leisure was vague where Pruette's was negative. Frederick merely advocated time for 'outside interests'. This fear of leisure and inability to give it positive definition was characteristic of much thinking about free time in the early twentieth century.[26]

Not all, of course, shared this anxiety. Those who had a positive attitude to leisure seemed to value it above mass consumption as a fruit of industry. Patten, for example, saw in free time the only possibility of forming community and character, given the alienating effects of the division of labour. Leisure did not necessarily involve consumption. Instead Patten stressed the need to revive folk traditions. As historian Daniel Horowitz notes, 'By opposing possessions but not passions, Patten could stand against materialism without continuing to emphasise restraints.'[27]

Tarde envisioned a three-hour workday while Hobson and Marshall argued that productivity should be allocated substantially toward free time. Hobson was satisfied that 'a very slender harvest of happy thoughts and feelings will justify much apparent idleness'.[28] Marshall advocated in his *Future of the Working Class* two six-hour shifts and, for especially fatiguing work, three four-hour stints. His ideal world was a place where 'no one in it should have any occupation which tends to make him anything else than a gentleman' – a status which required freedom from work. While, from the 1880s, he combated the job-sharing argument of short-hours advocates, in *Principles of Economics*, he noted that

> the coming generation is interested in the rescue of men, and still more women, from excessive work, at least as much as it is in handing down to it of a good stock of material wealth. . . . It is true that fewer know how to use their leisure well than know how to work effectively, [but] it is only through freedom to use leisure as they will that people can learn to use leisure well.[29]

The debate over consumption and leisure turned on attitudes toward democratisation and the capacity of elites to control it. But all of these authors shared a common perspective. Whatever may have been their feelings about mass consumption or free time, they assumed a distinction between true needs and false wants and expected a progressive expansion of free time. What distinguished them was how they assessed the potential of the 'educator' in shaping a mass culture of goods and leisure and the possibilities of realising in free time the individuality and community that was destroyed in a bureaucratised world of work. They projected their contrasting convictions upon the future, either in a utopia of met needs and cultural fulfilment or in a dystopia of false wants run amok under the leadership of a leisure class. Soon, however, the assumption that one could distinguish between needs and wants would be eroded and, with it, the intellectual possibility of a stationary state economy or leisure society.

ENDLESS ABUNDANCE AND THE BIAS OF MONEY OVER TIME

Both the positive and negative assessments of mass consumption and leisure rested on the distinction of true needs and false wants. But economists gradually abandoned this perspective as they slowly discovered that needs were not only unlimited but relative. If the desire for goods was not to be sated, then the demand for time free from wage work was problematic. One early theorist, even advocate, of limitless consumption was George Gunton (1845–1919), an English immigrant to the US and, in his early years, a publicist for American labour's goal of an eight-hour day. In his book, *Wealth and Progress* (1887), he developed a demand-side theory of economic growth, arguing that development depended not on profit but high wages and working-class consumption. Gunton identified the spending 'opportunities' of the 'most expensive' workers with the cutting edge of economic growth. While he insisted that these consumer moments required increased leisure, spending actually limited the demand for free time and increased the willingness to work. New wants induced workers into having 'such a conscious need for an object that its absence will cause sufficient pain to induce the effort and sacrifice necessary to its attainment'.[30]

Lujo Brentano, an influential European economist, shared the view that higher wages stimulated not only mass consumption but productivity. Employers, he claimed in 1894, no longer needed to maintain long hours or low pay in order to assure a profitable output – a traditional view of economists and employers. Rather advanced consumer needs, developed in leisure time, would motivate labour to work harder, not less. Leisure then posed no threat to productivity; instead, the prospect of unlimited consumption checked the growth of leisure. Not only did this view refute the backbending labour supply curve, but it abandoned the classical distinction between true and false needs. Consumption could be identified with civilisation and progress, with an upward spiral of work and spending.[31] These doctrines laid the intellectual foundations for a bias toward money *and* work over free time. This was more than a reformulation of the Enlightenment's justification of luxury for the rich as a stimulus for economic growth. It was a rationale for mass consumerism and, with it, the discipline of work.

Still, economists were reluctant to embrace the hedonistic implications of Gunton's doctrines. Marginal utility economics well illustrates this ambiguity. Marginalism, developed in the 1870s by the Briton W. Stanley Jevons and the French Léon Walras, and much later, by the American John Bates Clark, broke from classical economic theory at many points. Marginalism replaced production with consumption as the starting point of economics. Marginalists also began their analyses with the individual rather than historically determined classes, thus avoiding the presumption of social conflict.

But more important here, marginalists defined value in terms of subjective utility which varied relative to the satisfaction of competing scarce goods. This led to the abandonment of the classical distinction between real and false needs. There were no necessary ceilings on the quantity of goods which could be subjectively desired. While, of course, there was a limited demand for any *one* good (which diminished with each additional or marginal unit), that decrease was relative to demand for still other goods. Goods had value not because of their intrinsic qualities (or their embodied labour time) but because they were scarce relative to other goods. Economic rationality was reduced to the maximisation of choice between subjective preferences along an endless 'continuum of desire'; in turn, this eliminated the possibility of a stationary state economy where all 'true needs' would be satisfied and non-economic pursuits could take charge.[32]

To be sure, the concept of true needs reappeared in the hierarchy of desires rediscovered by Jevons and Marshall and charted by the consumer economist, Ernst Engel in his famous curve. With the satisfaction of 'lower' desires, utility shifted from basic biological needs to higher, less immediate, ones. Still, there was no theoretical limit to the needs engendered by the movement from the 'organic' economy (physical needs that eventually were sated) to a 'social' economy based on emulation. Marginalism's calculus of subjective preferences provided no moral or logical defence against endlessly expanding consumption. Marginalists had no economic argument against the intrusion of the market into activities where tradition or non-economic relations had previously prevailed. 'Economizing rationality' left no room for 'value rationality', as political theorist Nicholas Xenos recently noted. Marginal utility and its empirical refinements gained hegemony especially in the Anglo-American academy by the 1920s. With it came the logic of endless growth and a rejection of the distinction between true and false needs.[33]

Still the implications of this logic would not be fully developed until well after World War I. This, I think, was for two reasons: first, the marginalist theory of 'two-goods maximising' tended to reinforce expectations that prosperity would lead to reduced demand for goods and increased motivation for free time. This, at least, implicitly revived the traditional needs distinction. Prosperity meant the shift in the value of 'goods', in this case, from income to time, in so far as the marginal utility of the next unit of money decreased relative to a unit of free time. Jevons associated diminutions of worktime with changes in workers' income, not as most

labour intellectuals argued, with changes in the intensity or productivity of work. Higher hourly wages produced not the incentive
to work longer but to work less: 'Artisans, mill hands, and others
[even merchants, Jevons notes] generally, seemed to prefer greater
ease to greater wealth, thus proving that the degree of utility [of
consumables] varies more rapidly than the degree of painfulness of
labour.'[34] In other words, the democratisation of prosperity would
lead to mass disengagement from work. This both saved the back-
ward-bending labour supply curve and implied the stationary state
economy. Most important it undermined the idea of limitless consumption.

A second impediment to the logic of endlessly expanding needs
was the fact that economists retained moral assumptions that were
disconnected from theory. We have already seen this in that orthodox marginalist, Alfred Marshall. As economist Fred Hirsch notes,
early twentieth-century economists found rational the pursuit of
'individualistic economic satisfactions' but only within an implicit
'paternalistic enlightened framework' of a moral limit to needs.
Hirsch notes that John Maynard Keynes (1931) assumed the existence of a moral hierarchy that militated against a 'mercantile
populism' of undifferentiated needs. Keynes believed that the
satisfaction of absolute needs may allow us to 'devote our further
energies to non-economic purposes'. He recognised that

> man [then] will be faced with his real, his permanent problem –
> how to use his freedom from pressing economic cares, how to
> occupy the leisure, which science and compound interest will
> have won for him, to live wisely and agreeably, and well.

He looked forward to 'three-hour shifts or a fifteen-hour week'.
Like Mill, Keynes expected that the new leaders were not to be
the 'money makers' but 'those peoples who can keep alive, and
cultivate into fuller perfection, the art of life itself'.[35]

The two-goods maximising theory and a 'paternalistic enlightened
framework' shielded social scientists from the hedonistic implications of marginalism. But, more important still, these two
concepts were central to how elites responded to the democratisation
of time and money after World War I. The essential ambiguity of
classical political economy survived in social science. Prosperity
meant more than a high-wage economy: it raised the question of
whether affluence undermined or realised higher cultural standards;
and, because high wages seemed to lead to the progressive diminution of worktime, prosperity led to a debate over whether leisure

was an opportunity or threat. From both vantages, money and time appeared to empower rather than discipline the workforce. For some, like Keynes, an enlightened minority could teach the rest of us in the 'art of life'. But for others, this democratisation undermined growth and social order. Yet, by the 1930s, most social scientists had abandoned the assumptions upon which these debates were based: in the process emerged an economics biased toward work and consumption.

PRODUCTIVITY AND PLENTITUDE IN THE EARLY TWENTIETH CENTURY

In 1900, almost everyone shared a common view that prosperity would release wage-earners from work discipline. For proponents of a linkage between productivity and plenitude, mass industrialism meant a new citizenship of leisure and goods that would usher in an age of permanent social peace. Growth meant *both* material comfort and free time because market needs were satiable. Yet not only did business resist this vision of mass distribution (especially of free time), but progressive advocates of industrial democracy were themselves ambiguous about the shift of social values from work to leisure and consumption.[36] Only a revolution in thinking about the fruits of productivity would resolve these conflicts and ambiguities.

Since the 1880s, industrial productivity and its fair distribution were goals of social democrats and progressives on both sides of the Atlantic. The view of traditional liberals that productivity flowed from fear of want was gradually displaced by a social liberalism that conceived of growth as emanating from the scientific deployment of trained manual labour and managerial organisation. Accordingly, optimal output was governed by psycho-physical limits, i.e., fatigue. Thus efficiency was possible only with improved working conditions and especially shorter hours of labour. As important, a plenitude of goods and leisure was to flow from science. While challenged by revolutionary socialists and syndicalists for its reformist and bureaucratic implications, this broad productivist doctrine gained hegemony on the left by the end of World War I. And with it came an uneasy detente between organised labour and many efficiency reformers.[37]

This is more than a little ironic considering the well-known feud between scientific management and labour which peaked just before the war. As many have documented, Frederick Taylor and his disciples in the US and France attacked 'soldiering' or restriction of output when they attempted to control the pace and methods of production: time study was to determine optimal output while motion study was to institute the 'one best way' of work.[38] Labour responded forcefully to this threat to its skill and autonomy. In 1911, Samuel Gompers of the American Federation of Labor (AFL) condemned Taylor's time-study men for 'making every man merely a cog . . . in a big machine . . . with no need to employ more than a few mechanical motions'.[39] In 1913, French trade unionist Emile Pouget claimed that motion studies 'stifled the ingenuity of the worker'. Meanwhile, in Britain, few employers embraced scientific management before or even after World War I, and British workers were equally antagonistic to any mechanisation that threatened skill and employment.[40]

But the social conflict, sparked by productivity innovations, greatly abated during World War I when trade union leaders were brought into contact with managers on war production boards. After 1918, the efficiency of war production served as a model both of the possibilities of distribution and of social harmony.[41] But, even before the war, both industrial engineers and trade unionists were edging toward a less confrontational approach. In response to the opposition of American shipyard workers to his methods in 1912, Frederick Taylor claimed his system would usher in a 'mental revolution' by ending class conflict in the factory. Scientific management would increase 'the size of the surplus until the surplus became so large that it was unnecessary to quarrel over how it should be divided'.[42] Of course, Taylor's 'mental revolution' was simply management's promise of higher wages and shorter hours in exchange for labour's ceding control over production. Yet, by shifting from the microcosm of conflict between the stopwatch man and the worker, to the macro-level of economic progress, Taylor diffused his reputation as an enemy of labour and helped to set the stage for compromise.[43] Indeed, Taylor's 'mental revolution' became the basic rationale for the eight-hour day that was won in western Europe and in many American industries immediately after World War I (see chapter 4).

As early as 1908, Taylor's disciple Morris Cooke used this reinterpretation of scientific management to justify a new status for industrial engineers. Instead of serving big business, the engineer could become an expert adviser to industrial democracy and an enabler of growth. This idea resurfaced in 1916 in Henry Gantt's group of radical engineers, the 'New Machine', and, in 1932, in

Howard Scott's Technocracy Inc.[44] Prominent American liberals like John Dewey, Rexford Tugwell, Paul Douglas, Stuart Chase, and George Soule embraced technocratic ideas of 'rational production' in the interwar years.[45]

In their dream of harmony and plenty against the divisive and wasteful 'predators' of business, radical American engineers were even willing to ally with labour. In 1920, Morris Cooke (in a volume jointly edited with Samuel Gompers) stressed that industrial engineers should join with leaders of a 'new unionism' to raise productivity, increase wages, and reduce worktime. The Taylor Society, long hostile to the output restrictions of workers and unions, published conciliatory remarks by William Green, Gompers' successor, in support of the new technology.[46] In 1928, Rexford Tugwell argued that if American industry were to cut 'down the hours of men involved [in highly rationalised industry] to six or to four . . . , the increased product would enable us to maintain as high or higher wages'.[47]

Optimism that innovation could yield increased fruit were well founded in the US. While industrial productivity per American worker increased only 7.5 per cent between 1899 and 1914, it increased 37 per cent between 1919 and 1926, a rate that astonished contemporaries. Even the establishment figure of Herbert Hoover believed that such gains warranted an eight-hour day in basic steel and that shorter hours would raise both productivity and welfare. Inefficiency, he claimed, was primarily the responsibility of thoughtless management, a conclusion that American labour embraced as ammunition in their ongoing battle with employers over long hours and low pay.[48]

Of course, talk of an alliance between engineers and labour was brief, emanating from vastly different ideological and status concerns. And the principal goal of progressive productivism – the distribution of free time and higher wages – was largely a failure after the postwar gain of the eight-hour day in many industries.[49] Productivism was a complex product of cooperation between managers and trade unionists in the war, a more conciliatory view by engineers toward the 'human factor', and organised labour's need for allies in the anti-union climate of open shops and company unions in the 1920s.[50] Nevertheless, productivism was a controlling idea that guided the American and European debate over time and money in this period.

Labour's attitudes toward productivity, of course, were ambivalent. Workers were often slow to embrace the trade-off of increased productivity for shorter hours and higher wages. Improved output per worker often led to output restriction and resistance to innovation whenever jobs seemed to be threatened. Americans often associate this behaviour with Europeans: among the French, it was called economic Malthusianism and among the British, ca'canny.[51] But Americans also engaged in what Whiting Williams in 1925 called 'taking easy' in response to the 'paralyzing fear of the bread line'.[52] Parts of the American labour movement in the early 1920s associated increased productivity with technological unemployment and some even advocated the 40-hour week, not as a fruit of growth, but as a means of defending jobs.[53]

By 1925, however, American labour began to reject the linkage between productivity and joblessness. Instead, the AFL formally embraced industrial rationalisation as a way to raise wages and make possible the cultural benefit of increased leisure. The AFL Convention of 1925 declared:

> We hold that the best interests of wage earners as well as the whole social group are served [by] increasing production . . . and by high wage standards which assure sustained purchasing power to the workers. . . . Social inequality, industrial instability and injustice must increase unless the worker's real wages . . . is advanced in proportion to man's increasing power of production.

The AFL Convention insisted that shorter hours were also to be the fruit of productivity. Labour writers supported the 40-hour week, not as a means of preserving jobs or raising wages, but primarily as compensation for and release from the psychic effects of the advanced division of labour. Advocates of productivity, however, tended to stress the potential for high wages which, according to one union official, 'must stand upon its own feet'. A new orthodoxy had emerged: increased output per worker could alone raise wages. This (at least temporarily) replaced an older doctrine – that workers' share of income would increase if working hours were shortened because this would make labour scarce and thus more expensive. The new demand for a wage that rose with productivity had little impact on bargaining and largely disappeared from discussion during the Depression. But it became the foundation for acquiescence to managerial innovation and probably set the stage for the priority of higher wages over shorter hours. Nevertheless, until after World War II, American labour leaders continued to envisage a balance of leisure and consumer power as fruits of mass productivity.[54]

American readers may recognise these ideas as peculiar to their own 'exceptional' development. After all, the productivity movement was often named after two Americans, Taylor and Ford; and the corporatist practices of the AFL have often been contrasted to the class consciousness of European labour relations. Nevertheless, while Europeans did take a cue from Americans, they had their own largely indigenous productivity-reform movements. Rather than rehearse their complex histories, let me offer a few influential examples of western European patterns.

The wartime productivity of British industry prompted a dream of postwar prosperity. Lord Leverhulme's *The Six Hour Day* (1918) was perhaps as influential in Britain as was Taylor's 'mental revolution' in the US. This British manufacturer offered a vision of 'a symmetrically and proportionately increased' economic pie. A key to the solution to social conflict was a six-hour day in two or three shifts, a scheme that would both eliminate fatigue (and increase leisure) as well as maximise the use of machines.[55] In 1920, moderate British trade unionists similarly linked productivity to leisure time and mass consumerism.

Encouraged by the gain of the eight-hour day in 1919, Tom Mann and others endorsed Leverhulme's six-hour day and government-sponsored fatigue research. Worktime reductions, high wages, and industrial efficiency were inextricably linked.[56] During their reassessment of policy following the disastrous coal miners' strike of 1926, the British Trades Union Congress (TUC) joined the productivity movement which was sweeping Europe and America. Echoing American trends, the TUC's 'Memo on Technological Unemployment' (1928), refuted the fear that technology was creating unemployment. Instead joblessness was caused by lack of innovation which made British goods uncompetitive. Technology alone made possible a policy of 'high wages', which, in turn, would expand markets and create new jobs. At the same time, the TUC reflected the new reluctance of their American counterparts to pair time and money. Its memo pointedly did not recommend further reduction of the workday which, the TUC feared, might cause 'additional overhead charges' and 'hinder the movement of labour from a stationary or declining industry to an expanding one'.[57]

Even more in France, technocratic intellectuals and trade unions argued that efficiencies in management and production would allow a reduction in the workday and increases in wages. During the war, the socialist minister of munitions Albert Thomas had supported Taylorism as a blueprint for higher productivity in peace time.[58] In

1919, his reformist allies in the General Confederation of Labour (CGT) attempted to create alliances between technicians, labour groups, and consumers.[59] In the 1920s, the non-communist European left became a major advocate of industrial innovations. The objective was not only to increase the economic pie but to preserve the eight-hour day, a standard that was under nearly continuous attack from employers throughout the decade. Improved productivity, even scientific management, they argued, should remove any need to raise hours or lower wages in order to compensate for increased competition.[60] About the same time as the AFL was linking wages and labour output, the reformist CGT issued a 'Manifesto on Productivity' (October 1926). While denouncing innovation that made workers redundant or 'interchangeable', it applauded the potential of a productivity wage and lower-priced goods.[61] Like the CGT, the communist unions demanded that the benefits of increased productivity be shared by those workers who were forced to submit to more intense production.[62]

The emphasis on the linkage between productivity and the democracy of time and money may seem ironic: in the 1920s, there was practically no decline in worktime anywhere in the industrial world and the productivity wage was not the basis of labour negotiating.[63] Most commentators on this would-be alliance between the productivity movement and labour have stressed its corporatist and reformist implications in a period of retreat for organised workers.[64] But the appeal of a productivity-based wage and workday went beyond reformism. It reflected an effort to translate traditional notions about the value of labour into a mass-production age. That worth could no longer be expressed in a defence of craft skills, a fact recognised by most thoughtful labour leaders just before World War I. But, in the new context of mass production, labour's value could have meaning in the distribution of the fruits of *collective* effort in free time and money – and that worth increased in proportion to the intensity of labour. In this way, the technocrat's promise to labour was more than a compromise of principle. It represented a democratic and relatively balanced distribution of time and money.

LIMITS TO INDUSTRIAL DEMOCRACY

The productivist vision of shared fruits of leisure and goods depended upon three factors: an effective alliance of labour and humanistic engineers; an ability to find an alternative to the traditional work ethic; and the cooperation of business and policy makers. All three conditions, however, failed to be realised.

First, the alliance of labour and technocracy was fragile. It hardly assured a united front based on the idea of a linkage of productivity with a balanced allocation of leisure and high wages. Labour's attitude toward productivism remained ambivalent: not only did unions fear job and skill loss but, as bargaining agents, they had no reason to agree, even theoretically, to a ceiling on 'high wages'. Thus they had no clear doctrine of limited needs. This undermined their commitment to increased leisure. There remained great differences between organised labour and even the most sympathetic of its technocratic allies. Radical technocrats shared little of labour's concerns with working conditions and skill. Reformist engineers, for example, embraced the notion of combining increased free time with 24-hour utilisation of machines and other resources which few workers willingly accepted.[65] And with their social distance from the economic bargaining system, such intellectuals were able to honour a traditional ethic of limited needs.

The classical distinction between real needs and false wants was preserved in the American technocratic concern with eliminating the waste created by the capitalist market. Veblen was echoed in Stuart Chase's faith that when the engineering principles of 'order, discipline, and the consciousness of definite social aim' were established, 'wasteful' production would be eliminated and with the new efficiency 'four to six hours of work a day' would become the norm.[66] Engineer Arthur Dahlberg concluded that industrial efficiency would improve if business had access to *less* worktime.[67] Central to this analysis was the traditional assumption that the 'real' demand for goods decreased when biological needs were met. This natural process was frustrated when worktime did not decrease with innovation; in this 'irrational' situation, business would use its additional profits to create 'useless goods'. Dahlberg contended that the 'work ethic', by distorting 'efficiency' with needlessly long working days, was creating a culture dominated by frivolous consumption.[68] Finally Lewis Mumford in his well-known *Technics and Civilization* (1934) argued that productivity rose only with the 'reduction of trivial and degrading forms of work' and the 'elimination of production that has no real social use'. He argued that we must 'normalize consumption'.[69]

These three examples of technological optimism began with a doctrine of limited needs to advocate an ideal balance of goods and leisure. It is hardly surprising that labour leaders did not embrace this approach when we consider the material standards of wage-earners in that period. But this division between technocratic intellectuals and labour frustrated an alliance for the democratisation of time and money.

Even more problematic was the persistence of traditional attitudes toward work. In the 1920s, most trade unionists and technocrats affirmed innovation as the vehicle of leisure and plenty. Those defenders of craft work who had attacked Taylorism before 1914 had largely disappeared by 1918.[70] But few technocrats or labour leaders would concede that a democracy of free time and goods could replace work as the organising principle of personality and community. This, like the subtle divisions between labour and technocrats, impeded the realisation of the democratic implications of productivism.

American technocrats in the Veblen tradition insisted that a new culture of production should be developed as a counterweight against consumption life styles even when they advocated four- or six-hour workdays. Tugwell admitted, albeit from a traditional male perspective, that the trouble was that

> our social groups are consuming groups. . . . [W]e have almost completely divorced our producing lives from our consuming lives. At home and among our friends we have no approval for our productive efforts, and so our neighbors, and, tragically, our very wives and children come to estimate us according to our incomes. . . . [F]or the old morality of service, of workmanship, and of pride in skill, there is substituted the morality of display.

Against 'consumptive spectacles' Tugwell could only insist that we must change 'in the direction of making production more spectacular; of setting up measures of productive efficiency; of making it seem virtuous and worthy of approval to be productive'.[71]

Trade unionists shared this same inability to conceive of a society based outside the workplace. They too groped for productive spectacles. In the AFL, William Green followed Gompers by embracing the new technocratic values of 'service, the promotion of efficiency and elimination of waste'.[72] British trade unionist F. J. Maynard insisted that workers must abandon the old traditions of the individualistic skilled labour and understand that 'team work can be as enjoyable'.[73]

French machinist Hyacinthe Dubreuil shared a similar view as a propagandist for Fordism.[74] Following a lengthy tour of American factories arranged by Albert Thomas in 1927, Dubreuil wrote a series of well-received books advocating a new workplace 'democracy'. He praised the 'scientifically-run' American factory as an alternative to French 'discord and class war'. Industrial engineers should create a 'moral atmosphere' in the factory using the 'same technology that destroyed it'. They should improve physical conditions and social services in the plant and stress 'service' to the 'public' rather than class or privilege.[75]

The International Labour Organisation (ILO), directed by Albert Thomas, also advocated new forms of workplace solidarity. An ILO study stressed the need for, at least, the tacit cooperation of labour organisations and a rested and well-paid worker for efficient production and a mass-market economy.[76] Not only would high wages and leisure be the worker's reward for submitting to new methods designed to intensify work,[77] but the labour process itself could be rehabilitated in a technocratic age. Work had to have intrinsic value. But this was the rub. No one expected that work could be 'meaningful' in the ways that artisans experienced. An ILO report offered this simple suggestion as a remedy to boredom: 'as in the case of gang work, the spectacle of rhythmic movements of one's workmates may act as a stimulus that can be intensified by rhythmic sounds or singing'. Otherwise, the 'most important cause' of monotony was the 'incompatibility of some workmen's character to conveyor work'.[78] This could be addressed through personnel selection. Tests could identify that worker (to use Ford's words) for whom 'repetitive operations hold no terrors' and who 'above all . . . wants a job in which he does not have to think'.[79]

More positive were the views of the socialist Henri de Man. He insisted that satisfaction at work was essential for psychic and social stability. Without it, not only was socialism 'dead' but workers would continue to suffer a 'social inferiority complex' and seek relief in emulative spending. 'Joy' was to be found in 'fulfilling a duty'. The need to develop a group spirit in mass-production work went beyond job security, high wages, and leisure time.[80]

André Gorz has recently argued that this workplace ethic was the ideology of a new class of skilled labour who benefited from the newly mechanised factory and who ignored the interests of the unskilled or craft workers for whom mass-production work was inherently dissatisfying.[81] This viewpoint, however, ignores the context and the ambiguity of the emergence of modern work ideology. Many who affirmed a modernised work ethic in the 1920s were also advocates of increased leisure and consumption which benefited the less skilled.

In the 1920s, trade unionists attempted to modernise the traditional pride of the individual craftworker into the collective affirmation of mass-production efficiency. The alternative, according to Lafargue and Gorz, was not to glorify the 'right to work' but to treat labour time as a necessary and equitably shared means to the ends of autonomy in free time. But this notion was clearly not acceptable to many in those early days of the mass-production economy. A work ideology, which tried to cope with the implications of mass production, while rejecting a purely instrumentalist view of labour, reflected an uncertainty that social solidarity and personal integration could be achieved in the realms of free time and consumption.[82] These concerns obsessed the industrial democracies, the Soviet Union, and the fascist dictatorships. Still, this attempt to adapt the traditional work ethic to conditions of mass production placed a serious brake on the emergence of an ideology of free time.

A final impediment to the technocratic vision of the democratic and balanced allocation of time and money was the resistance of business. Employers were, of course, seldom enthusiastic about the distributionist implications of productivism. They were even more concerned about the impact of growth on the commitment to work. A democracy of goods and leisure seemed to undercut the disciplinary function of work. Despite the successful campaign in 1923 to replace the twelve-hour shift in the American steel industry with the eight-hour day, little was done to reduce hours in other long-shift industries. Ford's call for a five-day workweek in 1926 was ignored outside a few consumer service and product sectors.[83] In the 1920s, French and British business support for productivism seldom went beyond cautious innovations in management and mechanisation. European employers certainly did not embrace a trade-off of workers' acceptance of innovation for the equitable distribution of its fruits.[84]

Central to the employers' critique of this productivist social contract was the conviction that a share-out of time and money undermined the work ethic. Business leaders repeatedly blamed the leisure gained after 1918 for their economic difficulties and held the line against further erosion of work discipline. In the US, Ford's efforts to spread his gospel of the five-day/40-hour week in 1926 met with derision from other businessmen. In response to world competition and declining markets, the British coal industry tried to increase the workday from seven to eight hours. This effort was partially responsible for the General Strike and lockout of 1926, which so embittered British labour relations.[85] French employers continued to argue that work alone brought salvation: leisure would dissipate the majority who lacked the training and intelligence to make proper use of unregulated time. In 1922, industrialist André François-Poncet declared that the only beneficiary of the eight-hour day was the cabaret; and conservative Deputy M. Josse claimed that the eight-hour law had created a 'moral crisis', and was a 'symbol of laziness'.[86]

In the 1920s, technocratic reformers were unable to legitimise a trade-off of time and money in exchange for industrial innovation. Not only did business reject this vision and labour reveal ambivalence toward it, but even the technocrats were unwilling to embrace their own doctrine's radical threat to traditionalist ideas about work. That which continued to make this dream viable was the persistent notion that productivity led to a natural satiation of needs and thus to the growth of leisure (as well as consumption). This idea produced both hopes of balanced distribution and fears of economic stagnation. Only the refutation of this assumption would clear the way for the doctrine of limitless work and consumption.

THREATS OF OVERPRODUCTION, PROMISES OF MASS CONSUMPTION

For most business, both productivity and its distribution threatened economic stability and growth. But this produced a serious dilemma: if leisure and goods were distributed, long-term growth would suffer because work discipline would be undermined; but if they were not widely shared, productivity threatened a crisis of glut. New thinking about needs eventually overcame this apparently insuperable problem. And Americans clearly played the leading role.

A major concern of business and technocrats was the apparent saturation of American consumer markets in the 1920s. 'Overproduction', viewed by many as the source of the severe recession of 1920–1, appeared to result from an insufficient demand for consumer goods. In the midst of that recession, the National Association of Manufacturers asked the public to 'end the buyers' strike'.[87] But fears of overproduction continued throughout the 1920s. Walter Grimes, an American businessman, wrote in 1928: 'the middle class American already buys more than he needs. . . . Unless we have a greater outlet for our goods . . . as manufacturing efficiency increases, there will be larger groups with too much leisure.'[88] The unemployment resulting from overproduction was both an economic and a moral problem.[89]

But, while mounting inventories were disconcerting, most business leaders had a larger worry – that distribution in the form of high wages and shorter hours would undermine growth. Of course, Henry Ford argued that, by combining high wages with a two-day weekend (based on a 40-hour week), increased consumer demand would soak up inventory. As important, increased consumer need would lash workers ever more firmly to their jobs.[90] However, few businessmen in the 1920s were convinced. As a publicist for the National Association of Manufacturers wrote in 1926: no 'union man' would do 'one iota more per hour' with the shorter work-week.[91] The problem was to keep people working and, given the expectation of a backward sloping labour supply curve, shorter hours (and higher wages) would lead to less (or no more) output.[92]

But if Fordism were rejected, the only obvious alternatives were the ancient palliatives: maintaining long workdays and reducing (or dampening the rise of) wages to reinforce work discipline and prevent satiation. But this approach left business with a seemingly insuperable dilemma: the traditional medicine of blocking the empowerment of free time and money might have negatively increased the incentive to work but it guaranteed weak domestic markets and ensured overproduction (or underconsumption). However, as Ford recognised, this approach ignored the *disciplinary potential* of high wages and of consumer-based leisure.

A very different solution to the burden of 'overproduction' was to lift the cap on needs. This would create both mass consumers and disciplined workers. The central discovery was that unlimited consumption did not mean waste and declining effort. Rather, with increased spending, growth and labour discipline could become compatible. The result would be a more positive assessment of the democracy of time and money but also a bias in favour of consumption.

But, again, economists were reluctant to embrace this perspective in the interwar years. There were two broadly contrasting points of view about consumption and needs creation that, as we have seen, had a long pedigree. The more traditional approach can be summarised in a book by American economist Walter Pitkin, *The Consumer. His Nature and Changing Habits* (1932). Pitkin argued that physiology placed limits on basic wants. 'The greatest advances in living standards', he argued, 'come . . . from increases in leisure,

in health, in recreations, and in personal security.'[93] But because
of the interest of producers in 'volume consumption', there was
inevitably a 'war between maker and user'. Discontent was inevitable because unrestrained production undermined quality of life:
'Being compelled to dwell where he does not enjoy living [in industrial cities] . . . , the workingman cannot be made happy with high
wages.' Given this classical attack on consumerist materialism, the
reader may be surprised to hear Pitkin's solution. He advocated
suburbanisation which alone could give people 'security toned up
with a little speculation and adventure' and 'easy going self improvement'. The suburban home-owner would become the 'ideal
consumer no less than . . . a good citizen'.[94]

A second approach to consumer economics assumed the plasticity
of human needs. Hazel Kyrk's *A Theory of Consumption* (1923)
and Paul Nystrom's *Economic Principles of Consumption* (1929)
both began with the conflict and inequality between the producer
and consumer.[95] This was a perspective they shared with Pitkin in
opposition to orthodox economics. But Kyrk and Nystrom were
far less certain about the natural limits of consumer needs. Their
problem with orthodox marginal utility theory was its lack of a
psychology that explained the non-rational and social character of
consumer decisions. Kyrk insisted that 'The process of consumption
is organized according to certain standards of the appropriate and
the necessary. Luxuries thus can become necessities in the evolution
of that standard.'[96] But a major implication was that moral constraints could break down under affluence. Surplus removed limits
on the natural quest for variety in consumption and gave full play
to the desire for 'distinction'. This process was accelerated by the
presence of both social stratification and mobility: 'The more democratic the social spirit, the less restricted and limited is the concept
of what is or is not permissible for individuals of the different
classes to do and to enjoy.' While science and education might
encourage consumption of health-giving goods, Kyrk was clearly
sceptical that growth meant progress up a hierarchy of needs: 'What
safeguards are there that changes will be in the direction of
progress, or that a dynamic, expanding standard is really the
development of a higher rather than a more expensive standard?'[97]
The overriding problem was, as John Dewey noted, how to turn a
democracy whose 'main effect seemingly has been to multiply
occasion for imitation' into a more rational society based on clear
and limited needs.[98]

Despite her Veblenite pessimism, Kyrk had solutions that Patten would have embraced: in order to 'eliminate false values and establish new ideals and purpose', consumers needed more than 'formal freedom of choice'. They required 'positive freedom in the form of adequate income and a wide variety of goods and services upon the market'. This was to overcome the traditional sin of gluttony in food, drink and sex. But it hardly anticipated a problem of the unrestrained diversity of modern consumption. Moreover, Kyrk's thought raised the question: who was to make the choice. And here she offered a thoroughly Victorian response: the most effective 'experts' were those persons who have 'the time, information and skill that is necessary in order to avoid waste and carry out high standards of consumption'. Those individuals were 'women who are heads of households'.[99]

These solutions to the war between producers and consumers were perhaps unimaginative. But the idea of the suburban home as the 'natural' consumer unit and recourse to the restraining influence of housewives were surely consistent with expectations of the period. Home economics was built around these themes. In 1920, Christine Frederick's *Household Engineering* included consumer expertise as an essential (female) domestic counterpart to (male) production. It is more than ironic that Frederick would, by 1929, have shifted from attempting to 'professionalise' the housewife to consulting advertisers on 'Selling Mrs. Consumer'.[100] Despite Pitkin's certainty that needs were naturally limited and Kyrk's fears that they were not, the *ideal* of limited needs could not withstand the logic of mass consumption.

Fears of endemic overproduction in the early 1920s were gradually replaced with the belief that the gap in consumption was only a temporary problem in the US. Few expressed this new viewpoint better than the President's Committee on Recent Economic Changes in 1929 which claimed that 'wants are almost insatiable; that one want satisfied makes way for another. . . . By advertising and other promotional devices, by scientific fact finding, and by carefully predeveloped consumption, a measurable pull on production . . . has been created.' A 'New Gospel of Consumption' had emerged, in America at least.[101] And along with it came the discovery of the disciplinary potential of free time and high wages.

Undergirding this new thinking were changes in economic theory. The Briton, Lionel Robbins, for example, in 1930 abandoned the assumption that prosperity reduced the willingness to work. That theory, he argued, ignored the fact that higher wages made the price of each additional hour of leisure more expensive. Leisure was not the residue of diminishing utility of income but had itself an economic cost; wage increases raised the opportunity cost of additional units of leisure. As important, the desire for consumer goods was indeterminate: it obeyed no rational order of diminishing intensity. 'Any attempt to predict the effect of a change in the terms on which income is earned must proceed by inductive investigations' of the demand for income. Increased pay rates could lead to demand for more leisure, more work, or no change at all.[102]

Robbins' agnosticism provided, in effect, an opening for those who argued along with Kyrk that the propensity to consume was socially determined and grew with the ability of the masses to emulate the rich. While Kyrk and most consumer economists hoped for restrained expansion of need, others saw widening consumer demand as an opportunity to solve the potential problem of 'overproduction'.

Pioneers in this new thinking were representatives of the emerging consumer-goods industries and allies among the high-wage advocates of organised labour. For example, in a series of books published in the mid-1920s, William Foster and Waddill Catchings stressed that there was no limit on the potential for consumption. The problem in their view was to increase the velocity of consumption and to avoid the 'dilemma of thrift' – savings, especially of the well-to-do, that were not recycled immediately into consumption. Such money 'used twice in succession to produce goods' resulted in stocking 'the market beyond the capacity of consumers to buy at current prices'. The result was 'underconsumption' and unemployment. The obvious solution was a high-wage economy and, when necessary, supplemental government spending to assure the continuous flow of income. Although this analysis was subject to rigorous criticism, especially regarding the theory of the 'dilemma of saving', it found a receptive audience in the pages of the AFL's *American Federationist*.[103]

Foster and Catchings recognised no limit on consumer demand: 'the wants of most people grow as rapidly as their incomes'. Foster and Catchings dispensed with the ethical component of Kyrk's notion of a high standard of living, a concept which they defined as 'nothing but the using up of much wealth'. They echoed George Gunton when they condemned as bad economics the moralistic railings against 'improvident' spending by workers.[104] 'Wearing things out', R. Sheldon and E. Arens reminded their readers in *Consumer Engineering*, 'does not produce prosperity, but buying things does.' Money, and with it a commitment to work, they might have added, far more than pure leisure, would grease the gears of the machine of growth.[105]

While this thinking germinated on American soil in the 1920s, it was not entirely absent from Europe. For example, in 1926, British industrial engineers Bertram Austin and W. F. Lloyd popularised the Fordist ideas of a mass-production/mass-consumption economy based on the 'secret of high wages'. New methods of production allowed not only low prices for consumer goods but high wages as well. These British engineers assured their readers that American markets were nowhere near reaching a 'saturation point'. Britain, too, could emulate these Fordist practices by developing a high wage home market and thus eliminate the 1.25 million unemployed due to decreased international demand for British products. Austin and Lloyd's book inspired French trade unionists with the hope of high-wage/mass-consumption economy as an alternative to the status quo of high prices, limited markets, and low wages.[106]

To be sure, Fordism hardly won a large audience anywhere in Europe between the wars. André Citroën's attempt to emulate Ford's mass-marketing strategy failed in France. European employers were sceptical of Ford's claim that he could export his methods to Europe with its traditions of 'quality' production and, more to the point, with its relatively low wages. And Europeans were very sensitive and often hostile to the cultural impact of Americanisation. Mass consumption on the American scale, at least, as either an ideal or reality would come to Europe much later.[107]

Still, if high wages were to solve the problem of 'overproduction' from the consumption side, there still remained the question of technological unemployment. An ideological solution to this problem emerged in the late 1920s and was fully developed by 1940. Both the American Wesley Mitchell and Britain-based Colin Clark argued that technologically-induced productivity did not eliminate jobs (or reduce worktime); rather it created new employment. Colin Clark's *Conditions of Economic Progress* abandoned the stationary-state idea with its implication of a 'mature economy' for the notion of occupational migration: with increasingly high income per head, Clark found, not the expansion of free time, but the shift of factors of production (including labour) from extractive and industrial sectors to services. Efficiency led not to liberation from labour time but to new forms of work and consumption.[108]

Underlying Clarke's argument was the assumption that no economy could function without a common commitment to work and without meaningful 'full-time' employment. This perspective was made explicit in the writings of the American technocrat-New Dealer, Rexford Tugwell. In his *Industrial Discipline and the Government Arts* (1933), Tugwell declared that the depressed world economy was at a crossroads: mechanisation had so reduced the need for routine manual labour that people were obliged either to follow the path away from a work-centred society (via increased leisure) or to find ways of 'creating new and more satisfying jobs'. Given Tugwell's earlier fixation on the problem of making work meaningful and the dispiriting effects of involuntary 'leisure' in the Depression, it is not surprising that he advocated the path of 'human work'. The goal of government no longer was merely to encourage output and reduce work – the classic couplet of the productivity movement of the 1920s; rather it was to help create new occupations and mobilise resources in order to prevent the 'waste' of national energy. The great social projects of the future, Tugwell insisted, could not be realised in leisure (an essentially individualistic activity), but in collectivist productive processes. Tugwell was a key proponent of New Deal public works and vocational education. But he also shared with Clark a devotion to transforming efficiency, not into leisure, but into cleaner, less fatiguing, and more creative forms of work.[109] A new work ethic combined then with an ideology of unlimited needs to legitimise the bias toward work/consumption against free time/limited needs.

By the 1930s, most economists rejected the utopian vision of a four-hour workday advanced by technocrats; instead they foresaw a consumer economy – stimulated by advertising and the imagination of business – that would require endless quantities of labour. They argued that the socially-induced demand for goods produced an unlimited need for money. This, in turn, assured not only a willingness to work but reduced pressure to liberate time from wage labour.

In the 1920s, the promise of productivity created the problem of economic equilibrium: it raised the question of the distribution of time and money and the impact of that share-out on the work ethic and growth. The liberating potential of time and money seemed to overshadow their disciplinary possibilities. But soon fears that high wages and leisure would free the individual to the detriment of the economic order gave way to the discovery that consumption encouraged work. To be sure, as I shall discuss in chapter 4, advocates of distributing productivity in the form of free time persisted during the Depression, thus challenging the consumerist assumptions of Catchings and Waddell. A philosophy of limited needs which valued autonomy from commodity relations survived in more constrained forms in the politics of hours reduction and the ideas of the democratic organisation of leisure. But, by the end of the 1930s, these ideas had largely disappeared from discussion by economists, who were overwhelmed by a fixation on the distribution of goods and employment. For advocates of post-industrial economies like Colin Clark, the economic problem of the Depression was a disequilibrium between demand and supply of labour. It was not the imbalance of productivity and leisure.[110] Underlying this assumption was the abandonment of the theory of limited needs that Tarde, Hobson, Patten, and many others had addressed.

Marshall and Keynes had assumed a shift from work to leisure values in a mature capitalist economy. Behind this conviction was the faith that a learned class, at least, knew when 'satiation' of goods and 'disutility' of labour was reached. Most of these thinkers seemed to have believed that when the social emulation identified by Veblen and Tarde ceased to have a basic economic necessity it would disappear. But why should it? As the marginalists noted, there was no theoretical limit to the endless substitution of one sated want by another unfulfilled one and, given the dynamic of the social system of emulation and the economic system of accumulation, the only compelling reason for limits would be ecological devastation. Some thought that the Depression was just that opportunity for the discovery of real needs: it seemed to prove the flaws of accumulation and to offer a political/cultural alternative. Still, as we shall see, advocates of an expanded public culture had little impact.

In any case, how could a moral community be created out of the division of labour and the atomising effects of social emulation? And who was to say who were to be the 'educators'? Early twentieth-century economists may have had fewer doubts about the character of that community and their right to educate than their descendants would have. Nevertheless, these dilemmas haunted the self-proclaimed educators of the interwar years. The frustrations of these humanists in envisioning this community set the stage for our contemporary impasse. Their concerns and their impact will be addressed next.

3 Barriers and bridges: cultural elites and the democratisation of time and money

While social scientists were abandoning the notion of limited needs, humanists were struggling with the implications of mass culture. Economists came to reject the inevitability of the progressive and thus the democratic extension of leisure; at the same time, humanists began also to doubt the possibilities of a democratic leisure culture that encouraged popular participation and choice. This cultural pessimism, like the new growth-driven thinking of economists, had an impact on the ultimate fate of the political movements for reduced worktime and democratic leisure organisation (see chapters 4 and 5).

Keynes had predicted the emergence of new cultural and recreation leaders appropriate for a post-scarcity society. Instead, economic growth produced an elite of advertisers and impresarios of commercial entertainment. Of course, among both the traditional producers of high culture and new facilitators of popular recreation and the arts were passionate advocates of the democratic organisation of the new free time. But the democratisation of leisure time was essentially problematic for most intellectuals.

The intellectuals' ambivalence toward the prospect of free time for the masses was rooted in the conflict between their classical theoretical biases and the emergence of a modern industrial society.[1] Aristotle identified leisure with freedom from necessity and dependence; leisure was based on a negative evaluation of work and the command of an elite over a household of labourers. But modern productivity threatened these ancient ideas by making most people mutually dependent on each other in market and bureaucratic work; it created a majority who enjoyed some time free from necessity and, as a result, who crowded the cultural space of the elite. Moreover, attitudes of the privileged toward popular leisure had long been shaped by the Platonic habit of equating the masses with unrestrained appetite and the belief that elites of intellect and will were required to enforce enlightened social control. But industrial wage labour and democratisation gradually released these masses from the discipline of long hours of work and relaxed the patronage and regulation through which the governing classes had formerly controlled popular culture. The failure of humanists to resolve these dilemmas has shaped the debate about consumer culture throughout this century and has biased thinking about the possibilities of free time.

Despite emerging affluence, Victorian ideas, based on Aristotelian and Platonic models, survived into the twentieth century. Sabbatarianism lingered in American blue (Sabbatarian) laws and English prohibitions of Sunday cinema (until 1932). Efforts of both French and Anglo-Saxon elites to turn collective and anarchic play into rational recreation organised around individualistic and orderly activities were perpetuated in this century in bourgeois patronage of youth leisure. Even the nineteenth-century heritage of populism was often hostile to industrial progress and displayed thoroughly ambivalent attitudes toward the people's pleasures.[2]

Matthew Arnold's mid-Victorian call for a cultural elite to form a bulwark against the aristocratic 'barbarian', the bourgeois 'philistine', and especially the envious 'populace' continued to have deep-seated appeal to twentieth-century intellectuals.[3] Underlying the intensity of these fears of cultural democratisation was the obvious growth of leisure and income of the masses with the eight-hour day and 'high' wages.

The increasing reality of affluence and mass leisure raised three concerns for modern intellectuals: (1) the evident decoupling of economic growth from a philosophy of real needs and, with it, the disassociation of productivity from the possibilities of personal autonomy and social enrichment; (2) the competition between the intellectual 'educator' and the impresarios of pleasure over the shape of mass culture at a time when intellectuals both were pessimistic that they could affect that culture and perhaps felt diminished responsibility for it; and (3) the difficulty of rescuing personality and community from competition and the division of labour in work and from social emulation and mechanical passivity in play. These three concerns shaped the thinking of the broad spectrum of culture producers and recreation leaders in the early twentieth century. The failure of intellectuals to resolve these dilemmas radically reduced their potential role in creating a democratic leisure culture in the twentieth century.

INTELLECTUALS AND THE CROWD

The conflict between their high cultural bias and the democratic implications of mass productivity defined most of the problems which intellectuals had with the modern crowd. This conflict, however, did not produce a uniform response; and various approaches could not be identified with differences commonly separating the left and the right. Humanists seemed to gather loosely around two poles. The perhaps dominant response was a reaction against the democratic threat of mass production in the form of a defence of classical cultural standards. This group included not only besieged proponents of European elite culture but radical critics of the modern 'culture industry'. A second more flexible, but no less elitist, approach was taken by those who found possibilities for cultural redemption in mass industrial culture, but only under the leadership of the classically trained intellectual. Around this pole gathered advocates of vitalism and cultural adjustment to modern technological change (based on the 'cultural lag'). To be sure, these two broad approaches sometimes overlapped and they group together thinkers who otherwise differed profoundly; but these two frames of reference help us to conceptualise how intellectuals encountered the 'leisure problem' in the interwar years.

José Ortega y Gasset's famous *The Revolt of the Masses* shared with most intellectuals of the period what Patrick Brantlinger has called 'negative classicism', an intensely anxious response to the apparent decline of rationalist individualism in the industrial world. Classical cultural standards were threatened by an invasion of the 'barbarian from within' represented by a mass culture of welfare and hedonism that was supported by a self-interested state and capitalist purveyors of comfort.[4] The masses, contended Ortega, was a 'moral', not an economic, class. It was a 'spoiled child' who imposed 'its own desires and tastes by means of material pressure' on the cultured minority. This theme was often repeated: mass consumerism equalled passivity, decadence, and a naive affirmative culture. It emerged from a semi-literate public which had been uprooted from traditional popular culture and yet possessed neither the time nor training to appreciate the high culture of the minority; as a result, high culture was diluted or crowded out by the mass market.[5]

Conservatives had long associated democratic culture and aspirations with the irrational crowd. Gustave Le Bon's influential work, *The Crowd* (1895), updated this view.[6] Underlying the political motive, however, was Ortega's keenly felt belief that the formerly submissive masses no longer gave 'respect' to the elite. And this feeling was as common among progressives and populists like George Orwell, J. B. Priestley, Lewis Mumford and Albert Camus.[7] F. R. Leavis' *Mass Civilisation and Minority Culture* (1930) was squarely in this tradition.[8] This essentially psychological response was a reflection of an abiding social distance between the educated elite and the 'crowd'.[9] This image of the rational individual beseiged by the surging cauldron of the crowd governed much thinking about the democratisation of time and money in the early twentieth century. It was reflected in Emile Durkheim's fear that too much unregulated consumption and leisure would upset the delicate balance of egoistic drives and social obligations.[10]

Freud shared this view. His *Group Psychology* (1921) associated Le Bon's irrational crowd with unrepressed libidinal drives.[11] On the street, the masses regressed to the mental state of children.[12] Freud later claimed that mass affluence intensified the 'cultural frustration' of conflicts between self-control and indulgence. He projected this psychological tension onto the social arena in clashes between men and women and the rich and the poor. For Freud there was little doubt who played which psychological role. Women, he insisted were 'little capable' of 'instinctual sublimations' necessary for civilisation. Labourers shared this incapacity. Freud was doubtful that civilisation could withstand any significant liberation of the pleasure principle. Work alone could bind 'the individual more closely to reality'. But Freud also insisted that the

> masses are lazy and unintelligent; they have no love for instinctual renunciation. . . . It is only through the influence of individuals who can set an example and whom the masses recognise as their leaders that they can be induced to perform the work and undergo the renunciations upon which the existence of civilisation depends.[13]

The problem was that industrial productivity shortened the whip of work discipline, and, thus, the pleasure principle threatened to swamp civilisation. Monetary incentives may have raised output but they did not create social discipline after working hours. The democratisation of money and time threatened the thin veneer of restraint and progress.

This led Freud to a deep cultural pessimism, shared by other defenders of classical rational individualism. Instinctual drives in adults had to be repressed or sublimated into constructive activities through work and, to borrow the language of Chris Rojek, into 'permissible pleasure'.[14] Freud helped to transmit two closely related Victorian biases into the twentieth century: the belief that the liberation of the masses from the unrelenting discipline of work had a corrosive cultural effect; and that only individualised play, constrained by the responsibilities of family and led by 'rational' elites, was consistent with civilisation and progress.

But there was an even more pessimistic side to Freud. In *Beyond the Pleasure Principle* (1920), he extended his negative assessment of pleasure into the concept of the death instinct. Play was not simply a relaxation of work tensions or even the dangerous liberation of the pleasure principle; rather it could release the 'death instinct' of boredom, infantile longings, and self-destructiveness. The Freudian S. Ferenczi 'discovered' a modern problem, 'Sunday neurosis', a tendency of workers to indulge in anti-social behaviour on their day off.[15] Culture in mass leisure, Freudians argued, could be preserved only when the nihilistic implications of the play impulse were controlled and this could be done only by cultivated individuals.[16]

This defence of classical cultural standards is usually associated with conservatives. But it had also a 'radical' face in the 'Frankfurt School'. This influential group of central Europeans also condemned mass leisure even as it stressed the manipulation of the capitalistic 'culture industry'. The Frankfurt School combined a unique blend of Freudian cultural pessimism with Marxian notions of 'false consciousness' to explain what it saw as the passivity of working-class culture.

Most typical of this approach was the *Dialectic of Enlightenment* by Theodor Adorno and Max Horkheimer. The rationality which the Enlightenment had hoped would free humanity from nature had become, according to Adorno and Horkheimer, the instrumental reason of advanced capitalism. In the form of industrialisation, instrumental reason came to dominate the individual in both work and play. Because 'mechanisation has such power over a man's leisure and happiness . . . , his experiences are inevitably after images of the work process itself'. As a result, 'pleasure hardens into boredom because, if it is to remain pleasure, it must not demand any effort'. Industrialisation inevitably produced a passive, mass leisure culture. Moreover, merchandisers of mass consumption had become totalitarian 'by occupying men's senses from the time they leave the factory in the evening to the time they clock in again the next morning'. In language that echoed Ortega, Adorno and

Horkheimer condemned the presumed fact that intellectuals and artists became subject to 'their illiterate masters'. In turn, they argued, capitalism produced an ideological truce between 'the conformism of the buyers [of mass culture] and the effrontery of the producers who supply them'.[17]

Still Adorno and Horkheimer found that atomised deskilled workers were the victims of a culture industry that mass produced standardised art and music. Mass leisure promoted not transcendence but adjustment to life by creating an illusion of variety and choice. The culture industry, said Adorno in an article concerning popular music, was a 'circle of manipulation and retroactive needs in which the unity of the system grows ever stronger'. Adorno was among the most pessimistic when he claimed that the capacity of resistance 'has already been suppressed by the control of the individual consciousness'.[18] Ultimately the only form of dissent available to the Frankfurt School was 'negation', a cult of aesthetics raised against consumerism. This conclusion was nearly indistinguishable from the conservative self-isolation of Ortega. It was based on a similar defence of European high culture against the mass societies of both fascist Europe and consumerist America.[19]

Around a second pole can be gathered thinkers who were more open to the possibilities of leisure in mass industrial society. In contrast to Freud's therapeutic rationalism was a vitalist psychology that was less pessimistic about play in modern industrial society. A good example of this approach is the American psychologist, G. Stanley Hall. In his book, *Youth: Its Education, Regimen, and Hygiene* (1909), Hall insisted on the primacy of physical/instinctual life and the need to 'rehearse the activities of our ancestors' through play. This positive view of active leisure was inspired by a quest for an intensity of feeling and reflected a widespread reaction to the stifling respectability and moral rigidity of Victorian culture. It was also a part of the search for an 'irreducible core of individuality' that many European and American intellectuals desired early in the twentieth century. For Progressivists, who wanted to reform the childhood experience, play was to compensate for the debilitating effects of discipline in industrial work and to create new vehicles of social adjustment.[20] And, by the 1920s, these ideas were adapted to a wider concern for restoring play to the lives of adults as an antidote to the psycho-physical distortions of prolonged work and division of labour in the modern world.[21]

Americans were 'bottled lightning', said William James in 1900. The solution was new habits of physical relaxation in play. The 'moral tensions' of acquisitive urban life needed to be released.[22] Otherwise the freedom of modern leisure would be dissipated in passive amusements and indulgence. G. T. W Patrick's *Psychology of Relaxation* (1916) similarly stressed that adult play was necessary to balance the Dionysian drives with the 'Apollonian motive of balance, harmony, and repose'.[23] A major point of this literature was that leisure could restore what industrialism had destroyed.

In some ways then vitalism was the opposite of Freud's therapeutic rationalism. Yet Hall and his followers were hardly apologists of 'appetite'. Rather they found in play a means of channelling desire. Following the German gymnastic tradition, Hall believed that play and physical training 'mentalizes the body' and 'gives control over to higher brain levels. Thus physical training actually makes the mind rule the body and frees us from nervousness and anti-social behavior'; play would reduce 'sexual stress just at the age when its premature localization is most deleterious'. The point of delving into the vital sources of life in play, claimed Hall, was to prepare youth to be 'fitted to stand the strain of modern civilization'.[24] For both Freudian and vitalist, Coney Island and Blackpool threatened civilisation. While Freudians feared that unleashed play would lead to psychic disintegration, vitalists seem to have suggested the opposite, that industrialisation created 'excessive repression' and thus passive consumers. The antidote was play. But even the vitalists saw the need to regulate that play impulse, often in ways very similar to how work was to discipline play. They also shared with the more pessimistic Freudians a tendency to identify the educator with the existing ruling classes.

A doctrine closely related to vitalism was that of the 'cultural lag', introduced by the American sociologist William Ogburn in *Social Change with Respect to Culture and Original Nature* (1922). Even more than the vitalist, Ogburn believed that there was redemption in industrial modernity. Mass leisure was not merely a manifestation of infantile and conflicting psychological drives, nor was it the manipulation of a passive working class for commercial profit. Certainly the problem with mass culture was not its threat to classical culture. Rather, popular or 'adaptive culture' erred by lagging behind technological change. Indeed, established attitudes toward work, leisure, and society were a brake upon progress. At the same time, biological needs of the contemporary 'cave man' no longer fitted modern urban life. Ogburn, however, resisted the pessimistic implications of this thought. Like the vitalists, he held that city people could 'find adventure in modern life as truly as it was found in the hunter's life'.[25] Needs that could not be gratified in modern work life might find outlets in recreation:

Modern life provides a great many stimuli to desires which are not gratified. . . . Is it not possible that recreation may furnish an outlet for some of these instinctive tendencies? . . . In games, for instance, are seen fear, anxiety, anger, the desire for mastery, self-assertiveness, leadership [and] sociability. . . . Thus in the case of a factory 'hand', recreation will enable certain instincts to function which find little opportunity to do so within the factory walls.[26]

Ogburn's analysis shared the optimism of the vitalists in his conviction that the lag could be overcome in cultural 'adjustments'.

Many technocrats freely borrowed this theory. This was clearly expressed in the reformism of Charles Beard's, *Whither Mankind* (1929): 'the whole domain of culture . . . must yield or break before the inexorable pressure of science and the machine'. Still he concluded: 'Under the machine and science, the love of beauty, the sense of mystery, and the motive of compassion – sources of aesthetics, relations, and humanism – are not destroyed.'[27] They were to be modernised.

While adhering to a materialist determinism, the cultural-lag theory implied a greater plasticity of personality than was implied by others. It surely was more open to the possibilities of modern mechanisation than were the Freudians and other 'negative classicists'. But, nevertheless, it suggested another form of cultural 'frustration' in the conflicts between inertia and change, and most analysts believed that few individuals were equipped to manage this conflict. Elitism and disappointment were perhaps the inevitable end of this relatively optimistic perspective on mass culture. In the final analysis the differences between Ortega and Ogburn were far less important than were their similarities.

MACHINERY OF AMUSEMENT

The two poles around which turned most discussion of mass culture and the new leisure were the pessimism of the classicist and theorist of the culture industry and the reformism of the vitalist and the student of cultural lags. But for almost all thinkers, the release of the masses from the discipline of work and the democratic access to goods threatened cultural standards and produced 'frustrations'. Guiding most commentators was the threat of the modern machine

– the vehicle of the liberated libido, manipulated pleasure, distorted vitality, and ill-adapted culture. And, for all, the 'masses' were the emanation of the machine. In the interwar years, intellectuals oscillated in often bewildering confusion between treating the masses as cultural victims of mechanisation and as victimisers of culture who were set free from constraint by the machine. In the end, the only recourse for most intellectuals was withdrawal or preaching. This hardly set the stage for their participation in the creation of a more democratic leisure culture.

Clearly the new productivity had a cultural underside. The most pessimistic argument was that the machine by liberating the mass libido had destroyed high culture and 'true leisure'. An American psychologist and college president, George Cutten, wrote in 1926 of how mechanisation produced the 'threat of leisure'. While industry might free workers from the drudgery of labour, expectations of speedy gratification and reduced effort produced passivity: 'life of too much ease is not conducive to mental strenuosity and as modern man is finding substitutes for physical labor, he is also looking for substitutes for thought'. If there were no 'self-expression in creative work, may we not expect an expression of sexual looseness?' away from work, Cutten asked. In 1935, the English writer Cyril Joad wrote off cultural democratisation with the simple declaration: 'in proportion as pleasures increase the capacity for them decreases'. Even the liberal American technocrat, Stuart Chase, lamented along with the Freudians that, since Prohibition, the weekend for most industrial workers had become an 'endurance test' against boredom.[28]

The high wages and mass production of Fordism also seemed to swamp cultural barriers. Cutten insisted that wages earned on the machine created a new 'survival of the fittest', giving command over resources to machine-tending 'morons'. And, with standardised production, merchandisers created a Gresham's Law where the lowest common denominator drove out elevated taste. In 1933, F. R. Leavis and Denys Thompson condemned the commodification of traditional art forms in the 'purple prose' of advertising copy.[29]

The conservative critique of democratic play in the interwar years often focused on the commercial film. Both Americans and Europeans saw the cinema not only as a threat to local and family-based morality, but as a diluting agent on high culture.[30] Yet even the English writer J. B. Priestley, who had populist sympathies, dared to say in 1934: 'If the proletariat has money in its pocket now, it can lead the life of the satrap.'[31] The 'left' side of this coin was also well expressed in George Orwell's famous condemnation of consumer culture in 1937 as the ultimate pacifier: 'fish and chips, art silk stockings, tinned salmon, cutprice chocolate, the movies, the radio, strong tea and the football pools quite likely . . . between them averted revolution'.[32] The view that mechanisation released the libido from work discipline and produced passive and bored leisure presumed the conservative psychological models of Ortega, Freud, Adorno, and other defenders of classical high culture.

A rather more liberal notion was that the machine itself produced the social psychology that led to the disappointing consumer/leisure culture. When technocrats praised high-wage productivity, humanists argued that mass-assembly jobs disabled workers, preventing them from marshalling the initiative and imagination required for anything more than passive leisure. The English demographer Henry Durant held that the 'machinery of amusement' finished 'the industrial training of turning actors into spectators'. 'The new working class', lamented Lewis Mumford in 1929, 'can alas! neither produce art nor respond to it.'[33] André Philip, a young French socialist law professor, insisted in 1927 that the high wages and short hours of American workers at Ford's mass-assembly plants were achieved at the price of the workers' 'liberty, personality and intelligence'.[34] In *The Life of the Automobile* (1927), the Russian novelist Ilya Ehrenburg painted a dreary picture of the new mass-production labourer in France. When asked by a new worker if he were going to a political meeting, 'Pierre'

> shook his head. . . . The Newcomer was still green. He still didn't know anything. He believed in books, discussions, in self-education groups, and in the world revolution. Pierre no longer believed in anything. . . . Pierre no longer ran the machine, the machine ran him. Now he attached shackle-plates. He forgot about the brotherhood of man. He understood only one thing. Nothing could possibly change. The conveyor belt moved. Against that, all arguments were powerless.

For Ehrenburg, the analogue to the mechanised factory was the American cinema:

> [The men] watched a society melodrama permitted by the censors. This was art, the culture of the lower classes, this was Paris, the 'light of the world'. Thoughts writhed, legs went to sleep,

eyes were dazzled by the mother-of-pearl screen. The projector whirred. The belt kept moving.[35]

Although Ehrenburg was on the extreme left, this view conformed with the thinking of the orthodox French sociologist Maurice Halbwachs and the conservative social observer Jacques Valdour. Many shared the conclusion of the non-Marxian socialist Henri de Man that proletarian work did not produce 'class conscious' revolutionaries but a 'social inferiority complex': instinctual needs were left unmet and mass affluence only subjugated workers 'more effectively than before to the cultural standards of the social classes adjoining their own'.[36]

Purposeless work, Durant claimed, created impossible expectations in the frantic pursuit of free time: the hyperactive holiday-maker was only the obverse of the common cartoon image of the clerk sitting on the beach with a vacant face, 'waiting for lunch time'. The popular English writer on leisure, L. P. Jacks, insisted in 1927 that free time could never be 'free' if it was not coupled with interesting work. And Constance Harris in 1927 set out to prove this in her pessimistic study of the free time of the working-class district of Bethnal Green in London. There, boring work and a demeaning street environment created 'a grey treadmill, without much hope or many desires'. The young, reacting to the 'pressure of their work', preferred the 'dance halls where they can gratify their love for unhealthy emotion' to the evening institutes. They did not aspire to middle-class standards; rather young workers were satisfied with 'many and cheap clothes the same as everybody else buys, and as little work for as much money as possible'. Adults spent their free time sitting in windows vacantly 'watching the life of the streets' or whiling away their holidays in the littered, well-trod byways of the crowd. Harris revealed Victorian prejudices but her views were shared by influential sociologists like Maurice Halbwachs.[37]

Mass-production work diminished the capacity for spontaneity and community; it produced empty free time and money that not only swamped cultural barriers but pacified the wage-earner. Consumption without meaningful work, many cultural critics claimed, was inevitably frustrating. According to the American sociological teams led by Robert and Helen Lynd (1929) and George Lundberg (1933), leisure inherently fostered a deadly dialectic of extroversion and privatisation (as expressed in the American use of the automobile).[38] In anticipation of David Riesman's *Lonely Crowd* (1950),

Durant argued that the young sought individuality in leisure but instead experienced insecurity and loneliness. This produced a mad rush for 'approval' in traditional marriage. A white-collar correspondent told Durant that, although he looked forward to free time when

> it is practicable to expand one's personality by a variety of contacts impossible in the working day; . . . one is constantly driven back upon oneself by the tenuousness of any moral tradition. One can so easily be lonely in the crowd today.[39]

Even for this relatively privileged office employee, leisure could never compensate for meaningless work.

The theme of the 'threat' of popular leisure dominated the 'learned' discussion of the democratisation of free time: many expressed anxiety that mass production and its workers undermined cultural standards and that time and money without meaningful work was inevitably wasted or harmful. But behind *ad hominem* arguments and a confusing labelling of culprits and victims was a more fundamental conflict: the intellectual's own frustrated search for both community and individual distinction, for bridges to, and barriers against the people. These contradictions were often projected on to perceptions of the past and future – nostalgic recollections of pre-mechanised communities and personalities but also fearful anticipations of Americanised futures. These attitudes stood in the way of humanists contributing to a democratic leisure culture.

In the interwar years, nostalgia for the 'traditional' English countryside was widespread. This infatuation with 'Merrie England' crossed class and political lines in Britain: it attracted the socialist George Lansbury whose England was a 'land of hedgerows and lanes' as much as conservative Stanley Baldwin. Dreams of vacationing in country lanes in Devon filled the dreamworlds of Lancashire textile workers in the late 1930s who could afford nothing more than a few days at a tacky commercial resort.[40] In the English village F. R. Leavis found craftsmen who still mixed work and play and enjoyed traditional festivals. But the organic community was destroyed not only by the division of labour but by the 'gap in consciousness', a loss of memory.[41]

Similarly the Lynds contrasted the recently departed intimacy of the small town with the impact of mass consumption, mass media, and especially the automobile on 'Middletown' in the 1920s. If the car kept 'the family together', as one wage-earner reported, it did so at the cost of all other forms of recreation. And, among the more affluent of Middletown, the automobile split the family in so far as each generation peeled off on their separate motoring ways. The Lynds contrasted this with the social life of the generation before the car, about which one correspondent reported: 'In the nineties, we were all much more together. . . . We rolled out a strip of carpet and put cushions on the porch step to take care of the unlimited overflow of neighbors that dropped by.' But prosperity, the Lynds found, led to a retreat into the family, and then into individualised pursuit of standardised pleasure. Joad lamented that 'we are deprived of the social pleasure of those who live in a community'; instead we pass our lives 'in perpetual transit from workshop and dormitory' and, while on holiday, we destroy real Dorset villages with the 'all conquering car'.[42]

A key to these attacks on mass consumption was a pervasive opposition to 'Americanisation' in Britain (and France).[43] This was a theme as old as the writings of de Tocqueville and Arnold. For many Europeans, the US was the barbarian future of democratic and mechanical conformity and rootless superficiality. But, in the interwar years, probably the most influential propagandists were Americans themselves – literary exiles like T. S. Eliot and Henry James and sociologists like George Lundberg and Robert Lynd. This sensitivity to the American dystopia was reinforced, especially in Britain, by the American dominance of phonograph music and film.[44] Huxley's *Brave New World* (1932), often interpreted by Americans as a critique of totalitarianism, is probably more faithfully read as an attack on American mass culture with its passive amusements and the betrayal of the cultured to the 'democratic market'. Edgar Mowrer's *This American World* (1928) tirelessly equated mass culture with the US. European egalitarianism and individualism combined with the cultural deprivation of the frontier to produce an American society dominated by the masses who could 'enforce what mental and moral tyranny they like'. Cyril Joad fretted over what he saw as Americans turning England into a 'glorified park, studded with thatched cottages and preserved rustics and ringed with hotels, for the delectation of her tired and travelling rich'. In 1933, Leavis and Thompson condemned the hyper-American life of the California suburb where no one has 'permanent friends or permanent furniture' and where a 'bungalow court life' revolved around the ephemera of the *Saturday Evening Post*, listening to the wireless, riding in the car, and 'studying how to stay thin'.[45]

These themes of lost community and unfulfilled personality, of course, were the standard bromides of the besieged cultural elite: this encompassed disillusioned traditional liberals like Ortega, pessimistic radicals like Ehrenburg, and reactionaries like Eliot. Especially in the 1930s and 1940s, many intellectuals associated the growth of mass-consumer culture with the ultimate social and personal distortion, fascist totalitarianism. The suggestible and lonely crowd became the victim not only of the merchandisers but of the state.[46] Nevertheless the threat of Americanisation was surely a more long-lasting concern.

Concern about the unleashed mass libido was never distinguishable from merely the intellectual's ascetic dislike of the libertine taste of the masses; and attacks on mass-market play were often little more than a barely disguised resentment of the wage-earner's growing consumer sovereignty. If the image of the debilitating impact of mass-production work was a more sympathetic picture of the people, it still stressed passivity, degradation, and manipulation. The emerging consumer culture, so often staged between the lost community and personal integrity of the past, and the lonely and ephemeral crowd of the California future, left little room for action. The longed-for dream of social solidarity had few markers in the contemporary world. Rather what the intellectual saw on the street only justified retreat. Cures were few and the prognosis was not good for a public culture founded on an exchange of cultural elites and working people.

BARRIERS AND UPLIFT: DILEMMAS OF THE CULTURAL JEREMIAH

So what were the programmes of humanists in response to the democratisation of leisure? Mass production (and communication) both reduced the distance between high and popular culture and increased the speed of cultural output on a global scale. In response, elites attempted to reaffirm cultural hierarchy, timeless aesthetics, and local artistic traditions.[47] This 'distancing', of course, was a major dynamic in English literary circles in the first two decades of the century. We see this attempt to re-create a cultural hierarchy in the apolitical and ahistoric aesthetics of Clive Bell, Roger Fry, and the Bloomsbury circle in general. Literary academicians also attempted to build cultural boundaries in defence of high English literature.[48] From the 1920s on, T. S. Eliot insisted that elites from different social classes should seek to preserve their unique heritage from the threat of mass-homogenised culture. Mass education could 'adulterate and degrade' both high and low culture. Instead Eliot advocated a 'healthily stratified' and 'healthily regional' world. Aldous Huxley revealed much when he wrote in 1925, 'To extend privileges is generally to destroy their value.'[49]

The cultural jeremiah was not always so reactionary. For F. R. and Q. D. Leavis and the readers of their journal, *Scrutiny*, the solution was not the impossible task of restoring the 'organic community'. Rather it was to find a substitute for continuity in the writings that were inspired by that lost community. Literature was to offer not only 'memory' but 'critical awareness of the cultural environment'. Literary training would sharpen the eye to the appeals of advertisements and popular culture in the cinema. The Leavises were critical of capitalism and their notion of cultural training was nurtured by their experience from teaching in Workers' Education Association courses. Their motto was that modern education 'must be largely an education against the environment'. This notion has had a great influence on leftist cultural studies in Britain which since the 1950s has been dominated by Raymond Williams. But the appeal to a conservative elite was obvious. *Scrutiny* attracted the insecure English teacher and generalist in an age which increasingly rewarded scientific specialisation.[50]

Those who placed the highest barriers between high and low culture had the greatest fear of the release of mass libido. But, as we have seen, others argued that mechanisation reduced the worker's capacity to use free time creatively. This perspective offered less elitist solutions and drew from the relatively optimistic thinking of the vitalists and theorists of the cultural lag. Durant, for example, argued that the problem of leisure was that it was designed for the 'millions who know work only as an evil necessity' and was controlled by 'people who need not toil'. The remedy was obviously to change the relationship between work and play. Durant was hopeful that routine work would soon be eliminated and with it the 'machinery of amusement' for those who were psychologically disabled by such work. But he dreamed also that new voluntary social services would eliminate the division between the utility (but monotony) of work and the freedom but (passivity) of leisure.[51]

But Durant's ruminations, so similar to the ideas of the Greens in the 1980s, hardly had any serious auditors between the wars. More common was the idea that the 'educator' should counteract the machinery of amusement. Traditional nineteenth-century paternalism influenced those who thought that popular leisure could be uplifted. But it was often filtered through the language of vitalism and of the cultural lag.[52] One Anglo-American expression of this paternalism was provided by self-help literature devoted to improving leisure. Books and articles that offered advice on the best use of free time shared much with the salesmanship and success guides of the period.[53] These authors were often unsophisticated and were surely naive in their faith in the individual's ability to create a personal leisure culture. However, they generally also affirmed the need for a public alternative to prevailing commercial entertainment. American author of *A Guide to Civilized Leisure*, Henry Overstreet, believed that leisure must grow out of satisfying work and more humane environments; but he also agreed with Ogburn that recreation could fulfil needs that work could never express. Leisure could retrieve lost vitality by providing 'the fun of handling materials', the 'integrative experiences' of choral singing, the joys of 'building the skillful body', and the pleasures of 'adventuring with thought', of 'being alone', of 'taking something seriously' or 'just fooling around'. For Overstreet, such a diverse life of leisure would make a 'truly civilized' people in so far as it overcame the cultural lag: 'A new generation, bred to the friendliness and good sportsmanship of play, habituated to wider horizons of thought and creative imagination, may be more wisely equipped to confront the new adventures ahead of us.'[54]

This progressivist impulse survived in the interwar years among Anglo-American educators who advocated training for leisure. Educators were not embarrassed (as many would be today) to advocate a liberal-arts education as the best sort of education for life after working hours. These pedagogues abandoned the Arnoldian defence of a liberal-arts education as a cultural fortress of an elite. Instead they argued that, while vocational education prepared for jobs that soon would be obsolete, liberal-arts education prepared the individual for a life of intellectual curiosity and social sensitivity – the 'real' occupation of the future. Unlike the ancient Greek elite who depended on the work of slaves, the modern leisure class would be democratic and freed from work by the machine. During recreation the individual, who had been lost in the new world of mechanical work and boring labour, could be revitalised.[55]

For proponents of the 'cultural lag' theory, like Robert and Helen Lynd, the evils of mass-consumer culture were not the products of ill-disciplined libido but of 'new forms of social illiteracy' created by the merchandisers. More effective consumer education and informed 'self-criticism' among consumers was necessary.[56] Managers of the British Broadcasting Corporation and even elements within American commercial radio shared this hope for educating a more critical audience.[57] Even the French socialist André Philip, took a similar stance: in order to combat cultural Americanisation, socialists must not limit themselves to the struggle for material betterment. They should also be a *force d'éducation* to 'create men who are masters of themselves and capable of realising themselves'.[58]

Yet most writers were sceptical about the possibility of leisure as a compensation for meaningless work: 'The only ones who can be saved from the evil effects of the machine are those who do not require saving', said Cutten. Even Durant feared that without training in youth, workers would be 'unable to leave the old world of work or to enter the new world of leisure'. Still these same authors insisted that educated leisure was the only antidote to mechanical work.[59]

The democratisation of time and money was a threat to intellectuals. Their solutions vacillated between intellectual withdrawal or paternalistic education. Were the people simply a collective libido released from necessary constraints, or were they victims of mechanisation? Were they a threat to high culture or, despite their debilitating experience, did they possess untapped vitality and a capacity for adapting to an uplifting culture? However these questions were answered, mass culture was problematic and even a threat to most intellectuals. This attitude made it impossible for most humanists to contribute to an effective democratic alternative to commercial leisure.

CULTURAL POPULISM IN THE 1930s

Of course, not all intellectuals were so wary of the growth of free time in the twentieth century. A group of populists rejected the negative association of mechanisation and mass leisure and sought contact between intellectuals and the people. These ideas had a long pedigree and were hardly unknown in the 1920s in the vitalist followers of G. S. Hall and the humanistic advocates of efficiency like Bertrand Russell and Lewis Mumford.[60] But the Depression gave a great impetus to this populism. And it took many forms.

In France, the emergence of an alliance of intellectuals and workers is perhaps the most striking. It took place in the context of the growing threat of fascism and the formation of the Popular Front in 1935 (see chapter 5). The operative term, 'engagement', was perhaps best identified with Paul Nizan's *Les Chiens de garde*

(1932). Nizan condemned the vaunted independence of intellectuals and their self-proclaimed role as defenders of eternal truths. When Nizan insisted that all literature was political, even when authors attempted to stand above contemporary culture, he was attacking Julien Benda's *Trahison des clercs* (1927). Yet even Benda became a fellow traveller in the 1930s. Engaged French intellectuals, however, seldom confronted the concrete reality of popular culture; rather they were involved in popular political issues (especially in movements against fascism) and were concerned with the impact of political engagement on intellectual integrity.[61] For example, Emmanuel Mounier and his 'personalist' movement inspired a Catholic engagement with the 'people' against an individualistic and reactionary Catholicism. The writers for Mounier's journal, *Esprit*, participated in the labour movement's Colleges du Travail and doubtless other forms of improving leisure; they shared a vague ideology of anti-consumerist self-denial, European federalism, and an optimism that youth would produce a new European. But *Esprit* was not concerned with the theoretical implications of leisure practices and was extremely wary of direct involvement in working-class politics. Nevertheless the notion of engagement set the stage for the cultural and leisure movements of the Popular Front (see chapter 5). It surely inspired leaders of the contemporary popular culture movements in France.[62]

A similar populism was less dramatic in Britain and the US. But, perhaps because it was less active in politics, the Anglo-American variety addressed the problem of mass leisure more directly. In Britain, given the absence of serious Popular Front politics, a cultural populism thrived in such forms as the Left Book Club and Mass-Observation.[63] The 'political' act was to 'go to the people', not to educate and ally with country or factory folk, but, more modestly, to understand the 'other'. Many shared with J. B. Priestley an interest in the everyday life of individual working people, rather than the political potential of the 'masses'.[64] Symptomatic of change among American intellectuals was Matthew Josephson's call for a rapprochement between popular culture and intellectuals in his *Portrait of the Artist as American* of 1931. The expatriate artist must come to terms with American culture: the 'salvation and strength of artists' was found in their ability 'to incorporate themselves in the actual milieu'.[65]

In this context, populist intellectuals developed largely favourable attitudes toward specific forms of mass leisure. Some found virtue in what the middle-class outsider might have seen as 'degrading' leisure. By the mid-1930s, writers even defended such traditional 'bad boys' of popular leisure as the football pools and the commercial film as harmless excitements. Cinema, said the English sociologist Denys Hardy, was a means to 'extend and define our sympathies and so control our subtler emotional life' and to remind us 'of the more interesting possibilities of living'. John Hilton, an academic and BBC talk-show host, sponsored an essay contest on the theme, 'Why I go in for the pools', in the midst of a hostile parliamentary hearing on gambling. Respondents stressed that betting was done in a wholesome family setting on Thursday evenings, that it gave pleasure without great cost, and that winnings went into little gifts for the family. An overriding theme, however, was the hypocrisy of parliamentarians for preaching against working-class gambling when the MPs bet on race horses and speculated on the stock market.[66] This changing attitude toward popular leisure was reflected in a less didactic style in adult education in France and Britain (see chapter 5). In the early 1930s, popular pressure forced the BBC into offering more popular musical and educational formats.[67]

A greater openness to plebian pleasures was expressed in Ivor Brown's celebration of consumer culture in his *The Heart of England* (1935). The English were 'a cheerful people with a good notion of how to enjoy themselves'; when they vacationed at Blackpool, the 'capital of pleasure', or created cosy nooks in their otherwise monotonous houses, Brown insisted, they knew what they wanted. 'Urban intellectuals' failed to understand the people's resourcefulness and the meaning of pleasure. The Briton Jack Common mocked the moralising style of a Constance Harris and the pretentiousness of an Orwell or Mass-Observer who sought the proletarian 'savage' in the local pub. Working-class people, he claimed, were wilfully complex: they combined thrift with splurges, loose morals with sending children to Sunday School, and ardent individualism with love of the street crowd. They were hardly victims of work or merchandisers.[68]

Some populists went so far as to argue that industrialism made possible a more egalitarian and tolerant leisure culture. While John C. Hammond heralded the 'Era of Common Enjoyment' in 1933, a year earlier his English compatriot C. Delise Burns declared that 'leisure is the most valuable product of modern mechanisms'; the reduction of worktime had created a 'widening of choice of the majority', and a 'greater tendency to make experiments'. Everywhere Burns found blessings in new technology. Mass-produced clothing reduced caste distinctions especially after work: 'in leisure it is difficult to distinguish the factory worker from the doctor's daughter'. The wireless, the phonograph, and the cinema were 'bridging gaps' between peoples. Because 'most of the time' we must 'look at what others enjoy, in order to enjoy occasionally what we ourselves enjoy best', we broaden ourselves and experience a 'common feeling'. All this led to a 'democratic civilisation' and a 'freer and subtler community between all men'.[69]

While the American Lewis Mumford, in his classic *Technics and Civilization* (1934), railed against the nineteenth century's smothering of folk culture, he shared with Burns an optimism about 'new' mechanisation in the twentieth century:

> When automatism becomes general and the benefits of mechaniz-ation are socialized, men will be back once more in the Edenlike state . . . : the ritual of leisure will replace the ritual of work, and work itself will become a kind of game.[70]

C. C. Furnas, a Yale University chemical engineer, in 1931 adapted a similar technological dream, not to praise new consumer goods as one might expect, but to glorify a 'two hour [work]day'.[71] Lamenting the continuing prejudices in favour of hard work in a technological age, Furnas insisted that 'if liberal education does nothing more than render people harmless, it is worth while in our dangerous, mobile age'.[72]

The eccentric French leftist Jacques Duboin looked to electrifi-cation as the panacea. It would lead to the gradual disengagement from work and a new, more positive attitude toward free time: technology would lead to a decongestion of the city and create a suburban paradise. A little house with a 'patch of land' for gardens would replace 'industrial smog, noise of sirens, often dirty and inadequate lodgings, and the costly corner bistro'. With the electri-fication of the home, the suburban male worker could become an artisan again 'like his grandfather'. This was a curious expression of a common nostalgia for the village utopia. It was merely updated with 'neo-technical' modernisms and buttressed by a conviction that traditional community could survive mechanisation in leisure time.[73]

Burns, Mumford, Furnas, and Duboin shared a faith in a human-ising technology. Along with this went a democratic belief in the rationality of humanity. The conservative's negative psychological assessment of the 'mass man' was based on a 'profound ignorance of common life', said Burns. Aristotle's leisure elite was obsolete: 'The social function performed by a leisure class in the past can now be performed by those who have to work for a living' because of increased free time. The common folk could 'reach the frontier as much as we' intellectuals. The old ideals of the 'lady and gentleman' were developed in the seventeenth century in exclusive salons. But new models of culture must come from 'shops and streets, in buses and public libraries'. The new standards would emerge from youth and would be expressed in the ideals of the 'energetic' personality, 'variety', and 'fellowship with strangers'.[74] Bertrand Russell also condemned the traditional leisure class for its parasitism and its hypocritical preaching of a 'gospel of work'. That class might 'produce one Darwin, but against him had to be set tens of thousands of country gentlemen who never thought of anything more intelligent than fox-hunting and punishing poachers'. If all were to be able to join the leisure class, said Russell, 'every person possessed of scientific curiosity will be able to indulge it, and every painter will be able to paint without starving'.[75]

This optimistic assessment of new technology and its democratic cultural potential was closely linked with a belief that increased material security and free time released a positive, rather than negative, psychological core. When workers were less tired and less burdened with child rearing and home maintenance (with smaller families and modern flats), said Burns, increased leisure and income would lead not to boredom or nervousness but to an improved use of free time. Economic security would produce a more tolerant people: 'ordinary men and women, having the opportunity of a happy life, will become more kindly and less inclined to view others with suspicion', Russell predicted. Workers were passive because of the stress of modern labour, not their natural infantilism.[76] Even if mechanical work were disabling, populists were convinced that free time could play a compensatory role.

Burns' technological optimism and positive mass psychology laid the pylons for bridges between intellectuals and the people. But populist intellectuals did not build many bridges. Not only was the influence of this democratic impulse limited and brief, but it was itself riddled with ambiguity.

LIMITS OF CULTURAL POPULISM

The populism of the 1930s was always rooted in the conflict of intellectual leftists, torn, as Orwell put it, between their isolation from the 'common culture of the people' and their status as people 'who have never been and never expect to be in a position of power'.[77] This ambiguity led populist intellectuals alternatively into an uncritical embrace of 'common' consumer culture and a reactive rejection of popular leisure when they identified with the powerful.

Populist writers, in an effort to defend the democratic potential of mass leisure, slid easily into a rationalisation of mass consumption. Burns and others argued that increased spending led not to mass-market mediocrity but to greater variety of life; and even if most commercial recreation was escapist, that was not bad 'occasionally'. Films, for example, were an alternative to the pub and offered an opportunity for women to join the public world. Burns went so far as to argue that gambling provided an 'excitement' as valid as the tranquility offered by rambling. And, if the working class wasted its time, Burns reminded us, all classes have always done so. In any case we should not 'urge any one who is satisfied with the playing field to go further from the city of common life'.[78]

But, in *The Shape of Things to Come* (1933), H. G. Wells took this consumer vision even further with his enthusiasm for a future civilisation based on 'purchasing power'. A mobile people living in smaller houses would constantly seek 'changing scenery'. A 'clearing away' would define the new age. The 'real lesson of plenty' was not 'getting things' but 'getting rid of things'. The 'problem of socialising property' was to be solved in Wells' utopia not by the distribution of plenty but by 'use and consumption of material goods without the burden of ownership'.[79]

To be sure, not all were so uncritical of consumerism. In 1931, the American leader of the National Recreation Association, Howard Braucher, rejected the rising chorus praising spending and appealed to recreation leaders to promote leisure 'without the expenditure of large sums of money'. But his colleague Henry Pratt insisted that the Depression had created a 'duty of consumption'; he even advocated that a 'philosophy of waste' should displace the 'gospel of work'.[80]

The naivety of these appeals to mass consumption are immediately evident. Not only do these writers underestimate the power of social emulation, they hold fast to a naive progressivist faith in technology and democracy. For Burns, there was no real distinction between the impact of technology and the market on the one hand, and democratic and voluntarist action on the other. They would work together to create a more tolerant and egalitarian society. He set up a 'straw man', the cultural traditionalist, as the impediment to progress in the democratisation of leisure, rather than the

totalitarian or impresario. The result was an inability to conceptualise an effective alternative to commercial leisure built around non-
market and popular participation in public cultural and recreational
activities.

Probably a greater problem for populist intellectuals was, however, the opposite tendency – their difficulty in sustaining faith and
interest in the potential of popular culture and democratic leisure.
Because Anglo-American populism in the 1930s took primarily cultural rather than political forms (as in France), their cases are
especially instructive. Most revealing is the rich 'travel' literature
that depicted the everyday life of working people in work and
especially play.

An ambivalence toward British workers' leisure was surely
reflected in George Orwell's famous *Road to Wigan Pier*. Less
renowned but as indicative of the intellectual milieu of the later
1930s was Mass-Observation. This group of mostly well-educated
young English artists and self-taught anthropologists observed daily
life in the late 1930s in the industrial Lancashire town of Bolton
and its 'outcropping', the seaside resort centre of Blackpool. While
the objective was 'truth', undistorted by theory or class prejudice,
Mass-Observation made a radical political statement when it tried
to give ordinary people a voice.[81] Bolton was an ideal choice for
study in that it expressed for many educated English southerners the
essence of the grimy North.[82] The industrial northern environment
produced an honest, life-hardened proletariat, an inspiration for
the soft, jaded southerner.[83] The act of observation expressed a mix
of feelings – guilt, social concern, curiosity, and a search for the
'authentic' in the hardy North.

Even earlier in the 1930s, American literati shared with Priestley,
Orwell and Mass-Observation, a quest for communion with the
people. Abandoning the interior life of fictional characters and
the company of New York intellectuals, Louis Adamic, Nathan
Asch, Theodore Dreiser, Erskine Caldwell, James Rorty, Sherwood
Anderson, and Edmund Wilson travelled throughout the US in
search of real people and the data for social action. Their quest was
as much for release from the jaded existence of the intellectual.
'We do not want cynicism. We want belief', Anderson admitted.[84]

The American populist utopia was found, not as in England
among the urban proletariat, but in the rural heartland of farm
workers, lumberjacks and miners. Anderson found men 'from the
oldest American stock we have. It is the kind of stock out of
which came Abraham Lincoln.' In such people, the old values

of community at least were remembered. The same sort of nostalgia was evident in the topics chosen for photographs taken for the New Deal Farm Security Administration in the late 1930s and early 1940s.[85] Even the technocrat Stuart Chase sought a 'lost' society in the villages of Mexico. He found in Oaxaca and Tepoztlan a culture which integrated work and leisure, and where, he assured us, people had 'more fun' than in industrial America.[86]

The French Popular Front, a coalition not only of antifascist parties, but of leftist intellectuals, was the rough equivalent of the Anglo-American attempt at 'going to the people'. But that engagement did not occur in travels and published diaries; it took the form of participation in shifting literary organisations like the Association of Revolutionary Artists and Writers, many of which predated the formation of the political Popular Front in 1935. Journals like *Vendredi* provided leftist intellectuals with a forum for their populism. Mass demonstrations against fascism also had a cathartic effect on many intellectual participants: 'Never have I been loved in this way: loved by unknown people, because I am one of them. . . . Around us all, in us all, there is one absolute conviction: that's it, we are going to be happy.'[87]

But these gestures were essentially ambiguous. Mass-Observation's quest for the opinion and the audience of the 'everyman' was always tempered by pessimism toward popular leisure. According to Tom Harrisson, a leading Mass-Observer, modern culture was an adaptation of 'old superstitions to new conditions'. The Mass-Observers found many instances of this principle in the popular attractions of Blackpool. At the side-show stalls, they found the religious fatalism of the past directed toward modern science in the fortune-telling machine. And they believed that this quasi-religiosity was manipulated 'for commercial, political, or other reasons'.[88] Working-class culture as 'tribal life' hardly meshed with Burns' technological vision of a democratic cultural future.

American populist writers were similarly contradictory. While Anderson found 'very little bitterness' among jobless Americans, he attributed this to an irrational fixation on the work ethic: 'In America every man who is broke, down on his luck, is half ashamed of the fact' and obliged to 'explain' himself. Louis Adamic also discovered a chronic psychological malaise in the American city. An abiding sense of inadequacy dominated American immigrants, which he argued, was a result of an 'actual inferiority in character, mind and physique'. The only solution was confidence building in the acquisition of 'a knowledge of, and pride in their own heritage and makeup'. Still, he doubted that the American working classes had any potential for leading a collectivist revolution. Finally Rorty held that Americans were so conditioned by the make-believe of Hollywood and advertising that they were incapable of a sustained understanding of their situation or of doing anything about it.[89]

Ultimately these writers could not conceive of real change coming from the 'salt of the earth'. By the late 1930s, the American literati's hero was no longer the people but the isolated individual. Still this change hardly removed the longing for social commitment, especially in the context of the rising threat of fascism.[90] From 1936, many embraced the new fashion of defending prevailing 'democratic' culture from the 'foreign' threat of totalitarianism. As the historian Richard Pells notes, 'what began as an effort to find out where the country had gone wrong frequently ended as a celebration of all that seemed right'.[91]

Archibald MacLeish, Gilbert Seldes and others enthusiastically affirmed their 'belief' rather than their dissent; and they declared the superiority of American values over imported European 'doctrine'. To be sure, these authors were deeply hostile to the status quo and some even supported a gradualist 'planned socialism' in the face of the fascist threat. But the solution was less reform than, in MacLeish's words, 'democratic loyalty': both the scholar and popular writer were irresponsible in their failure to defend the 'common culture'. This duty required a 'rediscovery of the past'.[92] Gilbert Seldes combated the cultural jeremiahs with a 'countercharge': 'that the literary belittling of America has carried forward a propaganda for the destruction of the American political system and the abasement of the American standard of living'. He pointedly endorsed 'the common man against the intellectual . . . ; [and] increase, production, and fecundity against scarcity, limitation and sterility'. The real fun was to be had, not in Chase's machine-less Mexican villages, but in Danbury and Dubuque. To be sure, America was not perfect; but the central problem was one of recognising that workers had a right to a high wage. Increased disposable personal income, not collectivism or 'limitation', was the guarantee of American democracy. The American alternative to fascist capitalism and Marxist collectivism was 'eternal growth and increase'. Seldes not only linked the American Way of life to materialist aspirations, but he suggested that the very idea of a non-commercial democratic leisure culture was elitist.[93] Unable to maintain the tension between engagement and autonomy, these American intellectuals slipped from negation to affirmation, from a pride in self-exile to an admiration of power and conventional aspirations.

French intellectuals took a rather different turn but it led to a similar place. As early as 1934, the Association of Revolutionary Artists and Writers shifted its commitment from the revolutionary proletariat to the 'indivisible culture' of France. During the governing period of the Popular Front (1936–7), engaged intellectuals defended their Maisons de Culture not as centres of proletarian art but missions of the French cultural tradition.[94] Louis Aragon abandoned his surrealist ideas to defend French high culture – even if in service to the French Communist Party. An amazing array of theatre, adult education, and voluntary tour groups emerged after 1934 (see chapter 5). Their purpose, however, was not to find a common ground between popular and high culture, much less to explore new art forms, but to bring traditional and high culture to the masses. To be sure, Fernand Léger tried to use modernist art forms to build bridges between elites and the masses. But the more common approach was Aragon's attempt to revive French folklore.[95] The famous film of the Popular Front, *La Marseillaise*, was less a glorification of the French Revolution than of the unity of the 'real' people of France, the pre-industrial peasant and artisan, retaking their homeland in their march north from Marseilles to Paris in 1792. An opportunity for positive cultural exchanges between the intellectual and contemporary popular culture was obscured in a fog of Jacobin nostalgia and patriotic traditionalism.[96]

Populist appeals for community turned from the futurist and democratic visions of leisure with affluence in Burns and Mumford to the nostalgia for tradition in Aragon and Seldes. Dreams of bridging gaps between educated and popular culture drifted into intellectual elitism. Even Mumford's call for a neotechnological age was, in the final analysis, conservative: he envisaged a new community based on the collective management of resources and time; but ultimately it required a self-imposed stability built on 'normalized consumption'; and, despite protests that he was not a technological determinist, Mumford relied upon technology and a managerial elite to get us to that 'second Eden'. He ignored the people in their everyday lives. Indeed, by the end of the 1930s, Mumford too grew more pessimistic about the possibilities of cultural change and the democratic potential of leisure.[97] Gilbert Seldes may have corrected the earlier idealism by returning to the popular culture in its concrete detail. But he did so at the price of sacrificing the intellectual's critical distance and by indulging in both a sentimental nostalgia for Americana and a crude affirmation of consumerism as the equivalent of liberty and democracy. Neither extreme was able to bridge the distance between the intelligentsia and the people.

By the late 1930s, we see a return to the pessimistic assessment of popular culture that had prevailed in the 1920s. Robert Lynd's sequel, *Middletown in Transition* (1937) revealed serious doubts that 'the people' could develop an 'adaptive culture' to catch up to technology. Despite the growth of neighbourliness in Middletown during the Depression, Lynd found in his re-visit, not creative cooperation, but power elite manipulation, conformism, and a popular desire for security. He had lost hope that consumer education could overcome 'social illiteracy'. Advertisers were simply too influential.[98]

In his *Knowledge for What?* (1939), Robert Lynd wondered whether conflicting cultural messages could produce anything but frustration: part of that culture told people to save and another to spend; and a few powerful institutions and ideas exercised a disproportionate influence over a 'go-as-you-please culture'. Lynd agreed with Carl Becker that the distance between the people and the intellectuals had grown wider in the modern world:

> [T]here has emerged a new class of learned men, . . . whose function is to increase rather than to preserve knowledge, to undermine rather than to stabilize custom and social authority. . . . But within this enlarged frame of reference common men are not at home.[99]

The absence of social bonds made Americans both pathologically competitive and imitative. In Europe a similar situation led to Hitler's success with his appeals to 'the clean release of unequivocal action'. But in the US, 'modern merchandising manipulates our hunger for a way out, a fresh start, by selling us a new car, an Easter bonnet, or an electric razor as a momentary splurge into authoritative certainty'. Totalitarian and consumer psychology were the same.[100]

The implication was clear to Lynd: these 'common men' needed social scientists to counter the influence of the advertisers in order to create for them a leisure culture better adapted to modern conditions. But Lynd agreed with Harold Lasswell and Thurmon Arnold that the masses responded not to reason or even self-interest but to deeply embedded emotional symbols, which, at best, could be manipulated behind the scenes by rational and pragmatic leaders for the general good.[101] This vision of 'leadership by a caring elite of professional planners', as Richard Wightman Fox puts it, may have been implicit in Lynd's thinking since he wrote his first Middletown study; but it reflects also a growing pessimism in the possibility of spontaneous community between the intellectuals and the people in the late 1930s.[102]

An equally pessimistic approach was taken by the alienated left-wing American intellectuals around the *Partisan Review*, a highly influential group that emerged in the late 1930s. The best known expression of this American tendency was Clement Greenberg's attack on 'kitsch', both as a product of popular taste uprooted from folk culture and as a diluted form of high culture. Another contributor, Dwight Macdonald, lambasted the pseudo-seriousness of 'midcult' and Popular Front culture. Like Eliot, he preferred the honesty of mass-media escapism and pure high culture to this ersatz and pretentious attempt to mix the two. William Phillips insisted that intellectuals should abandon their embrace of the crowd for independent intellectual community.[103]

Thus the populist decade of the 1930s ended in the US with an intellectual retreat from social commitment and a return to the defence of classical elite culture. The threat of totalitarianism and frustrations with mass consumerism surely explain much of this. But, it may be fair to ask, did these American intellectuals ever make a serious attempt to build bridges to popular culture? The various idealised images of the 'people' were all too often based on nostalgia or a futurist utopia. In this avoidance of the present, they shared much with their more conservative counterparts. Seldes, of course, expressed a positive approach to popular culture, but all too easily fell into an uncritical affirmation of mass consumerism.

This failure to come to terms with 'real existing' popular culture was just as clear in Europe. Orwell and Priestley in their journeys of discovery found an abiding 'love of liberty', or 'deep tinge of Christian feeling' among the whist players and 'bawdy joke tellers' of industrial England. But they saw also people who 'nearly all looked as if life had knocked them into odd shapes' and who smelled. The new consumer culture was, of course, part of the problem: Priestley contrasted the joy of men singing 'glees over their beer' with the modern habit of passively listening for the latest hit. He was disgusted by Blackpool's amusement 'machines that laugh for us' and the shows that 'collect audiences and then get rid of them as soon as possible' in a 'catch penny process'. Priestley concluded: 'Monotonous but easy work and a liberal supply of cheap luxuries might well between them create a set of people entirely without ambition or any real desire to think and act for themselves, the perfect subjects for an iron autocracy.' Orwell worried about the rise since 1919 of an 'indeterminate social class' subsisting in a 'rather restless, culture-less life, centring round tinned food, *Picture Post*, the radio and the internal combustion engine'.[104]

That 'indeterminate class' was the problem. These English humanists saw a new social type, created, not as the Marxists had insisted, by the production process, but out of the world of leisure and consumption. Idealised images of a heroic human core or a noble savage thriving in the adversity of the industrial North clashed with the 'Worktowner' vacationing at Blackpool. Priestley fell back on a classic solution just as did many others: there were two working classes. The first, consisting of the 'less intelligent and enterprising', had become the 'fit patrons of the new Blackpool, which knows what to do with the passive and listless'. But a new sort of working class was now emerging that did 'not want the new Blackpool and would probably have rejected the old: it does not care for mass entertainment and prefers to spend its leisure in quieter places, cycling and walking and playing games in the sun'.[105] It was this new working class that leisure reformers would seek and that Mass-Observers perhaps hoped to find among the factory workers of Bolton.

But did this working class really exist, except in the imagination of populist intellectuals? The cultural wall separating that elite from the worker was breached only when temporary economic or political coalitions formed. These conditions existed especially in the early 1930s. They continued in distinctly national forms in Britain and France during and immediately after World War II. But they hardly led to a permanent cultural rapprochement or the possibility of a democratic leisure culture beyond the marketplace.

The underlying problem was frustration at the 'indeterminate social classes' and the apparent fact that the impresarios of pleasure, the Northcliffes and Disneys, had created an effective alliance of taste with the masses, and had given effective meaning to 'freedom' in leisure. The intellectuals' search for a 'new' working-class culture (especially among youth) was, of course, a quest for people who had somehow evaded that consumerism. There was a logic behind the hope that this 'new' working class might be found in 'traditional' areas (Middletown or Worktown), somehow perhaps less corrupted by change. But more honestly what the 'new' group had in common was the amalgam of tastes of the intellectual elite – 'modern' but nostalgic, comradely but uncomfortable in a raunchy crowd, and life-affirming but prudish and essentially ascetic. When this new class was not found, the only solution was to 'raise' the masses or to retreat from them. Thus the old nineteenth-century gap between 'culture' and 'anarchy' survived in the ditch between populist intellectuals and working people with their very different sensibilities toward leisure. The attempts of intellectuals to bridge the gap and to meet the people beyond paternalism led to discovery of the poverty of connectedness. An honest assessment of this gap (as in Orwell) appeared to be the only alternative to idealisation and blame.

A politics of democratic leisure possibly could have created an alternative or, at least, a popular language of alternatives to mass consumerism. But what was missing in the 1930s was an understanding between the intelligentsia and the people upon which such an alternative could have been built. This may now be obvious from the vantage of the late twentieth century. But these differences did not prevent attempts to forge a political alliance around a balance of work and free time and a culture of 'democratic leisure', as we shall presently show.

4 Time becomes money: the politics of distribution and recovery

By the twentieth century, the distribution of time and money had become a public issue. In different ways, its prospects obsessed economists and humanists. But this distribution also took centre stage in political struggles. Steady national economic growth combined with the concept of a democratic commonwealth legitimated political choices: productivity could be allocated in the form of investment, consumption, or time free from work. These options were already at the core of collective struggles over worktime and pay in the nineteenth century. To be sure, Malthusian wage doctrines and laissez-faire prejudice against economic democracy severely biased the choice toward investment. But, by the late 1880s, a loose coalition of social liberals and trade unionists had emerged throughout the industrial world. They forcefully advocated not only the democratic share out of time and money but the importance of such a distribution for further growth.

Essential to this perspective was the notion of an 'international labour standard'. This concept challenged not only the gross disparities in material living standards between industrial nations but asserted the idea of a 'right' to a universal minimum of time free from work. This doctrine gradually emerged in the nineteenth century. When industrial employers attempted to replace the informal pace and duration of labour by a standard and intense workday, they produced also its mirror opposite: a demand for an equally uniform and fully unimpeded period free from work. This international quest for time culminated in 1919 with the general concession of the eight-hour day (or 48-hour week) in industrial Europe and the US.

The asymmetry between capital and labour, and growing business competition made the market an inadequate arena for winning this standard. It inevitably became a political, and with the emergence of international trade, even a diplomatic issue. The Washington Eight-Hour Convention of 1919 was the first project of the International Labor Organisation (ILO). This convention attempted to enforce that standard as an entitlement to free time against the downward pressures of market competition. For ILO Director Albert Thomas, the eight-hour day was both a legitimate fruit of mass productivity and a guarantor of optimal use of labour power in a mechanical age. Thomas and his associates combined the democratisation of time free from work with scientific management for enhanced productivity. Indeed this linkage between non-economic time and productivity would form the base for demands for further distribution of leisure in the Depression.

Yet the idea of an international and progressive reduction of worktime was discredited in the 1930s. Instead, the debate over the allocation of productivity was lowered to the national, plant, and individual planes. It was reduced to the struggle between profit and wages which crowded out the democratic non-monetary implications of industrial productivity. During this period, free-time goals themselves were increasingly equated with opportunities to consume or to dream of a consumers' paradise. Leisure became a tool for achieving economic equilibrium in a mass-production age, a counter-weight to 'overproduction' and a means of distributing income-producing jobs. Free time lost its status as an end, a product of productivity but free from the iron cage of economism. Instead, it became the opportunity for mass consumption necessary to absorb the unlimited potential of industrialism. Time became money: distribution was transformed into the economic recovery of 'full-time' jobs and consumption in the 1930s. An essential part of this transition was the shift from the idea of a progressive expansion of daily free time to 'packages' of leisure at the weekend and during annual vacations. This was hardly anticipated by the many advocates of 'vacations for all' who saw in the democratic holiday an opportunity for freedom from industrialism and a site for a democratic leisure culture. Yet, for many, this packaged leisure became an intense dose of consumption time. During the interwar years, the choice between time and money was more clearly understood than before; but it was also a period which eroded the idea of the progressive improvement in the general standard of leisure and instead introduced individualised free time dominated by the annual vacation and consumption. The burden of this chapter is to explain this political transformation.

POLITICS OF TIME TO 1930

In 1900, the workweek in the US and western Europe varied greatly by trade and region, clustering around the range of 52 to 60 hours. At the lower end of the scale were skilled, unionised manufacturing and male-dominated occupations, especially in Britain and the US. The worktime of wage-earners in retail, transportation and seasonal (often sweated) trades was longer, sometimes much longer, especially in France. Not only was the workday long, but its duration varied dramatically. Many wage-earners experienced annual cycles of extreme overwork and under- and unemployment. There were no national hours standards.[1]

From at least the second decade of the twentieth century, organised workers and professional reformers shared a common perspective: technology made reductions in worktime both possible and necessary. Lost output due to hours free from labour could easily be offset by increased labour productivity; and shorter hours would stimulate further mechanisation and, in turn, prompt still more pressure to cut hours. Reduced worktime would not simply increase the number of jobs but lead to the social betterment of labouring families and the expansion of consumer demand. No longer was leisure merely a necessity for vulnerable mothers and children but, as a fruit of industrial society, it became a right for all, including adult males.[2]

The popular demand for leisure in the first two decades of the century was revealed in employers' complaints of increased absenteeism and turnover: in the US, new immigrants from eastern and southern Europe sacrificed wages for time with family.[3] Even during the emergency of war, British munitions workers would not abandon their holiday-taking customs. In France in 1917, women textile workers sparked two years of free-time agitation by demanding Saturday afternoons away from the factory.[4] The eight-hour day was on the international labour agenda from the spring of 1917: it spread from the US and Russia across Europe from late 1917 and by mid-1919 had become standard in France and Britain. In the US, 28 states passed hour legislation in 1919 and 48.6 per cent of industrial wage-earners worked eight-hour days by the end of that year.[5]

While for many moderates the 48-hour week was optimal, for other reformers and organised labour, the mass productivity of the 1920s was a reason for a still further disengagement from work. Probably because of the fact that the US economy was the most innovative, Americans led the short-hour movement in the 1920s.[6] Motivations were certainly ambiguous. In 1925–6, American Federation of Labor (AFL) officials stressed the need for a 40-hour week in order to absorb workers who were made redundant through mechanisation. William Green told the US President in the summer of 1926 that 'labor must have shorter working hours in order to meet this condition of overproduction'.[7] Soon, however, American organised labour had backed away from the anti-growth implications of this argument and more consistently embraced a productivism that they had long held: productivity was not to be condemned for leading to joblessness and thus reduced hours were not the remedy to shrinking jobs. Rather, increased output was primarily the source of prosperity for all, and only secondarily the opportunity for increased leisure. High wages gained priority over hours as a way to distribute that growth. This did not mean an abandonment of time for money. The demand for the 40-hour week found a different rationale. It became a trade-off for intensified monotonous work and for 'recreation and recuperation . . . necessary to sustain vigor'.[8]

This change in the thinking of organised labour reflected more than a tactical accommodation to increased public confidence in growth in the mid-1920s. It was a response to the janus face of productivity: innovation threatened jobs but also promised goods. Shorter hours were a means toward the conservative goal of preserving existing employment and work culture, while money or high wages became the fruit of a progressive embrace of productivity. Unions were instruments of both job sharing and the productivity wage despite contrasting implications for the politics of time and money. Within the context of early twentieth-century capitalism, the politics of free time could be understood as anti-progressive: demanding shorter hours in order to combat overproduction suggested a goal of economic constraint, a limits-of-growth ideology; and business critics were correct to point out the conservative objective of protecting the occupational status quo. By contrast, the politics of money was forward-looking, implying growth and material fulfilment. The fact that both were fruits of productivity with legitimate, if conflicting, claims was obscured.

This 'trade union mentality' necessarily limited labour's leadership in the politics of time and money; and this view impeded an alliance with the intelligentsia in a movement for a disengagement from work (see chapter 2). Labour attitudes toward the distribution of productivity were inherently contradictory. Unions sought both money and time (even if the latter objective involved the contrasting purposes of compensatory leisure and job preservation). To be sure, trade unionists understood that mass productivity made leisure a radical alternative to work that no longer was central to life. In this way, free time became an end, and mass production an argument for a progressive reduction of worktime. But the focus on job protection and the productivity wage implied the opposite: a strong commitment to work culture and endlessly expanding needs. All of this would haunt the movement for shorter hours.

Paralleling this quest for shorter working hours was a movement for paid holidays. Until 1919, the demand for extended paid leave from work was rare among wage-earners. Excepting printers', miners', and railwaymen's unions, vacations were not on the labour agenda in Britain and France. Regional annual shutdowns of plants which coincided with traditional English 'wakes weeks' had pre-industrial origins. But especially after 1870, these festivals increasingly shifted to seaside resorts like Blackpool which were accessible by cheap railway ticket.[9] In France, vacations were the preserve of public employees and the middle class.[10] In the US, the extended holiday was equally a mark of affluence, facilitated in the late nineteenth century by resorts linked to the railroad.[11]

But the nineteenth-century 'holiday' had little in common with the popular movement for paid vacations after World War I. Especially in Europe, these holidays were often derived from traditional religious celebrations or communal fairs and sporting events. With the exception of the British August Bank Holiday (begun in 1875), none was designed to relieve the monotony of industrial work. Nor did they usually provide the working classes with an opportunity for travel and escape from work and home environments. This was because workers did not enjoy an extended period of leave nor were they compensated for vacation time. Even the Lancashire holiday was financed by voluntary workers' saving, not the employer. Still most English workers were unable to go away for more than a long weekend. For many, an annual shutdown – in order to refurbish machinery or because of slack sales – was merely a seasonal 'lockout'.[12]

To be sure, by 1900, European and American civil servants and clerks often enjoyed an annual holiday of several weeks. In fact, this was a mark of white-collar status. Paid vacation rights seem to have extended gradually outward from employers to those closest to their social status and contact – managers, foremen, clerical staff, and senior craft workers in stable trades. Employers rationalised their denying them to production workers on grounds that salaried employees earned no overtime and that their work could be made up after the vacation. Moreover, seasonal employees were slow to be granted holidays because vacations could hardly be said to improve their productivity. For many employers, paid holidays appeared merely as a wage increase. Employers granted white-collar employees vacations because they were 'brain workers'. Apparently employers assumed that the body of manual labourers needed only to be fed; and short daily durations of time free from work were sufficient for physiological recovery. From the standpoint of wage-earners, however, this refusal reflected their low social position and the employers' view that manual workers were incapable of benefiting from more than brief spells of rest away from work.[13]

Since 1911, the demand for 'total and sustained freedom from toil' had been on the agenda of the British Trades Union Congress (TUC). Yet only in the postwar wave of collective bargaining for the eight-hour day were paid vacations won by 2 million wage-earners in well-organised British trades and, at that, usually only on a local level.[14] Far fewer French workers won a week's paid vacation. In fact, the practice was far more developed in central and eastern Europe – and long before the *Kraft durch Freude* of the Nazis.[15]

Even slower to trickle down were vacations for the American working classes. Trade-union demands for paid holidays lagged behind European workers. American employers argued that vacations did not appeal to their production workers, especially those of 'foreign extraction'. Indeed, in the 1920s most paid vacations were 'gifts' of management who hoped that this privilege would increase employee productivity and company loyalty.[16] Employers dropped about half of these vacation programmes during the early Depression years when fear of unemployment provided a cost-free form of creating 'loyalty'. Only 5 per cent of American wage-earners enjoyed a paid vacation in 1920, a figure that rose to only 10 per cent by 1930. By contrast, 85 per cent of salaried employers shared this benefit by the end of the 1920s.[17]

Inevitably American unions focused on the economic issues of wages (and more ambiguously hours). This may be understood as part of the legendary tradition of American business unionism and its lack of a strong social agenda. But it was also a measure of the impotence of organised American labour. Also significant is the fact that almost half of the unionised workers in the US were employed in seasonal industries like mining, textiles, and building where employers had no incentive to recognise the paid vacation. But the lack of an American movement for a legal right to paid holidays was surely a mark of the relative weakness of social democratic traditions in the US.

In Europe, by contrast, there was a close relationship between the movements for the paid holiday and the reduction of worktime. Both movements peaked during the postwar period of labour militancy and reform. Both emerged from the same international demand for increased free time. But their paths diverged after 1925. The holiday with pay gained widespread support from the mid-1920s in Europe, while the shorter workday became identified with the increasingly impotent labour movement and redistributionist economics. To conservatives, a shorter workweek meant inflation and a threat to international economic competitiveness. By contrast, the Right often embraced the paid vacation as a measure of social hygiene and a legitimate entitlement of leisure. The contrasting fate of the movements for shorter working weeks and holidays with pay is central to the eclipse of the politics of free time.

AMERICAN POLITICS OF LEISURE AND RECOVERY IN THE 1930s

The Depression of the 1930s was surely the turning point in the debate over time and money. While employers blamed the slump on high labour costs, trade unions and reformist allies argued that increased productivity in the 1920s had not been balanced by either higher wages or a sharing of worktime. The consequence was 'underconsumption' and massive unemployment (or, put in labour's terms, unfunded and undistributed leisure time). The solution for unions was to maintain wages and reduce weekly working hours. Thus soaring joblessness sparked discussion of the need to distribute leisure – not merely to prime the economic pump.

Underlying labour policy was the theory of the 'mature' economy: technological growth inevitably had reduced the demand for labour. In 1932, the American Louis Walker observed: 'now we face the necessity of substituting leisure for mass unemployment'. The problem was not structural but a cultural or an ideological lag: too few understood that leisure was a *product* of industrialisation as much as were goods and that it must be distributed to avoid the tragedy of massive unemployment.[18]

The joblessness of the early 1930s, of course, resurrected the old trade-union call for reduced worktime.[19] The American movement was particularly vocal given an unemployment rate of 25 per cent in 1932. The AFL congress of November 1932 embraced the 30-hour week without a wage maintenance provision as an essential work-sharing measure. Still advocates expected a six-hour day to create sufficient labour scarcity to maintain or even to raise hourly wages. The W. W. Kellogg company adopted the 30-hour week in a well-publicised experiment in industrial paternalism. Soft coal, textiles and some western building companies reduced normal hours along with wages in order to spread the burden. Senator Hugo Black's 30-hour bill, introduced in December 1932 and approved by the Senate in April 1933, was conditionally endorsed by the incoming Roosevelt administration as a means of work sharing.

There are many ways of interpreting this short-hours movement. The historian Benjamin Hunnicutt offers a powerful argument: the 'gospel of consumption' had been discredited in the 1930s, leaving only reduced worktime as a solution to the endemic problem of overproduction.[20] As we have seen in chapters 2 and 3, a number of *intellectuals* thought they were witnessing the emergence of economic maturity or, as Mill called it, a 'stationary state society'. Producing less and disengaging from work were the logical consequences of a mature economy that could now meet 'real needs' but that could not distribute still more 'wasteful' goods.

But this analysis was hardly the perspective of labour, business, or government. To be sure, articles in the *American Federationist* stressed the technological rationale for a progressive expansion of leisure. AFL thinkers clearly saw a choice between technological displacement of workers and distribution of leisure.[21] As the AFL's William Green put the point in 1932, 'The principle of relating the number needing jobs to the total number of man-hours of work available should be permanently incorporated in national policy and business procedure.'[22] Still the AFL's overriding objective was to reduce unemployment, not to expand leisure; and there were other ways of creating jobs than shorter working hours. Doubtless some employers sought to reduce the potential hardships of the jobless by spreading them among all of their workers in decreased paid worktime. But most businesses not only opposed 'rigid' legislated worktime reductions, but feared that such diminutions might become permanent. Finally the Roosevelt Administration first and foremost wanted economic recovery; they adopted a hodge-podge of remedies, only one of which was work sharing. Most important, job creation programmes in effect contradicted the logic of work sharing. These facts partially explain why worktime movements largely failed in the 1930s.

By early 1933, both American business and the New Deal government were already backing away from work sharing. In April 1933, key senators, cabinet officials, business leaders and economists concluded that the 30-hour week was impractical; instead, they advocated public works and collective bargaining rights as alternative methods of creating jobs and of stimulating spending. Hunnicutt may well be correct that the New Deal government in effect coopted the political forces behind the 30-hour bill when it supported the National Industrial Recovery Act (NIRA) of 1933. Of the first 64 'Codes', or industrial agreements under the NIRA, 50 established not a 30-hour but a 40-hour workweek (even when the average workweek was under 36 hours). The purpose was not job sharing but, as Roosevelt noted, 'a limited code of fair competition', eliminating those sweat-shop conditions that employers had used to gain a price edge. At the same time, the NIRA included a jobs creation programme. In 1934, Secretary of the Interior Harold Ickes made the government's objectives clear:

> No one can reasonably contend that the standard of living in this country is so high that we can afford to . . . require the employed portion [of the workforce] permanently to divide their work with the unemployed. . . . Our task is to find useful work and employment for all of our people by increasing the interchange of goods and services among them.[23]

When the NIRA was declared unconstitutional in 1935, Roosevelt embraced the Wagner Act (which encouraged unionisation and wage increases via collective bargaining), public works programmes, and an 'easy money' policy.[24] His goal was recovery of production rather than work sharing. The 30-hour bill of 1932 was transformed into the Fair Labor Standards Act of 1938. In its final form, that law did no more than create a minimum wage of 40 cents and a standard 40-hour week. The watered-down law reflected the intense lobbying of business and the growing conservatism of New Deal democrats. It was also a product of the 1937 recession and the emerging view that the economic goal should be not the *distribution* of time and money but increased production.[25] The Fair Labor Standards Act did not reduce the worktime norm below the industrial mean and thus it was merely a law against 'sweatshop' conditions. In Roosevelt's words, it protected the 'underpaid and overworked'. The only justification of short hours that today remains widely accepted is its humanitarian value of setting limits on exploitation.[26]

Until Pearl Harbor, the AFL continued to press for the six-hour day in collective bargaining. But, at the insistence of employers, Roosevelt declared a 48-hour minimum in February of 1943 in war industries. After the war, while unions endorsed 30 hours work for 40 hours pay, this demand was largely a dead letter. In any case, pent up demand for goods probably stimulated pressure from the rank-and-file for wage increases in place of reduced worktime. But a decade earlier, the New Deal had already successfully shifted the debate to a choice between higher wages (dependent on increased output) and shorter hours. To be sure, unions remained surprisingly loyal to the 30-hour concept. Yet, because organised labour linked short hours to re-employment and high wages, they accepted a 'recovery ' programme. By 1937, American unions had embraced the administration's alternative package of public works, minimum wage, and eventually a 40-hour maximum (with overtime pay).[27]

Surely political realities (especially southern opposition to more radical legislation) forced organised American labour to accept the New Deal programme. Yet, without a firm commitment to the technocrat's ideal of limited needs (see chapter 2), organised labour was susceptible to ideological alternatives to work sharing. The conditions that gave rise to the 30-hour movement were precisely the conditions that guaranteed its failure. A six-hour day implied 'sharing the misery', not an emerging disengagement from work. To many American workers, job creation via 'Keynesian' fiscal measures and a 'humanitarian' labour standard were acceptable substitutes for work sharing for they addressed both their 'conservative' job and 'progressive' wage concerns. The notion of 'distributed leisure' was an intellectual option but not a political one.

In any case, it encountered a powerful ideological opposition. Consider the response of public interest economists in the US. Members of the Brookings Institution generally admitted that the Depression was a result of economic imbalances but they stressed income maldistribution, not worktime. The Depression had 'weakened productive capacity with respect to plant and equipment as well as labor'. The path to take then was to stimulate spending (by lowering prices) and to restore investment and employment. Pointedly the objective was not to share work. In a 1934 Brookings study, Harold Moulton and his colleagues stressed that the unfulfilled desires for goods 'of the American people are large enough to absorb a productive output many times that achieved in the peak year 1929. . . . The trouble is clearly not lack of desire but lack of purchasing power. . . . [W]e have not as yet reached the age of abundance of which we all like to dream and that extensive leisure has not as yet been *forced upon us* as an alternative to a surfeit of goods and services' (my italics).[28] The 30-hour week would only reduce the capacity to produce.

In another work, Moulton noted that the 30-hour week would 'offer to the workers of the country *merely* a choice between more leisure and a more abundant consumption of goods and services' (my italics). To Moulton, this choice was irrelevant when the 'duty of the nation is to prevent want among the unemployed'. This could not be achieved by a 'compulsory reduction of the hours of work, which would freeze the possible volume of production below the level required to give all the people the abundance they desire'.[29]

Moulton not only disassociated productivism from free time but, by embracing a consumerist ideology of unlimited need, he revealed a bias toward work. These themes were already well developed in the 1920s in the works of Catchings and Foster and among the 'new unionists' who also embraced the linkage between high wages and increased productivity.[30] But they were intensified during the Depression. The dominant word was 'recovery' not 'balance' or 'distribution' and this entailed resumption of growth – of consumption and work.

But even a strong proponent of distributed leisure like Louis Walker shared much with Moulton. While his argument for a progressive diminution of the workweek assumed a 'mature' economy, in the context of depression, Walker gave a narrow meaning to free time: leisure was to be an essential component in solving the crisis of overproduction. Unlike commodities, 'leisure has one wonderful quality – it is entirely consumed'. It could not be overproduced. But Walker assured the merchandiser that free time was no threat to sales for 'if leisure is marketed only when goods can not be, there will be little danger of a shortage in the supply of expensive frivolities'. The problem instead was to make leisure 'usefully consumable' , i.e., time for spending. The best form of 'consumable' time was not, however, longer doses of daily leisure: 'We can learn to make more money and have a better time in life by turning out packaged leisure along with our packaged goods – as a principle of business operation.' His solution was not the seven-hour day when a worker would become a 'pest to his wife – and to himself' around the house. The answer was an expanded weekend and vacation. This was an unusually advanced position but it neatly summed up the ambiguity of distributed leisure. In the 1930s, time had become money.[31]

The Depression demoralised and reduced the 'capacity' of 'underutilized' labour. As public works administrator Harold Ickes observed in 1935, 'only during the past few years have we seen how closely bound together are happiness and work'.[32] Just as humanists began to doubt the value of free time, the economists and policy-makers gave priority to work and consumption. Together, these ideas laid the ideological foundation of the political irrelevance of time in the US.

INTERNATIONAL WORKTIME AND THE EUROPEAN 40-HOUR WEEK

The Depression also renewed the worktime debate in western Europe. Despite their vaunted radical traditions, French and British workers adopted the relatively moderate goal of a 40-hour week. The shrinkage of world markets in 1930–1 brought a sudden end to the infatuation with Fordist mass production.[33] Many wage-earners faced joblessness or short-time work (with corresponding reductions in pay). Others experienced overtime and more intense work when employers sought to reduce unit costs and to undercut competitors.[34]

While employers blamed the slump on the world market (especially their inability to compete because of high labour costs), organised European workers attacked 'underconsumption'. Increased output per employee had not been balanced by either greater wage income or job security. The consequence was demand inadequate to meet supply and thus depression. According to this common view, the only solutions were steady or increased wages and job sharing by means of reduced hours. Bertrand Russell put the issue simply. There should not be eight hours per day for some and zero hours for others but four hours per day for all.[35]

By September 1931, the British TUC called for a 40-hour week with no reduction in pay as 'one of the ways in which the workers may share in increased productivity'. Part of this project was also a call for later school leaving and reduced age for pensions. In the midst of deflation, the TUC's representative in the ILO, Arthur Hayday, bluntly demanded, 'cut work time, not wages'. Another official declared in 1933 'the problem of unemployment is in its essence a problem of undistributed leisure'.[36]

From one perspective, these thoughts might be interpreted as simply the revival of economic Malthusianism – anti-technological output restriction in order to preserve traditional skills and jobs. For example, repeatedly in the early 1930s, British trade unions presented evidence that jobs lost in heavy industry and textiles were due to recent mechanisation. While, in the 1920s, some unions expected that jobs lost to efficiency would shift to new industries, this argument won no adherents in the early 1930s. Shorter hours, at least, could preserve present jobs and industries.[37]

But the unions were also addressing a seemingly insuperable problem – that the labour market did not effectively distribute free time and goods. The only apparent solution to this dilemma was to find new mechanisms for allocating demand to balance supply. While some trade unionists favoured increasing the wages of those with jobs, most preferred to kill two birds with the same stone: increase aggregate purchasing power by reducing hours and thus oblige employers to increase jobs – without decreasing pay.[38] Commentators in and around the Labour Party insisted that shorter hours were essential, not only to relieve unemployment, but to resolve the long-term problems of mature capitalism. In 1936, Ernest Bevin supported the 40-hour week as a way to 'flatten out production' and thus to eliminate the radical swings in employment, which, with mechanisation, tended to produce ever shorter periods of 'full-time' work. Even business people F. S. Hayburn of Marconi Marine Company and Harold Browden of Raleigh Cycle argued that employment was no longer a sufficient means of distributing purchasing power.[39] Like the short-hour advocates of the 1880s, they asserted that it was morally superior to provide all wage-earners with both compensated work and autonomous time. This was the only alternative to a labour force divided between those suffering the poverty of idleness and those fatigued by overwork.

But the 40-hour movement in Britain scarcely extended beyond work-sharing ideas. The cultural value, for example, of the two-day weekend hardly entered the discussion in Britain. One exception was a curious communist pamphlet (1937), 'Friday Night Till Monday Morning', which stressed the personal advantages of the two-day weekend: it would allow the (male) worker to 'please the wife' and 'treat . . . the kiddies now and then'. The pamphlet featured a cartoon showing a man sleeping in on Saturday morning with the words of an old music hall song underneath, "Snice to get up on Saturday morning, but 'snicer not to!'[40] But most 'serious' labour leaders conceived the 40-hour week as an economic solution to an essentially 'Keynesian' problem – underconsumption and unemployment.

Reform-minded economists promoted this remedy. For example, Colin Clark in 1934 embraced the reduction of worktime (with the maintenance of pay rates and financial controls to limit inflation) as a way of expanding employment and more fairly distributing the costs of the slump. Clark insisted that any threat to exports and profits (e.g., from competing Japanese textiles), would be more than balanced by an increased domestic market and a larger public sector.[41] Shorter hours meant primarily a stimulated home economy. In still another way, time had become money.

The National Conference of Employers' Organisations (NCEO) summarised the response of British business: it was not mass purchasing power and productive capacity that were out of balance but rather wages and prices. Since the war, high wages and social-service costs created an unrealistic labour standard which was bolstered by government employment and 'sheltered' industries. A high wage bill had made British goods uncompetitive on the world market. According to the NCEO, a 40-hour week would only exacerbate this situation by raising already excessive wages (by 20 per cent) and forcing employers to expand facilities, increase supervisory staffs, and hire 'unemployable' workers. In response to a bid of unions for a 40-hour week, British engineering employers in May 1933 proposed their own remedy to the slump: lower taxes, reduced wages, and the abandonment of the gold standard, all of which would cheapen British goods on the world market.[42] In sum, the hours debate of the 1930s in Britain was subsumed under the old struggle between the advocates of the home market versus the world market. The 40-hour movement was largely defined as a variation on the doctrine of the 'high-wage economy'.

A nearly identical debate took place in France. Like Russell, Jacques Duboin called for distributive justice, 'jobs for all, leisure for all'. The goal of industrial society was to 'free mankind from the burden of unnecessary toil . . . ; [but] instead of more leisure we have more unemployment'.[43] In 1931, the reformists in the General Confederation of Labour (CGT) sought a solution in a 40-hour week. The new standard was to solve the 'disequilibrium of consumption and production' caused by 'disorganised rationalisation' and 'overwork'. The communists agreed, going still further in resurrecting the Soviet example of the seven-hour day. Even the French government (following Italy) restricted employers' use of overtime.[44]

This was not only a signal of revived economic Malthusianism. CGT leader Léon Jouhaux revived the old linkage between technical innovation and the progressive reduction of worktime. In February 1933, he called the 40-hour week a 'step' in the continuous reduction of worktime.[45] But again – as in the British case – shorter hours were primarily intended to stimulate consumption; both job sharing and new time to consume were objectives. A widely used CGT poster featured a bread line and the slogan '40-hours for lower unemployment'. What had disappeared were the old campaigns for family life and the image of the social struggle over time. A two-day weekend would encourage home buying and suburbanisation and, with these, domestic consumption. In the end, the leadership council of the CGT did not press for shorter hours as much as they advocated a minimum wage and the nationalisation of banking.[46]

In turn, representatives of French employers like Pierre Collet, Maurice Pinot, and Eugène Combaz countered that a 40-hour week would cause inflation, weaken French ability to compete, force employers to hire 'undesirables', and unfairly burden small businesses. The 40-hour week was purely a wage matter and intervention in labour prices was inherently disruptive. At base, employers objected to the 'labour mass theory', implied in the notion of sharing work, as inherently static and a threat to growth.[47]

By 1931, the 40-hour week had become a transnational issue. Not only was it adopted by the International Federation of Trade Unions as a solution to mass unemployment, but textile employers from poor countries advocated it in 1933 as a cure for overproduction. And, even if Americans largely remained isolated, Europeans often saw Roosevelt's NIRA codes regulating worktime as positive models.[48]

The principle international forum, however, was the ILO. In July 1932, the Italian government requested a special conference to consider a uniform hours standard in order to reduce competition and to re-absorb the unemployed. The governing body of the ILO responded by organising a meeting in January 1933 devoted to the international reduction of worktime. Both the Italians and the ILO staff conceived of this conclave as an opportunity to shape the agenda of the upcoming World Economic Conference. The ILO's report adopted the underconsumptionist interpretation of the Depression by arguing that the new productivity required that society choose between 'maximum of material wealth or a larger share of leisure'.[49]

But the national delegations of labour, management, and

government at the conference split over the familiar questions of the validity of the underconsumptionist theory and the short-hour remedy. An international caucus of workers' groups stressed the linkage between joblessness and the deflationary impact of low purchasing power. Employers raised familiar technical objections and denounced the attempt to redistribute wealth in favour of wage-earners rather than others, especially farmers. The proposal of the trade unions for 40 hours without pay reductions failed when Italy and other governments refused to agree. Mussolini's objective was to 'share the misery', not to impose a burden on profit by raising the wage bill. Because of the implacable opposition of business representatives supported by the governments of Britain, Germany, and Japan, short-hours advocates had no influence on the World Economic Conference.[50]

Instead of a general 40-hour convention, the ILO passed a piece-meal programme of special conventions for separate industries. In 1936, Mussolini, like Hitler before him, abandoned the ILO and international solutions to the employment problem. In any case, by 1937, the opportunity for global cooperation had long passed. Instead each nation adopted variations of a 'beggar thy neighbour' approach to creating markets and jobs. Eventually the fascist solution of economic nationalism and war economy prevailed.[51]

What had failed at the international level, however, was not entirely abandoned in the national arena. The British TUC continued to press for 40-hour standards through the usual channels of collective bargaining.[52] But unions were not blindly wedded to industrial remedies. British labour was extremely active in the ILO in the 1930s (as it had not been in the 1920s) and it supported international conventions. Ernest Bevin strongly advocated a legal reduction of hours through a national movement.[53]

But, in the 1930s, British labour was incapable of affecting national economic policy. This was obvious in its failure to win a 40-hour week in any important sector. Moreover the legitimacy of shorter hours shifted toward the economic margins, just as it did in the US. For example, note the tone of a leading article in *The Times* (January 1935): 'Proposals for reducing hours of work, if they can be carried without loss, will always be welcomed by the trade unions, as would any other social or industrial reform; but a greater concern of today is to maintain and improve the standard of living of those in employment.'[54] Thus worktime was reduced to a dispensable welfare issue, subordinate to economic recovery and consumption-driven growth.

On the continent, where political intervention had far greater legitimacy than in Anglo-American society, the pattern was quite different. The French labour movement embraced legislation for a 40-hour week with no reduction in weekly wages. In 1935, with the formation of the Popular Front, the 40-hour week became a cornerstone of an anti-deflationary economic programme. Along with agricultural price supports and legal encouragement of collective bargaining, the shorter week was supposed to increase purchasing power. Shortly after the election of the Popular Front government, a wave of strikes forced through a 40-hour law. By September 1938, the 40-hour week was, in theory, nearly universal (except in agriculture and the professions).[55]

Yet capital flight, declining productivity, and inflation helped to produce trade imbalances in 1937 and 1938. In response, labour inspectors tolerated widespread overtime. But business opposition to this unilateral disarmament of the French economy was unrelenting from the passing of the law. Trade associations pushed for repeal, delays, liberal overtime rulings, and a replacement of the 40-hour week with a 2,000-hour work year (advantageous to seasonal industries).[56] The collapse of the Popular Front in May 1937 began a gradual abandonment of the 40-hour week. This process culminated in November 1938 with far less regulation of overtime (especially in defence industries) and the restoration of the six-day week (which made extra hours easier to impose). While these measures led to protest strikes on 30 November, the pressure to mobilise the economy in anticipation of war undermined political support for the 40-hour week. In March 1939, new decrees allowed up to a 60-hour workweek in defence industries.[57]

World War II ended talk of worktime reform everywhere. In France, the 40-hour week was quietly shelved after a brief revival in 1946. It was rejected by all sides as incompatible with the 'Battle of Production' and the Finance Ministry's growth plan. Indeed the 40-hour week remained under a cloud until the 1960s. In Britain, the immediate postwar demand for a 40-hour week was scrapped in 1946 for a more modest 44-hour week.[58]

The failure of the European politics of free time in the 1930s is hardly surprising. The very idea of a standard workweek had met vigorous resistance in the 1920s and continued to be opposed in the name of the free market and growth in the 1930s. But the inauspicious international context was a principal culprit. Since practically the birth of the movement for reduced working hours, advocates insisted that it could succeed only on an international scale. That, of course, was one of the principal rationales for the founding of the First and Second Internationals in 1864 and 1889. The eight-hour day of 1917–19 was an international standard, and, despite the opposition of competing national business elites, it was successfully defended as such by ILO reformers and organised European labour in the 1920s. It was entirely natural that European trade unions went to the ILO with their 40-hour plan in 1933. But the failure of this international forum sealed the fate of the free time movement in each country.[59]

The French 40-hour act of June 1936 was the exception in Europe, a throwback to the era of 1919. Not only was it modelled after the French eight-hour law of 1919, but both laws shared similar origins in social crises. What was different was that the 1936 law was passed in international isolation.[60] The transnational combination of reformers from the governing classes and rank-and-file insurgency, which had made possible the eight-hour movement of 1917–20, was missing in 1936. The ILO had proven to be too weak, founded as it was on the doubly unrealistic principles of international and interclass cooperation. The international labour militancy of 1919 was also missing. When Hitler destroyed the German labour movement in May of 1933, a strong supporter of the international short-hours movement disappeared. The political impotence of British labour in 1936 sharply contrasted with the political climate of 1919. The TUC was hardly capable of international leadership. This severely weakened the prospects for the success of the French Popular Front. Shopfloor or ballot-box victory in France was as insufficient in the 1930s as a similar socialist experiment would prove to be in the early 1980s. Little could advance the labour standard in one country if that nation faced an unfavourable international market and hostility from other states. Ironically, by 1938, the United States – that nation that had abstained from the 1919 legislation – had adopted a 40-hour law. This proved not the success of the international movement for hours reform but the isolation of the U.S. from those economic and military events engulfing Europe. In any case, the 40-hour week was hardly a meaningful reduction in the context of the American Depression.

Since 1937, economists and politicians have blamed the 40-hour week for the economic failures of the French Popular Front and even the German conquest of France in 1940. Most noteworthy, perhaps, the Vichy government accused Popular Front leader Léon Blum of weakening France at his trial in 1942.[61] Blum and another Popular Front official Pierre Cot defended the 40-hour week as a necessary response to the social upheaval of the Spring of 1936. They denied that it contributed to reduced productivity or reduced defence output. Cot insisted that opposition was 'purely political'.[62] Since the 1940s, the debate has continued, but the evidence on this question remains inconclusive.[63]

Underlying the debate over the technical effects of the 40-hour week on the French economy are its social and political implications: on one side, historian Michael Seidman argues that French workers rigidly defended the reduction of labour time as part of a 'revolt against work'. They rejected overtime and 'recuperation' of hours which were lost to production shutdowns (despite the needs of defence or even at the cost of embarrassing the Popular Front government).[64] In contrast, Herrick Chapman insists that workers understood the linkage between the 40-hour week and the need for increased output: in fact, the rank-and-file actively embraced the productivist ideology of the trade unions. Workers' opposition to 'flexible' application of the law was a political statement against managerial attempts to destroy this benefit.[65]

Both views have some merit. The militant defence of the two-day weekend may well reveal a decline of the work ethic (or even the relative failure of French employers to impose work discipline on labour, especially in the context of increasing work rationalisation). But this analysis does not take into account the extremely politicised character of the conflict over worktime in France or the fact that the work slowdowns often reflected workers' fears of unemployment. The late 1930s were hardly auspicious times either for testing the economic effects of worktime reduction or for measuring the social meaning of increased free time.

In any case, it is both simplistic and biased to lay the disasters of the Popular Front at the door of shorter working hours. Rather it seems more reasonable to put the inadequacies of this reform in a broader context. In this century, any real improvement in a national labour standard has almost always occurred on the international level. This, of course, was impossible in the 1930s when Europe was torn by economic and military nationalism.[66]

I stress these international dimensions of the problem because political and social historians usually neglect them. But the failure of the free-time movement in the 1930s revealed also deep ideological fissures. Employers and policy-makers believed that this movement was an attempt to restrict production. As we have seen, there were elements of economic Malthusianism in the motives of advocates of the 30-hour bill in the US and the 40-hour week in Europe.

Business argued that shorter hours (especially without reduced pay rates) would simply produce inflation. Economist Lionel Robbins wrote for many when he condemned legislated leisure as a disruption of factors of production and an interference in what should be an 'individual choice'.[67]

Most important, policy-makers had an alternative to share-the-work (or wealth) schemes in government spending to stimulate demand. While we are accustomed to associate this idea with John Maynard Keynes' theories published in 1936, John Hobson in 1930 supported increased purchasing power through progressive taxation and fiscal policy as an alternative to shorter hours.[68] This 'commercial Keynesianism' had a powerful influence through American economists like Alvin Hansen during the 'Second New Deal' after 1937. This policy had the advantage of not imposing on capital the burden of job creation. It also promised to preserve the traditional work ethic (see chapter 2). To be sure, neither shorter hours nor Keynesianism was acceptable to British Treasury officials. Keynesians were unable to withstand the business backlash to the Popular Front in France after mid-1937. And Roosevelt backed off from his pump priming just before the 1937 recession. Nevertheless the long-term solution would be predominately Keynesian. And work sharing and the broader idea of the progressive disengagement from work were discredited.[69]

HOLIDAYS AND THE ALTERNATIVE QUEST FOR LEISURE

The demand for additional leisure, however, in the packaged form of vacations was a great success in the 1930s. The holiday could be understood as an alternative to the far more expensive concession of a shorter workweek. Yet the vacation movement was more than a consolation prize; it was the site of an expanded language of leisure, albeit clothed in consumerism.

Americans were not immune to this international romance with the vacation in the mid-1930s, even if they were slow in adopting it. Company vacation plans tripled from 1934 to 1937, reaching about half of wage-earners by 1940. A well-organised union drive prompted steel management to concede a paid vacation in 1936.[70] Some 736,893 AFL members obtained it by 1937, although about 383,000 of these were government employees. Nevertheless, few workers in seasonal industries won or (apparently actively desired) the paid vacation. Management generally granted vacations in hopes of increasing labour productivity. Workers still preferred shorter days – by 75 per cent in a survey by *Fortune* in 1936. The attitudinal chasm between the white-collar and manual worker remained.[71]

However, wartime conditions of overtime strain, full employment, and government wage controls all encouraged organised American labour to press for vacation time. As early as 1941, an informal survey of steel workers found a preference for vacation time over increased pay. During the war, when the War Labor Board sought to control wage increases, some unions shifted their bargaining efforts to paid vacations. The Board, in turn, often complied in hopes of increasing labour productivity. A study of major companies found that 93 per cent of union contracts included paid holidays by 1949. Perhaps the suggestion in the radical labour song, 'Take Your Kids to the Seashore', reflected the need to *teach* workers the value of vacation time. But they were quick learners.[72]

American wage-earners, like Europeans, embraced the idea of a paid holiday. But in the US, the length of vacations was (and remains) part of the labour contract. Paid holidays were generally linked to period of employment. The American worker's vacation was not to be an entitlement of citizenship but a privilege, rewarding loyal service at work in the most organised sectors of the economy (government and big business). American companies have been notoriously stingy with paid vacation leaves.

By contrast, in spite of massive unemployment and deep ideological fissures, the vacation became a near universal ideal in industrial Europe in the 1930s. The holiday with pay responded to deep needs that transcended ideology and economic system. In the generation after World War II, the vacation became the leisure concept of choice for most Europeans when the one- or two-week holiday expanded to four or more weeks in the prosperity of the 1950s and 1960s. During the Great Depression, the paid vacation in Europe had far wider support than the 40-hour week even if conservatives in both France and Britain tried to delay legislation.[73]

Employers found that the vacation was a perquisite that could raise work discipline (by denying it to workers who had not been on the job for at least a year or to workers with bad records of absenteeism). It could also instil loyalty. A group of perfumers in London adopted a holiday with pay to 'implant in the minds of the employees that they are actually part of the business in the same sense as a Civil Servant is a permanent servant of the State'. Vacations also did not necessarily threaten annual production goals: they often coincided with seasonal slowdowns in demand or production. Perhaps most important, vacations reduced worktime per wage-earner by only about one tenth of the hours lost in the shift from a 48- to 40-hour week. Frequently this meant that employers would not have to hire new workers and supervisors, or be obliged to make new investments in facilities or machinery, especially when vacations were not granted individually but taken collectively during a plant or district shutdown.[74]

Beyond these practical advantages of the vacation, the right to leisure gained broad political legitimacy in the interwar years. The thinking of the advocates of the 'new leisure' and 'distributed leisure' encouraged a positive understanding of the holiday – not as a simple byproduct of collective bargaining – but as right of citizenship in an industrial democracy. By the early 1930s, the British work-science journals, *Industrial Welfare* and *The Human Factor*, were beginning to focus on the inadequacy of everyday recreational opportunities. Not only were urban workers in need of a sunny environment (a major British obsession in the 1930s), but industrial labourers required time to 'relax mentally altogether'. A holiday would relieve a 'sense of anxiety which dogs the town dweller'. Articles noted the health-giving and social potential of Fascist and Soviet leisure programmes even when they attacked state-controlled culture. These proponents of work efficiency clearly recognised the need for release from work environments for an extended period of time.[75] Of course, the ILO became a centre for legitimising the paid vacation.[76] Even the conservative old opponent of the eight-hour law, French deputy Louis Duval-Arnould, favoured the 1931 holiday bill for 'vacations are necessary in the modern world'.[77]

Political conflict, of course, impeded rapid enactment of holidays with pay. The British government especially was a reluctant participant in this movement.[78] A law of July 1938 only gave Trade Boards and other statutory bodies the right to provide holidays with pay in upcoming labour contract negotiations. However, in this context of threatened national legislation, employers widely conceded at least a week's paid holiday in collective bargaining: the number of wage-earners with a paid vacation increased from 1.5 million in April 1937 to over eleven million by June 1939.[79]

In France, the habitual log jam of the reactionary Senate was broken in the labour insurgency of June 1936. Along with other reforms, parliament passed a two-week paid-holiday bill on 21 June with little opposition. And, unlike the 40-hour week, it survived the Popular Front. It was recognised as an entitlement. The quest for time had shifted from the workweek to the vacation.[80]

The leisure goal of shorter weekly hours, which prevailed in the 1920s, was largely eclipsed in the Depression decade. Mass unemployment and the failure of labour diplomacy helped to transform the international movement for free time into a national economic demand for income and employment. In Europe, industrial and political opponents defeated the 40-hour week until the 1960s, producing a policy bias toward 'full-time' job creation (and mass consumption). That was true even of the 40-hour standard workweek that became law in the US in 1938. These events ended the dreams of a progressive disengagement from work. The postwar 'Battle for Production' in Europe only reinforced these trends. To be sure, the less threatening measure of paid vacations was modestly successful in the decade after 1936. The vacation rather than the workweek became the focal point for an important movement for democratic leisure even though the holiday would be especially adaptable to mass consumerism.

This may seem obvious, even predictable from the vantage of the end of the century. Still, in the early decades, the politics of time was part of an economic struggle that pointed beyond the place of production to a public debate over culture. It was part of a shift from struggles that were fought strictly on the political and economic terrain to battles waged in the arena of culture. Especially in the 1930s, interest in leisure and free time produced prototypes of late twentieth-century 'new social movements' – community and other social formations beyond the state and marketplace. In particular, the holiday was to become a point of ideological coalescence in the 1930s around themes of anti-urbanism, health, social and familial solidarity, and especially the democratic organisation of leisure. The vacation became a site of the struggle against economic time, and a recognition of a need for a new political strategy centred on culture. Even though the politics of free time had disappointing results, it led to a politics of culture and leisure. The fate of this movement is our next topic.

5 Democratic leisure and the failure of cultural politics

Paralleling the short-hour movements were debates about how free time ought to be organised. For many, time liberated from production was the only possible setting for the restoration of family life and social solidarity, especially given more intense and specialised work. Groups across the political spectrum were obsessed with how to organise mass leisure beyond the market. They focused on the leisure of the waged (mostly male) worker, largely, but not entirely, ignoring the domestic and family labour of women. While they shared much with nineteenth-century 'rational recreationists', in the interwar years they focused on two related innovations – the paid holiday and the idea of organising leisure.

One of the ironies of the 1930s and 1940s was the fact that the paid vacation became an ideal nearly everywhere in Europe and, to a lesser degree, in the US, Fascists, communists, and liberals all agreed that modern work required compensatory leisure. The holiday was to 'recover' lost values of family and community. It was to create a public culture of commonly-held virtues of filial piety and patriotism. This was not merely an escape from the factory but from the psychological insecurities of urban life. The vacation was to fulfil a new need of seasonal release no longer provided by religion or agricultural festivals. The holiday away from home was to be a new pilgrimage to refresh a life where personal fulfilment in work was vanishing.

Was this common view a reflection of 'deep structures' that transcend politics? In one sense such an interpretation is surely wrong. The political contest was still the animating factor in leisure policy, especially in Europe. Consensus was primarily a recognition of the growing cultural centrality of leisure as a terrain for the struggle over control of popular opinion. Especially after World War I, when the eight-hour working day became nearly universal, elites of

both the Left and Right recognised the potential political significance of organising leisure time. All sides used youth, family, and
leisure-interest groups for creating solidarities beyond the workplace. For the French Popular Front, the holiday movement was
an attempt (perhaps belatedly) to create an alternative to bourgeois
or fascist control of leisure.

In another sense, however, the holiday movement clearly did
transcend politics. It was nearly as evident in countries where ideological conflict was relatively weak – especially in Britain and the
US. The holiday fitted the needs of a familial and gender ideology
embraced by the Left and Right: vacations would provide family
time away from domestic routines for the homemaker and enable
the father to play paternal roles.[1] Leftist leaders had long shared
with conservatives a desire to 'uplift' the masses; and both groups
saw commercial leisure as a potential threat to shared cultural
standards. All agreed that popular sports and the return to nature
would renew national energies; vacations would give 'dignity' and
'joy' to the worker. In those years, American authorities filled state
and national parks with nationalist lessons and symbols.[2] But a
century of 'rational recreation' had taught elites that pure didacticism had little appeal to increasingly more independent working
people. The paid vacation was a response to workers who, in the
1930s, had clearly included a 'real holiday' on a growing list of
essentials defining 'social citizenship'. The paid vacation was an
accommodation to a new generation of youth-oriented holiday-
makers. It represented a condensation of complex objectives – both
solutions to elite concerns and compromises with popular demands.
The holiday was a free-time ritual that ventilated social space,
promised release from routine behaviours, and inculcated shared
goals of familial and national reconciliation.

The 1930s also presented a new view of recreation – born ironically of the Depression – that we can call 'democratic leisure'.
Elites on both sides of the Atlantic adopted more positive attitudes
toward workers' free time, addressed the disruptive effects of free
time without adequate income, and advocated 'distributed leisure'.
Non-communist leftists, in Europe especially, embraced these
views. They hoped not only to broaden their political base beyond
the narrow social world of labour through the appeal of enhanced
recreational and cultural programmes, but to wage a cultural battle
with 'totalitarians'. Yet this populism retained the paternalism that
the leftist elite shared with the Right. By investigating the intellectual origins of 'democratic leisure' in the US and especially western

Europe, we can see the full irony of the holiday with pay and the limits of the public culture's challenge to commercialised leisure.

ORGANISING FREE TIME

In chapter 3 I stressed that elite fears of the democratisation of time and money had moral as well as economic dimensions. Puritanical Americans responded to the temporal and material release of the mass libido with Prohibition in 1919. And in England that Victorian holdover, the Lord's Day Observance Society, resisted attempts to legalise cinema showings on Sundays until 1932.[3]

More effective, however, were conservative efforts to 'organise leisure'. A prominent French employer Léon Pasquier advocated building cultural and exercise centres designed to counteract those urban 'social diseases that threaten the race: alcoholism, immorality, Neomalthusianism, and tuberculosis'. Organised recreation would help workers 'rise up the social scale' and employers would thereby gain an improved 'quality of labour'. M. R. Georges-Picot appealed for a popular housing programme that would offer more and better designed space: a 'living room' would provide a 'place of refuge or free activity' and draw husbands away from the cabaret (or union hall). The garden would 'reunite the children around their parents'. Abbé Lemire and his French League for Garden and Home encouraged employers to provide 45,000 workers' gardens by the 1920s. Georges-Picot put the matter plainly, 'the worker's garden is an excellent element of social defence'. In 1930, Maurice Lacoin, a recreation specialist working for the Citroën company, reiterated this rather threadbare paternalism: the more the worker 'finds in his home a large complete life, the more he will have the ability and place for the education of his children, [and] the more he will accept the subjections and difficulties of the discipline of the factory'.[4]

French conservatives hoped also to shape the play of youth. This concern had roots dating back to 1883 when educators and the clergy began to organise summer youth camps.[5] Jacques Guerin-Desjardins, an organiser of summer youth programmes for Peugeot, recognised the limits of domesticity and family leisure: children 'have the right to leave and their parents cannot stop them'. The young had the 'natural' need for adventure and this was incompatible with the parent–child relationship. But that 'spirit of youth' was easily distracted into 'temptations' especially because adolescents had so much unsupervised free time (as a result of school leaving at fourteen and the decline of apprenticeships). One solution was for employers to sponsor youth activities. Guerin-Desjardins advocated that employers abandon their accustomed authoritarianism in the running of company youth camps. By 'giving [young workers] the impression that they are in a "chic maison" which thinks of them, of their distractions, of their happiness', the employer would bind them to the company. Camps could create 'friendly links' between adolescent workers and older supervisors (who also should attend the camp as leaders). The key was that indirect methods of control were to be used. Youth should participate in setting rules; and leaders should suggest, not demand, improved manners.[6]

French industrialists of the north and east had long advocated these 'environmental' solutions to social questions. After World War I, they continued to expand the number of social *oeuvres* – workers' gardens for adult men and musical, theatrical, and sports facilities for youth and families. Yet these efforts were mostly concentrated in mining and heavy industrial regions where the paternalism of large industrialists like the Wendels and Schneiders had long reigned.[7] One observer found that, outside of the mining areas, workers mistrusted recreation facilities sponsored by employers and the church. They identified leisure with 'liberty' and thus resisted any collectivisation of spare time.[8]

English philanthropy similarly focused on the 'training' of youth through patronage of sports clubs, company-run summer camps, and playground centres. Traditional upper-class support of sport survived in the Duke of York's Camp where equal numbers of public (elite) school- and industrial boys shared games and bonfires. The key was a controlled but *pleasurable* setting where organisers encouraged self-discipline and group loyalty.[9] Despite frequent calls for national policy in the interwar years, organised recreation in Britain remained a local and philanthropic endeavour.[10]

American patronage of youth recreation was, if anything, more developed than in Europe. It combined the conservative values and fears of the employer class with a progressivist ethic of efficiency and democracy. The summer youth camp became a peculiarly American institution where, by 1929, a million children yearly met nature in the sheltered moral environment of about 7,000 camps.[11] More important perhaps was the urban playground movement. With roots in philanthropy, the Playground Association (founded in 1907), became the advocacy body of a new group of recreation professionals. Municipal governments employed playground staff to organise games and sports in hopes of luring youth from the unsupervised street.[12] The ideology of this new class was well expressed in the 'Principles' of the Playground Association (1910):

> Delinquency is reduced by providing a wholesome outlet for youthful energy. Industrial efficiency is increased by giving individuals a play life which will develop greater resourcefulness and adaptability. Good citizenship is promoted by forming habits of cooperation in play. . . . Democracy rests on the most firm basis when a community has formed the habit of playing together.[13]

Here is both the vitalist theory of directed 'energy' and the progressivist notion of play as a form of social education. But underlying this social liberal discourse was a traditional paternalism, a belief in the need for a tutelary agent to carry out the child-rearing function abdicated by working-class parents.[14] Professional recreationists combined conservative concerns – expressed in the language of 'child saving', class harmony and regulated play – with their own progressivist discourse of efficiency, social education, and non-partisanship. In Europe, similar conservative values were embodied in more confrontational organisations. In France especially, leisure organisations reproduced confessional and political divisions. Since their military defeat in 1871, French patriots adapted German methods of using sport for nationalist purposes. Catholics had also long recognised that sport was an excellent vehicle for preserving the flock – an insight not lost on their secular opponents at the village public school who, as early as 1894, had organised their own sports clubs.[15] In the interwar years, Italian and German fascists also found that leisure was an excellent vehicle for fostering political loyalty. The *dopo lavoro* and *Kraft durch Freude* organised tours and youth summer camps, using methods that were scarcely distinguishable from those employed by Guerin-Desjardins to instil a 'politics of consent'.[16]

Examples of private employer- and church-run leisure programmes in the US would be easy to find. Welfare capitalists in large non-union companies employed recreation to promote plant loyalty and to break down ethnic or neighbourhood identities. But they generally lacked the more obvious political purpose of their European counterparts.[17] This may be a valid example of the impact of the diffuse American class system which militated against the formation of an extensive network of political, clerical or employer-dominated leisure organisations.

In any case, the Left, especially in Europe, shared a similar approach to the problem of organising free time. In the 1920s, the

French and British Left defended the eight-hour day as a vehicle for wholesome suburbanisation and proposed activities that would reduce dependence on drink. In language indistinguishable from their conservative counterparts, French socialists lavished praise on workers' gardens and rabbit husbandry as uplifting alternatives to the lure of the cabaret.[18] Not only did unions and leftist parties organise their own separate leisure activities, but, in doing so, they often shared the paternalistic perspective of the Right. The French Left competed with church and employers for the people's leisure time. Socialists and communists launched various activities in the fine arts and cultural education in the 1920s.[19]

More influential in France, however, were leftwing sports clubs, designed to counteract the appeals of both commercial spectator sports and conservative athletic clubs. In the 1920s, French socialist sports leagues sometimes gained the aid of sympathetic local governments. According to a socialist advocate of athleticism, Pierre Marie, they stressed 'healthy and vigorous formation of the young' and tried to counteract the 'recruiting drives of reactionaries'. Workers' Olympic Games were held in Frankfurt (1925) and Vienna (1931). After 1924, French communists and their trade unions also used sports and cultural groups to 'train for struggle' and to create loyalty to union and party beyond the workplace. Especially important were efforts to link the whole family and not just the union member to the cause. Later, in 1937, communist Benoit Frachon insisted that unions should 'give satisfaction to the daily needs of workers and their families'.[20]

Of course, the influence of these efforts can easily be exaggerated. Leftwing French sports groups had to compete with 20,000 non-partisan athletic societies. As one witness noted, many a worker refused to be 'parked in amusements especially created for his use'. Even the miner, 'ardent for his union . . . goes fishing or hunting in preference to a dance or cinema because he wants to be alone'. While workers may have increasingly valued sports, contact with nature, and even domestic togetherness, individualism and the lack of resources impeded the expression of these values in leisure organised by unions or leftist parties.[21]

As historian Stephen Jones has shown, a similar pattern of politicised leisure survived in British labour circles in the 1920s. Since the 1880s, organised workers' leisure had been built around cooperative societies, trade unions, socialist Sunday schools and the Clarion movement. After the war, Labour Party activists united around regular rounds of 'brass bands, teas, rambles, excursions, . . . and most popular of all, the annual rally and carnival'. Beatrice Webb even organised a 'Half Circle Club' for wives of Labour men and women organisers in order to provide an alternative to the temptations of 'London Society'.[22] The Labour Party, the trade councils, and the cooperative societies used sports to attract youth to their organisations.[23] Still the long and heralded English tradition of workers' education was fractured and ultimately rather ineffective.[24] And class-based leisure was mostly centred on the relatively apolitical pub and workers' clubs.[25]

Organised leisure and education was less common among American unions. Adult and labour education was even weaker than in England.[26] But American unions, like their European counterparts, found that sports and culture were helpful in organising efforts. Historian Lizabeth Cohen has found extensive programmes of sports activities (especially bowling) and family picnics in Chicago's CIO unions in the 1930s. These activities appeared to copy similar efforts of welfare capitalists in the 1920s but they used leisure to create inter-ethnic solidarity and union loyalty. And CIO leaders widely exploited the new media, especially radio, to reach their audience in the 1930s.[27]

In these three countries, leisure remained class-bound and the Left, when it competed with paternalistic and commercial attractions, tried to keep it that way. The goal was often less to satisfy popular pleasures than to shape those desires through education and uplifting activities; in this way, they shared much with the leisure programmes of conservatives.

AN ALTERNATIVE: DEMOCRATIC LEISURE

A movement for democratic leisure offered a quite different approach to free time. It was embraced by a diverse group of European socialists and American progressives. But its best known European proponent was the moderate socialist Albert Thomas, Director of the International Labour Office (ILO) from 1919 to 1933. Thomas insisted that neither government, business, nor even trade unions should attempt to control free time. Workers were too individualistic to submit to this patronage and its hidden agendas. Thomas was appalled by the attempt of the Right and Left to construct blind loyalty through the subversion of 'joy'. He favoured leisure programmes, organised by local, self-managed agencies composed of representatives of church, labour, management, and others. Government was to facilitate, not direct, activities. He also opposed leaving leisure to the marketplace and hoped to raise the cultural standard. Thomas admitted that he had no problem saying 'what is good leisure'. He advocated 'a well-directed use of spare time' – 'physical and moral education' as well as the cultivation of general education. His was a vision of a public culture, rooted in conventional Victorian values, but sustained by new voluntarist organisations with indirect government assistance.[28]

Thomas had a notion of 'efficient' leisure (as well as work) that certainly was comprehensive: he and his followers stressed the need to regulate access to alcohol, to improve home-economics instruction, and to reduce commuting time. He supported garden cities and housing programmes to encourage a 'harmonious development of the workers' family life' and a do-it-yourself domesticity. Thomas understood gardening or home-improvement projects not as work, but as family-centred and self-improving leisure. He even encouraged more compact workdays as a way of creating more 'efficient' and healthy leisure time.[29] The ILO repeatedly encouraged mixed-group and international leisure organisations even though they seldom provided more than sounding boards for opinion. Thomas found French allies in the Education League, a group of secular teachers who favoured lifelong education and improved recreational facilities.[30] In 1929, Thomas joined a broad-based National Committee on Leisure in France (organised first by the consumer cooperatives). He also convened international recreation congresses in Liège (1928) and Los Angeles (1932).[31]

On the surface, these efforts had much in common with Nazi recreation ideology. The World Congress for Leisure Time and Recreation, convened by the Nazis in Berlin in 1936, had official links with the Olympic Games and included representatives from British and American sports councils. Speeches focused on the theme of the 'triple harmony of work, community, and recreation'. Resolutions called for 'restoring the balance disturbed by the physical and spiritual strain of work'. This meant not only time away from the machine but the reorganisation of space: 'both the place of work and the home [should be] so situated as to allow . . . contact with nature'. This fascist-dominated meeting called for the 'restoration of the balance of the spiritual and physical sides by giving brain workers exercise and manual workers intellectual facilities in leisure'. But it was in the 'family circle that the worker finds the most satisfactory form of recreation'. This required not only an 'adequate free week-end' but family-oriented holiday camps (instead of tours by male workmates which did 'not always tend to improve family life'). All of this would have inspired Thomas. But the authoritarianism of the congress' sponsors was hardly concealed: the object of the state should be to 'further the community as a whole' and to organise play.[32]

The ILO-backed International Recreation Commission, founded in 1934 with the involvement of the (American) National Recreation Association, was at first willing to include its fascist counterparts. But in 1938, following the Nazi display of propaganda at the 1936 Berlin Olympic Games, a group with similar members deliberately distinguished 'democratic' from 'totalitarian' leisure. The problem was that the fascist idea of 'community' encouraged uncritical loyalty to the state and regime. By contrast, these democrats stressed voluntarism, local initiative, and individualism. Most would have agreed with the German exile A. Sternheim, who claimed that *Kraft durch Freude* tolerated 'no social contradictions' and 'obscure[d] the real differences in the position of the social groups' with its celebration of unity. Capitalism, he argued, had shorn the family of all its social functions, allowing it to survive only in the 'free choice in the use of leisure'. But totalitarian control over play destroyed even this last vestige of the family in 'private interest and pleasures'.[33]

Although the advocates of democratic leisure wished to 'improve' workers' recreation, the solution was not self-forgetfulness in the joys of group identity. Rather it was to train individual workers to use their leisure 'wisely' and to provide them with a wide variety of recreational choices.[34]

An old problem remained, however: how did choice and training mesh? Despite organisational innovation, the movement for democratic leisure remained paternalistic. This fact reflected the ambiguity of intellectuals everywhere toward mass culture (see chapter 3). Moreover, democratic leisure had obvious links with the traditions of rational recreation of the mid-nineteenth century.[35] Like their Victorian forebears, early twentieth-century reformers sought not to restrict leisure time but to organise it and to redirect it into individually uplifting and familial directions. The problem was that these values were only partially shared by the working classes.

The American recreation movement had much in common with European advocates of democratic leisure, even though different origins produced somewhat different results. The American movement emerged in the second and third decades of the twentieth century from a class of career professionals centred in local and state recreation and education departments. The American recreation movement between the wars retained a pedagogical, even salvationist, language. Most distinctive was its professional temper that produced an elitist, administrative viewpoint, rather than the broader populism of the Europeans. Without a serious challenge from totalitarians, the American recreationists focused on the other, more formidable enemy – commercial entertainment. Moreover, this group extended its scope from redeeming urban immigrant children through play to the wider task of organising the free time of adults. Still, despite its social-service rhetoric, this American version of democratic leisure had political implications as significant as those in Europe.

In the interwar years, the tutelary ethos of the professional child saver continued to permeate the American recreation movement, even in thinking about adults. Leisure was to help people 'adjust' to changing environments. In sociologist William Ogburn's words, recreation was 'to give direction to social change itself and to achieve a better social order'. The problem, of course, was that leisure time was often a vacuum that easily was filled by dysfunctional activities.[36] Sociological studies, conducted at the University of Chicago concerning urban dancehalls, saloons and vice, all made a similar point: disorganised play groups produce 'maladjusted' people.[37]

But this thinking went beyond the paternalism of the playground movement. American adult educators, sociologists, librarians and recreation professionals recognised that they faced a powerful opponent in commercial entertainment and they sought to create an alternative public culture. They repeatedly attacked commercial amusements for encouraging spectator passivity, for denying creativity and the intimate culture of the neighbourhood, and for exploiting sex and violence. Note the assessment of the President's Research Committee on Social Trends (1933):

> Business, with its advertising and high pressure salesmanship, can exert powerful stimuli on the responding human organism. How can the appeals made by churches, libraries, concerts, museums and adult education for a goodly share in our growing leisure be made to compete effectively with the appeals of commercialized recreation?[38]

Mass marketing assured a standardisation of play and undermined the individual; and advertisers appealed to the status anxiety of the insecure. In the words of Eugene Lies, the individual confronted 'inner and outer stimuli'. Cultivation of the 'inner man' of course required training. Simply put, 'leisure is choosing time' and people needed skills in making choices.[39]

In the interwar years, American recreationists extended their mission from 'training' children for making 'good' choices to facilitating non-commercial adult leisure: play was to fulfil a creative and compensatory function in the lives of those whose work was dissatisfying. Recreation was to make people feel 'something like the free agents that human beings were intended to be'.[40] Hobbies were perfect expressions of 'good' leisure for they fostered both individual creativity and were an alternative to 'bad' commercial pastimes. The key, as historian Steven Gelber notes, was that the hobby could 'reintegrate the spheres of work and leisure that had been separated by the industrial revolution'. It disciplined time while offering a compensation for alienating work.[41]

In many ways these objectives were little more than modernisations of Victorian rational recreation. Still, the democratic leisure movement in the 1930s partly transcended the conservative social agenda of its late nineteenth-century founders. The overriding concern with disorder partially gave way to a broader service and participatory ethic. The secretary of the New York Committee on the Uses of Leisure said in 1934: 'More and more it would seem as if the community must assume responsibility for providing privileges and opportunities which otherwise the individual cannot obtain.'[42] According to Edward Lindeman, 'freedom means interdependence, collaboration, relatedness'. Because work was so atomised, the 'democratic spirit' could only emerge in free time. Lindeman echoed Albert Thomas when he argued that a democratic leisure movement required an integrated programme: income and time distribution, ample housing, a 'comprehensive plan for human welfare', and recreation administrators 'who have been trained to view government as a social service'. The National Recreation Association was committed to non-partisan local and state leisure programmes.[43]

These American leisure activists stressed diversity and accessibility. For example, during the early Depression years, American recreation and cultural advocacy groups conducted a number of empirical studies of changes in recreational behaviour. These studies were preference polls of what people enjoyed doing and thus served as appeals for more democratic programming. Investigators were open to a variety of popular leisure-time pursuits. But they also implied that the market could not satisfy individual interests.[44]

Leaders of the National Recreation Association largely supported the short-hours movement in the 1920s and 1930s; they saw reduced work as an opportunity to develop personal creativity against the 'gospel of consumption'. Yet they also insisted that leisure had to be a form of 'social education' that would help to overcome the 'cultural lag' and modernise social values. These contradictory liberal and regulatory themes permeated American progressivism and the New Deal.[45]

Adult education well expressed this ideological mix. An example was the Boston Center for Adult Education founded in 1933 with support from volunteer teachers from Harvard University. Its founder Dorothy Hewitt insisted that instructors be aware of adult modes of learning. She stressed the need for informality, discussions, and even non-pedantic course titles. But workers' education was increasingly attached to university-based schools for workers and most forms of adult education remained within the control of professional educators.[46]

More than in Europe, professionals and government dominated the American recreation movement. In the second and third decades of the twentieth century, career recreation reformers were successful in expanding youth programmes; they also gained funds for public golf courses, libraries, and museums. Along with this growth emerged a welter of government agencies which administered these programmes.[47] Far more impressive were New Deal public-works projects. Roosevelt spent 1.5 billion dollars by 1937 to build a wide array of playgrounds, parks, tennis courts, swimming pools, and cultural centres. A public-works staff of some 40,000 recreation workers served perhaps 5 million people by 1939. The Civil Conservation Corps provided 680 work camps devoted to building and improving 867 public recreation areas, employing about 3 million young males by 1939. The National Youth Agency (NYA) developed recreation programmes as a part of a workfare policy. By 1940, over 9,000 public libraries, museums, and other cultural facilities had been improved by NYA labour. Works Progress Administration projects included jobs for music teachers, actors, and adult educators (that reached about a million students). Still all of these efforts were meagre compared to the 2 billion spent on commercial recreation in 1930 alone. Also much of federally funded recreation simply replaced scaled-back local and state projects.[48]

The voluntarism that pervaded the European movement was curiously muted in the US. At the same time, Washington divided public recreation into a dozen competing federal agencies.[49]

Lindeman complained that there was no department of leisure and physical education (as there was to be in France in 1936). Nor was there an effective semi-public planning agency as would emerge in Britain after the war. This combination of social-service professionalism along with divided authority and a lack of national planning is a well-known part of the American New Deal legacy.

In Europe, democratic leisure advocates shared a similar mix of democratic and authoritarian impulses with American recreation professionals. In Europe, however, it was expressed through the political struggles of the Popular Front and without the public works/bureaucratic dimensions of the New Deal programmes. The result was perhaps less impressive initiatives than appeared in the US. But, in Europe, new forms of public culture seemed to have been based on a broader active population than was the case in the US; and that culture was associated not with emergency employment, but with free-time voluntarism.

To be sure, the French Popular Front revived the old effort of the Left to organise loyalty through leisure. Socialist and communist youth groups like the Red Falcons and the local officials of the red-belt suburb of Bezons organised hikes and camps for youth. The communist daily, *L'Humanité*, was the impresario for a massive outdoor festival in the Paris suburbs to celebrate the end of summer.[50] In the late 1930s, the communist-controlled Metalworkers of Paris organised festivals and tried to create leisure committees at each factory in order to promote sports and cultural activities. The General Confederation of Labour (CGT) embraced the motto, 'a club in every factory'; by April 1937, it had organised 21 football teams in the plants of Renault. The objective was to facilitate the '*cégétisation* of the smallest detail of the workers' lives'. The Metal Workers' union also bought land for camping and even provided a chateau near Paris for members' use.[51]

Behind these efforts was an older cultural battle. The 'great fear' of June 1936 with its massive sit-down strikes revived employer interest in organising leisure in France. Business organisations encouraged members to develop their own leisure clubs. Conservative front groups like the Central Committee for Family Allocations created umbrella leisure and tourism organisations that paralleled the efforts of the Left. Familiar appeals to workers' gardens, home-improvement training, and youth camps reappeared in the conservative press.[52] In December 1936, the trade-union weekly *Syndicats* warned that the metal and mining *patronat* sought to forge 'new chains' of class subordination through manipulated leisure. In response, *Syndicats* argued, unions ought to organise their own theatres, libraries, and camping clubs.[53]

Nevertheless, not all organised leisure in the Popular Front period was so deliberately class-based. In France, moderate socialists around the CGT sought to realise Thomas' concept of democratic leisure beyond the divisions of occupation and crude paternalism. In the early 1930s, the CGT's Centre for Workers' Education ran courses led by socialist intellectuals to dispense classical literary education to wage-earners. These rather elitist efforts naturally had little impact.[54] Soon, however, the CGT adopted more populist and diverse approaches to mass culture. Following the lead of Thomas, the CGT's Georges Lefranc advocated that local trades councils, rather than union federations, should organise workers' leisure in order to build wider social ties. Umbrella groups, in which unions were only one participant, were even better.[55] By 1935, the CGT's Workers' Colleges offered basic education in 686 informal classes. Soon thereafter Lefranc had embraced a more populist model of cultural training by accepting tourism and hobbies as appropriate settings for adult education. For a while, he even beamed a radio programme from the Eiffel Tower twice a week.[56]

The French Left clearly was opening up to popular culture. In 1936, the CGT daily *Le Peuple* began to run sports columns, movie reviews, and even a '*page du Foyer*'. The socialist *Le Populaire* expanded its sports coverage from a half to one-and-a-half pages and offered a half page to 'women' and an equal amount for the radio. Despite some objection from purists, in 1936 the socialist daily featured front-page coverage of the Tour de France. As educator Edouard Dolleans put it:

> The new culture is not a luxury. It is within reach of the humble and the most distant; . . . vision, sound and silence, the cinema, records, radio and photographs have all powerfully contributed to the formation of the new culture, the culture of the total individual.[57]

An ally of these Paris-based groups was the Education League. This rural-based organisation coordinated tourism programmes with Paris and promoted cultural and sports activities in small towns. In 1936, this teacher-led group began constructing communal halls for leisure activities and even had a model hall built at the Paris Exhibition of 1937 to encourage imitation. But their Catholic rivals embraced similar goals: the desire to inculcate within the young a taste for wholesome exercise, fellowship, and home-based hobbies to counteract the allure of commercial leisure. Catholics shared with the secular leaders of the Popular Front a desire to promote domestic life through family camps and an abhorrence of state-directed leisure on the fascist model.[58]

British adult educationists adopted a similar a multi-class model. They too rejected the didacticism of the past for informal outlets of individual expression. Hobbies, E. B. Castles argued, were the best antidote to the 'deadening compulsion always to be in a crowd'.[59] W. E. Williams of the British Institute of Adult Education defended non-vocational education for 'living' and for making people 'less dependent upon externals'; this alone would create 'a state of mind that can be at rest without a toy'. A pamphlet which publicised the Workers' Education Association clearly expressed the new philosophy: 'The end of all work is leisure, and leisure is what we have least been educated to enjoy.'[60] Advocates of adult education in Britain shared with Lefranc the view that these self-initiating activities were the only antidote to passivity.

British adult education took on new forms: the BBC, for example, encouraged 'wireless groups' to discuss educational radio programmes and articles in the BBC's *Listener*. Local education officials promoted classes on popular topics like crafts, folk dancing, and practical commercial skills; they encouraged teachers to shift from formal lectures to participation and discussion. The National Council of Social Services published detailed plans for the building of village halls for athletic and cultural activities. Like their French equivalents, these halls were to be constructed with local labour and funding. Indeed that was part of the idea of building community.[61]

It is, of course, possible to interpret these European trends in the 1930s as merely an update of the paternalism of Victorian rational recreation. They shared a similar individualistic and improving ethic and an antipathy to commercial mass entertainment. Both also embraced the language of social reconciliation and participant initiative. In a sense the European democratic leisure movement simply adapted these ideas to the new conditions of mass production where the psychological satisfactions of work were increasingly displaced on to leisure. The result, one might conclude, was merely a new form of social control which allowed a ruling class to retain power in the workplace while conceding 'circuses' after hours to be directed by the ringmasters of leisure.

But I think this interpretation ignores the complexity of the democratic leisure movement and its potential for stimulating political change. The movement both challenged commercialised free time and offered models for social interaction outside the state and workplace, especially in Europe. In these ways, it anticipated the 'new social movements' of the 1980s and 1990s. Democratic leisure advocates were responsive to popular desires for free time. They looked toward a public culture that somehow would bridge the chasm between high culture and working families. That this failed, of course, is essential to the story. But it is not the whole story. The European vacation movement makes this clear.

VACATIONS FOR ALL

During the 1930s peaked a generation of growing interest in extended periods away from work and the home environment in western Europe. Few workers actively desired either a shorter workday or even a two-day weekend *as leisure time* as opposed to work sharing. The failure of community recreation programmes suggested disillusionment with the benefits of daily doses of free time.[62] This undermined the logic of a public cultural politics built around regular experiences of education, fine arts, or sports. Apparently people preferred a radical discontinuity of experience rather than a free-time culture that was integrated into everyday life. Thus the holiday became a major site for the organisation of leisure.

The Depression decade was marked by an extraordinary interest in affordable holidays and camping in Britain. As is well known, the British practically invented the modern pleasure holiday in the nineteenth century. Still, the popularity of the seaside holiday reached new heights during the Depression. In 1937, Blackpool served 7 million tourists. But, in 1939, Southend also had 5.5 million visitors and Hastings, 3 million. The highly profitable Butlin holiday camp, first appearing in 1937, quickly captured the public imagination. About 200 new commercial leisure camps had emerged by 1939.[63]

More important for the development of democratic leisure was the parallel growth of non-profit holiday programmes in Britain. The Youth Hostel Association appeared only in 1929 (reaching 20,000 members with facilities at 150 hostels by 1932 and growing to 281 by 1938). Both hikers and cyclists travelled in groups from hostel to hostel for low-cost holidays of interclass fellowship and nature-loving. With subsidies from the Carnegie Foundation, the Youth Hostel Association even provided a camp for adolescents on the dole for 'training' purposes. Writer and broadcaster C. E. M. Joad publicised the hostel, helping to attract white-collar youths with appeals to the 'lost heritage' of communitarian rural life. Less paternalistic and more plebeian was the Ramblers Association that was founded in 1932. Its spirited rhetoric condemned the 'pluto-crats' who denied the people access to pathways on private property. Of course, this group represented only a fraction of the half million ramblers who took to the road each summer in the 1930s. But many shared the association's sentiments. Hikers some-times clashed with wealthy grouse hunters who owned the moors beyond the polluted air of the towns in the industrial north.[64]

One solution to this conflict was the group tour and vacation centre. An important organiser of collective tourism was the Holi-day Fellowship. Although its lineage dated back to 1891, the Holiday Fellowship's greatest growth was in the interwar years, serving, in 1938, some 45,169 guests. By 1939, this nature-loving com-munity of about 100 rambling and excursionist clubs accommodated members in some 90 guest houses in England and abroad with a volunteer staff. Its 'Creed of the Open Road' called members:

To love the fields and the wild flowers, the stars, the far open sea, the soft, warm earth, and to live much with them alone; but to love struggling and weary men and women and every pulsing, living creature better.[65]

Although most members of the Holiday Fellowship were clerical and skilled workers, some manual labourers were attracted to the promise of relief from the dreary industrial horizon. The romantic image of the rural landscape was widely popularised in railway-station murals, designs on boxes of prepared foods, popular countryside novels, and guidebooks for automobile tours. The Eng-lish countryside was, as historian John Lowerson notes, 'an untidy museum of the quaint'.[66]

But foreign travel had already entered the dreams of English wage-earners in the interwar years. The Workers' Travel Associ-ation (WTA) was founded in 1921 and attracted about 26,000 members by 1931. In an effort to democratise travel abroad, it booked exchanges of labour activists and others at Swiss resorts.[67] In a 1937 study, Lancashire factory workers revealed a keen interest in overseas travel even if they had an opportunity for no more than a short boat trip to the Isle of Man. By the end of World War II, that longing for overseas travel set the stage for the extraordinary shift of the English working classes away from their accustomed holidays at Blackpool and to Spain and Greece.[68]

In France, this vacation culture was rather less well developed.

Not only was the seaside holiday still inaccessible to the manual labourers, but few wage-earners actively sought the paid holiday.[69] Still Marc Sangnier, a well-known veteran of Christian democracy, founded the first French hostel in 1929. The movement grew rapidly in the 1930s despite being divided along confessional lines. The secular wing had 325 hostels by the end of 1937 and the Catholics ran about 505 cheap vacation centres. In the non-Catholic hostels, the familiarity of sexually mixed groups scandalised conservatives and gave the hostels a uniquely youthful character. In 1933, French railroads began to offer tours for their workers. Le Touring Club de France owned 1,200 camps by 1938 with 300,000 members. These outdoor activities especially attracted those young adults with fond childhood memories of the scouts and other youth groups. Clearly, even in the depth of the Depression, the idea of leisure as a social necessity and even a right was gaining legitimacy.[70]

Vacation advocates focused increasingly on the need to accommodate the desire of youth for autonomy. In 1938, an executive from Lever Brothers, a British company long noted for its progressive social policy, made this point: 'as soon as the . . . [young] are earning their own living, they like to go off on holidays on their own'. French authorities shared this perspective.[71]

But others stressed the needs of young families. English adult educator Marie Butts argued against the exclusive development of youth-oriented leisure; she insisted that children needed to 'be proud of parents' and to share play time with them. She even proposed 'family training courses'. In response to popular demand, the Workers' Travel Association and Holiday Fellowship upgraded their accommodation to satisfy family needs; and, in the mid-1930s, even a few town councils in England constructed holiday camps for low-cost family vacations. The Guinness Trust equipped their Holiday Home with double rooms for young families and dormitories for older children 'to give the mother a rest from her duties'. Married women were attracted to the Butlin camps for their promise of relief from domestic duties; mothers appreciated Butlin's 'Auntie Peggy's' playgrounds and games for small children. The French reformist group *Musée Social* called for sea and mountain resorts for family holidays which should include dining halls and housekeeping services to free mothers from domestic work.[72]

How do we account for this surge of interest in the family and mothers? During the Depression, widespread unemployment meant that 'free time' ceased to mean merely recuperation from and compensation for wage work; it took on new meanings for the entire family, not just the male 'bread winner'. For example, the jobless situation of the father or adult child produced the tensions of a forced family togetherness; the inability of different ages and sexes to find means of common enjoyment became acutely apparent. Of course, sociologists observed that parental role reversal threatened patriarchy when jobless fathers sometimes lost status while being supported by wage-earning children or wives; but they also stressed that the 'unemployed man's wife [has] no holidays' because husbands failed to adjust to their jobless state by contributing meaningfully to the domestic work. While both French and British writers advocated that men assume greater housekeeping roles, an obvious palliative for the wife was a holiday. In fact, British social workers idealistically advocated that volunteers 'adopt' children in order to give wives a chance for a 'real change of scenery'. The French socialist educator George Lefranc hoped that increased free time would erode 'male egotism' and create a new home life. 'If women work outside the home', he suggested, 'then the men should do their share of domestic work'. But Lefranc also advocated that cooperative child care allow couples time together on Sunday and even that holidays with pay be coordinated so that families could share time together.[73]

Despite this growing awareness of the non-waged domestic work of women and the equity of sexual symmetry in work and leisure, the Victorian ideal of separate spheres still prevailed. The French Popular Front's Léon Blum, reflecting upon the 40-hour week in 1942, provides a good example. He argued that additional leisure produced

> not idleness but rest after labour. The organisation of leisure and increases in the purchasing power of wages . . . allow the workers' family to maintain its health by exercise and its spirituality by games, to give more time to domestic occupations and affections; and one day they will make it possible for working class mothers to give all their time to their homes and families; in other words, they strengthen, in fact, the moral factors of society.

All of the Victorian associations of time and gender remained: the rest after labour belonged to the male wage-earner; ideally free time was to be devoted to domestic privacy; and, economic progress would 'one day' create the bourgeois utopia of the housewife in the French working class where many married women never ceased being wage-earners.[74]

The central image of democratic leisure in the 1930s was the paid holiday, the 'vacation for all'. This was particularly true in Europe where the idea of the workers' holiday quickly captured the imagination of both the French Popular Front and the British Left. But, as many historians have recently pointed out, few French wage-earners actually took a vacation away from home during the Popular Front; and those that did, visited relatives in the country or went to the nearby coast of Normandy, not to the Riviera. Most French wage-earners could not surmount the psychological barrier of actually leaving home for an extended period of time. They found it difficult to believe that they actually would be paid for 'doing nothing'. Fewer still would embark on a vacation without the social cocoon of the trade union or other familiar group. One may well question the view of Michel Verret that, like most consumer goods, the vacation culture simply trickled down to working people. But, by the 1950s, the decline of ties to the extended family and workplace surely helped to create the private leisure that is typically expressed today in the extended summer vacation.[75]

This interpretation, however, seems to neglect a vital point about the character of leisure in the 1930s. Not only were workers conservative in their slow embrace of individualism in free time, but powerful political forces tried to create an alternative to private commercialised free time. What occurred in the 1950s was not simply the 'modernisation' of workers' culture or even a cultural response to social fragmentation; rather, what happened was the eclipse of a programme of public culture of free time that had been championed by those many organisations for democratic leisure.

We can begin to explain the fate of that culture by analysing the irony and ambiguity of the Popular Front's image of the vacation. Consider an issue of the socialist daily, *Le Populaire*, in August 1937 that offered the incongruous image of a large group of metalworkers leaving their Paris factory for a two-week vacation in Boulogne while singing the 'International'. The foremen ignored this transgression of discipline because they were too busy rushing out of the plant for their own holiday. The popular magazine *Vu* featured an issue on popular holiday-making in the midst of the strike wave of June 1936, scarcely noting this major political event.[76]

Repeatedly the vacation represented class victory but also an escape from politics. The Popular Front press loved to mock the presumed discomfort of the old leisure class as it encountered the *congés payés* or workers on paid holiday: a cartoon showed the meeting of the bourgeois poodle and the '*chien de congé payé*';

and another had a hotel keeper telling the rich tourist that all 'your rooms have been rented'. Few observers noted that the paid vacation would create a new mass market for commercial leisure. Indeed conservatives feared that when the French masses invaded the seashore, rich English tourists would flee in horror. Yet the non-confrontational images of family togetherness and friendship were also common vacation themes. In the summer of 1937, *Le Populaire* interviewed a worker gleefully departing Paris for Brittany with his wife and child to 'see the old ones'. Even the communist *L'Humanité* in August 1936 stressed that the vacation afforded the family, who 'live under the same roof but as strangers and without having the time to know one another', an opportunity for togetherness. This article expressed the hope that new friendships between families created during the strikes of June 1936 would become strong while sharing holiday pleasures. *Regards* offered photographs of the 'first paid vacation' of families relaxing on the 'little beaches' in the Nord 'without arrogant luxury, without casinos'. The old came to enjoy a 'long merited' rest in the shade while children ran along the beach with their parents.[77]

Politics and pleasure were not distinguished. In the summers of 1936 and 1937, the Left press in France alternated reports on the Spanish Civil War with articles recommending sea and country resorts and features of French provincial towns worthy of tourism. They combined patriotism and play: 'We discover the beauties of our country thanks to the paid vacation.' In popular tourism, abstract classroom history and geography would become a reality to workers. But the learners would also become teachers: Parisian workers off on holiday to the four corners of France were 'bringing to their home towns the generous and advanced ideas of the great city'. The vacation was an opportunity to dissolve the divisions of labour and region: the 'broad shouldered athlete and the long haired intellectual', the peasant, and the metalworker were to meet and learn from each other.[78]

Vacation discourse revealed an extraordinary mix of ideas – class struggle, family togetherness, nature worship, and patriotism. It stimulated the growth of a variety of decentralised labour-related organisations that encouraged popular vacations in France. The Popular Tourist Association of the Parisian Region attracted 30,000 families for whom it found cheap holidays in 1937. This group promoted not only tours to the provinces but, in anticipation of postwar enthusiasms, it organised winter vacations to the Alps and even trips to Tunisia. In April 1937, the CGT organised a Tourism

Office and even sponsored a vacation savings bank for members. During the summer of 1937, the Paris Exhibition provided the opportunity for organised tours of Paris for up to 700,000 provincials. Teachers' unions organised the club, Vacations for All, with camps and youth hostels.[79]

Behind much of this activity was Albert Thomas' concept of democratic leisure. It was faithfully followed by the 36-year-old Léo Lagrange, the Popular Front's Undersecretary of State for Sports and Leisure. Lagrange's office offered support for voluntarist holiday and leisure programmes. To be sure, the Popular Front's commitment to mass leisure was flagging as early as March 1937 when appropriations were substantially reduced. In June, Lagrange's activities were shifted to the ministry of education. But Lagrange's policy was of great political importance to the Popular Front and many of his programmes continued under the Vichy regime.[80]

Lagrange shared the familial and youth orientation of the leisure movement of the 1930s. He cajoled railway companies into accepting a programme of inexpensive family excursion tickets, which attracted 1.5 million by the summer of 1938. He also administered the building of 400 sports arenas by the end of 1937. His office introduced physical education in nearly half of the *departements* during the Popular Front in the hope of encouraging lifetime interest in sports. Lagrange even popularised tennis, skiing, flying and other traditionally elite forms of physical fitness. He made common cause with the growing youth-hostel movement by subsidising both laic and Catholic associations. The Popular Front's Ministry of Health in 1937 proposed the use of country schools as bases for an expanded programme of children's summer tours and camps.[81]

Yet the Popular Front opposed 'directed leisure'. Rather, as Lagrange put it, 'we must make available to the masses all kinds of leisure which they may choose for themselves'. The weekly *Vendredi* insisted that government programmes were not to create a '*corvée de joie* but to give to the people the taste for what they like'. Lagrange supported autonomous municipal Leisure Clubs to express the new 'social maturity' of the people. The political core of democratic culture was the absence of partisanship and manipulation. And, Lagrange was intent on proving that a parliamentary state was capable of creating a 'vast organisation of sport and leisure' as successful as that of the fascists.[82]

Lagrange stressed participation rather than spectator sports and simple playing fields rather than ornate stadiums. He insisted that

'Joy can not be imposed. It is self-acquired and self-merited.' Lagrange emphasised not a 'joy' or national 'unity' under the flag of national self-promotion or voluntary obedience. Rather 'joy' meant 'spontaneity'; and 'unity' was the 'breaking down of the walls' which separated intellectuals and workers. He insisted that his objective was to create a harmony of youth based on 'a sympathy and respect necessary for fair play'. Leisure and sport were to fulfil the fragile dream of interactional solidarity. His idea of unity was the apolitical hostel movement which he called a 'republic of youth'. And, by taking control of participant sports and cultural activities, workers would become free of bourgeois paternalism. Alice Jouenne typified the Popular Front leisure ideology. In August 1937, she wrote that the more democratic the access to leisure, the less prone will societies be to make war: 'Leisure promotes peace for it magnifies life and makes one love life.'[83]

Yet Popular Front leisure policy was hardly undirected. Lagrange stressed the Hellenic ideal of 'equilibrium' between the 'health of the body and the health of the spirit'. Like so many before him, Lagrange emphasised that 'specialised labour' required the corrective of physical culture and sport. Again he rehashed the old biological argument for leisure as a means of reversing the decline in the birth rate. And, like his Nazi counterparts, he stressed the critical role in national renewal to be played by a physically fit 'new generation'.[84]

The French Popular Front stressed voluntarism, local initiative, and individualism against the authoritarianism of fascist culture. But it also sought to organise the 'masses' and to enlist them through leisure into their vision of the future. It was an attempt to give a socialist content to culture and to supplement abstract and even divisive economic programmes with socio-cultural solidarity. An ambiguity remained unresolved.[85]

The British case was, of course, very different. Britain's conservative government did not follow the French Popular Front's democratic leisure policy or enforce universal paid vacations. Also missing was the ideological fervour across the Channel. Still the British enthusiasm for leisure and tourism in the late 1930s paralleled that of the French. By 1937, thanks in part to new paid holiday contracts, a little under a third of Britain's 46 million citizens took one or more weeks holiday away from home. The National Savings Committee, which had long encouraged 'thoughtful spending and purposive saving', attempted in the 1930s to enlist business support for holiday savings clubs. The Industrial Welfare Society with labour and business backing advocated non-profit travel bureaus and summer camps. In the summer of 1937, the Labour Party (with volunteer help from cotton factory workers) held demonstrations complete with 'gay streamers' at vacation spots in favour of holiday legislation. Trade unionists even advocated that the government make troop-ships available for international cultural exchanges.[86] The holiday movement was certainly international.

Lagrange's language and policy had British equivalents. As early as 1931, the Ministry of Public Works, led then by Labour leader George Lansbury, proposed numerous projects for bathing pools and playgrounds. Labour Party activists lobbied for relaxation of Sunday prohibitions of film showings and football matches; they favoured also improved access to hiking trails. By 1937, the Labour Party declared that leisure was to be one of the 'four great benefits' to be gained by their next government. Proposals for a British Ministry of Sports and Leisure failed in 1937; but laws, passed in 1937 and 1939, promoted physical fitness and protected parks and camping grounds. After the war, when Labour finally came to power, leisure policy planning absorbed key party officials.[87] For example, Labour leaders, along with the resort and rail industries, promoted the extension of the traditional holiday season to ease congestion in the seaside towns in August.[88]

The *Labour Magazine* recalled Lagrange's leisure ideology. An article published in June 1937 predicted the end of the 'beanos, the fun fairs, and the noisy makeshift hilarity which has done duty for the holiday of the many'. In its place would emerge a popular tourism which would give the people a chance to explore nature and understand others from different trades and nationalities. Notables of the Left, including G. D. H. Cole, Clement Attlee, and Harold Laski, supported the 'National Committee to Provide Holidays for Unemployed Workers in Distressed Areas'. A fund-raising leaflet for the Committee (1938) argued that 'industrial refugees . . . need to get away from the misery and drabness of their everyday lives'.[89] The holiday was to be for all.

These sentiments reflected a broad, if ill-formed, international movement for democratic leisure. In 1938, the International Commission of Workers' Spare Time, an earnest convocation of progressives from the western democracies, hoped to combat rising chauvinism through recreation; they called for international exchanges for inexpensive and progressive social interaction between workers. Yet, while delegates expressed frustration that they lacked those government resources which their fascist and

Soviet counterparts enjoyed, they were adamant that leisure, like freedom, was to proceed from the individual, not the state.[90] How to do this was, of course, the problem.

DILEMMAS OF ORGANISED LEISURE

These innovations in public leisure policy met with many, perhaps insuperable difficulties in the 1930s. As we have already noted, the movement for the reduction of worktime was largely defeated. But the theory of democratic leisure also met with unanswered questions and dilemmas.

First, if freedom meant individual choice, could organised leisure compete with consumer sovereignty? Labour leaders often recognised that individuality could be best expressed in time away from the job rather than in the work experience itself. A British miners' union pamphlet (1938), celebrating newly won paid holidays, featured pictures of a young miner showering away the last of the coal dust for a week, collecting his vacation pay, packing his wife and two small children on to a train, and ending with an image of the miner frolicking on the beach with his tots, over the title 'Then a dip . . . Happy!' For fathers, the vacation was to be a gift to the family and an opportunity to experience parenting outside the routine stress of the industrial world. And for many married women, it represented temporary freedom from domestic concerns. In responses to an essay contest on the theme of the ideal holiday, British workers offered strictly private images – varying with the infinite variety of age, family situation, gender, and personal proclivity. The vacation was a chance for romance, chumming with childhood mates, and even simply just 'letting the world go by' in a brief escape from the world of the clock. The idea of organisation by any meaningful definition had little place.[91]

This may help explain why the public recreation movement seldom was able to compete against commercial leisure. British travel and holiday-camp cooperatives lacked the capital and perhaps managerial skill to prevail over the commercialised fun of Billy Butlin's holiday camps. But more fundamentally, their didactic proclivities stood in the way of pleasure-making. How many workers would choose the international exchange of workers over the Golden Mile of Blackpool? For many, Butlin's camps were simply more fun than the Holiday Fellowship. At least one Mass-Observer found the Butlin camps in the late 1930s to be fun (contrary to the American image of them as regimented and even masochistic); by contrast, another observer found the Workers' Travel Association guest house to be unfriendly and cliquish. In fact, the Butlin camps were in many ways simply adaptations of earlier non-profit holiday camps but with greater comfort; they accommodated popular taste by adding bars, dance music, and opportunities for heterosexual encounter. The adult educationalists and groups like the Holiday Fellowship or Vacations for All were certainly sensitive to the needs of providing the poor with opportunities for familial expression in leisure. Yet the Butlin's camps and later the Disneylands were far more successful in exploiting this market.[92]

Rational recreation was far from the minds of most workers. On this point, many sociologists of working-class culture are right. The continued prevalence of gambling suggests that the traditional quest for excitement in leisure had hardly been 'civilised'. Of course, some categories of 'improving' leisure like gardening and amateur participation in football, cricket, or softball grew during the inter-war period. Catholics in France were able to preserve their flocks through an ambitious network of youth and sports groups. And, in the US and Britain, church attendance remained a counterculture to male pub or saloon sociability.[93] But, as the writer Richard Hoggart argues, the English working class of the interwar years had a love for a 'sprawling, highly-ornamental, rococo extravagance'. This was particularly evident in the holiday-making of exotic Blackpool. As I will note in later chapters, working-class 'materialism' was a moral necessity in a drab life of stress-filled routine.[94]

A second dilemma for democratic-leisure advocates can be noted. Not only did the market outcompete non-profit play, but it sometimes coopted the leisure movement. This was particularly obvious in the US, where recreation professionals dominated free-time discourse. American idealism for the 'new leisure' in the early 1930s gave way to an accommodation to commercial interests in the 1940s. Instead of the earlier harsh criticism of the entertainment industry, recreation professionals later seem to have reconciled themselves to a subsidiary or, at least, a complementary role in the consumer society. In the 1940s, apologists for public recreation stressed its potential for creating jobs, increasing real-estate values, and stimulating economies. The need for public provisioning remained; but no longer was it an alternative to the market. Instead it was part of the infrastructure for that market:

If America is to realize the fullest social and economic benefits from recreation, the country will have to dig down deeply and provide funds both through public appropriation and the 'contributed' dollar. In such an expansion of recreation, building materials of many kinds will be needed and workers will be required to construct and maintain physical plants. . . . . Americans know what they want. They want homes, jobs, and an opportunity to live abundantly. They have demonstrated their willingness to pay for all three. The current upswing of nationwide interest in recreation is a manifestation, and perhaps advance notice of that new market – one in which the demand far exceeds the supply – is emerging.[95]

New Dealers linked public leisure to the process of job creation through public works projects. It was a short step after 1945 to understand recreation as an industry and thus part of a broader programme of economic expansion.

Ultimately the contest was not between totalitarian and democratic leisure but between 'organised' and market leisure. But few saw it that way in the interwar decades. British adult educator Lancelot Hogben believed that the problem of capitalism was its 'stagnation'. For him, like so many of his contemporaries, the possibility of the endless growth of the commodity form simply did not exist. And while, in the same period, the challenge of the market was much more evident to Americans like Jesse Steiner, the wall between public and commercial leisure was never high; and those differences evaporated in the new ethos of growth and 'recovery'. Instead, democratic recreation advocates feared far more the manipulation of totalitarians and did so long after the 1930s. Thus the complex problems of market leisure were often evaded.[96]

And there remained still a third problem (especially in western Europe): if the advocates of democratic leisure were successful in bringing the people pleasure, how were the social values of the Left to be inculcated into this leisure culture – and not to cede this terrain of values to the merchandisers? The key, of course, was how to organise leisure and yet to guarantee its freedom; how to uplift and yet not be undemocratic; and how to create joy without alienating people by patronising manipulation. But the problem also was how to 'make' people feel fellowship and act for the common good in and through play.

The failure of a real reconciliation of the intellectual and the people is a profound, if obvious, source of these problems. Julian Jackson and Michael Seidman are correct in stressing the contradictions between the Popular Front's 'productivist vision of leisure' with its advocacy of a radical separation of work and play, on the one hand, and the 'premodern' resistance of many workers to that vision, on the other. Some French workers failed to return to their jobs at the end of their *congés payés*. Others took jobs during their vacations. These responses might also explain why some labourers were reluctant to exchange continuous and intense work for long blocks of time free from labour. The self-improving cultural goals of Popular Front leaders had little measurable impact on these workers. The holiday ethic was slow to develop (at least in France). Instead leisure organised around daily encounters with alcohol and gambling persisted.[97] Many workers were surely 'unorganisable'. Attempts at 'uplifting' these people were manipulative and inevitably disappointing.

If democratic leisure was to uplift, it was also to guarantee 'liberty'. This meant not only popular participation and accommodation to the needs of youth and family, but acceptance of popular taste: free time was meant both for studying Racine and listening to Maurice Chevalier. The problem was that an effort to transcend the garrison mentality of party and union may have inadvertently encouraged a withdrawal from politics. After all, for Lagrange, the non-partisan friendliness of the Youth Hostel was his 'republican' ideal; and his stress upon sports rather than the critical intellect had an apolitical effect.[98] Pleasure, even of the social kind, had no necessary relationship to broader commitments. Still it might be fairer to say that the Left failed to avert depoliticisation while attempting to address the individualistic needs that led to political passivity.

The holiday was a focal point of this dilemma: it was to be organised but free, to serve a national purpose but also provide an escape into pleasure. People on vacation sought the private intimacy of loved ones, fragmented by age and marital status. They may have longed for re-aggregation, but only in the apolitical crowd along the seaside promenade or shopping arcade. Free time seems to have depoliticised in private, cyclic rites of the weekend and vacation. Attempts to reorganise politics around leisure made sense given the decline of workplace and community solidarities. But was it really possible?

While some of the ideas of democratic leisure were revived after World War II, they had little immediate impact. In any case, the cultural bond between populist intellectuals and workers, never very strong, had broken when most intellectuals returned by the late 1930s to the pessimistic analysis of mass leisure that had prevailed in the 1920s. In the vacuum left by this abortive politics of public culture emerged a consumer culture that progressively absorbed the people's time. Intellectuals contributed to the consolidation of mass consumerism by perpetuating boundaries between high- and low-brow culture. But the failure of democratic leisure went beyond the fears and pride of the intelligentsia. It was also rooted in the experience of the people and the traumas of capitalist transformation. This may help explain choices made between time and money that led to mass consumerism. And so, these experiences and traumas will be my next theme.

6 Traumas of time and money in prosperity and depression

The movements for shorter hours and democratic leisure were defeated by their own contradictions. But these ideas also failed because of their inability to attract working people. An explanation common since mid-century is that wage-earners had little interest in free time or its 'improvement'. Instead they wanted goods and were willing to sacrifice free time to wage work for access to them. This interpretation, however, is biased by the victory of consumerism after 1945; and thus it is not a useful analysis of the historical origins of mass-consumer society earlier in this century.

As we have seen, most business people and intellectuals in the 1920s saw things quite differently. They feared that increased productivity would produce mass access to goods and free time, which, in turn, would threaten economic growth and moral standards. Only a few saw that the democratisation of time and money would create a renewed commitment to steady work; rare was the person who realised that mass consumerism would assure economic equilibrium, even if not the purity of high culture. Was this common reading of the masses simply wrong? Or did something change between the 1920s and the 1950s? Doubtless, the earlier interpretation failed to recognise the disciplinary potential of Fordism. But a series of traumatic events seems to have transformed or, at least, shaped popular attitudes toward free time and goods leading to what became the consumerist consensus.

How do we assess the real desires of wage-earners for free time and goods? Frankly no very clear answer to that question is possible. The two-goods maximisation theory of the marginalist school presumes a long-term balance between time and money: after wage increases satisfied wants, given the onus of work, wage-earners would favour free time.[1] The combination of intense work, overtime, and rising wages that was experienced by many during World

War I may have produced a desire to 'buy' leisure time in 1919. However, after this goal was realised in the eight-hour day, further increases in productivity could be expressed as increased consumption (and investment/profit).[2] But this theory ignores obvious structural constraints on 'choice'.[3] Economic historian Chris Nyland argues instead that the intensification of the labour process forced the diminution of working hours.[4] But, despite continued pressures to increase labour intensity, the demand for free time has hardly kept pace; and this theory does not explain why workers demanded a share of increased productivity in higher purchasing power. A wider historical context must be introduced that shows the economic and political limits on choice during the traumatic interwar years. This analysis should reveal psychological constraints that biased most families toward money rather than time. These traumas were based as much on wage-earning families' understanding of themselves as consumers as on their identities as workers.

CHOICE AND DISCIPLINE IN THE INTERWAR YEARS

Attitudes of wage-earners toward free time and wages were surely plastic and depended upon factors often out of the control of wage-earners. Choices can be understood only in a broadly political context. Between 1917 and 1923, demands for the eight-hour day expressed, not merely a trade-off of income for leisure, but also a quest for a permanent *right* to personal time. Union leaders insisted that hour reductions were not to be bargained away for economic concessions. In the French building trades, for example, workers proposed compensatory free time instead of income when employers obliged them to do extra work. British wage-earners reasoned that if a 9:00 a.m. start, a 40-hour week, or two-week vacation were appropriate for management, workers should share that right. Variations in the intensity and fatigue of work ought to be reflected in different wages, not in hours. Even marginalised black domestics in Kansas City won an eight-hour day in 1919. In the post-Armistice blossoming of democratic claims, labour defended the new workday as a right of citizenship, a concrete expression of social equality beyond political liberties.[5]

The eight-hour day (or 48-hour week) was also a culmination of a 'modern' quest for leisure, built around a uniform and compressed workday with continuous periods free from work and its authoritarian environment. This is not to say that the traditional play of community-centred festivals or lengthy rest breaks and frequent, but irregular, voluntary absences from work had entirely disappeared.[6] But workers in seasonal and cyclical trades (including construction, dockwork, and even steel and automobile manufacturing) increasingly resisted 'flexible' work years and insisted on a standard day of labour. In July 1919, transportation workers in Chicago went on strike against a workday which was spread over fourteen hours for eight-hours of paid labour. They demanded a continuous workday. Wage-earners often sought to compress the workday (even to sacrifice traditional 'coffee breaks') in order to free as much of that day as possible from labour. British textile workers rejected the compromise proposed by industrial reformers: shorter workdays on a two- or three-shift system. Such a schedule might make reduced individual hours more acceptable to business. But to women labourers especially, the shift system disrupted family life, increased the number of meals to prepare, and destroyed 'natural' rhythms of life. The veteran American labour leader, Mother Jones, surely reflected the views of many steel workers on twelve-hour shifts when she said in 1919: 'What we want is a little leisure, time for music, playgrounds, a decent home, books and the things that make life worthwhile.'[7]

Of course, the quest for free time could not be easily separated from the demand for money wages. Most short-hour strikers in 1919 were also fighting for increased pay in order to compensate for inflation. Often workers desired reduced workdays in order to protect jobs and to lower the threshold when overtime rates would take effect. Fears of job loss and competition certainly motivated workers during that stressful postwar period when the conversion of war industries and entry of veterans into the job market threatened employment. This largely explains the 40-hours strike in Glasgow, Scotland, in January 1919. The American coal miners' strikes later that year for the six-hour day had several purposes: to combat overproduction and, with it, underemployment, low wages, and the insecurities of a seasonal workyear.[8] The old artisan's ethic survived in the demand that all local males in a trade should have sufficient time at paid work to be able to maintain a family before anyone should work more hours. But in France, at least, war casualties and a low birth rate produced labour shortages. Unemployment was hardly a long-term problem. Moreover French workers were not quick to take advantage of this situation by demanding overtime bonuses.

Everywhere organised labour had an ambiguous attitude about the choice between time and money. This was hardly a utilitarian decision to maximise personal or group advantage; rather it was a response to the discipline of the market, which, for the most part, employers dominated. A central fact was that management responded very differently to workers' demands for free time as compared to money income. While employers resisted granting concessions in either hours or wages, generally they were far more reluctant to tolerate reductions in worktime. Shorter hours increased training and benefit costs and limited the ability of business to respond quickly to orders without maintaining large inventories or making capital improvements. Reduced worktime also diminished the dependency of labour upon any particular job. By increasing the demand for labour, shorter hours lowered the value of any job in comparison to other activities, paid or not. Thus hours' diminutions meant less labour discipline. In contrast, wages were more easily raised or lowered with the market (either directly or through inflation).[9] Probably most important, economic competition impeded the reduction of working hours. Businesses, threatened by the cheap goods of others who continued a long workday, would not risk reduction of worktime.

These were powerful biases against the redistribution of time even when productivity increases made it possible and work intensification made it desirable. The opportunity for free time was brief and unusual. This context of market discipline explains the 'choice' between leisure and work and thus time and money.

A quest for free time was feasible in the labour upsurge immediately after World War I. But it faded when economic pressures and political impotence dissolved labour solidarity later in 1919. Strikes for advanced hour demands were defeated everywhere. British engineers and French construction workers failed by summer in their efforts to win a 44-hour week (with a Saturday half-holiday) and American coal miners got wage increases rather than the prized six-hour day in December. American steel workers were doomed to continue to toil on two, twelve-hour shifts despite a massive union drive and strike in late 1919.[10]

Accompanying these defeats were decreased job and income security. The number of jobless Britons increased from 250,000 in the autumn of 1920 to 2 million by June 1921 or (16.9 per cent of the workforce). In 1921, American factory workers lost almost 18 percent in real earnings with one in five jobless.[11] Real wages fell, at least briefly, in Britain in 1921; and in France (with inflation), purchasing power dropped sharply between 1922 and 1926.[12] All of this produced the market discipline that led workers to reject a sacrifice of paid worktime for the right of leisure or the noble principle of sharing work with the unemployed.

Of course, sceptics and employers have long argued that reduced worktime was merely a pretence for raising wages by applying overtime pay rates earlier. Typical was the view of the French observer Paul Rives who wrote in 1924 that the eight-hour law was 'only a minimum wage law'; workers expected that income beyond the subsistence level was to be earned on overtime or through moonlighting. Trade-union leaders often shared this view of the rank-and-file.[13]

But market discipline often determined behaviour. For example, decreases in real wages undermined the eight-hour standard in France. Employers took advantage of those dependent on wages by offering overtime rather than increased hourly pay for a standard workday.[14] Historian David Brody found that American steel workers, 'particularly where wage rates were falling, . . . preferred the extra hours. Nothing mattered more than the maintenance of accustomed living standards.'[15] And they worked the notorious twelve-hour shift! Many wage-earners had to adjust to a seasonal or erratic workyear, despite efforts of unions to create greater uniformity by insisting on a regular eight-hour day. 'Middletown' wage-earners often experienced the roller-coaster ride of periodic plant shutdowns. Even in the prosperous year of 1923, 28 per cent of adult male wage-earners were laid off some time during the year. Leila Houghteling found most of the 'regularly-employed' factory workers in Chicago to be jobless at least a month in 1924. Such wage-earners had little choice but to maximise income when jobs were available by working as long as possible.[16]

The collapse of the labour movement after 1919 is essential to understanding these responses. Throughout the 1920s, unions naturally insisted on full enforcement of overtime limits (in France especially) and high overtime bonuses in order to discourage their use. Still, organised labour was hardly in an auspicious political position after 1920. In France, the schism within the Left and the massive influx of immigrant workers nearly destroyed the labour movement. The number of American workers in unions dropped from the 1919 peak of 5 million to less than 3.5 million by 1923; and the percentage of the industrial workforce in unions sank 50 per cent in the 1920s, declining to merely 10.2 per cent by 1930. Almost completely unorganised were major manufacturing industries, especially those who competed in the national marketplace. In the US, pro-management courts, plant displacement to the south, welfare capitalism, and conservative governments strengthened business control over work schedules. Splits within the American unions let management eliminate the 44-hour week in New England textiles. This decline of American labour power shifted leadership of the short-hour movement from unions to church and business reformers. In 1923, philanthropists were instrumental in winning the eight-hour shift for steel workers; and Ford gave his unorganised factory operatives the 40-hour week in 1926.[17] Even in Britain, union membership declined from a postwar high of 8.3 million to 6.6 million in 1921; it slid to about 5 million after defeat in the coal strike of 1926, not to increase much until World War II. Along with this decline was stagnation in hour reductions and, for miners, a longer official workday.[18]

Weak unions meant that workers reacted individually to the desire for time free from work: wage-earners conducted informal slowdowns and breaks from work, hopped from one monotonous routine post to another, and were late or absent from work. All of these patterns increased during the 1920s.[19] But in the organisational vacuum, personal economic security became paramount. In the Netherlands, by contrast, a strong trade-union movement created an elaborate network of leisure facilities. There, a political alternative offered a choice. In its absence, 'individualist rationality' prevailed – and, with it, the bias of money over free time. Without a strong workers' recreational culture, Lynd's Middletown workers could not imagine what they would do with more leisure.[20]

Just as important was the desire to preserve existing living standards, which seems to have motivated the bias toward money. At least in France and Britain, there is little evidence that this choice had much to do with the promise of consumerism. According to neo-classical theory, increased access to goods would have raised the opportunity cost of free time and thus lured people into accepting more hours at work. But that access had to be tangible to make much difference in motivation. Otherwise, the threat of joblessness and income security would be decisive in the 'choice'. To be sure, in the decade up to 1924, British working people enjoyed a net gain of national income (partly because of the great deflation of 1921). They broadly shared in the rising productivity when consumer expenditure per capita grew in each of the interwar years. A 1938 government survey found a mean of 29.4 per cent of working-class household income went to 'non-essentials'; but 40 per cent still went to food[21] However, a subsistence mind-set survived in France even in labour economist and engineer, Roger Francq.

In 1919, he declared that a 'shortening of the workday is the only way for workers to gain from rising productivity', implying no possibility of an increase in real income.[22] This was a realistic assumption when real wages in France fluctuated from an index number of 115 in 1920 (1914 = 100) to 99 in 1927 rising only to 116 by 1930, despite substantial gains in productivity.[23] The European preference for money in the 1920s was based, not on Fordist consumer expectations, but on the more traditional discipline of subsistence.

By contrast, from the 1920s onwards, observers have found a burgeoning consumerism among American workers. In the period 1925–9, real wages were about 60 per cent higher in the US than in Britain and roughly 2.5 times the purchasing power of the French.[24] The 'desire for higher earnings became more dominant in the minds of the workers than the feeling for industrial freedom and independence', claimed one contemporary scholar.[25] In fact, real-wage growth in the US was exceptional in the 1920s. While real wages scarcely increased between 1900 and 1920 and good years were often followed by bad, during the 1920s wage increases persistently outstripped the cost of living. Mean real wages rose by 40 per cent between 1910 and 1929, and, even when unemployment losses were deducted, purchasing power grew by 27 per cent during the 1920s.[26] Much of that American growth was directed toward new consumer goods and especially leisure products.[27] As a proportion of total expenditures, spending on recreational goods and services increased from 3.2 per cent in 1909 to 4.7 per cent in 1929.[28] Similarly in Britain, higher productivity stimulated a 7.8 per cent increase in real wages in the 1920s and a 7.7 per cent rise in the 1930s.[29] This may have been a pale reflection of the American standard; but it placed the British in an intermediate position between the European continent and the US.

Yet these developments hardly implied the emergence of a consumer society among the working classes even in the US. To be sure, with increased income came rising expectations. Persistently sharp differences in income heightened the pain of low earnings for unskilled workers and farmers. One solution was that American families increasingly bought on hire purchase. Automobiles paid for on the instalment plan accounted for three-quarters of sales by 1925 and helped to put on the road one car for every 1.3 families by 1929.[30] Still most of the consumer debt owed by *wage-earners* was for medical and other emergencies, not cars or furniture. Consumerism was a middle-class phenomenon early in the century, even in the US. In the 1920s, Chicago workers continued to shop in neighbourhood stores and attend local theatres; they stayed away from the commercialised chain or department stores and downtown movie palaces.[31] Only marginally did creeping consumerism explain choices against free time. Rather it was the whip of job and wage insecurity and the absence of a viable alternative that drove the bias toward money.

And socio-psychological traumas of the Depression exacerbated that prejudice. In many ways the slump of the 1930s had its most disruptive impact on France. This led to the socio-political explosion of the Popular Front. Yet the traumas of joblessness and income deprivation were surely greater among Anglo-American workers. The French jobless rate increased slowly from a mere 4 per cent as late as 1931 to 8.5 per cent in 1936.[32] By contrast, the number of the jobless in the US rose from 1.55 million in 1929 (3.2 per cent of the workforce) to over 12.8 million by 1933 (24.9 per cent), never dropping below 7.7 million (14.3 per cent) in the 1930s. The unemployment rate peaked in Britain at 22.1 per cent in 1932 and decreased slowly to 10.5 per cent in 1939.[33] The French wage-earner also did not suffer decreased consumer opportunity, not having realised it in the 1920s. In fact, the real income of French workers scarcely declined between 1930 and 1935.[34] In any case, there is considerably more sociological evidence of the social effects of the slump in the English-speaking countries and thus they necessarily will be stressed.[35]

The Depression had a major impact on wage-earners' attitudes toward income and worktime. But this effect was uneven and, in part, psychological. Anglo-American jobless rates varied enormously by occupation and region. For example, in 1931, while 30.5 per cent of unskilled British manual workers were unemployed, only 14.4 per cent of skilled and 5.5 per cent of white-collar workers lacked jobs. And, for the unfortunate, unemployment was not of short duration. In 1933, the average period of joblessness in the US was 65 weeks for men and 47 weeks for women. While, in 1929, only 53,000 Britons were unemployed for the whole year, by 1933 that figure jumped to 480,000.[36] But, because of the dole in England and a complex work and welfare system in the US, few of the jobless experienced health-threatening misery. Instead unemployment was an experience of social and psychological deprivation. Those sociologists who observed the jobless did not find the economic destitution described in the late-Victorian investigations of Rowntree and Boothe; rather these witnesses found workers with

'time on their hands'. Workless and unfunded time was a psychological disability in a society that valued paid labour and where
many of those who kept their jobs actually grew more affluent. As
Orwell saw it, 'So long as Bert Jones across the street is still at
work, Alf Smith is found to feel himself dishonoured and a failure.
Hence the frightful feeling of impotence and despair which is almost
worse than the demoralisation of enforced idleness.' This had an
impact on everyone associated with the jobless.[37]

The experience of unemployment and job insecurity had a very
profound but subtle effect on attitudes toward worktime and wages:
this trauma tended to diminish the value of free time while it
reinforced the attractions of money and the goods that it could
purchase. Unemployment disrupted routines and made free time
something more to dread than to long for. It intensified the linkage
of status with work, wages, and the goods that money could buy.

THE TRAUMAS OF JOBLESSNESS AND THE DECLINING
VALUE OF FREE TIME

During the Depression, for many, time free from labour became
not leisure but idleness; and it was identified with the indignity
of joblessness and disruption of family routines. This experience
reinforced the ideology of work and gender roles as organising
principles of personality and society.

Like most historical sources, much of what we know about these
phenomena is seen through the lenses of elites. When British philanthropic foundations commissioned studies of the jobless, they
were primarily interested in the disruptive effects of unemployment,
especially how joblessness led 'in stages' to despondency and dependency. These investigations went beyond the usual fixation on the
presumed 'pauperising' effects of charity; instead they argued that
'empty' unstructured time undermined work discipline, eroded
skills, and reduced general work-worthiness. Joblessness made 'free
time' demoralising and even undesirable to workers.

This was a common view also in the American literature. Surely
it bolstered the arguments for the massive programme of work
relief for which the New Deal is especially noted. In Britain, however, work camps and retraining efforts played a relatively smaller
role. Instead philanthropists (often linked to the National Council
of Social Services) used this analysis as a moral backdrop to cajole
the 'fortunate' to support 'occupational clubs'. These local centres
provided hobbies and crafts for the jobless; they were to help

preserve the self-respect and manual skill of the jobless in anticipation of the worker's re-employment. Keep-fit classes, boot repair-
ing, and minor carpentry dominated these centres. At their peak
in 1936, they may have attracted 200,000 participants.[38] These
efforts were surely designed to defuse political pressures from the
jobless; and the supporting ideology certainly psychologised unemployment and ignored underlying responsibility for the economic
crisis.[39] But they were to give the jobless structured time lost when
they became unemployed.

The theory that guided the occupational club movement had roots
in empirical research. The belief that joblessness led to a progressive
disintegration of personality emerged from a study of Marienthal,
Austria (1933). There, investigators found universal depression.
One year after the town's major employer, a textile factory, had
closed, old social networks had nearly disappeared. The central city
park that formerly had been the pride of the town was allowed to
fall into disrepair; and people even reduced their activity level and
slept much more than normal. This team concluded that free time
'proves to be a tragic gift. Cut off from their work and deprived
of contact with the outside world, the workers of Marienthal have
lost the material and moral incentives to make use of their time.'[40]
A major contributor to this study, Paul Lazarsfeld, emigrated to
the US and had a very important influence on American and British
sociology of unemployment. These Anglo-American studies stressed
that protracted joblessness led in stages to withdrawal from society,
despondency, and an inability to find or hold jobs.[41]

Certainly this literature betrays a heavy cultural bias that denied
to the labouring classes the resources necessary to cope with time
that was not structured by others. Even to Orwell, 'Joe', a single
unemployed man, 'looked more like a neglected little boy than
a grown-up man'. Orwell speculated: 'it is the complete lack of
responsibility that makes so many of these men look younger than
their ages'.[42] This fixation on 'unstructured' time led investigators
to focus on those youth who had never experienced regular work
discipline. A culture of unemployment retarded the development
of the youth's superego (for they lacked the model of a working
father or shop mate). Their childishness was necessarily prolonged
without the work experience. According to these authors, organised
leisure was one solution, but a better solution was work.[43] The
Depression diminished the value of leisure time for wage-earners.

British historian Ross McKibbin is correct to stress the distorting
mirror created by this literature: the British working classes did not

fit the picture of the Marienthal jobless with their passive despair; instead, he suggests, a large number of unemployed Britons became absorbed in their gardens and in reading; and a surprising number of women joined keep-fit classes.[44] In any case, the psychological consequences of joblessness varied with the skill and mental state of workers.[45] As McKibbin notes, the evidence of this sociology points to a more complex picture of how the jobless used leisure times than does its theory.

How then does one sort out the ideology from the insightful observation? First, I think that it is easy to overemphasise the bias of this literature and even the paternalistic function of the 'occupational clubs'. The 'unwanted worker' was a real socio-psychological problem; part of any solution was to find social outlets and an opportunity for self-initiation in otherwise unstructured time. And, despite its upper-class sponsorship, even the National Council of Social Services (NCSS) was inspired by the Workers' Educational Association with its participant-directed programmes. The line was blurred between the ideas of 'democratic leisure' (chapter 5) and paternalist manipulation of the jobless. NCSS literature repeatedly stressed that the clubs were to be part of a permanent alternative to commercial and passive leisure.[46] This thinking was surely naive. But it was not necessarily manipulative. For many active members, the clubs were empowering.[47]

Second, we should acknowledge that joblessness in the twentieth century did, in fact, pose particular problems. In contrast to nineteenth-century antecedents, the Depression affected all sectors of the economy. Thus unemployment did not simply shift the wage-earner to another job (as, for example, in the tramping or itinerant labour system) or to petty trade or farming (except, of course, in France and rural areas of the US). Rather it meant mostly workless life on the dole or similar programme. Sociologists were right to stress that income without meaningful labour posed unique and potentially debilitating problems. It disorganised time and diminished the value of leisure.

But the social science of unemployment was wrong to assume that joblessness led to permanent withdrawal and despondency. Rather, it reinforced loyalties to *routines* of public worktime and private play time. Unemployment undermined the value of free time because it destroyed routines of both work and play. 'Time', one unemployed Briton complained, 'is my worst enemy now.' E. Wight Bakke found that unemployed Britons had a 'sense of being "out of stride" '. The ambitious suffered the most from prolonged failure to find a job.[48] At the same time, jobless Britons made a tenacious effort to maintain a leisure schedule structured around the now absent workweek; they continued to attend the cinema on the same evenings as when they had been in jobs. They also 'worked' at finding employment during 'normal' working hours (or stayed home to avoid being discovered with 'nothing to do'). The Mass-Observers found their 'Worktowners' preferred to keep jobs in the mills even if they earned less than what they could earn on the dole. Contrary to middle-class prejudice, few of the jobless actually 'loafed' or drank in pubs.[49] The great embarrassment was to be without purposive (waged) time. The unemployed 'has seen the clock go around but he has nothing to show for the hours that have passed', observed the American Eli Ginzberg. As Marie Jahoda recently noted, the absence of a 'succession of events' and 'intentionality of action' made the workless day long but forgettable.[50]

A logical, if ironic, consequence of the Depression was a growing interest in the hobby, a 'job you can't lose'. As American historian Steven Gelber has noted, hobbies were a cure for alienating work; but, for the unemployed they could also be a substitute for a job by filling time with a work-like activity.[51] But with no employment to structure their time, men especially were frustrated in their attempts to follow accustomed routines in leisure hours. A skilled English wire drawer reported that 'there is very little for me to do beyond looking after the house and the child during my wife's absence' at work. He dropped out of the union because its decisions 'do not touch me'. He asked, 'Is this a man's life?' The old hobbies of a lathe operator grew stale, for these activities 'which are the necessary antidotes to the debilitating effects of modern industrial life' made no sense without work.[52]

André Gorz's characterisation of today's jobless surely would have been understood by the victims of the Depression: 'I cease to experience this private existence as my personal sovereignty because it is no longer the obverse of compelling social obligations.'[53] To the jobless male in particular, unemployment destroyed the oppositional character of time: it obliterated the division between public 'obligation', which justified the individual with a wage, and private freedom, where men displayed themselves as chums and providers.

Joblessness created the irony of underutilised free time and self-imposed isolation. The passivity produced by enforced leisure was not simply the consequence of mass society's failure to prepare people for free time. Rather it was a rational (or at least understandable) withdrawal from a social world based on reciprocal meanings of time. Bakke found an English lad who had been jobless for eight weeks and on the dole; he promised his mother that 'as long as he isn't doing anything to earn money, he isn't going to spend it'.[54] This was surely an extreme response. But the unemployed, especially those socialised to work, felt that they had no right to enjoy public leisure time without participating in public worktime. Psychological retreat to the home was inevitable.

This withdrawal was also natural to a working class conditioned to accept a radical separation of space and time between domestic and public spheres. Many outsiders have been impressed with the exclusiveness of the labourer's home. As one of Bakke's English correspondents explained:

> I wouldn't want my next door neighbour in here [his house]. No one but my very closest friends. This is where I live, and my family lives. . . . [Others] will go away and talk about what we had in our home and it's none of their business.

Bakke's later study of American working-class neighbourhoods found a similar lack of community feeling: despite common status and interests, families feared that gossip and quarrels were the inevitable byproduct of too much social contact in their closely packed neighbourhoods.[55]

This attitude may reflect a decline in community feeling in the Depression. The inability of churches, fraternal orders, or even neighbourhood credit and retail businesses to provide for the people's needs may help explain growing inwardness. As Lizabeth Cohen stresses in her insightful study of the Chicago working class, this breakdown forced people to turn both inward on the family as well as outward to the state. During the Depression, the 'outside world' was particularly threatening to Britons on relief who faced the humiliation of the 'means test man' who had access to the home and personal records.[56]

In the 1930s, social scientists began to recognise the impact of suburban 'dormitories' in breaking up work groups and the failure of neighbourhoods to replace the sense of community that formerly may have been built around work. Commuting time, stressed Briton Kate Liepmann, constituted a loss to recreation, family and self; this travel was wasted time that did not lead, as promised, to a utopia of community life. Ruth Durant's study of the London suburb of Watling in the 1930s found a contrast between the 'daytime hurry' which was 'followed by apathy in the evenings'. While 'calls on and from relations living in London are habitual', 'the majority of men spend their free time exclusively with their family. Mutual visiting of residents is rare.' Social contact centred on the tube station to London, not on the community centre with its transient, relatively privileged, and cliquish core membership.[57] The Depression's denial of the community of work surely reinforced these trends toward the privatisation of leisure time.

Only in places like the mining region of Rhondda, Wales, which had reputations as 'hotbed of institutions' and where family life was relatively open, did community thrive around the occupational club movement. But even in Rhondda, few of the young joined the occupational clubs; and those groups that did well relied on the leadership of a few.[58] In other places like Liverpool, where jobless centres depended on the support and leadership of the philanthropic, members were often 'tainted' by loser status. Even with encouragement, few of the unemployed used their time free from work to join community groups.[59]

Instead the unemployed retreated to the home and family. This pattern tended to accentuate the traumas of broken temporal routines: English husbands found themselves filling an 'hour in the morning with the "pram" in the park' and tending to housework chores, sometimes in a 'complete reversal of roles'.[60] 'To see your wife busy', noted a jobless Briton, 'makes you feel ashamed.' And another complained: 'I hate being chained to the home most. There is no substitute for work.' A character in Brierley's *Means Test Man* spent whole mornings tending a small potato patch in order to avoid the 'humiliation' of housework.[61]

The disruption of accustomed domestic routines also unnerved many American homemakers as Bakke noted:

> Apparently this shift of the husband to domestic duties is desired neither by the husband nor by the wife. She is conditioned as much as he is to the fact that the husband's business is to earn money and not to do the household tasks. Several of the wives expressed the wish that their husbands would help them more, but very frequently they would add, 'but I suppose I'd lose my respect for him if he did'.

'Excessive' togetherness was hardly welcomed: 'Just being together is not enough. You have to be together with some purpose, and when that ain't true it ain't any fun', admitted an American woman.[62]

Unemployment befell women, of course, even though they were

more capable of obtaining jobs in low paying textile, garment, and especially service jobs. But even for the homemaking majority, the Depression brought not free time but more domestic work because these women had to do without 'store-bought' goods. Moreover, homemakers found their routines disrupted and made more time-consuming by the presence of unemployed husbands at home who often refused the 'indignity' of doing housework. Mirra Komarovsky found American homemakers resentful of their jobless husbands' interference in childrearing or housekeeping details. She concluded that 'again and again would the complaint be made by both husband and wife that his continuous presence at home puts a great strain upon their relations. Work relief is superior to money relief from this point of view as it is also in many other respects.'[63]

The joblessness of men put the burdens of women's household work in sharp relief. As one of Margery Spring Rice's English women interviewees pointed out, 'I believe myself that one of the biggest difficulties our mothers have is our husbands do not realise we ever need any leisure time. It isn't the men are unkind. It is the old idea we should always be at home.'[64] The English philanthropist S. P. B. Mais observed that the 'unemployed man's wife . . . has no change of scene, no fun except for an all too rare burst to the pictures to keep her sane'. Not only should the middle class 'adopt' the children of the jobless so that mothers could get away, but unemployed men should go to occupational clubs to get them out from underfoot of their wives.[65] Moreover, for some women, domesticity paled without an alternative. Marienthal women eagerly wished for a return to jobs, and not only for the money: to be 'stuck here alone between one's own four walls one isn't really alive'. Note these words of Marie Butts of the International Bureau of Education that sum up the problem, if in an exaggerated way: 'The family do not get on particularly well together and prefer to enjoy their leisure with companions whose tastes they share. . . . Can anything be done to get shy, reserved, inarticulate and rather uneducated people of several ages to enjoy life together as a family?'[66] She certainly doubted it – especially when the male provider lacked a job.

Work anchored the personality of most wage-earners. Leisure was both a compensation for and an extension of work. English educator Alison Boyd admitted that the 'prospective of an ever increasing reduction in the demand for labour . . . is menacing the well-being of all unwanted people'. Many shared Ginzberg's view that the work relief of the WPA benefited Americans 'who otherwise would have deteriorated from idleness. . . . We learn from contrast. We learn from unemployment the true significance of work. Work establishes the basic routine of modern living.' According to another observer, English workers resented the 'university youth trying to organise them' into clubs. 'The men do not want charity (much less how to use leisure). They want jobs.'[67]

Most important, the Depression reinforced a commitment to the values of work and the things that wages could buy. Instead of a militant class of the jobless, numerous British and American studies discovered that workers were humiliated by unfunded leisure. Komarovsky found none of her jobless family men

> who welcomed freedom from the lifelong routine of work, to whom this freedom was a compensation, however slight, for the curse of unemployment. . . . [Q]uite apart from economic privations, the unemployed man suffered from loss of daily routine. . . . Furthermore, for most of the men in our culture, work is apparently the sole organizing principle and the only means of self-expression. . . . They feel that hobbies are trivial and undignified when they form the main content of life. This derives, in part, from the dominant philosophy of life which glorifies work. . . . While theoretically, economic activities are supposed to be the means to the good life, as a matter of fact it is not the end, but the means themselves, that have the greater prestige.[68]

This surely must have reinforced a commitment to work and the income that wages brought. As the Lynds observed in their second study of Middletown in 1937,

> enforced leisure drowned men with its once coveted abundance, and its taste became sour and brackish. Today, Middletown is emerging from the doldrums of the Depression, more than ever in recent years committed to the goodness of work. . . . [S]o nobody today is wanting more time off from work. . . . It is this . . . sour background of too much leisure that prompts local workingmen to insist that they 'don't want relief, but jobs'.[69]

WAS THERE LOVE ON THE DOLE?

While the Depression undermined the value of free time, it reconfirmed the worth of money. When unemployment became a mark of social difference, the resulting loss of income became a symbol of social exclusion. As I have already noted, this was particularly true because the impact of economic hardship was very unevenly distributed. Moreover, daily contact with the affluent on urban streets and nearly universal access to the mass media that continuously displayed luxury only increased the humiliation of poverty.[70]

Those who continued to hold full-time jobs in the US suffered little. In fact, *hourly* wage levels were relatively stable (compared to the massive cuts of earlier depressions). Between 1929 and 1932, hourly wages declined only 13 per cent while cost of living decreased 20.7 per cent. The problem was with the jobless and those placed on short-time schedules. Average hours were cut 24 per cent and by 1932 the wages in manufacturing were 59 per cent of the 1929 level. The more steadily employed groups of salaried workers, however, saw earnings drop only a quarter.[71] The British pattern was similar. Some regions experienced drastic declines in employment. For example, in 1936, joblessness reached 28 per cent in South Wales but touched only 6.5 per cent in London. Many communities where unemployment was widespread became passive and lowered expectations. But, because prices dropped faster than wages, the steadily employed sectors of the British workforce were often better off. Their access to transportation, entertainment, and clothing increased.[72]

Many of the Depression's victims were in daily contact with the more affluent. This probably only intensified the longing for goods among those who experienced real decline in purchasing power. As American sociologist Glen Elder notes (1974):

> Comparisons with past gratifications and standards only served to intensify discontent in deprived families. . . . The higher the climb before the Depression, the greater the investment in the way things were at that time, and the more intense the frustration of downward mobility.[73]

The result was that all associated status and even adulthood with goods.

It is, of course, difficult to find direct evidence to support this thesis. But the fact that 'luxury' consumption did not always drop as fast as did income is a significant indicator. While spending clearly declined during the early Depression years for expensive items like cars (by 70 per cent between 1929 and 1932 in the US), people kept up spending on gasoline for older cars. Smokers hardly reduced their dependency on cigarettes: American sales dropped merely 6 per cent by 1933 and rose 22 per cent over 1929 levels by 1936. Americans bought new electrical appliances, especially refrigerators. As economic historian Winifred Wandersee notes, 'To many families a radio, the latest movie, a package of cigarettes, or the daily newspaper were as necessary to the family well-being as food, clothing, and shelter.'[74]

Contemporaries often stressed the 'escapist' character of working-class leisure consumption in the 1930s when the jobless bought cheap magazines, went to sensational films, and gambled to 'forget their troubles'. 'Schoolboy adventure' for men and fashion and gossip magazines for women dominated reading hours. Orwell claimed that 'twenty million people are underfed but literally everyone in England has access to a radio'. John Hilton's *Rich Man, Poor Man* (1944) found that extra income of British workers went to better clothing, housing and food, but it also was spent on 'pools, perms and pints, on cigarettes, cinemas and singles-and-splashes; on turnstiles, totalisators, and twiddlems: and on all manner of two pennyworths of this and that'.[75] Sympathetic labour historians, however, often emphasise that indulgence in cheap luxuries, like films and betting, sustained life and that, in any case, austerity was unrealistic. American and British middle-class magazine readers may have been treated to the virtues of thrift (and the benefits of home-canning). But few working people had either the equipment or the will to make much use of this advice. In the early 1930s, one unemployed Briton asked his readers to think of how humiliating it was for the jobless to hear the admonition to 'scrape together a few bones and cabbage leaves . . . [to] make a good dinner'.[76]

Even if the 'escapist' theory is unfair, we cannot entirely discount the psychological effects of poverty.[77] The experience of reduced income on people who expected expanded access to goods 'must have made the pinch of hard times seem intolerable', noted the American sociologist Jesse Steiner in 1937. Steiner and other advocates of the 'new leisure' hoped that old sociability and pleasure might be revived. He was encouraged that surveys showed that Depression-era Americans were spending much more time on cost-free home recreations. But he was ignoring the implication of his own insight about the need for luxury.[78] His counterpart, the Briton C. Northcott Greene, made the same observation: joblessness meant not destitution but a 'lack of a few extra shillings [which] cramps [the jobless] in every way'. Yet too he hoped that this problem could be solved by replacing tea with cheaper cocoa and other forms of domestic economy. But, again, as Orwell made abundantly clear in *Road to Wigan Pier*, poverty increased the need for luxury.[79]

A revealing pattern of 'irrational' consumer behaviour during the Depression was popular gambling in Britain. During the 1930s, gaming gained strength when otherwise unemployed men served bookmakers as runners, gathering bets at pubs. Littlewoods football pools were especially popular, drawing on the 'tanners' of millions; bets were small and the mail-in coupon due the Thursday before the Saturday games became a weekly ritual for perhaps 40 per cent of the adult male population by 1935. Talk on the line at the labour exchange, noted Bakke, was mostly about 'horses and the dogs'.[80] Commercial gambling was, of course, widespread among other urban working-class peoples. For example, in the 1930s, blacks from south Chicago patronised some 500 'policy Stations' (almost as many as churches) which provided an illegal, but 'protected', lottery for these poor people. And, in the American West, the gambling towns of Las Vegas and Reno expanded to serve the population centres of southern and northern California.[81]

What attracted people of marginal and insecure income to gamble? As English observer H. L. Smith opined (1935):

> certainly more pleasure is gained in anticipation than is lost in disappointment. The pleasure lasts for some days; but the disappointment is momentary and easily forgotten. Also the fact that many people are excited at the same time about the same event increases the pleasurable excitement of each.

James Hilton's survey of football-pool bettors found few expected more from winnings than the purchase of small gifts for the family or for the financing of home-improvement projects. Historian Ross McKibbin notes that many male British workers despised bingo and the lottery as mindless, preferring their 'learned guesses' based on information gleaned from sporting magazines and 'inside' tips. Winners gained status as skilled practitioners. Betting gave men without public stature one of their few opportunities to make decisions. The competitive tension released in gambling filled a need, denied by the modern division of labour.[82]

But all of this is secondary to the essential purpose of gambling – the winning of money that was otherwise unattainable. When, as during the Depression, hard times seemed as arbitrary as did the unearned income of the rich, workers could believe in the possibility of fortuitous gain, no matter how long the odds. The football pools and the Irish sweepstakes seemed 'democratic' opportunities for the people to share in good fortune instead of just hard luck. For many, especially because the cost was nominal, gambling appeared to be a wise investment. 'Why not me?' they asked. As McKibbin notes: 'it was this irregularity of income which generated a rhythm of debt and credit of which gambling was to become an intrinsic part'. British workers gambled rather than saved (except for burial insurance). 'Though the working-class attitude to time was probably fatalistic it was also optimistic.' The future would take care of itself; but it might also bring good luck.[83]

More central still to the social meaning of money was the association of wealth and its display with respectability. This has been a major theme of social historians of the late-Victorian worker. English historian Paul Johnson, for example, stresses

the positive desires [of workers] to display the extent of savings and wealth because these were so important in determining the ranking of individuals in the working-class hierarchy. So ornaments were collected and arranged in the parlour for display to visitors, and 'Sunday best' was worn even by the irreligious.[84]

This attitude, of course, survived in the 1930s.

Moreover, spending was psychologically liberating and its lack was devastating. For wage-earners in Jack Common's *Seven Shifts*, Saturday night was not only free from work but it was the time when they could dress up and spend: 'even if the surplus is tiny, people will relax on it, and there's a difference in the way they walk and talk with each other'. Thus the despair of the jobless in Walter Greenwood's novel, *Love on the Dole* (1933), becomes intelligible: he was 'suddenly wakened to the fact that he was a prisoner. The walls of the shops, houses, and places of amusement were his prison walls; lacking money to buy his way into them, the doors were all closed against him.' The jobless or underemployed experienced scarcity in a world of semi-affluence and remembered pleasures. The 'other' was not the employer or powerful but consumers. A young Greenwood character 'felt resentful of everybody who was prosperous'. And, by this, he meant new apprentices, the bookie, and the 'cadaverous pawnbroker'.[85]

Resentment was tempered by identification with those who could buy. The jobless dreamed of the respect and freedom that came from the ability to consume. This is why, noted F. Zweig in the 1940s, English workers resisted any effort by government or social elites to control leisure or consumption. For them, 'the spending of money in a spectacular way is marvelous'. Recreation meant freedom and it must constantly change. So-called male 'providers', claimed Zweig, placed great stock in their own spending money; they even reduced the percentage given to their wives for household management when their wages increased. Sons were allowed to withhold much of their apprenticeship pay while parents kept their demands 'more or less on the level of a lodger's pay'.[86] Fathers and teenage boys defined freedom and even manhood in terms of choice in spending. Doubtless many workers shared the explanation of a 'leading citizen' of Middletown of why people judged others by their houses and cars: 'It's perfectly natural. You see, they know money, and they don't know you.'[87] Reduced personal income and the social isolation of joblessness probably reinforced the tendency to make such judgements. This helps explain why the Depression (and postwar austerity) produced neither sustained challenges to capitalism nor support for the cultural alternative of 'democratic leisure'. Instead these crises heightened the disparity between socially defined consumer expectations and the personal experience of scarcity.

The trauma of austerity centred on frustrating efforts to maintain consumption routines. English workers tried to stick to the 'right sort' of cinema when the family occupied their regular 'pew' on Saturday night. Bakke found that the unemployed of Greenwich, England, still spent 2.6 hours per week at the films and 'the influence of these hours extends far beyond the time spent in the theatre'.[88] Others attempted to carry on the annual habit of summer holidays.[89] Some American families tried to maintain consumption routines through deficit spending. Instalment buying, that had became habitual in the 1920s, continued in the Depression decade. By 1932, about 60 per cent of furniture, autos, and household appliances were bought on hire purchase as were up to three quarters of radios and half of other electrical domestic goods. Instalment sales comprised nearly 15 per cent of consumption. Particularly sharp decreases in food prices produced savings that could be used to keep up spending on 'extras' like women's clothing and car maintenance. As the Lynds pointed out, 'car ownership stands to [Middletowners] for a large share of the "American Dream"; they cling to it as they cling to self-respect'.[90]

A major cause of distress was the inability of the jobless to keep up social obligations in spending. For men, this often meant an inability to play the roles of 'mate' and provider. Bakke's jobless men in Greenwich dropped out of the old gang when they could no longer participate in the informal code of reciprocity: 'I like to keep my end up. I can't do it and I know what they think of me even if they don't say it.'[91] This impeded the normal pub life of the jobless who were unable to participate in the ritual of 'standing rounds'. The Briton Max Cohen, in his *I Was One of The Unemployed*, was humiliated by having to borrow from others and frustrated by his inability to join old friends 'somewhere bright and gay, lively and happy'; he had only six shillings per week after rent while on the dole. This same sense of social obligation affected families too. An American couple without work complained:

> you can't even have a card game without serving sandwiches and coffee, . . . but all that costs something. We had some people with whom we kept up our contacts, and by common agreement we decided that we wouldn't serve refreshments. Somehow it wasn't much fun any longer and very soon we broke up.

But this humiliation particularly obsessed men. Some abandoned old hobbies like photography, embarrassed at having to look at the pictures taken by others.[92] A jobless Greenwood character 'would slink round the by-streets . . ., glad to be somewhere out of the way of the public gaze, any place where there were no girls to see him in his threadbare jacket and patched overalls'.[93] Part of the male's identity, developed since apprenticeship years, was the ability to participate in a fraternity of casual consumption with fellow workmates. And, this symbol of manhood faded with unemployment.

The frustration of reduced income, of course, extended to the male 'provider' role. English and American fathers were humiliated by their inability to provide children with fashionable clothing for Sunday outings or even 'pennies' for their small offspring.[94] As a jobless English father noted:

> It gets on your mind, to see the kids around and you know you're not bringing anything to them. I used to like to have them run to meet me when I came home from work. But now . . . well – I almost wish they wouldn't come. It's hell when a man can't even support his own family.

Note also this comment from a husband: 'It is getting me under to see the wife supporting us, and me who is supposed to be the head of the family doing nothing but look for work.' Manhood was identified with being the provider. An American wife admitted that 'maybe it is not [her husband's] fault that he's unemployed, but it's a man's business to support his family'. Ginzberg found that some women denied sex to their jobless husbands. According to Komarovsky, unemployed American fathers sometimes expected to lose the love of their children while they were jobless, especially if their relationship with their offspring was based on coerced respect. Income provided breadwinning men both power and 'a margin of toleration' from wives and children for their human frailties. Not only did joblessness mean for men a loss of social status and authority in the family, but it seemed to undermine their masculinity and to cause psychosomatic illness.[95] Given this domestic culture, it is hardly surprising that politicians could make points by advocating that married men be given priority over women in lay-off decisions in order to preserve male roles as providers.[96]

The provisioning function expressed more than male vanity and the man's domestic power. Money greased the wheels of family life. Speaking about American families, Bakke noted:

A large proportion of our problems is solved customarily by the expenditure of money. . . . The necessity for undertaking a special campaign for funds every time a necessary expenditure must be made places a tremendous strain upon the organisational and planning abilities of the family.

Spending for, and keeping goods within, the family created cohesion.[97] Wandersee observed that 'the man who worked to pay for an automobile, a refrigerator, or a radio was contributing to a family identity, but that identity was maintained through possession rather than production'. The absence of that income reduced not only the status of the provider but threatened the unity of the family. As Margaret Mead would comment some years later, 'when people did not have enough work, no money, and so no symbolic right to play, entertainment was curtailed, movie money was short, dates lacked gaiety, and child bearing was postponed'.[98]

Consumption was part of a complex culture of domestic respectability. Despite the public routine of cinema-going, the Depression led to a turn inward on the home. The English (and American) working-class fixation on keeping 'intact the front room' is well known.[99] The trend toward domestic consumerism was increased by access to cheap radios in the 1930s.[100] The Pilgrim Trust and Mass-Observers were impressed by the efforts of poor families to cling to the dignity and independence symbolised by keeping up life-insurance payments. This traditional obsession with a respectable burial was to avoid the indignity of the 'final dependency'. This, like so many other forms of working-class consumption, expressed a will to privacy and freedom from humiliating reliance on the state or charity.[101]

This quest for familial autonomy doubtless also contributed to the long gradual trend toward married women entering the workforce. The Depression simply exacerbated a complex and still poorly understood movement of mothers into the labour market in the twentieth century. Slowly these women replaced wage-earning children as sources of supplemental family income. Not only reduced domestic production made this possible and necessary, but rising expectations of consumption seem to have propelled this trend.[102]

But, even when married women held jobs while their husbands did not, role reversals did not necessarily follow. Komarovsky found that in only 13 of the 58 families that she studied did the husband's authority actually decline markedly. Wage-earning married women were far from gaining domestic power, much less independence to pursue outside activities. Many women, as documented in the oral history collection, the 'Voices of American Homemakers Project', filled the gap left by their husband's unemployment with a harried mix of money-making and goods-producing: they sewed, cleaned the homes of the more fortunate, and gardened. They realised the frustration that their granddaughters would later experience – compounded duty in house and wage work.[103] As Wandersee observes, these wage-earning wives 'faced the double task of maintaining [the home] both economically and emotionally. . . . It is thus no wonder that few women exulted in this enforced leadership; it was undertaken at great cost to themselves and their families.' This strain was even more apparent for many women during World War II when the conflict between job and domestic obligations was often unbearable.[104]

It is hardly surprising that this experience, even if short lived, tended to reinforce the prevailing sexual division of labour, especially among the children of the Depression. Glen Elder's study of American offspring of families of the 1930s suggests that daughters were denied support for further education and were socialised early to domestic roles, rather than to 'enforced' independence. Responsibility, not fulfilment, was the learned value. Boys were more likely to be freed from parental control, especially if they found jobs at an early age when fathers were laid off. Thus, for males, both the fraternity of spending and the work ethic of the provider were reinforced. The 'feminine mystique' and the ideology of male providing which dominated the 1950s was reinforced by the experience of the 1930s. This gender system was founded on consumption and 'full-time employment'.[105] For many, the Depression solidified the gender order by revealing its stress points: the wife's domestic domain and the male's role of provider. The slump showed that neither women nor men wished to abandon these roles. This gendered system created the ideal 'balance' of wage work and consumption time that emerged after World War II around the 40-hour workweek.

It never made sense for populist intellectuals to project on to working people their nostalgia for an ascetic community of neighbours around leisure. But neither was it accurate for more conservative observers to presume that wage-earners with free time would do nothing but become victims of the con men of consumerism or, in the frustration of unstructured time, escape freedom in overtime and moonlighting. That intellectuals vacillated between these extremes is proof of the persistence of the chasm that separates intellectuals from working people. In reality, wage-earners seemed to respond to the opportunities of time and money in the ever changing context of their concrete lives. Openings for the quest for free time have been very brief, coinciding with unusual periods of organisational power and consciousness. In their absence, the disciplinary power of the market reduced the range of choice to a defence of present living standards within the prevailing gender system.

A nascent mass consumerism in the 1920s, in the US especially, may well have begun to lash wage-earners to the wheel of work. But the traumas of the Depression decade which followed also had an impact. In that situation, where poverty was not general but restricted to 'deindustrialising' regions, economic scarcity meant loss of self-respect. Workers defined themselves less as jobholders and more as consumers. Instead of creating a militant class against capitalism, unemployment humiliated working families with unfunded leisure. This was inevitable in a society where, especially for men, free time was a compensation for work and leisure was inherently dependent upon income beyond subsistence. Not only was the value of free time diminished and money endowed with special social power, but commitment to work was reinforced. Few jobless families found that 'all of our friends are in the same boat'. Many believed that others in their status group were better off. This made deprived families unwilling either to accept relief or to identify with the jobless even if they themselves were among the unemployed.[106] Despite the emergence of new social solidarities of trade unionism, these movements only temporarily reversed the logic of individualism: free time became, if anything, more privatised; and money increasingly became the mark of personal and family status. Even if some recognised the value of non-waged domestic labour in the 1930s and the economic disruptions to the sexual division of labour made possible a domestic power shift, the Depression tended more to reinforce the existing status quo in gender relations. The identity of men as providers and women as keepers of a private domestic order was re-confirmed.

Finally the interwar experience advanced the notion of personal fulfilment through consumption. Advertising, the media, and instalment buying created a precocious consumerism in America from the 1920s. As historian Richard Fox summarises, by the 1950s: '[A]ll seemed united by their commitment to acquiring the mass-marketed tokens of "the American standard of living".'[107] Britain and later France were not far behind. The identification of leisure with consumption won many to hard and steady work in disagreeable jobs.

But the relative deprivation experienced by the unfortunate in the Depression surely intensified this association of free time and money. In reaction, after World War II, millions of working-class Americans and even Europeans sought to join the middle class in sampling the satisfactions that advertisers and their more fortunate neighbours had continuously displayed during the lean years.

Nevertheless, the social bias toward goods was not merely a product of the traumas of market discipline or even the distortions of the Depression. Rather that prejudice reflected the social power of consumerism that extended far beyond social emulation. This neither the intellectual nor activist of democratic leisure recognised. Commodities did not simply subvert 'traditional' ways of life; rather consumerism met accustomed social needs while undermining social contacts. Through mundane domestic consumption and exceptional purchases for vacations, spending both comforted and fulfilled dreams. And, the tensions between free time and consumption that intellectuals insisted on maintaining were attenuated. To these themes, we now turn.

7 The consumer's comfort and dream

Early in this century, the democratisation of time and money seemed to threaten cultural and economic hierarchies. Fordist and conservative economists argued over the need to restrain this process and the possibilities of turning it into a new social order. At the same time, humanists and advocates of democratic leisure emphasised tensions between leisure time and mass consumption. Almost all shared a belief that economic growth would soon fulfil limited consumer needs while leading to reduced worktime. Where supporters of democratic leisure differed was that they valued this trend as an opportunity to develop a personal and social life less dependent upon possessions purchased in the market. But time freed from work did not become time freed from goods for most wage-earning families. Rather these people filled their leisure with consumption.

A key to the success of consumer capitalism in this century has been not only its success 'delivering the goods' but its satisfying and prompting people's expanding longings. This process, however, few intellectuals understood very well. Work in a Fordist economy may have been dissatisfying, even coercive to many. But it was also 'free' in so far as it produced new moments of consumption and the means to enjoy them. This may be an inadequate definition of freedom. Ernest Bevin was surely right to complain of the 'poverty of desire'. But that impoverishment must be explained, not merely condemned in the neo-Aristotelian biases of leisure jeremiahs like George Cutten. Nor should it be wished away as in C. D. Burns' faith in an emerging democratic leisure class.

In chapter 6, I offered one explanation of the consumerist 'choice' by drawing on the negative impact of market discipline and the Depression's traumas. But this, of course, is incomplete, especially for an understanding of why working people positively preferred domesticity to community centres, or Blackpool to the Holiday Fellowship. In this chapter, I argue that working people actively participated in the formation of the consumer society even as they were being manipulated by it. As important, leisure time and consumption were reconciled in that comforting nest of goods, the modern home, and in the consumer's holiday dream of a community of spending. Time has partially collapsed into money.

THEORIES OF MASS CONSUMERISM

A nascent mass consumerism inspired explanations early in this century that persist today. These theories focused on three sometimes overlapping and generally negative themes: the cultural degradation of the experience of mass-production work; the market-driven manufacture of needs for a vulnerable collective psyche; and the dynamics of emulation in mobile urban society. Despite their insights, these explanations betray how most intellectuals failed to grasp the positive meanings of consumer goods and their linkages to the use of time. A brief critical review of these theories (and a few more recent ones) will set the stage for a more thorough analysis of the advent of the comforts of consumerist domesticity and the dreams of holiday spending.

Perhaps the most conservative approach linked mass consumption to a rather negative interpretation of the working-class experience in the mechanised factory. The deskilling of labour, a trend exacerbated by the emerging assembly line, produced not a revolutionary proletariat, but a class deprived of the ability to resist the allure of new consumer goods. This theory was especially powerful on the European continent where the biases of high culture and the cultural divisions between economic classes were especially great. The French sociologist Maurice Halbwachs (1877–1945) well represented this perspective when he challenged Ernest Engel's suggestion that cultural standards converged with the rise and equalisation of income. Instead, Halbwachs argued that working-class aspiration for 'higher', more diverse consumer goods was slow to develop despite increased wages: the 'warping effect of [workers] being kept in isolated contact with inanimate matter' and infrequent association with other social classes limited their desire for higher living standards. Even the quest for free time was weak because wage-earners 'no longer quite know what they would do with their time if they had it at their disposal'. Thus, Halbwachs claimed, French working-class families did not spend more on housing when income rose (in the way that Engel had predicted). Instead, wage-earners consumed their surplus on the street rather than in the family. There, according to Halbwachs, the worker expressed 'needs for fantasy, ostentation, distraction for the enlarged social life'. Because the worker was less 'bound up' with old culture, new gadgets, whatever their defects, were 'accepted the more submissively'. Halbwachs saw the American working class as a vanguard in mass consumption. This was because, he believed, the American home was weak; and thus religion and culture were too superficial to serve as an antidote to consumerism. The non-Marxian socialist Henri de Man echoed these views in his analysis of the 'social inferiority complex' of workers whose alienating labour produced conformist consumption rather than class consciousness.[1]

Halbwachs was sophisticated in recognising the material and social roots of working-class 'taste'; and he was aware of the psychological need for luxury. Still he betrayed a traditional European and especially French bourgeois bias: contradictory assessments of working-class attitudes toward change; the juxtaposition of the 'good consumption' in the home and the 'bad' in the street; and the identity of cultural superficiality with consumerism *à la Americaine*. Halbwachs failed to transcend his French experience, where relatively rigid social distinctions prevailed, to recognise the potential of consumerist emulation between social classes (already developed in the US). Most important, his writings on French working-class domesticity betrayed the backwardness of French sociology of the period, particularly its ignorance of popular domestic aspirations.[2] Halbwachs' views survive today in the insights and prejudices of Pierre Bourdieu and others who emphasise the linkage between the working-class experience and mass culture.[3]

A second analysis, based on social structural and psychological theory, is rooted especially in the American context. In the US, two nearly simultaneous trends appeared to create a consumer society: while an emerging mass-production economy produced a need for mass markets, the erosion of the ascetic Victorian personality created an American psyche susceptible to the appeals of merchandisers. Economic concentration, rapid transportation, capital-intensive production and mass communications made national advertising a vital tool for creating wants to which Americans were especially receptive.[4] Many observers in the 1920s argued that only mass consumption could absorb the increasing capacity of the American economic machine to produce.[5] But advertisers had a special obligation to use psychology to induce consumers to buy things they did not need.[6] Beginning with Walter Dell Scott before World War I and followed by the social psychology of Floyd Henry Allport in the 1920s, these 'captains of consciousness', to use historian Stuart Ewen's potent phrase, 'attempted to turn the consumer's critical functions away from the product and toward himself'.[7] Through the powerful forces of association, advertising sold not merely goods but 'personal adequacy', 'romance', sexual potency and antidotes to ageing and death.[8] Merchandisers accepted the sociologist's claim that patriarchy, based on the family's role as a production unit, was in decline. In response, business consultant Christine Frederick, for example, advised advertisers to appeal directly to women who, she noted, had become the purchasers of 80 per cent of American goods. Advertising increasingly focused on a distinctively youth market with copy suggesting the incompetence of adults.[9]

Critical social theorists like Robert Lynd largely accepted the claims of advertisers that consumers were essentially passive objects in the process of generating demand to meet the supplies created by new mass-production industries. Lynd argued that manufacturers were 'compelled to create "acceptance" to keep ahead of the production curve'. Advertisers manipulated the contradictions of the individual consumer who was 'only a partially rational bundle of impulses and habits shaped in response to an unsynchronized environment, with resulting tensions'.[10] Social change had produced frustrations to which consumption was a form of 'adjustment'. In 1928, economist Paul Nostrum noted that the rationalisation of modern business and work resulted in a 'lack of purpose in life' which had the effect of 'concentrating human attention on the more superficial things that comprise much of *fashionable* consumption'.[11]

This theory that consumer goods have become signs of contradictory longings of essentially irrational individuals has had a major impact on contemporary critiques of consumerism.[12] But David Riesman, and more recently, historians Christopher Lasch, Warren Susman, and T. J. Jackson Lears have developed more subtle linkages between structural economic change and the emergence of a new social psychology. They have argued that early in this century the American ethic of individual integrity or 'character' was replaced by a morality of adjustment and self-fulfilment. A fundamental shift in Anglo-American society was responsible: an entrepreneurial, production-oriented economy which required self-control and thrift gradually gave way to a bureaucratic and consumer economy which demanded co-operative and more spend-free attitudes. 'Personal magnetism' and 'team-playing' on the job combined with 'social adjustment' and 'life-affirming' consumption after working hours. A quest for intense experience led to an attachment to the new. But that desire also produced a nostalgia for the rural and the simple in the hope of recovering vitality. By the 1920s, these authors argue, these contradictory longings informed advertising and gave new meaning to the consumption of goods.[13]

This broad analysis of the origins of mass consumption has the virtue of historical specificity: it combines the impact of socio-economic structural change with the emergence of a new psychology of needs creation. But these structural-psychological arguments surely overemphasise the rationality of the social order (if not of the individual). As the Depression showed, a mass-consumption society did not necessarily follow from new productive capacities. And the stress upon manipulation certainly assumed that consumers were radically passive and, even more, that advertisers had an influence that many contemporary scholars have forcefully denied. Finally, this analysis tends to assume that the mass market prevailed when, in fact, class and other divisions continued to shape spending decisions.[14]

A third approach to mass consumerism was to stress the social psychology of spending. This perspective spanned the two continents and reflected the growth of social imitation in urban, increasingly mobile society. Particularly important here were the American Thorstein Veblen (1857–1929) and the German Georg Simmel (1858–1918). Veblen's discovery of consumerist emulation among the 'leisure class' of new money in the 1890s is well known. That analysis, of course, was easily extended to the status seeking of lower social strata.[15]

While Veblen focused on the psychology of wealth accumulation, Simmel came to similar conclusions from an analysis of the social impact of the emergence of money culture. Money used in the exchange of labour and goods freed the individual from personal dependence on others and democratised social distinctions; but it did so at the price of intensifying the pace of life and at the cost of everyone becoming instruments to each other. Ever expanding commercial stimuli and choices forced newly urbanised people into adopting a 'blasé' attitude toward a modern world that constantly assaulted the senses.[16]

The only apparent way that one could recover oneself was to pursue ephemeral marks of fashion in the marketplace. Fashion, Simmel argued, 'combines . . . the attraction of differentiation and change with that of similarity and conformity'. Social distinction and identity were merged: 'Every fashion is essentially a fashion of a social class; that is, it always indicates a social stratum which uses similarity of appearance to assert both its own inner unity and its outward differentiation.' Fashion, Simmel stressed, was inherently dynamic. Humanity's 'universally imitative character', accentuated by both class society and urban social mobility, produced a chase: 'insecure classes' (and especially women because they lacked a fixed economic calling) imitated the fashion of the more secure. This, in turn, obliged these fashion leaders to create fresh innovations in order to assert their collective unity by distancing themselves from the crowd.[17]

These views were widely shared in the interwar years. The French sociologist E. Goblot (1926) wrote of luxury consumption as creating both social 'levels' (or standards) and 'barriers' which together declared the 'collective superiority' of the classes over the masses. Ernest Fluegel's *Psychology of Clothes* (1930) argued that presentation of self in fashion was the basic form of discretionary and open-ended consumption. In all cultures, clothing expressed both modesty and decoration, conformity and distinction. But the dynamics of social emulation in an open and competitive society extended the fashion game from the court to the boulevard where the lower orders imitated the rich. This, in turn, forced elites to separate themselves with new costuming. Mass production broadened and intensified the competitive and conformist dynamics of fashion. At the same time, democracy reduced the influence of merchandisers and the aristocratic elite. The former had to cater to new democratic and informal tastes and the latter was obliged to cede fashion leadership to a 'stage Bohemia' of entertainers.[18]

With their usual perspicuity, Robert and Helen Lynd observed these new democratic forms of social emulation. The satisfaction of status goods, like the horizon, remained forever out of reach no matter how far ordinary people 'got ahead'. And this frustrating experience, the Lynds argued, increased as social barriers decreased:

> In 1890 Middletown appears to have lived on a series of plateaus as regards standards of living . . .; it was a common thing to hear a remark that so and so 'is pretty good for people in our circumstances.' Today the edges of the plateaus have been shaved off, and every one lives on the slope from any point of

which desirable things belonging to people all the way up to the top are in view.[19]

This argument continues to shape much thinking about mass consumerism. For example, Fred Hirsch writes that the democratisation of goods led neither to social harmony nor to higher cultural aspirations. Rather the upward striving and downward self-distancing inherent in the fashion system produced frustrations without leading to demands for economic redistribution. Consumerist longings could be satisfied in the emerging Woolworth's culture of inexpensive luxury and in the vicarious pleasures of identifying with royalty or the 'stars'. Resentment, these writers stress, was more likely to be directed toward those still further down the consumers' hierarchy, those who lacked the aspired-to respectability and threatened to crowd out access to scarce status goods. At the same time, the democratisation of goods created what Jean-Christophe Agnew has recently called a 'single sign system of status', fused with displayed goods. An unwelcome consequence is that sociability means little more than individuals 'reading' each other through the surface signs of goods. Commodities were increasingly used to convey these purchased messages, deftly read by modern people schooled in 'ways of seeing'. As a consequence, interpersonal communication declined and opportunities for manipulation grew.[20]

This analysis succeeds in those areas where the other two fail. It recognises the internal dynamics of consumption in an era of social mobility. Thus it can explain how consumer needs expanded beyond physiological needs without recourse to moralising or assuming the all-powerful manipulation of advertisers. But, in the end, the theory tends to deny the tension between the quest for distinction and conformity upon which Simmel began his interpretation. Instead, it obscures that conflict by overstressing the drive for status through social exclusion. Simmel and Goblot insisted that individualism was expressed only in membership in a consumer class. However, the social meaning of consumption surely extended beyond invidious comparison; and consumption had other, non-social functions. Harold Blumer (1959) argues that Simmel overemphasises the influence of fashion leaders and fails to complete his own analysis of the democratising impact of money. Designers in the clothing fashion industry succeed when they capture the moving aesthetic edge between the new and the customary. Fashion, says Blumer, provides an 'orderly preparation for the immediate future' which consumers instinctively desire. It reconciles ambiguous attitudes toward the past and future as well as reduces social anxiety.[21] Finally underlying this view of mass-consumer society is the questionable assumption that social contact can and should be free of goods.

Theories of mass consumerism based upon social emulation, the manipulation of advertising, and the debilitating effects of mass-production work all strongly imply the passivity of consumers; they also imply that social life constructed around goods is somehow inferior. In fact, few intellectuals in the interwar years (except perhaps some populists considered in chapter 3 above) recognised the centrality of goods as positive vehicles of social expression.

This has only been corrected by a fourth interpretation of mass consumption, promoted by cultural anthropologists since the 1970s. Mary Douglas and Baron Isherwood, for example, have noted that goods make 'visible and stable the categories of culture'. There is little communication that excludes goods and their signs. Pre-industrial street life, they insist, has been romanticised. Rather, social interaction actually improves with affluence. Only relatively wealthy individuals can increase the frequency of rare consumer events, reduce the number of routine tasks, and thereby extend their social networks. The rich not only set barriers and cultural standards but, through their freedom from routine and their access to a variety of goods, are able to create consumption symbols. Poor people are obliged to be passive recipients of these symbols (via advertising or mass communications).[22]

This view, however, may overemphasise the social function of spending by abandoning Simmel's stress on distinction. A correction is provided by another anthropologist, Dan Miller, who emphasises that, when consuming, working people engage in 'self-production'. Thus they can overcome the alienation of the modern division of labour. Goods then, cannot be reduced to social 'markers' – much less emulation. They give meaning to the private worlds of individuals, families, and friends. The degree to which persons are able to produce themselves through goods depends on the time available to 'work' on these things and to control their own 'cultural environment'. These factors, not the goods themselves, are critical in shaping social and personal life.[23] The task, Miller seems to suggest, is not to shed the fetishism of money that masks the social origins of goods (as Marx would have us do). It is rather to liberate the symbolic meanings of goods (inevitably and happily alienated from production) from the control or influence of elites. This approach builds upon the populism of the 1930s and offers fresh paths for theory. But it also surely underestimates constraints on personal choice. It seems to neglect the insights of the older theories – the 'social inferiority complex' of the proletariat, the manipulation of merchandisers, and the impact of emulation. Moreover, it ignores the complex historical limits on choice discussed in this book.

In sum, each of these theories speaks to a portion of the problem of explaining mass consumerism: Halbwach offers an analysis of the constraints of work and class; the structural-psychological perspective provides a historical understanding of production-driven consumption; the theory of social emulation explains the frustrations of mass consumerism; and modern anthropology offers a more positive interpretation of the social and individual meaning of goods. But separately, they fail to specify the linkages between the work experience and the social functions of consumption. Halbwach's social psychology of work cannot explain why wage-earners joined the fashion game; but Veblen and modern anthropologists underestimate the linkages between the quest for goods and modern work. The first three interpretations imply a passive, blind participation in the social ritual of consumption; but the anthropologists seem to neglect historical constraints on consumerist meanings. None of them completely satisfies our need to explain the popular embrace of consumerism over time. A more comprehensive approach may be found by returning to a theme often touched upon in this book – the linkages between labour productivity, leisure, and needs.

In the 1920s, economists reluctantly began to recognise that the productivity of Fordism shifted the motivation to work from fear of impoverishment to the allure of goods, made available through 'high wages' and increased leisure time. The most reliable workers were those who earned relatively large salaries in an economy where many others took home much less or were jobless.[24] While high wages tied labourers to work, off the job, shopping has increasingly filled the time that technology had freed from domestic drudgery. In these ways, Fordism has disciplined time and money, lashing labour to wage (and consumption) work and limited choice in the use of leisure.

But, as critics of Fordism often ignore, high wages and free time were also liberating. Perhaps we should forgive French socialists of the 1920s for believing that Fordism transcended the dual economy of subsistence and 'arrogant superfluity' and replaced it with a mass market, symbolised by a Ford factory parking lot full of workers' cars.[25] Still, the 'asymmetry' between capital and labour had always

limited that empowerment.[26] But the meaning of inequality was radically changed in the transition from subsistence to Fordism because the locus of dependency shifted from the workplace to free time. To be sure, the 'golden chain' of instalment buying had replaced the stick of hunger; in exchange for those goods that equalised and privatised, families sold their future time. But the new discipline was obviously more attractive to workers than the old.
[27] Of course, the deskilling process at work spilled over into passive leisure; advertisers and impresarios manipulated consumers; and the logic of social emulation constrained freedom in play. At the same time, however, consumerism expressed a personal liberty in a complex and still poorly understood individualism that both reacted to and reflected changing work patterns.[28]

It is true that Fordism created a systemic bias against the expansion of free time that inevitably produced strains on family and personal life. As we have seen, social crises arose from the disequilibrium between work and leisure in the unemployed. And, as social critics have pointed out throughout the century, consumerist emulation has produced compulsive patterns of both work and leisure. We might even concede that consumerist imitation has swamped the work ethic to the competitive disadvantage of 'old' consumer economies like the US.

But Fordism, combined with Keynesian interventions, has assured growth with surprising equilibrium; it has created a new and relatively 'open' social hierarchy in play and the game of consumerist emulation; it has shifted people's expectations from work to leisure even if the job continues to weigh heavily on choice after working hours. Leisure became a realm of practical freedom where domestic goods could express individuality and social identity and where holiday spending could realise cyclic and measured moments of pleasure. The upshot, however, is that Fordism has also produced a new scarcity of time and money and concealed alternative ways of living.

This complex analysis may help explain the failure of democratic leisure in the interwar years. After working hours, people sought social contact as well as distinction and privacy. The quest was not for the intellectual's dream of social interaction in high-minded discussion groups or didactic holiday tours; rather, people strove for a society of consumer symbols, where their individuality was projected on to goods. Indeed, consumer items probably provided a valued balance between social identity, on the one hand, and individual freedom from social intrusion, on the other. Commodity 'signs' created belonging without the risks of intimacy or totalitarian self-denial. Moreover, as we found in chapter 6, people longed not merely for free time but also for alternative uses and meanings of time. Their objective was not the intellectual's vague dream of a progressive reduction of work and a new leisure of self- and social-realisation. Rather the goal was for public work alternating with private time and self-chosen entry into the public arena of play and consumption. This use of time was consistent with alternating periods of routine work and limited moments of freedom. Certainly for family providers, free time was meaningless without work structuring the day; and, as the experience of the jobless in the Depression showed, men especially understood free time as a reward for labour.

Thus 'time became money' to many wage-earners. But this phrase was understood not simply in Franklin's sense of the opportunity cost of unproductive time. Rather it expressed both the equivalences of the workday and wages and of leisure and spending. Time at work became an instrument of spending while free time was expressed in those social and private acts of consumption. Money became then the two-sided symbol of discipline and freedom while time alternated between compulsion and liberation.

But in the specific forms of free time we see something more, the realisations of the consumer's comfort and dream: domestic time provided continuity and memory through accumulated goods while holiday time suspended temporal routines and was expressed in the magic of uninhibited spending. Multiple temporalities combined with both social and private meanings of goods. In this complexity, free time assimilated consumerist needs.

Modern mass discretionary consumption cannot be reduced to the home or vacation.[29] But these two realms provide an efficient means of exploring a central theme of this chapter: the reconciliation of time and money. I hope that this theme will reveal more about the contradictions of consumption than the traditional bourgeois concept of 'bad' spending and the modernist notion of 'fashion'. By briefly investigating domestic and holiday spending on the eve of mass affluence, I hope to shed some light on the complex question of the contemporary balance between leisure and consumption and thus between work and free time.

SHAPING CONSUMERISM: NATIONALITY, CLASS, AND GENDER

The following analysis of domestic and holiday consumption necessarily must be rather abstract, eclectic, and even speculative. Examples will be drawn from my three countries when appropriate. Again, thorough-going comparison is not possible. But, before proceeding, I must briefly consider three factors which shaped domestic spending: these are the common themes of nationality, class, and gender.

As I have noted throughout this book, national economic and cultural conditions produced distinct paths to consumerist modernity. The contrast between French and Anglo-American patterns has often been noted. Those differences were no more clear than in domestic consumption. The detached, owner-occupied dwelling was far less common in France in the interwar years than in Britain and especially the US. French schemes for cheap public-financed housing in the late 1920s produced only a modest number of austere apartment blocks.[30] Relatively low real wages meant that food continued to absorb over half of French workers' income. Moreover, in the mid-1930s, the share of family budget in France devoted to housing actually declined with the rise in income. The common belief that the French placed higher priority on ephemeral pleasures like dining and quality clothing rather than on domestic improvements seemed confirmed. Poorly paid manual workers used just about the same low percentage of income for housing as did higher-earning white-collar employees (12.8 per cent and 11.4 per cent). By contrast, American surveys from the period of 1933 to 1936 found that the proportions of income devoted to household expenses ranged from 25.5 per cent to 33 per cent. Prominent French home economist Marguerite Lamy embraced a domestic economic 'Malthusianism' when she insisted that French women should minimise household expenditure rather than aspire to greater conveniences.[31]

To be sure, Paulette Bernège, French proponent of mechanised homes, and Jules Louis Breton, organiser of a popular annual salon devoted to domestic products, worked tirelessly for the modernisation of the French home.[32] Paul Chombart de Lauwe confirmed the influence of these ideas in a detailed survey of working-class domestic aspirations in the early 1950s. And still more recent studies of French popular culture suggest that consumerist domesticity had certainly penetrated the French working classes by the 1960s.

Family income, rather than deeper cultural or class factors (as suggested by Halbwach) seemed to explain the French exception.[33] But because of the late entry of the French into the modern ways of consumerist domesticity, I will concentrate on Anglo-American examples.

It is a truism that the household, as a centre of consumer escape and display, was a middle-class creation. The Victorian home was certainly a material expression of the middle classes' desire to define themselves against both the 'degenerate' aristocracy and 'irresponsible' lower classes. The suburb became the ideal form of domesticity with the growth of the 'alien' city and improved transportation from urban workplaces. Bourgeois domestic culture succeeded in defining itself as modern, normal, and 'national'. As American historians Colleen McDannell and Gwendolyn Wright show, middle-class Victorian women created in the home a material expression of traditional moral and religious values. According to Swedish anthropologists, Jonas Frykman and Orvar Loefgren, domestic goods provided a 'silent socialisation' about the 'essential ground rules of bourgeois culture' in western societies. These possessions taught the 'sanctity of property and the meaning of gender and authority'. And 'rituals of their use' confirmed these values. Most of all, the bourgeois home 'was both a showcase for the world and a shelter against it'.[34]

But that domestic standard spread to the working classes in aspiration, if not always in reality. To a degree, this merely was another phase in the long history of the working-class quest for 'respectability'. For the upwardly mobile Victorian working class in Britain and the US, that desire for privacy and display was expressed in the 'proper burial' and the Sunday suit. In the twentieth century, that combination of autonomy and participation was increasingly realised in the home and its accessories – aided by instalment purchase.[35] Not only did conservatives sell home ownership as an antidote to urban ethnic radicalism, but skilled workers and their unions embraced it as the essence of respectability.[36]

Home ownership was not, however, simply another form of emulation. Working-class adherence to outdated bourgeois styles of domestic respectability were not merely imitative, if sometimes awkward, responses to cultural insecurity. Instead, as Frykman and Loefgren note, working-class culture was essentially defensive: wage-earning families 'fought a two-front battle, against both the middle class and lumpenproletariat, and in this process of culture building, firm rituals and rules of social life were quite rigidly defined'. The ceremonial parlour represented not *embourgeoisement* but a retreat from work and the shopper's market where the social 'other' threatened.[37] The particular dilemma of the respectable poor was their difficulty in distancing themselves from the unrespectable poor.[38] Still for both the working and middle classes, domestic consumption was a way of combining social and private impulses. My discussion will focus on working families (broadly defined) but relate their aspirations to others.

If class shaped consumerist modernity, the gender-based division of labour helped to reconcile leisure and spending. The central reality was that the home was the principle workplace for most married women. In the interwar years, for example, never more than 12 per cent of married women in Britain had market jobs while that figure hovered around 90 per cent for men.[39] American figures were similar even if the less industrial French economy registered a much larger percentage of 'economically active' married women.[40]

This meant that it was primarily the woman who orchestrated domestic consumption. Not only was she manipulated by advertising, but, in the act of shopping, she found an opportunity for social expression. She worked with purchased goods and transformed them into displays of status and into individual expressions of familial privacy. Women left their personal mark on domestic space when they were trying to create comfortable places for family members in living areas. They used goods to organise those 'special' times that all family members longed for on the weekends and holidays; women provided refuge from routine, even if these efforts were, in fact, routine for many women. If men of all classes sometimes spent free time 'self-producing' in hobbies and home improvements,[41] domestic consumption remained largely under the control of females; and, it often was associated with work. Suburbanisation radically sharpened the sexual division of labour because it separated production from consumption, paid work from the home. Thus, according to American historian Dolores Hayden, the suburb 'made gender appear a more important self-definition than class, race or ethnicity'.[42]

Three obvious points may be drawn from these observations. First, because domestic consumption was for many women inextricably bound with labour rather than leisure, the anthropologist's claim that consumption is 'self-production' can be best applied to female homemakers. For men, consumption was inevitably more passive and, following Halbwachs, bound more closely to the wage-earning experience. Second, time and goods at home had hardly the same compensatory role for many women as they did for the working male provider. Homemakers largely accepted these obligations to shape the uses of goods and time for breadwinners and children; this was surely central to an emerging modern 'feminine mystique'. But the meanings of time and money (and their reconciliation) were organised around the needs of male breadwinners. In large part, this was because men, through their market work, mediated between public and private life for the family, a point not lost on feminists who have long insisted on equal economic opportunity as the basis of domestic parity. Third, the home could not have played its distinctive role without women homemakers. The only practical alternative was a radical transformation of the division of labour and time; and this would have required that men spend more time and do more work in the home, thus calling into question the normality of the eight-hour 'workday'. Without considerable housework, domestic goods could not be endowed with social and personal meanings nor could home time become an alternative to wage-earning routine. The division between male providers and female domestic consumers was the foundation of the harmonious balance of time and money, of acquiescence to discipline in wage and home work for a consumerist freedom.[43] Underlying the seeming universality of domestic ideas, then, are dynamic factors of nationality, class, and gender.

HOME, DISPLAY, PRIVACY AND TEMPORALITY

In many ways, twentieth-century domestic consumption resembles Simmel's analysis of fashion. Household spending encompasses both social and individualistic impulses, and thus it reconciles privacy and sociability in isolated but general rituals of consumption. Although home-based consumption in the new suburbs was dynamic, that domesticity was still a quest for stability. Time had far more complex meanings than was suggested by the futurist implications of fashion; and, in the interwar years, the quest for 'comfort' went far beyond emulation.[44]

The home was surely at the heart of the promise of mass consumption. Improved housing was part of what Lloyd George meant immediately after World War I by an England 'fit for heroes'.[45] Between the wars, an average of 33,000 units per year were built in Britain, mostly by private speculators for middle-income families. But, after 1932, lower interest rates and down payments and long-term mortgages made home ownership accessible to even lower-income strata. If only 10 per cent of British families owned homes in 1914, that figure rose to 21.5 per cent of manual workers and 51.9 of white-collar employees by 1949.[46]

In the US, cheap versions of the bourgeois Victorian railroad suburb became available to over 7 million mostly lower middle-class families in the 1920s. The American Victorian house, with its multiple living areas and formal entry halls, gave way to smaller houses, often bungalows.[47] Los Angeles alone opened 3,200 subdivisions to midwestern migrants seeking a promised land of sunshine and lawns, and freedom from immigrant-infested cities. The linkage of 'good citizenship' with home ownership was enshrined in Herbert Hoover's successful presidential campaign and his 1931 Commission on Home Building and Home Ownership. His successor, Franklin Roosevelt, provided loans to distressed home buyers, encouraged the 30-year mortgage that made home ownership feasible to many working-class buyers, supported highway construction that laid the foundation of modern suburban sprawl, and, in 1939, signed legislation that offered tax deductions on mortgage interest.[48]

Anglo-American sociologists, obviously influenced by Veblen, were quick to notice these new suburbs and their rituals of consumerist domesticity. As early as 1926, the American F. Stuart Chapin established social-status scales based on numerically weighted counts of household objects. Chapin and, a generation later, the Briton Dennis Chapman, found that the contents of front parlours were objective markers of social status. The presence of writing and coffee tables reflected less practical need than status statements. Curtain style and quality defined social rank and aspiration.[49] In the 1950s, Erving Goffman described parlour rituals as 'front stage performances' in contrast to the 'back room' intimacy of kitchens and sitting rooms.[50] Aspiring classes bought into higher status by imitating (often excessively in the view of the superior class) the consumption styles of their betters; in the early 1930s, George Lundberg found that upwardly mobile housewives from Westchester County, New York, vicariously experienced their domestic ideals in the women's club 'home' with its richly adorned sitting lounges, tea services, and fresh flower arrangements.[51] Helen and Robert Lynd linked social aspiration with purchase of automobiles: 'the make of one's car is rivaling the looks of one's place as an evidence of one's "belonging" '.[52]

Skilled manual and white-collar workers distanced themselves from their social inferiors when they moved to the suburbs; in turn, they imitated those who had literally already 'arrived' in the new neighbourhood. Instalment buying, according to an English study in 1944, was concentrated in upwardly mobile neighbourhoods, where young couples were 'starting a home'. Restrictive covenants, subtle gradations separating one development from another, and status-laden touches such as snobbish street names all contributed to the spatial dimensions of emulation.[53]

Status seeking, of course, was driven by the relatively privileged. But working-class families were also active participants. In the early 1950s, for example, English sociologists Michael Young and Peter Willmott found these patterns of social emulation in the migration of lower-income families to the London suburb of Greenleigh. Mortgage costs of a new home (a three-fold increase over the old rentals) and greater transportation costs required men to provide their wives with increased 'housekeeping allowances' and to reduce their spending at the pub and football game. Home purchases necessitated new furniture: wives even bought 'Dunkley prams' for 'smartness calls for smartness'.[54] Social life that 'centred on the house not people' created a new consumer consciousness. New residents naturally looked 'for guidance to their neighbours'' houses. Character, family and background, known through lifelong contact in more stable communities, could no longer be the basis for judgement. Instead, social relationships became 'window-to-window, not face-to-face'. In suburban Greenleigh, Young and Willmott concluded, the social control of neighbours was 'all the greater because they are anonymous'. Affluence may well have allowed privacy but social linkages were increasingly based on external similarities rather than mutual needs.[55]

This sociology offered a powerful interpretation. However, domestic consumption, especially among the working classes, was not identical with emulation. First, for most families of English wage-earners, domestic consumerism before 1950 or even 1960 was extremely modest and was based on relieving serious inconvenience. A study of a crowd of skilled English workers at a home furnishings show in 1946 revealed that few aspired to owning refrigerators or washing machines. Most of the manual labourers who viewed rooms of modern furnishings and appliances longed only for a new armchair or a modern kitchen and bathroom. The majority were either content with their living standards or realistic about their options. Status seeking was hardly the dominant motive in domestic spending.[56]

Second, these sociological analyses of the new suburbs shared deep prejudices with the cultured elite. In Britain, autobiographical writers unfavourably compared the new housing with the old terraces in nostalgic accounts of home life: they contrasted memories of old street games, friendly storekeepers, and the Sunday-evening gatherings of the family around the piano with tales of boredom and isolation in the new suburban housing. In the 1930s, homeowners replaced memory-rich, if mismatched, Victorian furniture with the 'veneered walnut suite', bought on hire purchase.[57] In the US, a similar nostalgia for neighbourly small-town get-togethers clashed against images of the empty porches and full garages of suburban culture.[58] However, these romantic accounts often ignore the fact that the good old days were marred by family feuds, couples who seldom shared free time, and homemaking that required clothing to be washed in a 'boiler' in the scullery.[59]

The attack on the new popular suburb came from another predictable quarter, the modernist intellectual: for example, the English critic Osbert Lancaster condemned endless rows of nearly identical houses as an eyesore: 'the largest possible area of countryside is ruined with the minimum of expense'. American urbanist Lewis Mumford attacked the suburban 'wilderness' as a false escape from the city's ills. As historian John Stilgoe notes, American urban intellectuals in the 1920s transferred their earlier hostility toward the 'cultureless frontier' into a caricature of the new outlying suburbs. In both countries, modernist planners offered a contrasting domestic ideal: open spaces, and opportunities for casual social interaction even if that meant high-rise construction.[60] Architectural historian Paul Oliver and his British colleagues argue that this hostility to the suburb was rooted in upper-class snobbism, the self-interest of architects (working for the wealthy), and a lack of understanding of popular domestic values.[61]

Whatever may have been the reasons, these biases have tended to blind observers to the complex purposes of domestic consumerism. The Anglo-American suburban home embodied a widely shared nostalgia for rural life. English interiors often included arched hearths; these, according to I. Davis, were designed to 'awaken impressions of Devon fires or inglenooks'. But tradition was to be combined with modern convenience. The electrified pseudo-Tudor semi-detached was precisely what people wanted.[62] The American attitude was similar. East-coast buyers sought pseudo-colonial exteriors but modern floor plans. With affluence came a taste for still earlier housing styles – 'stockbroker Tudor', for example.[63]

More important, the new homes also expressed longings for privacy as well as social identity. British house builders recognised that buyers wanted both individuality and belonging. According to one English developer, interiors should leave an 'impression' on visitors; builders should also vary the fronts to 'link them together with a slight unifying theme'.[64] Few English intellectuals, except Ivor Brown (1935) and John Richards (1946), recognised this. Richards insisted that the 'semi' was 'an accumulation of happy accidents' and a 'landscape from within', created by its inhabitants.

After 1945, it was new affordable homes that returning veterans expected.[65] Surely domestic consumption was not only a means of affirming economic and social status; it was a way of creating a familial emotional tone, recalling personal experience, and forming identity. It expressed private longings, not merely a 'haven from a heartless world' or status seeking.

Recent social psychology provides tools for analysing these complex desires for private space and distance from others. In so far as status was measured by personal access to exceptionally large private space, the democratisation of social life necessarily entailed the extension of personal territory to everyone.[66] Late Victorian reformers insisted on the normalcy of private family life. Note their almost obsessive attack on the working-class custom of taking in boarders, a habit that largely disappearing in the 1920s in the US.[67]

This nearly universal desire for privacy is illustrated in a 1943 survey of the English *Daily Express*: half of respondents wanted suburban housing (and 40 per cent preferred country homes) as compared to only 6 per cent who favoured the town in this most urban of countries. A Mass-Observation survey of housewives found a widespread desire for front halls and passages between rooms for enhanced privacy; they insisted on their 'own front door' as opposed to a common gate. Homemakers wanted 'friendliness but not friends' in the neighbourhood.[68]

Even those sociologists who stressed social emulation acknowledged this quest for private space. English sociologists J. M. Mogley and D. Chapman noted that working-class couples purchased complete rooms of furniture at marriage. The purpose was not merely to make a social statement but to express a private emotional world. Homes did more than display status; they functioned as 'symbols of security', especially during social or political crises. By differentiating spatial function and 'quality' between rooms, couples created a sense of security through 'symbolic order'.[69] 'Ritual objects from the past' expressed, according to

Warner, more than heritage. These artefacts linked 'the sentiments of the living with those of the dead' and did so in often highly personal ways.[70]

Anthropologists who study household objects have recently stressed that owners place little value in status consumer goods as compared with highly personal artefacts. Consumer goods are often merely 'pecuniary trophies rather than . . . objects of personal significance'.[71] The home provides a nearly unique site for continuous individual contact with objects made or cultivated by the dweller and associated with family, friends, and ancestors. It should not be surprising that the 'do-it-yourself' movement grew during the Anglo-American suburbanisation of the 1920s. Simple carpentry and gardening skills allowed home-owners to create a personal statement. The formal English front garden and the male's domain, the back garden of flowers and vegetables, became centres of this self-expression. English 'semis' generally came with a picture rail, mantel, and bay window which allowed the display of feminine bric-a-brac.[72] The American middle class was fascinated with antiques and restoration of old houses in the second and third decade of the twentieth century. But magazines and tool makers also promoted home-improvement projects as vehicles of domestic togetherness for working-class families as well.[73] Consumer goods made possible a private world.

Probably the most important domestic consumer good in the interwar years was the radio. The wireless surely contributed to that inward trend while also vastly increasing the frequency of shared, if passive, experiences. At first, in the 1920s, radio sets were so expensive that broadcasting probably encouraged social contact in so far as people gathered at bars or relative's parlours to listen. In the early 1930s, however, dramatically lower prices brought the radio into most working-class homes.[74] If, in 1930, only 35 per cent of British homes had a radio licence, by 1939 71 per cent had this permit. An American survey in 1938 found that 40 per cent of households on a typical winter evening had the radio on. The radio became as much a domestic appliance as it was a creature of mass media (or, in the US, of mass marketing).[75] Social research found that the wireless relieved the isolation of women in homes that were increasingly devoid of relations and children. And, because evening schedules mixed programmes designed for different ages and sexes, families were encouraged to listen together. The radio was the new family hearth and often looked like one. Most of all, the wireless wonderfully reconciled privacy with longings for a community of information and symbolic worlds.[76]

Time at home became an occasion for the accumulation of goods that displayed and expressed the self. But the home was also a site for experiencing social meanings of time that were available only in private life. As Maurice Halbwachs argued, 'there is not one universal and unique time. A society breaks down into a multiplicity of groups, each with its own duration.' French sociologist Georges Gurvitch (1964) noted that the temporality of the home is realised in 'long duration and slow motion, sometimes cyclical time, and finally, time held back on itself'. In home life, modern people attempt to stand outside of the time flow of public life, of mechanical regularity, and of progression. In the English front parlour, Mogley noted, the clock 'will be fast or stopped and a calender will hardly be seen'.[77]

For wage-earners, contrasting meanings of time were particularly sharp early in this century. Time at work inevitably dragged; anticipation of the 'red light' or bell signalling release at the end of the day or week dominated consciousness. The image of the boss 'hanging from the hands of the clock', retarding the longed-for hour of escape, is a common one; and efforts of mass-production workers to evade routine by accelerating and retarding the pace of production is well known.[78]

The reguiated, calculated character of market or worktime required that private leisure retain an irregularity even if that meant that people 'wasted' home hours. Domesticity offered free time to accumulate experiences of memory and continuities. The home became a 'private museum of treasures' as noted one English memoir of the 1920s. It included 'ugly souvenirs from seaside resorts and all kinds of bits and pieces Grandad had picked up during his soldiering years'; sitting rooms were decorated with 'trophies of rod and gun' and the 'flower entwined Gothic lettering of some pithy saying from the scriptures'. These artefacts guarded against the intrusion of society and change. They provided a refuge from the ongoing 'sensory overlading of consumerist culture and fashion'. As Halbwachs put the point, 'the permanence and interior appearance of a home impose on the group a comforting image of its own continuity. We doubt that so much time has passed. . . . The group . . . becomes enclosed within the framework it has built.'[79]

These alternative meanings of time were especially concentrated on the weekends. Wage-earners had long devoted Saturday evening (or afternoon where the half-workday was practised) to frenetic activity – shopping, especially for women, or male socialising around club and sports.[80] But carnival time on Saturday evening turned into solemn time on Sunday. English sabbatarianism survived in late rising and afternoon naps (for men, at least); the reading of multiple newspapers (if not scripture); and dressing in the Sunday best for family afternoon strolls to the pub (if not always to church). Weekday patterns were reversed: homes and gardens were full of activity and the streets were relatively empty. In some English households, fathers might even 'mind the baby' or 'help with the washing up'.[81] This weekly cycle served a psychological function that transcended its religious roots. Yet it also perpetuated religion's insistence that repetition and reversal (birth following death), rather than natural entropy, governed life.[82]

Still, it was only 'real' time in the market workplace that gave meaning to these domestic moments, especially for providers. The pains of labour gave breadwinners permission to enjoy leisure; and work schedules structured those 'sacred' moments of freedom.[83] This dichotomy, of course, did not exist for most married women. Indeed, it was their routine work that made the home a haven for their family's freedom. In the twentieth century, consumption work was increasingly central to the homemaker's identity and to her husband's evaluation of her.[84]

Modern domesticity reconciled free time for spending with the discipline of worktime for earning. But, if this symbiosis was most evident for male providers, it had a home-based parallel among female homemakers. To be sure, the survival of 'task oriented' domestic work is well known; and women surely spread their work throughout their waking day. Nevertheless historians and sociologists of housework stress that, not only was 'women's work' directly determined by wage–work schedules, but that a woman's self-esteem was based on her contributing as much (if not more) time to housework as her spouse provided in wage-earning. This was especially the case because men could claim that their time was worth more than the unpaid hours of wives. Semi-economic calculations of time inevitably entered the home and made domestic work a disciplined and regulated activity. The wife's hours of housework justified her access to her husband's money and her enjoyment of the private time that she largely created. For both men and women, time and money were reconciled in the home even if in different ways.[85]

Domestic consumption combined privacy and social identity. It provided rich alternatives to routinised worktime and did so through those cyclic and measured moments of weekend freedom. These temporal experiences were realised in and through goods. Spending and cyclic free time reinforced the commitment to steady work. Without wage work and routine time, spending and free time were impossible and meaningless. With the emergence of mortgaged housing, families bought membership into an intimate community of private spaces and temporalities. They also sold their futures and lashed themselves to the time clock at work. A Woolworth's culture guaranteed universal consumer participation while it confirmed a social hierarchy of consumption; it induced a seeming endless chase up the ladder of spending and working. A sense of belonging and freedom was confirmed along with the necessity of work to obtain the forever scarce material tokens of participation and choice. Time at home became 'full' because it was justified with time at work. And, they were bridged with money.

HOLIDAY'S DREAM OF SPENDING AND FREEDOM

A second arena for the reconciliation of time and money was the holiday. By the 1930s, the modern idea of the vacation as 'vacating' one's home and work had surely captured the imagination of the working masses. A 'real holiday' increasingly required 'getting away' from the routine and environment of the everyday. To be sure, it was no longer a 'holy day'; rather the vacation was time nominally freed from all moral authority. Still the holiday remained 'magical'. As anthropologist E. R. Leach notes, without a regular shift from 'profane' to 'sacred' time or a 'discontinuity of repeated contrasts', even modern people feel 'cheated of time' and deprived of the means of 'marking' time. The vacation had become the 'transcendence' of modern industrial people for whom an afterlife had become less tangible and for whom progress from wage-earning to bourgeois autonomy (much less a liberating social order) seemed increasingly remote. The transition to and from the holiday 'pilgrimage' required ritual markers – 'needlessly' elaborate preparations, tensions, unaccustomed behaviour and an 'obsessive' collection of souvenirs. As ritual celebrations, Carol Werner argues, holidays 'entrain' cyclic and linear temporal rhythms and evoke particular sensibilities to past, present, and future. Elements of the eighteenth-century aristocratic Grand Tour of Europe and the 'bath' survived in the mass vacation with its educational and healthful appeals. But it also incorporated the carnival and even the pilgrimage. To many working people, the vacation was identical with bourgeois freedom. As a French worker recently put it, 'To live is to travel.'[86]

But the holiday was also to become a perfect 'metaphor' of the consumer moment. The seaside vacation especially offered hundreds of magical displays to be seen along the super-boulevard of the promenade. In the interwar years, the seaside resort was a spectacle, a perfect expression of the consumerist 'gaze'; it was an experience of sight (and other senses) rather than ownership. The late Victorian 'seaside girl' with her associations to rejuvenation and desire remained the central symbol of the resort's self-advertising in the twentieth century. She was, as historian Thomas Richards observes, a key to the seaside's attraction as a 'therapeutic ethos of individual fulfilment through a manufactured utopia of commodities'. 'Postmodernity' in the resort long pre-dated the intellectual's discovery of cultural 'bricolage' in the contemporary shopping mall.[87]

As I note in chapter 5, the holiday culture appeared later in France and the US than in Britain. The seaside holiday, or at least 'day trip', had become common in the British urban working class from the 1880s. But, even in Britain, certain areas were still more 'precocious', especially the mill towns of Lancashire. Almost archetypical was the holiday mecca of Blackpool on the western coast of England where about 7 million visited in 1937. Mass-Observation's detailed reports of this 'outcrop of industrial civilisation' in the late 1930s provide a unique, if not entirely representative, picture of 'the bright mirror of how the workers spend their week of freedom from factory and mine'.[88]

Holiday spending like domestic consumption combined desires for individual distinction with a quest for group identity. The vacation became an extension of the department store and boulevard; and the seaside resort provided a space for contained, but dynamic, displays of fashion – exhibitionism and conformity in shared signs. Holiday spending anticipated a 'future' of material fulfilment when workers shared in the daily luxury of the rich. This may have helped to create a social solidarity between the classes – even if hierarchy was re-established in limitless consumer choices and distinctions of place, service, freedom, and 'authenticity' that visibly divided poor from affluent tourists.

According to the Mass-Observers, the Lancashire 'Worktowns' were devoid of a sense of common purpose or 'progress'. An almost random change-obsessed individualism dominated English popular culture. The 'decline in church attendance, pub visits, voting, and the birth rate' was evidence of this pessimistic withdrawal into the self:

> In a world that now seems to nearly everyone to 'have gone crazy' and where all the older institutions seem impotent in the face of new powers, the individual increasingly believes only in himself. . . . Private life and its rhythms have grown enormously.

This cynical individualism fuelled not only the growth of astrology and the football pools with their obsessions with personal fate, but also the holiday oasis of Blackpool. The vacation resort 'attempts to form the largest possible group of consumers, but does not attempt to establish any social relationship between them'.[89] Instead Blackpool provided the 'progress' missing in everyday life with a constantly changing arena of new variety shows, rock-candy gags, and freshly decorated facades on the featured attraction, 'Noah's Ark' in Pleasure Beach. The resort satisfied an unquenchable individual desire for the new. Blackpool also created a libertine environment that tolerated endless expressions of individuality. Here one could throw balls at 'traffic lights' in games along the promenade, 'learn' about one's unique personality in the booths of one of the two 'real' Gypsy Smiths, lick 'Mae [West]'s Vest' in rock candy, or get rolling drunk without fear of embarrassment in a town where police were exceptionally indulgent.[90]

Yet the vacationing act was also 'a communal affair'. It was anticipated in savings clubs and in plans discussed in pubs as early as February of each year. Worktowners experienced the social meaning of the vacation in their frantic collective preparation for the massive 'holiday exodus' by bus and rail on a single Saturday morning in mid-summer. As the train from the mill towns passed onto the sandy coastal flats and Blackpool's Tower came into view, quiet self-absorbed travellers became 'bound together as "fellows" by this common rallying point'. People began sharing cigarettes and candy; spontaneous groups formed to sing religious and popular songs. While a small survey by Mass-Observers found only 24 per cent of Worktowners who claimed that they wished to go to the popular resort, 69 per cent actually went there. To be sure, Blackpool entrepreneurs replaced the convivial pageantry of the feast days of the old Friendly Society and village 'wakes week' with a far more passive form of consumption during the holiday week. But holiday makers chose boarding houses in Blackpool because 'pals are going there or because the management came from their home town'.[91] Whole towns, released annually from the mills for nine days, recongregated at the seashore in a modernised wakes week. One Observer claimed that on the streets of Blackpool, 'people are on the look out for one another to prove to one another that they have come too; then their neighbours cannot claim superiority'. The same motive prompted people to buy souvenirs which displayed the Blackpool Tower.[92]

People expressed this act of belonging in Blackpool by consuming goods and adventure. One popular hairdresser in Bolton had been booked solid until 2.00 a.m. from January for the week before the holiday when mill town stores were 'jammed with girls buying dancing frocks'. Tourists dressed in their Sunday best for the journey to Blackpool; and many headed immediately for the 'World's Greatest Woolworth's' store opposite Central Station in Blackpool to buy swimming suits that few would bathe in.[93]

The binge was as necessary to these industrial people as it was to the anthropologist's 'primitives'. It expressed not only a release from everyday want but represented a dream of a democracy of goods. According to F. Zweig, a 'real holiday' to the London worker was a good time without thinking about money, an opportunity to behave like the rich. Otherwise 'he wants to stay at home'. In the 1940s, Zweig met a postal worker who spent over four times his weekly pay on a week's vacation in London.[94] In *Love on the Dole*, Greenwood's 'Joe' during the Depression spent at an annual rate of £750 for a week's holiday with his new bride even though he earned but £104 per year: 'here, by the sea, everything had been ideal'. Joe believed that 'marriage would be one long repetition of the holiday'.[95] Luxury, even if infrequent, was a key to expectation and the meaning of freedom. Without it, life was not worth living. A main difference between the classes was the frequency and intensity of this experience. What was intolerable was the total absence of luxury. A 45-year-old woman weaver said to a Mass-Observer:

> During holiday time, I and my sister use scented soap and never look first at a menu to find what a thing costs but just order it, because once in a year we want to smell and behave like ladies.[96]

Yet the vacation was a constant reminder to all that they were not quite ladies and gentlemen. Holiday makers would make a point with their 'less fortunate neighbour' by asking him or her to watch the garden while they were away, bringing back a 'bar or two of [Blackpool] rock [candy]' in payment. Those who could afford a holiday on the Isle of Man (30 miles off the Lancashire coast) mentioned it in the pubs in winter. And, those tourists on limited means were continually reminded of that fact by the inconvenience of their lodgings (often self-catered) and their need to watch others spend their 'pennies' in the countless stalls, amusement rides, and slot machines.[97] Hierarchy was created by distance from profane time and space: the freer from routine and scarcity and the further from real life, the higher the vacationer's prestige. Even so, all strove and, to a degree, enjoyed that proleptic realisation of full time and fullness of goods. Blackpool was a democracy of delights that encouraged the display and submersion of self along the promenade.

The holiday also linked spending with 'sacred' time. In a distinctly modern yearly cycle, the holiday suspended clock discipline (even if it was difficult for people to give up their habit of looking at their watches). During vacations, time was experienced in depth as past and as future. A jobless Worktowner explained that people go on holiday

"to escape from the old dragon". He pointed to a wall no more than a foot high in the back garden, and said that he felt that the [wall] symbolised a boundary for him, a tying down; and it was only by walking into the country that he managed to get rid of that feeling, and his worry.

People sought in the holiday not only spatial extension but freedom from regulated and mechanical time. One 'card-room girl' wanted a vacation

to forget the clock, the newspapers, the public – and I cannot even tell you how I want to spend my holiday, because that would be planning and all my working is done according to plan. Just this. The movements of a flow of the river almost explains how I feel about a holiday.

A working-class homemaker commented that 'a large number of people go [to Blackpool] because it revives past memories, love affairs'. The theme of rejuvenation appeared again and again in Blackpool postcards, in the tableaux of the autumn 'Illuminations', and in health remedies peddled in stalls on Central Beach. The idea of 'cheating time' was well expressed in extending the hours of drinking and dancing. Blackpool's Illuminations in October defied the onset of winter night by 'magically' emblazoning the promenade with neon and flashing light to the delight of dense crowds.[98]

But 'sacred' times were essentially consumer moments. Pursuit of exotic time, nostalgic time, and future time were all evident in the attractions along the promenade. In an afternoon, one could purchase the strange in the Indian sharma, childhood memory in the Punch and Judy show, and the new in the 'Telepathic Robot, the Scientific Miracle'. In Blackpool, adults could relive the past while sharing rides with children on donkeys (mothers) or building castles with them out of sand (fathers). But they also participated in the collective (if distorted) re-creation of history when they bought a ticket to the wax museum. Despite the efforts of Blackpool business reformers, age-old spectacles survived even if dressed up in modernity: the tightrope-walking 'Stratosphere Girl' or the fortune-telling 'Green-ray Television Wonder'.[99]

In Blackpool, the visitor also got glimpses of the 'future'. To be sure, Blackpool was not a pure form of the anticipatory consumer moment. Unlike the world's fairs of New York and Paris of the late 1930s, it did not provide a systematic glimpse at the comforts and convenience of the future. But Blackpool's motto was 'Progress'; it was here that England had its first trolley and cinema; and, in the 1930s, the normally earth-bound could take an airplane joy trip.[100] Novelty as well as custom was worshipped.

A more subtle attraction was what Gurvitch called the 'diffuse time of irregular pulsations, of unforeseeable fluctuations between the appearance and disappearance of rhythms'. This experience was best expressed in the milling crowd.[101] Despite bourgeois and reformist preaching, holiday makers sought a time of the masses. In Britain, factory workers, far from avoiding the throng that they knew at work, seemed to have enjoyed taking holidays at the same time and going by crowded trains to the same packed seaside resorts.[102] But at Blackpool the dreary mass labouring at machines and silently rushing to and from work had magically changed: 'The crowd has an automatic tendency towards release from the constraints of time', noted the Mass-Observers, when individuals at Blackpool merged into the packed streets and promenade that blocked traffic from nine in the morning to eleven at night. Groups formed to 'gaze at a man shying at [Belisha] beacons, a little boy lost, splashing waves, a tame pigeon, or a man rolling up his sleeves'. 'Gazing', not 'laughing', meeting new people, or even seeking the thrill of casual sex was the principle occupation of members of Blackpool crowds.[103]

That 'gaze' may have been shaped by elites as recently suggested by sociologist John Urry.[104] But those who had merely spectated during the day sometimes became actors under cover of darkness and the glow of artificial light. At night, 'whirlpools' of people appeared and disappeared around drunken singers; and 'chains' or 'crocodiles' of youths 'silted' their way through the streets. What provided pleasure was the ebb and flow of time in the crowd, not the 'messages' contained in the Illuminations at Blackpool.[105]

Despite its 'educational' themes, the New York World's Fair of 1939–40 was also a spectacle of the fantasyful and infinite variety; and it too created 'whirlpools'. As the *Architectural Record* noted, the New York Fair's 'designers found that the crowd's greatest pleasure is in the crowd'. The people apparently wanted a Blackpool: in its second year, the Fair's tone became distinctly less educational, and was promoted as a 'super country fair'.[106] But the catalyst of all these temporal meanings was the consumerist gaze. In many ways, then, the difference between 'sacred' time and the dream of spending vanished on holiday.

Finally, the conflict between the work-a-day world and the holiday were reconciled in the saving and spending cycle of the annual vacation. Mass-Observers found that Worktowners displayed a tenacious adherence to the rituals of seasonal change, despite the fact that generations of urban English people had been alienated from the natural world of the peasantry and from a lived religiosity. Secular town-dwellers flocked to the cinema on the eve of Lent and gave their children pancakes on Shrove Tuesday. Following this abbreviated carnival, they went meatless for 'forty days commemorat[ing] an incident about which they know very little indeed'. But the annual cycle in twentieth-century England was dominated by neither the agricultural nor the religious calendar but by the summer holiday trek, and the cycle of saving and spending that made it possible. Money ordered the year in the way that weather and religion once did. The weekly collective rite of holiday saving survived even if it was transferred from friendly societies to the modern savings clubs centred at banks.[107]

'After a week from home', a Worktown housewife claimed that she was 'always glad to get back home. Still home to me, thankful to get back and begin saving again.' Austerity, the ordinariness of everyday life, and even the burden of saving were relieved in annual luxury. And holiday makers eased the transition back to 'reality' by accumulating souvenir 'relics from Holy Blackpool'.[108] 'Holy' days had become a duration of intense interaction with goods. Full time was full of magical displays of goods. Blackpool reconciled work and play; routine and the extraordinary; time and money.

Suburban domesticity and Blackpool vacations were only windows into the emerging world of mass consumption. The Blackpool experience, shaped by constraints of income, time, and transportation in the 1930s, has radically declined since the 1960s with the coming of greater affluence, automobility and cheap air flights to packaged Mediterranean resorts. But it offers insights into why goods prevailed over free time. Indeed, as Urry notes, many of the elements of the Blackpool spectacle have entered into the daily practices of contemporary consumerism.[109]

Spending served needs that went far beyond the manipulation of merchandisers and compensation for meaningless work. Its meaning transcended the constraining psychology of work and of emulation. Consumption fulfilled a general quest for privacy and sociability without the risks and awkwardness of individual disclosure or of the self-forgetfulness and austerity of the organised group. This may explain the ultimate failure of totalitarian manipulation of leisure. But it also provides clues as to why the institutions of democratic leisure had so little apparent influence. Goods prevailed because they reconciled time and money. Worktime wages and play-time consumption were roughly balanced. Goods and 'sacred' time become fused in the cyclic rites and museums of domesticity and in the vacation time of the consuming crowd.

8 Consumerist modernity, an end of history?

A consumerist consensus emerged after 1945. It had been built upon mass production, balanced with high wages, and buttressed by Keynesian macro-economic management and manipulated needs creation. But that culture was also inextricably bound with uses and meanings of time: the triumph of consumerism meant the eclipse of the movements for the progressive reduction of worktime and democratic leisure as legitimate fruits of productivity. Consumerism is not only the basis of both the modern economic order and public culture, but it defines how most people organise their time around working and spending. Alternatives perhaps never had much of a chance in those decades of austerity, political upheaval, and war before 1945. But it remained a question whether and when they might be revived.

The postwar boom could have resurrected the debate that followed 1918. Demobilisation might have produced a demand for reduced worktime just as peacetime conversion did after World War I. Unions had hardly abandoned their short-hour demands from the 1930s: calls for the 40-hour week in Britain and its restoration in France were widely heard; and American unions still insisted on the 35-hour standard as a means of work sharing. Leftist governments in Britain and France could have returned to the cultural populism of the democratic leisure movement. Indeed, postwar progressive electoral victories encouraged fresh thinking about leisure planning in Britain and prompted the rebirth of Lagrange's vision of volunteer cultural activity in France.[1]

But neither work sharing nor democratic leisure had any serious role in the postwar recovery. The obvious explanations are that the pressing demand for reconstruction and fulfilling pent-up material needs, that had long been deferred by the Depression and war, precluded the 'luxury' of free time. But this eclipse of the free-time option long outlasted the postwar emergency. Instead, a political consensus quickly emerged around expectations of 'full-employ-ment' and unlimited consumption. In the late 1930s, the American political elite opted for 'commercial Keynesianism' and, after 1940, military Keynesianism; it chose indirect monetary and fiscal stimu-lation (increasingly defence spending) rather than some form of democratic economic planning to achieve this goal. The failure to win effective job-creation and public-housing legislation greatly weakened social welfare politics within the American unions; and legislation restricting trade-union activities reduced the ability of labour to continue to raise the option of work sharing. The re-emergence of American business unionism during the Cold War was hardly an auspicious setting for free-time movements.[2] But universal commitment to higher levels of personal consumption probably was more important than the conservative drift of Ameri-can politics in the late 1940s. After all, it was broadly shared by the left-wing British welfare statists and French economic planners, even if without the entrepreneurial enthusiasm of the Americans.[3] In all three countries, this new consensus had roots in the 1930s in the appeals of full employment and the disillusionment with free time. While the Depression and especially the War might have led to a permanent transformation of gender roles, women returned to the security of the home to bear large families and to participate in the promise of domestic consumerism. Even if intellectuals rejected its cultural consequences, no one had a serious alternative to the work-and-spend ethic, 'harmoniously' divided between the male public provider and female domestic consumer.

But, by the 1960s, challenges to the consumer culture and signs of a 'cultural shift' suggested the possibility of post-materialist options. These trends might suggest that we should re-interpret the interwar debate over time and money. Predictions that affluence would lead to a 'stationary state society', where non-economic cultural options would flourish, may have been merely premature in the 1920s and 1930s. The victory of full employment over work sharing and limit-less mass consumption over non-commercial leisure may well have been temporary. One might argue that this consensus was founded on a unique confluence of a mass-production economy and a mass-consumer social psychology that peaked in the generation after 1945. But more recent technological changes may have permanently undermined full-time employment. Despite the valiant efforts of merchandisers, there may indeed be a limit to consumer demand in advanced industrial countries. Those who dreamed of democratic leisure simply may have been premature. Affluence and time freed from work and other forms of social obligation may have created conditions suitable for the emergence of a new 'mutualism' in leisure, voluntary social service, and other non-market activities. Even the intellectual's cultural elitism may have begun to give way to a more positive 'postmodernist' assessment of popular culture. Recent signs of change in the sexual division of labour may have finally undermined those distinct gender roles that perpetuated a segmented and fixed balance of work and leisure.

Another view may, however, be more accurate. Predictions, emerging in the mid-1960s, that a postmaterialist society was unfolding have not been realised. Powerful political and social pressures in the 1980s have frustrated advocates of work sharing and self-management of time. Despite the growth of social movements outside formal political structures in western Europe, such groups have not yet had an important impact on shifting politics away from economic distribution; surely they have had little success in creating a self-initiated network of voluntary institutions organised around time free from work, much less realising greater gender equality at home and work. In the US, not only has there been an increase in worktime for the average family in the 1980s, but the social movements so often noted in Europe have few American equivalents.

Social forecasters usually project their own (or sponsors') prejudices on to the future. That, at least, should not be the historian's vice. But if, as I believe, history can inform choice, then a review of trends since 1945 may not only add meaning to my historical interpretation but shed light on the constraints and potential of 'time and money' in the future.

MASS CULTURE AND THE POSTWAR INTELLECTUAL

The political appeal of consumerism in the generation after 1945 is obvious. That humanists would respond negatively to it is also understandable. But this hostility had origins long before postwar affluence and took forms that revealed as much about that intelligentsia as they did about the cultural consequences of consumerism. Most intellectuals abdicated any creative role in forming an alternative to the politics of consumption. Instead, many linked mass culture to both commercial manipulation and totalitarianism. Probably because consumerism was far more pervasive in the US than in western Europe after the war, the intellectual's negative obsession with mass culture was far greater in the US. Antifascist American liberals easily transformed themselves into cultural soldiers in the Cold War. American liberals developed a fortress mentality that reduced the distance between them and conservative apologists of cultural and economic privilege.[4]

In many ways the American attack on 'mass culture' was little more than a reprise of the interwar discussion (see chapter 3 above). Ortega's fears of democratic time and money reappeared in the American Dwight Macdonald's attack on 'midcult' in the 1950s. This commercialised culture lived off debased forms of high culture and, because of the people's 'fear of difference', midcult was hostile to the spontaneity of the popular arts. The merchandiser's quest for a broad market led to a merging of taste; the result was an 'infantile regression' of adults and 'overstimulation' of children.[5] Ultimately these attacks expressed a common fear of collapsed cultural hierarchies: anglophile Macdonald, like Leslie Fielder and T. S. Eliot, called for a return to class divisions in western culture to free us from a deadening conformity.[6]

Even David Riesman, one of the most subtle students of popular culture, argued that a 'general lowering of barriers' between regions, classes, and ages produced general expectations of a 'standard package' of goods. This association of cultural levelling with emulation and anarchistic hedonism took many forms: in the 1950s, the middle-class Anglo-American adult was obsessed with the influence of working-class (or Black) consumer culture on their offspring (via rock music, for example); and the cultured elite lamented that broadcasting and national advertising reduced American television programming to the lowest common denominator.[7]

This fear of mass-cultural pollution took still other forms: a pervasive theme was that an indulged population had lost its willingness to work. In 1961, sociologist Harold Wilensky claimed that only the managerial class still put in long hours; the masses, by contrast, enjoyed the leisure formerly reserved for the elite. This reversal of historic class roles obsessed Herman Kahn and Anthony Weiner's forecast, *The Year 2000* (1967): they predicted that future mechanisation would produce a society of drones, where the masses would be required to work very little, but where people would have little capacity for self-cultivation. A minority of educated technicians would have to monitor and support the rest of the population. Concerns with the decline of delayed gratification and rise of status seeking among the American working and middle classes permeate the studies of leisure in the 1950s and early 1960s.[8]

The old idea that production work led to consumerist passivity was given fresh voice in the 1950s. Clement Greenberg doubted that improved productivity could yield culturally valuable free time for working people. Only a leisure class unimpeded by the world of work, it seemed, could revive 'true' leisure.[9] The French sociologist Georges Friedmann agreed that the division of labour limited the possibility of the 'integral' individual; leisure was less an opportunity for personal fulfilment than the release of 'permanent nervous tension'.[10]

By the late 1950s, Riesman had grown even more pessimistic about the future of leisure. In *The Lonely Crowd* (1950), Riesman still expressed hope that free time could compensate for meaningless work. But, with the emergence of a decentralised suburban culture in the 1950s, he found that leisure's potential to liberate was reduced. Riesman was unusually sensitive to the resistance of working people to the rigid separation of instrumental work and passive leisure. He recognised that wage-earners often rejected the status seeking observed by Packard and Whyte in middle-class suburbs. But he insisted that leisure has become so unsatisfactory that it is now 'what workers recover from at work' rather than serving any positive purpose.[11]

These forms of cultural pessimism were deep and persistent. But not all shared fully in their implications. A long list of liberal pluralists, including Reuel Denney, Paul Lazarsfeld, Robert Merton, Edward Shils, Gilbert Seldes, and David Riesman, insisted that mass production did not led to mass culture. Diversity survived in the multiple uses and meanings that different social groups gave to goods and the popular arts. Indeed consumption helped the young and minorities to dissent in relatively harmless ways and to adjust to adult and majority culture. Lazarsfeld's studies of radio audiences concluded that the 'culture industry' was not manipulative, but rather reinforced common beliefs and longings; culture merchandisers were subject to unpredictable changes in popular taste.[12] The American Herbert Gans adapted this liberal pluralism to more populist ends in his extensive work devoted to the diversity of popular taste (especially in the 'conformist' working-class American suburb).[13]

This literature was especially well developed in the US. But English and French cultural and social critics also balked at extreme elements in the theory of mass culture. From the late 1950s, Raymond Williams and even Richard Hoggart stressed the tension between mass and popular culture. This discussion gave rise to a rich ethnography of contemporary working-class life that revealed the adaptability and resilience of work, community, and youth sub-groups in spite of the appeals of mass consumption.[14] From the mid-1950s, Paul Chombart de Lauwe and René Kaes offered detailed analyses of French working-class 'needs' that suggested complex aspirations and cultural meanings. Later Pierre Bourdieu's *Distinction* rejected the oversimplification of the mass culture in this exhaustive dissection of aesthetic subgroups.[15]

But populism in any form was surely a minor voice. Not only did attacks on mass culture permeate the Left throughout the 1960s and 1970s,[16] but the democratic leisure tradition scarcely had any intellectual support. Again, Riesman's views are instructive. In an essay published in *Abundance for What?* (1964), he could see the coming of a time when consumerism would fade. But Riesman placed little faith in the improving leisure offered by adult edu-cators. The only alternative to a spending that sated was the security of work. Still he had little hope for job enhancement, given the instrumentalist attitudes of both managers and union leaders. He offered this pessimistic conclusion: To 'stave off the fear of sati-ation' we scan 'the technological horizon for new goods that we will all learn to want'. This leads to a

> state of suspended animation in the discussion concerning the quality of life a rich society should strive for; social inventiveness tends to be channeled into the defense of past gains rather than into ideas for a better proportionality between leisure and work.[17]

Pessimism pervaded this literature of the postwar generation of humanists just as it did the interwar generation. As Andrew Ross points out, negativity reflects the beleaguered status of the human-ist, especially in the US, where the intellectual and the people received little 'respect' from each other.[18] This only left the field to the merchandisers and productivists.

CONSUMERISM AND ITS CELEBRANTS

In contrast to the cultural jeremiahs were the celebrants of con-sumerism. Again this perspective was more common and appeared earlier in the US than in western Europe. Not only did these apologists of consumerism counter attacks on popular culture with charges of elitism, but they resurrected Harold Mouton's praise of limitless growth whenever unions proposed work sharing. The glorification of capitalist productivity and consumption was, of course, part of the conservative reaction to New Deal welfarism; it was a reassertion of traditional business prejudice against the 'sterility' of public spending.[19] But this view was also deeply rooted in New Deal liberalism itself. Most American liberals linked increased consumer spending to full employment. As Chester Bowles put it in 1945, 'our standards of living must rise steadily year by year to match the increase in our productive capacity'. Walter Reuther, the leftwing leader of the United Auto Workers, abandoned his union's commitment to the 30-hour week in 1945, arguing instead for a 'balanced economy of full employment – full production – full consumption'. He had adopted the equation popularised by Catchings and Foster in the 1920s. Reuther also shared with many liberals an anxiety about new leisure:

> we will get the four-day week long before we can use it intelligently unless we begin to work hard now on how people can use their new leisure creatively and constructively. . . . We always make more progress in working with machines than we do with men.[20]

Of course, enthusiasm for mass consumption went well beyond the proponents of 'full employment'. The editors of *Fortune* whetted their merchandising appetites on the seemingly boundless demand of Americans for goods in their *Changing American Market* (1953). In this book, they also linked mass consumerism to the genius of American democracy: old luxuries were becoming mass-consumer goods and all Americans were joining the 'rich middle-income class' to the envy of world. Academic sociologists predicted the convergence of social classes as an inevitable consequence of post-industrial consumer society.[21] In the 1960s, American economist George Katona insisted that the American lesson for Europe was the promise of a bigger pie rather than reapportioning the slices. While attacking critics of individual consumption, Katona declared:

> It is precisely the wanting and striving for improvements in private living standards that forms the solid basis of American prosperity. Only if the so-called private opulence increases still further can we hope to overcome public poverty.[22]

W. W. Rostow's famous last stage of economic growth – 'the age of high mass-consumption' – was, in effect, the end of history, not the four-day week advocated by those he labeled as 'utopians'.[23] 'The mass society', said Daniel Bell, 'is the product of change –

and is itself change. It is the bringing of the "masses" into a society, from which they were once excluded.'[24]

But the rationale for consumerism went beyond ideologies of 'full employment' and commercial populism. Economic orthodoxy (shorn of older paternalism) implicitly supported the same position. Economic choice rested on the personal 'sovereignty' of the individual consumer and a natural 'craving for variety'. Most economists found it beyond their 'competence' to consider the possibility that choice might be manipulated or have ecological, social, and cultural costs.[25]

In France, J. -J. Servan-Schreiber (1967) saw the American model of mass consumption as a 'challenge' to the social rigidity of Europe; 'growth' not 'protest' over the economic pie was the wave of the future. Despite more sober American prospects in the 1980s, P. Yonnet still gloried in the consumerist Americanisation of France. He too identified liberty with consumer choice and democracy with mass access to goods. Unlike politics which was based on conflict, consumer choice was an 'anti-promethean game'; and 'massification' of culture was really the work of individual consumers building the road to real democracy.[26]

Underlying this ideology of consumer sovereignty was the reality of an unprecedented broadening of access to durable goods. In the US, the share of personal income absorbed by perishable essentials (mostly food) decreased from 37.7 per cent in the decade after 1938 to 28.4 per cent between 1974 and 1983. Disposable household income (in 1982 dollars) rose from $15,110 in 1940 to $26,313 in 1970 to a peak of $28,607 in 1979. If, in 1946, only 54 per cent of American families owned cars, a decade later 73 per cent were 'auto-mobile'. Eighty-six per cent owned televisions as early as 1956. Between 1950 and 1970, largely suburban developments increased the housing stock in the United States by half, with as many houses added in the 1970s. In the 35 years after 1935, home ownership nearly tripled for white wage-earning families and doubled for black families.[27]

Advertisers and the government prepared Americans during the war for this splurge with the message that they were fighting for the 'glorious future' of 'mass distribution and mass ownership'.[28] Pent-up demand for consumer goods was released after World War II in filling these homes with, what Thomas Hine has termed, 'populuxe' possessions. The extravagant tailfin on cars, the flying-saucer lamp, the two-tone refrigerator, chip-and-dip, the lounge chair, and the sheer magic of the 'push button' in thousands of products 'celebrated confidence in the future, the excitement of the present, the sheer joy of having so much'.[29]

Paralleling this explosion of American consumption was a decline of free time. John Robinson found that disposable time per week decreased between 1931–3 and 1965–6 from 40 to 34 hours for men and 38 to 35 hours for women. Still free hours devoted to the supreme commercial media, radio/TV, rose from four to thirteen hours for men and from three to ten hours for women. Most of this increase was taken from social interaction.[30]

But perhaps most telling was the apparent unchallenged victory of consumerism among workers. In 1947, male breadwinners employed at W. W. Kellogg's cereal plants acquiesced to a 40-hour week in exchange for higher wages, thus abandoning their famous 30-hour standard that had been won during the Depression. By contrast, it took almost 30 more years to root out the 30-hour week in female-dominated departments, a fact that reflects the persistence of the gender division of household labour. Despite the paper commitment of many unions to a shorter workweek, a 1963 Gallup Poll found only 42 per cent of American union members in support of a 35-hour week, the majority apparently preferring higher incomes. And most trade unionists at an AFL-CIO Conference on Shorter Hours of Work in 1956 agreed that higher wages and overtime pay rather than more leisure concerned members.[31]

Those social pressures that encouraged mass consumerism in the interwar years reappeared after 1945. Suburbanised privacy reinforced the American consensus around the 'family wage' of male providers and the priority of disposable personal income. Consumerism offered stimulation to bored housewives, pride in providing and participating to husbands, and belonging to children. The suburban ideal compensated for bureaucratic work and offered security in the nuclear age. As historian Elaine May notes, consumerism assured a balance of work and a safe form of indulgence that did not seem to violate traditional values – even as consumerism introduced constant change.[32] There is little doubt that the shopping culture in the US has had a greater impact than in Europe. By the 1970s, not only did Americans spend as much as four times as many hours shopping as did Europeans, but Americans devoted far more space to shopping malls and other retail commercial activity. The distinction between leisure and consumption for many Americans had disappeared as time and money had become one.[33]

Pressures of postwar reconstruction delayed the advent of mass consumerism in Britain and France. Real wages in Britain rose 40 per cent between 1950 and 1965. But only about 1960 did this growth translate into new forms of working-class consumerism (which partially supplanted spending on necessities and the older male leisures organised around drink, tobacco, gambling, and sport). While planners in 1945 hoped for a more open community built around new non-exclusive public housing, Britons largely rejected the tower blocks; instead, they longed for the suburban comforts of the semi-detached houses. Interviews with young British women just after the war found the same commitment to domesticity that had attracted young American wives. These British women aspired to practical marriages with good providers/husbands; they hoped to avoid the humiliation of the Depression years when fathers had often been unemployed and mothers had sometimes been forced to engage in domestic-service work.[34]

A sign of this new domestic consumerism was the rise in the share of family income devoted to housing costs from 13.9 per cent in 1953 to 18.9 per cent in 1968. Home ownership rose from 42 per cent in 1960 to 55 per cent by 1980. Even if television was slower to enter family life than in the US (in 1959, only 66 per cent of British homes owned one), within a decade a full 90 per cent possessed a television. A BBC study in 1974 found that half of leisure time was spent watching the screen.[35]

French spending trends followed the Anglo-American pattern. While in 1950 food comprised 49 per cent of the average household budget and housing absorbed merely 14 per cent, by 1985 food decreased to 19 per cent and housing costs rose to 26 per cent of family income. Automobility was slowly but firmly implanted, rising from 10 per cent of households in 1950 to 75 per cent by 1980. The well-known French tradition of urban apartment living and indifference to Anglo-American 'lawn culture' was eroded during the 1970s when new housing was increasingly suburban and detached. Household goods, long desired by working people, gradually entered their lives: if, in 1963, only 30 per cent of households owned televisions, by 1976 86 per cent had the box. By 1980, the French watched television for an average of 2.3 hours daily.[36] Finally, the demand for free time seemed to disappear in France; a 1964 survey showed that two-thirds preferred higher incomes to increased leisure – although this attitude was particularly pronounced among those with lower incomes, presumably striving for middle-class living standards.[37]

AN EMERGING CRITIQUE OF THE WORK AND SPEND CULTURE

A new critique of consumerism had begun to emerge, however, as early as the late 1950s. We should not be surprised to find a revival of Veblenesque critiques of emulative consumption in popular American sociology (Vance Packard and William Whyte, for example), and a renaissance of German critical theory in Theodor Adorno and Herbert Marcuse. These traditions had hardly disappeared in the debates over popular culture in the 1950s. Humanistic technocrats like the aged George Soule continued to predict that material needs would be sated and that society should cultivate positive and active forms of leisure. J. K. Galbraith produced a classic reformation of the cultural-lag theory in his *The Affluent Society*. There, he argued that the excesses of American consumerism were a consequence of the survival of an outdated scarcity mentality.[38]

Cultural jeremiahs and celebrants of growth were especially prominent in the US, where they shared a common experience with mass consumption. In contrast, Europeans were probably more open to a revival of thinking about free time. A particularly revealing case occurred when developmental economists began to predict increased leisure. The French economist Jean Fourastié, long an advocate of economic growth and critic of the 40-hour week, argued in 1965 that the French could expect dramatic increases in free time: based on a modest growth rate of 2.3 per cent, within 30 years, wage-earners would enjoy a 30-hour workweek in a 40-week year for a worklife of 35 years.[39] Such forecasts were embraced by leftists, who into the 1980s, predicted a 1,000-hour workyear by the end of the century.[40]

This fresh evaluation of free time was reflected in the emergence of Anglo-French leisure studies in the early 1970s. Echoing the democratic leisure movement of the 1930s, Joffre Dumazedier and his colleagues heralded an emerging 'leisure society' based on individual choice and time freed from economic necessity and social authority. A cultural (rather than a political) revolution emerged from 1968, Dumazedier insisted, in the massive growth of self-directed and commercial leisure activities in France. This trend was irreversible, independent of even economic trends. Free time, rather than work or even formal politics, would be the centre of new social change and fulfilment. Leisure freed workers from routine and obligation. It provided conditions for the re-emergence of individual choice in play and new festive communities. Dumazedier rejected the cultural jeremiad and even looked forward to the opening of 'EuroDisneyland'.[41]

Leisure studies produced, of course, more critical perspectives in the 1970s. Sociologists William Gossin and Stanley Parker, like Henry Durant almost 40 years before, linked work- and free time: the experience of regulated worktime reduced the ability of individuals to construct their own time; only if jobs offered greater autonomy and creativity could we expect more diverse and self-managed leisure. According to Mihaly Csikszentmihalyi, the 'flow experience', that 'holistic sensation' of acting with total involvement, defined both satisfying play and work. It was an error to presume that work was an obligation and that leisure was desirable, but useless. Ideally both activities should express responsibility and autonomy. This analysis produced, not a pessimistic critique of mass culture, but an insistence that work be 'humanised' and free time be extended.[42]

Leisure studies shifted the problem of the democratisation of time and money from the threat of manipulated mass culture to the experience and use of time at work and leisure. But it did not directly address a central problem of this book – the linkage between free time and consumption. Questions remained: Gossin showed that affluence did not seem to produce satiation nor did it reduce the willingness to work. Indeed, his survey of piece-rate workers found that 51 per cent considered at least 40 hours a week ideal![43] But why? And, why was 'free time' increasingly experienced as rushed – a scarcity – even as it was extended and aided by 'labor-saving devices'?

The economists Gary Becker (1965) and Staffan Linder (1970) addressed these problems in fresh evaluations of marginalist theory: with rising real wages, the 'cost' of free time rose, obliging 'rational' workers to opt for overtime and moonlighting; economic maximising induced them also to intensify their 'consumption' of leisure time and to choose time-saving devices to aid in their leisure. This meant a saturation of free time with leisure goods and their maintenance, thus creating a 'harried leisure class' of consumers. People might long for community and self-expression; but goods got in the way of their enjoyment of time and each other.[44]

The French cultural critic Philippe Barou d'Iriburne (1973) offered another approach to these questions. His answer to why affluence did not satisfy the craving for goods was that commodities had become primarily symbolic, meeting needs of those seeking a place in the cultural hierarchy. Consumption signs had invaded all sectors of life from rites of passage and tokens of familial or social solidarity to the elusive quest for status. These signs particularly took hold, Barou insisted in memory of Halbwachs, among the less secure members of the working class. Reduction of worktime would only lead to the new manufacture of consumer signs which would gradually re-saturate time. But the intellectual's condemnation of 'false needs' was hypocritical, Barou argued; and it ignored the fact that signs provide real 'cultural comfort'. Barou noted that everyone may have an interest in 'making peace' in the frustrating quest for 'signs'. But no one could do anything about it as an individual. Meanwhile the ideology of growth, promoted by national economic elites and international competition, only intensified the problem.[45]

The American economist Fred Hirsch (1976) offered a third explanation as to why affluence did not satisfy. While many had predicted that growth (supported by the welfare state) would create social harmony and personal security, this had not occurred. Mass affluence placed environmental limits on personal enjoyment (crowded highways on Sundays, for example) and reduced the value of status goods which declined in proportion to the degree that others had acquired them. The subsistence economy of physical needs had transformed into a 'positional economy' of status goods and services. The result was not simply open-ended growth but perpetual frustration. Affluence, Hirsch insisted in the tradition of Veblen, did not produce social harmony; instead, it reduced support for the welfare state: improved distribution only seemed to intensify competition for status goods in the positional economy. Thus self-regard, encouraged by the commercialisation of most needs, diminished a sense of social obligation.[46]

Whatever else these and similar critiques of affluence may have suggested, they implied the bankruptcy of, or at least social and psychological limits to, state-sponsored growth: not only did they question productivist policies of the Keynesian/Fordist state, but they suggested severe constraints on the possibilities of coherent political alternatives. Barou's solution was to create a coalition across traditional political lines. This alliance would support consumer education, ecological measures to reduce growth, and inter-enterprise agreements to eliminate competition that led to 'sign' marketing. He even advocated controls on the introduction of new luxury products.[47] But this was hardly the stuff of winning political campaigns.

These views paralleled the return of utopian anti-productivist thinking in the late 1960s and 1970s; Ivan Illich's call for 'tools of conviviality' and personal competence against the therapeutic state and its twin, commodity culture, shared much with Henri Lefebvre's appeal for 'enhanced forms of democracy' in a decentralised participatory society and the 'Small is Beautiful' school of E. F. Schumacher.[48] More recently, Briton James Robertson, in a techno-logical update of William Morris' *News From Nowhere*, has advo-cated that neighbourhoods and households become 'more self-reliant and conserving' and less dependent on money. A harmoni-ous combination of work and leisure in 'ownwork' could replace their rigid segmentation.[49] Each of these writers advocated a break from unlimited emulative/manipulative consumption and the forma-tion of non-political/non-market social and temporal 'space'.

Others attacked the other end of the productivist/consumerist consensus – 'full employment' – and the constraining power of the 'work ethic'. From the late 1970s, predictions of a 'collapse of work' were increasingly heard. British trade unionists, including Clive Jenkins and Ivor Clemitson, forcefully argued that an emerging 'third' industrial revolution would not create sufficient jobs for full employment (as had previous technological upheavals). Not only was the computer chip simplifying the assembly of industrial goods and thus reducing the demand for labour, but robotics and program-mable machine tools were about to eliminate millions of production workers. Jenkins and many others resurrected the old theme of technological unemployment by challenging Colin Clark's theory of occupational migration: they argued that it was illusory to hope that new technology would simply be followed by a further transfer of full-time jobs from the industrial to the service sector as had happened earlier in the century. Instead, computers would reduce white-collar jobs. Increased production and productivity did not mean more (if different) jobs. Jenkins even doubted that the new technology would generate those levels of consumer demand that were created during the second industrialisation and had produced automobiles and electrical goods. The rise in unemployment from the recessions of the 1970s was structural, not cyclic. No one could expect that investment in new technology would produce sufficient numbers of new jobs. In fact, the Labour Party erred in perpetuat-ing the productivist/full-employment myth. Innovation was necessary, this group insisted, for British competitiveness; but it could not create enough jobs to avoid higher unemployment rates and all the social disruptions that they caused.[50]

Another group that was critical of the 'full-employment economy' rejected the standardised workday. Since 1919, the eight-hour day-time shift had organised family life largely around the needs of male providers. However, increasingly diverse family and life-stage patterns prompted calls for a 'revolution of chosen time'. A French group, Echanges et Projets, in 1981, challenged the equity and efficiency of present allocations of free time. Not only were manual labourers relatively overworked, but women's 'free' time was disproportionally absorbed in household work. And synchronised blocks of work and free time produced waste – both dead time in commuting, and underutilised machinery. Most important, the 'monochronic' schedule ignored the real needs of most individuals. Some might prefer money to time in overtime bonus work, for example, and embrace rigidly segmented blocks of hours; but most wage-earners required other arrangements: women preferred shorter, more flexible, workdays and child-care leaves; many male manual workers wanted reduced workweeks and longer vacations; and older workers sought early withdrawal from the workforce and less abrupt transitions to retirement. Time, even more than money, Echanges et Projets insisted, was a fruit of productivity and should be distributed fairly and according to individual need.[51]

The dead weight of the work ethic stood in the path of expanded and more flexible free time. As theoretician André Gorz (1989) put it:

> We are . . . faced with a social system which is unable to distribute, manage, or employ . . . new-found free time; a system fearful of the expansion of this time, yet which does its utmost to increase it, and which, in the end, can find no purpose for it other than seeking all possible means of turning it into money.[52]

The solution for Gorz and his British counterparts was to cease glorifying work and romanticising the working class. Historically these dogmas had created the false hope of humanising work. Now they perpetuated long hours of alienating and subordinating labour that drained people of much capacity for self-management outside of work. These dogmas also humiliated increasing numbers of people who were excluded from the dignity that a job endowed.[53]

This line of reasoning led Gorz to saying 'Farewell to the Working Class', rejecting the traditional Marxist notion of a revolutionary class. The majority of workers had lost the capacity to change society because of the disabling impact of division of labour; at the same time, the paternalist (socialist) state could only increase their dependency. Liberation from the contradictions of a capitalism that created free time, but denied its use, could only be realised by a 'non-class of post-industrial proletarians' outside of the labour market and the state. These people, Gorz argued, would not sacrifice themselves for the socialist future; rather they would insist on an individualism freed from hierarchy, aggression, and competition. While 'heteronomy' in work could not be suppressed (indeed, it is the foundation of free-dom beyond work), it could be subordinated to 'autonomy' in free time. Gorz was, of course, not thinking of Dumazedier's individualist leisures, but of new forms of political participation and mutuality in production and consumption. This, Gorz insisted, was the final message of Marx, so long obscured by productivist ideas.[54]

The key was job sharing to make time available for new activities. Few advocates were sanguine that this could be achieved simply by across-the-board cuts in daily hours; Jenkins claimed that a 2 per cent reduction in worktime produced only a 1 per cent increase in jobs. And Gorz stressed the need for financial incentives for less productive sectors to reduce hours. All agreed that new social services were required to encourage 'local group culture' and to provide greater access to 'convivial tools'. Sometimes this thinking led to radical proposals: instead of 'waging' household work, Gorz suggested, let men and women join the abbreviated work world and then share in private domestic/family labour. Shorter and more flexible hours could even encourage greater involvement of employees in plant and office management in order to facilitate new work patterns. But all agreed with Jenkins that a 'concerted national decision to opt out of the consumer race' was a difficult necessity.[55]

NEW CULTURAL POLITICS AND BREAKING THE 40-HOUR BARRIER

The intellectual's discovery of the 'collapse of work' and call for self-managed time paralleled the emergence of new movements for non-commercial leisure and reduced worktime. All four trends challenged the claim that the market had successfully colonised everyday life.

The old debate about the distribution of productivity reappeared in the 1970s and 1980s. It was not merely a reaction to a generation of unbalanced consumerism; but it grew out of social movements that pointed away from commercial leisure and reflected pressures for reduced worktime. In a limited way the ideas of democratic leisure of the 1930s were revived after a generation of consumerism.

As early as 1958, Galbraith noted the emergence of a 'New Class' of professionals who preferred autonomous and limited work to status consumption. But it was the late 1960s that seemed to be a turning point. It was at this time, according to political scientist Ronald Inglehart, that a transnational 'postmaterialist' cohort began to emerge, especially in Europe. The gradual disappearance of those age groups which had been shaped by the economic insecurity of the Depression signalled a 'cultural shift' toward the post-scarcity values of the children of affluence. This transition meant also a decline of the traditional Left and a period of protracted political confusion. But it may lead yet to a more positive assessment of public and non-material 'goods' (environment, time, and cultural activities, for example). Eventually it may mean a redefinition of the 'boundaries of the political', shifting politics from questions of distribution, growth, and security (implicitly based on a privatised family and gender stereotypes) toward the issues and style of new, mostly European, social movements. These groups have been organised locally around uses of space and resources, sexual and ethnic identity, consumer rights, and greater participation in a new voluntary sector. At least implicit in these movements is the need for expanded time free from employment obligation, public authority, and the market. And often these movements are founded on new public roles for women.[56]

A related change is the erosion of the sexual division of labour of industrial society: many have described the decline of the fully employed/fully providing male worker and its mirror opposite, the homemaking/consuming female upon which depended the time/ money compromise of the 'normal' workweek. Not only has the household become less dependent upon the male's 'family wage', but married women have entered the workforce while men have been slowly leaving it. Labour-saving domestic machines and smaller families may have reduced the homemaker's worktime; but the need for income to cover increased costs for housing, transportation, and recreation probably contributed more to women's flight from domesticity.[57] This has not eliminated the household economy so much as complicated it: the decline of the homemaker has led to increased pressure for shorter worktime (or part-time jobs with benefits) for women, but also for men. It has also created a demand for new worktime arrangements in order to accommodate domestic needs. While adjusting to these schedules remains mostly the duty of women, increased time of wives in employment places moral pressures on husbands to contribute more in childcare and domestic work.[58]

Another complex trend is the emergence of an 'informal economy'. R. Pahl, C. Offe, and J. Gershuny have argued that technological change in the 1970s and 1980s has unexpectedly stimulated self-provisioning activities. Because of different rates of productivity, manufactured goods have become cheaper relative to services. Thus households have an incentive to purchase domestic 'capital goods' and to do their own domestic jobs and improvements (using vacuum cleaners and home workshops, for example). This phenomenon has reduced the marginal utility of income for those with good jobs and has increased interest in self-initiated domestic activities. Thus the demand for time free from wage work increases. As the trade-offs between household time and wage income shift, the time of men and women may be redivided between paid and unpaid work. Thus existing gender inequalities both in and outside the home may also decrease.[59]

These trends suggest a re-evaluation of this history of time and money. In particular, a cultural lag may explain the failure of democratic leisure in the interwar years. The survival of nineteenth-century cultural paternalism (in the political elites of the Left and Right) and the persistence of a scarcity mentality (common in all classes) blocked the formation of the 'culture society' advocated by Burns and Lagrange. But, as Inglehart and others suggest, the divisiveness of cultural elitists and the moral power of the work ethic began to be overcome after the mid-1960s. Classically trained humanists have lost influence and cultural educators have grown more sympathetic to popular arts, as Andrew Ross notes. This might indicate the possibility of new cross-class alliances built around the ideals of individual autonomy and postmaterialism. Finally, changing balances within the family and between wage work and household activity may lay a foundation for an expansion of autonomous activity. All of these trends point to the possibility of a new balance of free time and consumption.[60]

In fact, there is evidence that the ideals of democratic leisure have not been crushed by consumerism. Especially in Europe, there are increasing signs of non-commercial and active uses of free time in the 1970s and 1980s. Up to 39 per cent of Britons joined in participant sports in a 1977 survey. By 1980 in Britain, there were roughly 36,000 football clubs, and 50,000 other sporting clubs, as well as 1,000 local history libraries, 4,000 working men's clubs and 20,000 women's institute branches, to mention just a few examples of voluntary activities.[61] While a 1982 survey of leisure in Britain found 80 per cent engaging in gardening, and 25 per cent participating in non-sports clubs, only 14 per cent admitted to gambling. A mere 9 per cent undertook a second job. Do-it-yourself activities, a clear sign of self-provisioning familialism, increased sharply between 1959 and 1981 in Britain (rising from 55 to 81 per cent of men and from 48 to 60 per cent of women).[62]

Sociologists Jeff Bishop and Paul Hoggett found in the mid-1980s that people came together whenever they found the 'slightest opportunity for organisation'. Out of 85,000 living in a middle-class English community, some 28,500 adults joined groups organised around one 'enthusiasm' or another. Clubs existed for activities as varied as mouse fancying, caving, morris dancing, lace making and lapidary. They adapted to shifting leadership and widely diverse group cultures and activities. These clubs displayed 'almost perverse distinctiveness'; this encouraged comparison and allowed individuals to 'place themselves' in relation to others. But members also shared a 'mateyness' that often explicitly rejected the competition of trophy-seeking 'pot-hunters'. What they all had in common was a desire simultaneously to produce and consume something and to do it together. Clubs shared much with a lost 'informal economy'; but they also began only 'beyond need': 'It is precisely this freedom from economic measures, and from the trappings of the commercialised world of leisure, that attracts people into such groups, and enables them to consider what might seem to be work . . . as leisure.'

These activities, Bishop and Hoggett insisted, should not be understood as 'markets' to be served by manufacturers or governments but as social groups that deliberately stand outside the role of customer and constituent. Members of these clubs realised what the advocates of democratic leisure in the 1930s had been groping for – a non-market leisure that embraced the needs for identity and distinction outside the cycle of working-and-spending. Most important, these clubs suggest that the tension between free time and consumption has not been entirely effaced.[63]

Similarly French investigators have catalogued an explosion of social and cultural activities since the 1960s. While there were only 2,008 registered sports organisations in France in 1960, by 1982 there were 7,237. During the same period, cultural clubs increased even more dramatically from 600 to 4,116. An active cultural education policy, encouraged first by André Malraux's famous tenure as cultural minister, bore fruit in rising attendance at artistic and educational events. Weekly do-it-yourself activities of French men increased from 34 per cent to 41 per cent between 1967 and 1988.[64] While commercial tourism has attracted millions of Frenchmen (note the 1950 founding of 'Club Med'), non-profit groups like the Peuple et Culture and Fédération Léo-Lagrange revived the Popular Front ideas of social tourism and leisure. Especially since 1968, the old popular-education tradition has been revived by those 'animators' and volunteers who helped to organise and support cultural organisations (like regional centres of art and *maisons de la culture*). French promoters of popular arts and recreation may have sought to perpetuate loyalty to church or political party; but all stressed wide participation. Government facilities and educators have contributed to the growth of amateurism in music and the other arts. Recently French social scientist Henri Mendras has observed an increase in self-initiated social activities and, with them, a decline in the authority of political parties and churches.[65]

There is much less evidence of these trends in the US. Still, as sociologist Robert Stebbins has shown, the American amateur in sports and the arts provides a vital link between the professional and spectator. Although torn between play and the quest for professional standards, the amateur offers a non-market choice. And Americans continue to find a wide variety of ways through which to express themselves in hobbies, social service, politics, and neighbourhood activities that suggest that there is indeed life beyond the shopping mall.[66]

Even though seldom acknowledged, the cultural politics of the 1970s and 1980s had much in common with the ideas of democratic leisure. Contemporary authors, like Gorz and Roger Sue, share with Russell and others from the 1930s an abhorrence of 'spade socialism' and economic Malthusianism; they have affirmed the power of technology to deliver humanity from insecurity and necessity. Both generations rejected a conservative defence of existing jobs and technologies; instead, they argued that productivity should combine with new social policy to create both free time and goods – not simply turn time into money. Both groups agreed that new leisure required finding alternatives to market work – as ways of distributing wealth and of creating social cohesiveness. Both argued that slavish adherence to a work-and-spend ethic only promised deepening social divisions between the fully employed and the jobless and, for all, increasing frustration in a consumerism that can never fully satisfy. Both groups also recognised that free time could not cease to be anxiety-causing until people found ways of countering the 'Sunday Neuroses' of empty and passive time. Alternatives to consumption were needed to refute the belief that 'outside paid work there can be only inactivity and boredom'. The radical Gorz has advocated that free time could resurrect a 'private sphere' through individual and associated labour. This, he identified with the old cooperative and mutualist traditions of nineteenth-century socialism; but the idea of a 'private sphere' had also much in common with the hobbyists of the 1930s.[67]

Paralleling these trends away from consumerism was the rebirth of the short-hours movement, especially in Europe. This emerged, however, only after a generation of reversal. The French 40-hour standard was *en principe* restored in 1946. But, in order to win the battle of production, officials tolerated up to 20 hours of weekly overtime in industry. In fact, mean real workweeks increased from 45 hours in 1945 to 47.2 by 1963. But, beginning with the labour accord that followed the upheaval of May 1968, hours were gradually dropped to a 40-hour standard by 1980. French law lengthened paid holidays to three weeks in 1956, to four in 1962, and to five in 1982. The workyear had dropped by 10 per cent between 1974 and 1982; and worklife may have decreased by a third in 20 years, especially because of the trend toward early retirement.[68]

British conditions were somewhat more auspicious for hours reductions after the war. Still, between 1946 and 1948 trade-union negotiators abandoned their earlier goal of a 40-hour week and settled for a 44-hour norm. But, in a series of labour contracts between 1964 and 1970, nominal hours per week were generally reduced to 40 hours. However, because of the 'systematic' use of overtime in male-dominated trades, shorter holidays, and a later retirement age, Britain lost its role as European leader in providing its citizens with free time. By 1979, the workyear for British workers remained 2,030 hours; but the French level was only 1,834. In Denmark, it was only 1,498![69]

However, the most dramatic trend was the failure of the US to keep pace. While the American 40-hour week standard of 1938 remained exceptional until the 1960s, thereafter working hours did not drop while they did in Europe. Vacation rights of Americans scarcely improved while they were dramatically expanded in Europe. This is perhaps the most obvious effect of the failure of American social democracy. Indeed, as Juliet Schor has shown, Americans experienced a lengthening workyear in the 1970s and 1980s (by a month of work). There are a number of plausible explanations: stagnant mean family income, lacklustre productivity, a social order that emphasises disposable personal income rather than social entitlements, and the relative dominance of consumerism. In any case, a dramatically longer workyear in the US by 1989 was the result: Americans worked 1,989 hours as compared to 1,646 hours in France.[70]

Clearly Europeans led the movement for reductions of worktime in the 1970s and 1980s. Despite their success in reaching the 40-hour week standard by the end of the 1970s, Europeans wanted still more leisure time: surveys conducted in 1977 and 1982 revealed slight preferences for more time over higher wages (even though reduced daily hours were less favoured than early retirement, longer holidays, and other packages of free time).[71] Nevertheless, there was no articulate public demand for a policy that sacrificed consumption for free time. It is not then surprising that the new hours movement had traditional origins in the labour movement and its concern with unemployment.

As early as 1957, growing fears of automation led labour leaders in Europe and the US to argue once again for a linkage of the new technology to work sharing (and increased leisure). Locals of the American auto-workers' union, for example, resurrected the old demand for the 30-hour week in the late 1950s and the AFL-CIO endorsed the 35-hour week in 1961.[72] But it took increased joblessness following the 1973 oil crisis and the growing impotence of Keynesian policies to make work sharing again a popular option.[73]

Calls for job sharing and flexitime (as opposed to the more extensive notion of work sharing) had somewhat different origins. These proposals often involved pay decreases along with reduced hours when eight-hour jobs were divided between two people. New work schedules were sometimes more beneficial to management than to employees. Even when union members favoured flexible hours (especially where women predominated and problems of coordinating family and work time loomed especially large), varied schedules undermined collective bargaining and diverted attention from work-sharing proposals which were designed to create jobs. Still these ideas often overlapped with those of work sharing.[74]

In 1979, the European Trade Union Confederation proposed the reduction of the workweek by 10 per cent, a six-week paid holiday, and an option of retiring at 60 years of age. John Conyers even introduced a 35-hour week bill in the US House of Representatives following renewed trade-union interest.[75] In 1981, the new French socialist government proposed a gradual introduction of a thirty-five hour week and, in 1984, German metalworkers struck for the same goal. Others, like Frank Cousins of the British TUC, called for a 1,000 hour workyear to be phased in by the year 2000 with great flexibility as to how it would be allocated between reduced workdays and weeks, increased vacations and sabbaticals, and early retirement.[76]

In 1983, Yves Barou and Jacques Rigaudial recognised the need for avoiding the destructive political confrontation between business critics and cultural advocates of free time that had hampered earlier short-hour movements. They, like H. M. Vernon and other reformers of the 1930s, insisted that reductions must be accompanied by better utilisation of capital (for example, in shift work and staggered vacations).[77]

But economists offered contradictory forecasts as to the effects of reduced worktime on prices, employment, and productivity. Expectations that the 35-hour week would solve the unemployment problem proved disappointing in France after the official workweek dropped to 39 hours in 1982; fears that further reductions would hurt France's position in the world market led to the reversal of plans to lower hours to 35 by 1985.[78] Although British engineers won a 39-hour week in 1979, their goal of a 35-hour standard failed, as did attempts to reduce systematic overtime. The efforts of British unions to win flexible hours and work sharing met with a stone wall of opposition led by the Thatcher regime. The Reagan years were equally discouraging to American short-hour advocates. Particularly troublesome was the lack of a unified front on how to distribute free time and the apparent unwillingness of waged workers to sacrifice income for the 'greater' good of work sharing. Even more problematic, however, was the old difficulty, the unwillingness of employers to accept the costs of work sharing in the face of increased international competition. In the late 1980s, the idea of 'chosen time' degenerated into employer-imposed temporary and shift work (sometimes offered as an alternative to lay-offs); and these schedules often disrupted family and social life. In 1991, a group of sociologists concluded that there was no evidence of a 'clear and strong secular trend' for leisure instead of income.[79] Still this attitude is hard to isolate from the context of negative economic and political pressures against free time. Moreover European trade unions continue to press for a 35-hour standard. The jury is definitely still out on the fate of the recent short-hours movement.[80]

TIME, MONEY, AND HISTORICAL LEGACY

The question remains: do events and trends emerging since 1945 force us to modify the conclusion that time has been subsumed by money? The post-scarcity ideas of the time option had origins in the early years of mass productivity; but have they been defeated or merely postponed? A generation of depression and war followed by another two or three decades of mass consumerism nearly killed these aspirations; and persistent misunderstandings between cultural elites and the consuming public has exacerbated these problems. But have those complex economic and cultural changes which emerged from the 1960s set the stage for, at least, a revival of a meaningful debate about time and money?

Based on the historical legacy, there are many reasons to be doubtful, especially in the US. The same business interests that opposed the principle of a progressive diminution of work in the interwar period reappeared in the 1980s. Shorter hours would give a competitive advantage to any nation or firm that did not join the movement. A European parliament might partially resolve this problem by instituting an hours standard. But, as has been shown in the arms race, only the capitulation of the Soviet side has led to any serious movement to reducing nuclear arsenals. Will the economic race produce greater cooperation? Anne Lapping's surveys of employers in the early 1980s found no one willing to 'experiment' with time-reduction benefits. The apparent decline of fortress capitalism with the end of the Cold War may open space in national politics for the expansion of choice between time and money; but the old theme of military competition and national security may well be simply replaced by appeals to economic competition and national efficiency. Stagnation in the US may give rise to anti-consumption sentiment; but that feeling may well be directed toward the goals of harder work and capital formation rather than more free time. International economic 'disarmament' remains essential to meaningful change even if that is almost unimaginable without the strengthening of international institutions and much more serious commitment to postmaterialism.[81]

The question remains how such commitments would emerge. The 'poverty of desire' beyond the 'comforts' of consumption is surely a basic problem. In this century, cultural critics have vacillated between blaming this poverty upon manipulating merchandisers, deskilled work, or, more abstractly, an 'instrumental reason' that produces goods, but turns time into money. However, as recent scholars have shown, all of this ignores the subtle attractions of the shop. The market has penetrated free time and channelled social space into domesticity and the lonely and segmented 'crowd'. But few consumers really object. Free time and spending are easily reconciled in the cosiness of domestic consumption and dreams of holiday spending. The dominance of the market over the language of liberty and, in the twentieth century, the hegemony of mass distribution over the discourse of democracy, has long been a frustration to advocates of a popular public culture. Fears that the masses would become victims of either totalitarian bureaucracy or monopoly capital appear to be exaggerated now that party states have collapsed and Fordist mass-consumer economies have declined. But the *ideals* of market 'freedom' and consumer 'democracy' everywhere have been in ascendance since the 1980s. Some might suggest that cultural critics should abandon their Rousseauean quest for a community not dominated by goods, and exchange it for the market where discipline and freedom each play their appropriate role in creating a community of interest and choice.

But is the market bound to prevail over everything else? Advocates of the time option have usually protested that they too reject the asceticism and authoritarianism of the republic of limited needs; but they have not been able to convince the people that their social model could go beyond divisiveness and bring real joy. Democratic leisure proponents recognised, as did the impresarios of pleasure, that the 'masses' were really families, young, old, male and female, and, despite their longing for certainties and belonging, that they were basically secular. People wanted pleasure without commitment to past or future. They were attracted to festivals freed from rituals of time and place. But democratic leisure advocates could not deliver the goods. Groups like the Holiday Fellowship declined after the 1930s when their animators aged; youth clubs faced the constant ambiguity of being controlled by adults. Is there any reason to believe that new social movements will be any more successful? Ironically, cultural groups may be less flexible than markets in adjusting to change because of their democratic participatory ethic. When groups are dominated by their participants, they easily exclude others or become fractionalised. How much easier is the task of merchandisers who stand outside the markets they organise!

The failure of communism is a good example of the relative success of market 'indirection'. Not only could a command economy not find a mechanism to induce sacrifice that was not nakedly coercive, but the communist elite could not serve as a model of consumerist emulation without appearing to be 'privileged'. In these essential ways, capitalism was vastly superior: markets could provide both labour and consumer discipline without necessarily appearing authoritarian or unfair. As Simmel noted, consumer choice frees us all from personal dependence and limited options. And, if markets make us into strangers, there is much to say for gazing from within the teeming crowd. Merchandising has disassociated cultural elements and repackaged them in the Blackpools and suburbs of modern marketing. The anthropology of consumption shows that mass consumption allows the fulfilment of contradictory longings, the wearing of many roles, and endless experimenting – even if experiences are manufactured to meet consumer expectations and business profitability. It was utopian for advocates of democratic leisure to imply that free time ever could be entirely beyond the market.[82]

Diversity of choice, of course, was central to the movement for democratic leisure in the 1930s just as it was to French cultural animators and to those cultural programmers who worked for the Greater London Council in the early 1980s. But one person's self-expression is another's perversion; and thus public support for organising free-time activities is often weak. Business and conservative control of the financing and regulation of leisure services continue to be useful means of channelling pleasure into 'permissible' arenas, largely dominated by the market. In any case, non-profit cultural groups have had notoriously little control over either public space or time.

But the imbalance between the cultural animator, and the impresario or merchandiser is not the only factor in the power of the goods: the discipline of the market impedes the emergence of choice. It is not that I am 'compelled' to define my freedom in the purchase of a new car but I may well be obliged to work longer hours than I would choose in order to make it possible for a real-estate agent to buy that luxury automobile if I want to buy a house. As Juliet Schor notes:

> consumerism traps us as we become habituated to the good life, emulate our neighbors, or just get caught up in the social pressures created by everyone else's choices. Work-and-spend has become a mutually reinforcing and powerful syndrome – a seamless web we somehow keep choosing, without even meaning to.[83]

Consumerism may well be a trap. But with the failure of Soviet Stakhanovism and apparently of technocracy, the only obvious economic order consistent with productivity and individuality is a market. The live question is whether this must be accompanied with extremes of wealth and poverty which fuel consumerist emulation and the commodification of free time. The fact that intellectuals attack abundance while the corporate world embraces it has been a tragic, if explicable, diversion: humanists may be correct that the *real* ideology of capitalism is heedless hedonism, but they have done little to help people sort through their own complex situation or to achieve a balance of goods and time. The great difficulty has been to create alternative forms of individuality and community in leisure time. Clearly the task of creating conditions for personal and social expression relatively unmediated by goods is hard work even if all insist that it should also be play.

Part of the task, Australian Donald Horne suggests, is to counter the jobs and growth utopia with a new 'myth' of a 'full employment policy of the self': this would require going beyond work-dependent access to the storehouse of mass productivity and necessitate winning public support for a declaration of 'cultural rights'. This policy would mean mobilising the social and psychological resources necessary for concrete alternatives to the comfort of goods. But where would this new myth or utopia come from and who would organise free time? The old culture of solidarity and respectability rose from the people, even though it was articulated by cultured elites. A new myth would require a similar alliance and also be based on faith in the possibility of improvement.[84]

But again where is the basis of such a coalition and optimism? Surely we will not find it in the Marxist expectation of a revolutionary class emerging out of the industrial division of labour. Heteronomy at work can hardly not affect free time; a rationality of economic maximisation can not be taken off like a business suit before dinner for a rationality of self-constraint and spiritual fulfilment. Unfortunately that progressivist coalition cannot be found in the boulevard crowd of popular culture. There, people may protest but they cannot organise against the humiliations of consumerist emulation or the promethean obsessions of modernity. The question remains: when a functional language of belonging does not exist, Michael Ignatieff asks, can people even feel the need for fellowship?[85]

And, where are the intellectuals who could adapt the 'people's language' to the idea of a community even partially outside the realm of the market and state? Humanistic populists of the past are marginalised in secular capitalist society; and their language of 'nostalgia, fear, and estrangement from modernity' is increasingly irrelevant to postmodernist diversity. Advocates of the time option lack the focused constituencies of the 'special interests' of business and single-issue political groups. The 'critical culture' has become increasingly isolated in esoteric irrelevance – even as its members claim to 'learn from Las Vegas'. And that isolation is self-imposed.[86]

The real elite remains the fashion leaders in the media and in merchandising; they understand that belonging has little to do with the nostalgia (or nirvana) all too often sought by intellectuals. These trendsetters realise that community is transient and driven by insatiable change even as consumers express a desire for stability. And the political Right has, and may continue to have, more success in mobilising the quest for privacy in appeals to unfettered economic self-interest and in dividing competing groups over mutual fears.[87]

A key to the transformation of the jobs and growth culture is a realignment of gender. But the decline of Fordism may lead only to a new inequality: the dual-/high-income family with resources to engage in a diverse life of self-provisioning and postmaterialism may simply coexist with the unskilled, often jobless, and single-parent family, for whom free time remains empty and passive. Instead of a more balanced life, new technology may well only accelerate the turnover time of production and sales – and thus increase the intensity and anxiety of work.[88] Demands for profit may simply dictate a temporary and part-time workforce to accommodate the segmentation of the market rather than 'chosen time'. Even job sharing and disengagement from market work may not transform the sexual division of labour. Self-managed time may only reinforce the status quo; it may lead women to adjust wage and domestic worktime to minimise disruptions in their 'traditional' domestic and family obligations rather than create symmetry between men and women's roles.[89] A revitalisation of the 'private sphere' may continue to be blocked by the prevailing 'male career model' of work. This model, when transferred to the new economy, may simply lead to new social divisions between middle-class women: careerist females, by adopting that model, may come to rely on service labour for domestic needs. Other privileged women may reject the male career pattern, and, because of their superior family resources, may be able to choose to remain at home. Meanwhile women in disadvantaged families may simply be simultaneously overworked and underwaged.[90]

These pessimistic assessments are largely drawn from the experience of this century. But is there not an optimistic side to that history? Hobson may be correct that the democratisation of goods (if really realised) might undercut the emulative dynamic of consumerism and finally eliminate the scarcity mentality that dominates even the apparently affluent. Perhaps Russell is right that expanded leisure time will create sufficient freedom from alienating work to set the stage for a new civil society partially beyond the marketplace. This gradual change might lead to the social foundations for democratic/postmaterialist politics. Even more encouraging, mutualist groups have learned something about the need to address demands for participation beyond consumption; they have gained some experience in confronting those complex dynamics of individual distinction and social identity that commodity culture so well satisfies. They could learn even more if they studied the ways in which consumerism expresses people's longings for diverse meanings of time. Evidence that a majority would desire alternatives to the 'work-and-spend' culture should also inspire some hope.[91]

Solutions may be piecemeal and cumulative: carving out cultural choice in the arduous struggle to expand public support for local arts and sports programmes; winning more rigorous regulation of advertising and product development; finding ways of helping people to read the meanings of goods; turning a flexitime designed to maximise profit into time management that facilitates a blossoming of personal autonomy; and winning political consensus around solutions to the problems of families who are overstretched with job and domestic obligations. There are a number of innovations that are relatively simple to implement: wider use of compensatory time off the job rather than paid bonuses for overtime work; increased benefits for 'part-time' workers, and shorter hours in place of *future* wage increases.[92]

But in order to convince anyone that freedom and democracy are not coterminous with the market and that leisure has a value beyond its price, intellectuals must do more than alternatively condemn or embrace those whose lives are consumed by working and shopping. They need to understand why consumerism works and yet how its 'comforts' frustrate and are but poor substitutes for social solidarity and self-expression. Less dependence on goods might free us from heteronomy at work and manipulation at play. It should also help overcome ecological waste and danger. But intellectuals must join with the people in finding a language and a practice that expresses this alternative. This has not happened yet. It may not happen in the future. But then again it might.

Notes

1 MODERN DILEMMAS OF TIME AND MONEY

1 Mary Ferguson, a Washington DC area mother, interviewed in the *Washington Post* (12 May 1991), p. A18. See also John Robinson, 'The Time Squeeze', *American Demographics* 12 (February 1990), pp. 30–3.

2 Nicholas Xenos, *Scarcity and Modernity* (London, 1989), chs 1, 4, and conclusion; Fred Hirsch, *The Social Limits of Growth* (Cambridge MA, 1976), chs 1 and 6; and Carmen Sirianni, 'The Self-Management of Time in Postindustrial Society', in Karl Hinrichs, William Roche, and Carmen Sirianni, eds, *Working Time in Transition*, (Philadelphia, 1991), pp. 240–5.

3 S. Linder, *The Harried Leisure Class* (New York, 1970); Hirsch, *Social Limits*, ch. 5; David Harvey, *The Condition of Postmodernity* (London, 1989), chs 16 and 17; and Echange et Projets, *La Révolution du temps choisi* (Paris, 1981), ch. 1.

4 Juliet Schor, *The Overworked American: The Unexpected Decline of Leisure in America* (New York, 1991), ch. 2 details the popular media treatment of the time squeeze. Her calculations of the 'extra month' translate into 163 hours and are based on annual government employment data, excluding part-time and jobless workers. If the entire population were included, the increase in total worktime per year would still be 47 hours. Schor estimates that women have borne the major brunt of this increase in paid work (305 extra hours as compared to the 98 hours for men) even though when housework is included the increased burden is almost equal. The estimate is nearly the same if only paid employment is counted or if household labour is also included. She attributes the recent growth of worktime not only to the expansion of married women's employment (rising from 40 per cent to two thirds between 1970 and 1990), but to real declines in vacations, increases in overtime, and rising rates of child and youth employment due to weaker unions and increased economic competition. See pp. 24–38. However, demographer John Robinson finds a continued expansion of free time based on surveys that include the growing numbers of early retired and older workers who enjoy considerably more leisure than do the younger workforce. See John

Robinson, 'Time's Up' and 'Who's Doing the Housework', *American Demographics* (July 1989), pp. 32–5 and (December 1988), pp. 26–8.

5 Pioneer sociological treatments of this phenomenon are in Robert and Rhona Rapoport, *Dual-Career Families* (Harmondsworth, 1971) and the sequel, *Dual-Career Families Re-examined* (London, 1976). American analyses include J. Hunt and L. Hunt, 'The Dualities of Careers and Families: New Integrations or New Polarizations', *Social Problems* 29 (June 1982), pp. 499–510; Shelley Coverman, 'Gender, Domestic Labor Time, and Wage Inequality', *American Sociological Review* 48 (October 1983), pp. 623–37; Cynthia Rexroat and Constance Shehan, 'The Family Life Cycle and Spouses' Time in Housework', *Journal of Marriage and the Family* 49 (November 1987) pp. 737–50; and Arlie Hochschild, *The Second Shift: Working Parents and the Revolution at Home* (New York, 1989), pp. 1–11, 159–72, and 271–8. See also Schor, *Overworked American*, pp. 34–8 and ch. 4.

6 Michael Ignatieff, *The Needs of Strangers. An Essay on Privacy, Solidarity, and the Politics of Being Human* (New York, 1985) explores the sources of our inability to articulate social needs.

7 I am referring to Francis Fukuyama's 'The End of History?' *National Interest* 16 (Summer 1989), pp. 3–18 and his *The End of History and the Last Man* (London, 1992); as well as Daniel Bell's, *The End of Ideology: On the Exhaustion of Political Ideas in the Fifties* (Glencoe IL, 1960).

8 Simon Schama, *The Embarrassment of Riches, An Interpretation of Dutch Culture in the Golden Age* (New York, 1987); Neil McKendrick, John Brew, and J. H. Plumb, *The Birth of Consumer Society, The Commercialization of Eighteenth-Century England* (Bloomington IN, 1982); Michael Miller, *The Bon Marché: Bourgeois Culture and the Department Store, 1869–1920* (Princeton NJ, 1981); Rosalind Williams, *Dream Worlds: Mass Consumption in Late Nineteenth-Century France* (Berkeley CA, 1982); and Richard Wightman Fox and T. J. Jackson Lears, eds, *The Culture of Consumption, Critical Essays in American History, 1880–1980* (New York, 1983).

9 A classic is Richard Hoggart, *The Uses of Literacy* (London, 1957). Good brief critical histories of this literature are essays by Richard Butsch, 'Leisure and Hegemony in America', and John Clarke, 'Pessimism versus Populism: The Problematic Politics of Popular Culture', in Richard Butsch, ed., *For Fun and Profit: The Transformation of Leisure into Consumption* (Philadelphia, 1990), pp. 3–27, 28–46; Chas Critcher and John Clarke, *The Devil Makes Work. Leisure in Capitalist Britain* (Urbana IL, 1985), especially ch. 6; Tony Bennett, 'The Politics of "the Popular" and Popular Culture', in Tony Bennett, G. Martin, Colin Mercer, and Janet Woollacoott, eds, *Popular Culture and Social Relations* (Milton Keynes, 1986), pp. 6–20; Michael Denning, 'End of Mass Culture', *International Labor and Working-Class History* 37 (Spring 1990), pp. 5–17; and M. Debouzy, 'De la production à la réception de la culture', *Mouvement social* 152 (1990): pp. 33–45.

10 G. Stedman Jones, *Languages of Class* (London, 1983), pp. 86–7; Richard Johnson, 'Culture and the Historians', in John Clarke, Chas

Critcher, and Richard Johnson, eds, *Working-Class Culture: Studies in History and Theory* (New York, 1979), pp. 75–102.

11 Major contributions to this substantial literature have been British and focus on the nineteenth century. These include: Peter Bailey, *Leisure and Class in Victorian England: Rational Recreation and the Contest for Control, 1830–1885* (London, 1978); R. W. Malcomson, *Popular Recreations in English Society, 1700–1850* (Cambridge, 1973); and Eileen and Steven Yeo, eds, *Popular Culture and Class Conflict, 1590–1914* (Brighton, 1981). Among the useful American histories are: Michael Denning, *Mechanical Accents: Dime Novels and Working-Class Culture in America* (New York, 1987); Lawrence Levine, *Highbrow Lowbrow. The Emergence of Cultural Hierarchy in America* (Cambridge MA, 1988); Kathy Peiss, *Cheap Amusements: Working Women and Leisure in Turn-of-the-Century New York* (Philadelphia, 1986); Roy Rosenzweig, *Eight Hours for What We Will: Workers and Leisure in an Industrial City, 1870–1920* (New York, 1983); John Kasson, *Amusing the Million* (New York, 1978); and Lewis Erenberg, *Steppin' Out: New York Nightlife and the Transformation of American Culture, 1890–1930* (Westport CT, 1981). French sources include: Adeline Daumard, *Oisiviété et loisirs dans les sociétés occidentales au xixe siècle* (Amiens, 1983); and André Rauch, *Vacances et pratiques corporelles* (Paris, 1988). A valuable analysis of French consumer cooperatives as reactions to capitalist consumerism is in Ellen Furlough, *Consumer Cooperation in France: The Politics of Consumption, 1834–1930* (Ithaca NY, 1991).

12 I borrow this term from Schor, *Overworked American*.

13 National Bureau of Economic Research, *Recent Economic Changes in the United States*, vol. 2 (New York, 1929), pp. 625–6. See also Martha Olney, *Buy Now, Pay Later: Advertising, Credit, and Consumer Durables in the 1920s* (Chapel Hill NC, 1991), ch. 3.

14 David Potter, *People of Plenty* (Chicago, 1954). European infatuation with American productivity is expressed in Bertram Austin and W. F. Lloyd, *The Secret of High Wages* (London, 1926) and Hyacinthe Dubreuil, *Standards* (Paris, 1929; New York, 1929), translated as *Robots or Men?*, trans. B. Grasset (New York, 1930).

15 Marshall Berman stresses the twentieth-century origins of the rigid division between developmental optimism and the cultural jeremiad. I argue that this dichotomy did not gel until the mid-twentieth century and that the debate over time and money was central to this conflict. Marshall Berman, *All that is Solid Melts into Air* (London, 1982), pp. 17–30.

16 For the best analysis of this see, M. A. Bienefeld, *Working Hours in British Industry, An Economic History* (London, 1972), pp. 145–8, 162–78, 193, and 197.

17 Thomas Hine, *Populuxe* (New York, 1986), ch. 2.

18 Mary Douglas and Baron Isherwood, *The World of Goods* (New York, 1979), pp. 90–1.

19 For example, note the influential B. Rosenberg and D. White, eds, *Mass Leisure* (New York, 1967). A good discussion of this literature

is in Andrew Ross, *No Respect. Intellectuals and Popular Culture* (London, 1989), chs 1, 2 and 4 especially.

20 This literature, often loosely identified with postmodernism or anthropological approaches to the history of consumption, is immense and growing. Some examples are Colin Campbell, *The Romantic Ethic and the Spirit of Modern Consumerism* (London, 1989); Grant McCracken, *Culture and Consumption: New Approaches to the Symbolic Character of Consumer Goods and Activities* (Bloomington IN, 1988); Elizabeth Wilson, *Adorned in Dreams. Fashion and Modernity* (London, 1985); Chandra Mukerji, *From Graven Images. Patterns of Modern Materialism* (New York, 1983); Douglas and Isherwood, *The World of Goods*; Marshall Sahlins, *Culture and Practical Reason* (Chicago, 1978), ch. 5; Arjun Appadurai, ed., *The Social Life of Things* (Cambridge, 1986), ch. 1; G. Poujol and R. Labourie, eds, *Les Cultures populaires* (Toulouse, 1979); N. Gérôme, 'L'Ethnologie, la "culture de masse", et les ouvriers: fragments d'une perspective', *Mouvement social* 152 (1990), pp. 53–6; O. Schwartz, *Le Monde privé des ouvriers. Hommes et femmes du Nord* (Paris, 1990); and Michel Verret, *La Culture ouvrière* (Saint-Sebastien, 1988). Note especially Daniel Miller, *Material Culture and Mass Consumption* (Oxford, 1987).

21 For elaboration of the Kulturgesellschaft see Peter Glotz, *Manifest fuer eine neue europaeische Linke* (Berlin, 1985), pp. 54 and 92; and André Gorz, *A Critique of Economic Reason* (London, 1989), pp. 93, 183, and 196.

2 THE MODERN MORAL ECONOMY OF NEEDS

1 David Lloyd-George, Public Records Office, CAB 23–8, meeting of cabinet, 6 December 1919, cited in Keith Middlemas, *Politics in Industrial Society*, ed. Royal Economic Society (London, 1979), pp. 142–3; J. M. Keynes, *The Economic Consequences of the Peace*, in *Collected Writings*, vol. II (London, 1971), pp. 11–13; and R. H. Tawney, *The Acquisitive Society* (London, 1920), pp. 139–40.

2 David Potter, *People of Plenty* (Chicago, 1954); and Michael Schudson, *Advertising the Uneasy Persuasion* (New York, 1984), pp. 180–5. European infatuation with American productivity is evident in Bertram Austin and W. F. Lloyd, *The Secret of High Wages* (London, 1926); Julius Hirsch, *Das Amerikanische Wirkschaftswunder* (Berlin, 1926); André Siegfried, *America aujourd'hui* (Paris, 1927); and Hyacinthe Dubreuil, *Standards* (Paris, 1929), translated as *Robots or Men?*, trans. B. Grasset (New York, 1930).

3 John Hammond, *The Growth of the Common Enjoyment* (London, 1933).

4 John Edgerton, 'Forty-Hour Week', *Pocket Bulletin* 27 (3 October 1926), pp. 2–12, cited in Benjamin Hunnicutt, *Work Without End: Abandoning Shorter Hours for the Right to Work* (Philadelphia, 1988), p. 40.

5 This thesis was first and most fully developed in E. A. Furniss, *The Position of Labor in a System of Nationalism* (New York, 1919), especially pp. 118, 120–54, and 233–335. For the pre-classical economic

theorists who insisted that workers preferred leisure to income and thus that subsistence wages alone would assure an adequate level of production, see Arthur Young, *Northern Tour* (London, 1770), pp. 289–91; Josiah Child, *New Discourse* (London, 1693), Preface; William Petty, *Political Arithmetic* (London, 1755), p. 132; and Nicholas Edmund Restif de la Bretonne, *Les Nuits de Paris* (1739; Paris, 1963).

6 Not only did Bernard Mandeville's notorious *The Fable of the Bees, or, Private Vices, Publick Benefits* present a case for the economic benefits of luxury but Smith, Hume, and Voltaire largely supported these views. See Thomas Horne, *The Social Theory of Bernard Mandeville: Virtue and Commerce in Early Eighteenth Century England* (New York, 1978), chs 1 and 5 especially; and Gordon Vichert, 'The Theory of Conspicuous Consumption in the 18th Century', in Peter Hughes and David Williams, eds, *The Varied Pattern: Studies in the 18th Century* (Toronto, 1971), pp. 253–67.

7 J. J. Rousseau, *The First and Second Discourses* (New York, 1986), pp. 4–5, 175, 180–1; David Hume, *Treatise on Human Nature* (Oxford, 1978), pp. 357–65; and Adam Smith, *The Theory of Moral Sentiments* (Oxford, 1976), pp. 182–3. See also Nicholas Xenos, *Scarcity and Modernity* (London, 1989), pp. 3–22; Patricia Springborg, *The Problem of Human Need and the Critique of Civilization* (London, 1981), pp. 37, 38, 46–50, and ch. 5; Michael Ignatieff, *The Needs of Strangers* (New York, 1985), p. 21, chs 3 and 4; and Joyce Appleby, *Economic Thought and Ideology in Seventeenth-Century England* (Princeton NJ, 1978), especially ch. 7.

8 Benjamin Franklin, *Autobiography* (New York, 1932), pp. vii, 93–5 especially; A. Daumard, *Oisiveté et loisirs dans les sociétés occidentales au xixe siècle* (Amiens, 1983), pp. 9–21; and Philip Scranton, *Proprietary Capitalism* (New York, 1982).

9 J. S. Mill, *Principles of Political Economy* (1848; Toronto, 1965), pp. 753–96 and *Essays on Politics and Culture*, ed. Gertrude Himmelfarb (Gloucester MA, 1973), pp. 257–64. See also Graeme Duncan, *Marx and Mill* (Cambridge, 1973), ch. 7.

10 Karl Marx, *Grundrisse* (Harmondsworth, 1973), pp. 521, 611, and 706. See also Xenos, *Scarcity*, pp. 49–53, and 64; and Springborg, *Human Need*, pp. 4–5 and 95. For additional background, see Agnes Heller, *The Theory of Need in Marx* (London, 1976); and G. S. Cohen, *Karl Marx's Theory of History: A Defense* (Princeton NJ, 1978), especially pp. 306–7.

11 Edward Bellamy, *Looking Backward, 2000–1887* (1887; repr. New York, n.d.), pp. 158–60.

12 John Ruskin, *Unto This Last and Other Writings*, ed. Clive Wilmer (Harmondsworth, 1985), p. 158. See also James C. Sherburne, *John Ruskin, or The Ambiguities of Abundance: A Study in Social and Economic Criticism* (Cambridge MA, 1982); Paul Lafargue, *The Right to Be Lazy*, trans. Charles Kerr (1907; Chicago, 1989).

13 Anatole Leroy-Beaulieu, 'Le Règne de l'argent' *Revue des deux mondes* (1894), pp. 721–42; Louis Weber, *Le Rythme du progrès* (Paris, 1913); Emile Durkheim, *Formes elementaires de la vie religieuse* (Paris, 1912), pp. 323–30; Charles Booth, *Life and Labour of the People of London*

(Edinburgh, 1889); and Benjamin Seebohm Rowntree, *Poverty, A Study of Town Life* (London, 1902). I rely especially on Rosalind Williams, *Dream Worlds: Mass Consumption in Late Nineteenth-Century France* (Berkeley CA, 1982), pp. 298–333.

14 Thorstein Veblen, *The Theory of the Leisure Class* (New York, 1953), especially pp. 70–1, chs. 2, 13 and 14; and *Instinct of Workmanship* (New York, 1964), pp. 318–20. See also Daniel Horowitz, 'Consumption and its Discontents', *Journal of American History* 67 (September 1980), pp. 307–10.

15 Charlotte Perkins Gilman, *Women and Economics* (New York, 1898); and Lafargue, *Right to Be Lazy*, pp. 42–60.

16 See James Gilbert, *Work Without Salvation. America's Intellectuals and Industrial Alienation, 1880–1910* (Baltimore MD, 1977); and Daniel Rogers, *The Work Ethic in America* (Chicago, 1978).

17 Play and work were not antithetical in Patten's mind. Simon Patten, *A New Basis of Civilization* (New York, 1907, repr. 1968), pp. 211–15, 128, 138, 140, and 143. See also Simon Patten, *The Consumption of Wealth* (Philadelphia, 1889), p. 24 and *Production and Climax* (New York, 1909), p. 52. Note also the popularisation of abundance theory by Walter Weyl, *The New Democracy* (New York, 1912). Other sources include: Daniel Fox, *The Discovery of Abundance: Simon N. Patten and the Transformation of Social Theory* (Ithaca NY, 1967), especially pp. 47–55, 69–75, 155–65 and his introduction to the 1968 edition to Patten's *A New Basis of Civilization*; and Horowitz, 'Consumption', pp. 304–6.

18 See Ellen Furlough, *Consumer Cooperation in France: The Politics of Consumption, 1834–1930* (Ithaca NY, 1991), pp. 83–93 for Gide's role in the French cooperative movement.

19 Charles Gide, *Les Sociétés coopératives de consommation* (Paris, 1910), pp. 264–76 and *Principes d'économie politique* (Paris, 1921), translated as *Principles of Political Economy*, trans. E. F. Row (New York, 1924) pp. 482–91 and 495–501, quotation from p. 501. For further interpretation, see Williams, *Dream Worlds*, especially pp. 78–82 and 268–83.

20 Jean Gabriel Tarde, *Laws of Imitation* (1890; repr. New York, 1903), pp. 239 and 322–44; Tarde, *La Psychologie économique*, vol. 2 (Paris, 1902), pp. 151–6, 256, and 264; and Tarde, *Fragment d'histoire future* (Paris, 1904), pp. 74, 81, and 96. For an excellent analysis of Tarde, see Williams, *Dream Worlds*, pp. 350–84.

21 John Hobson, *Work and Wealth* (London, 1914), pp. 298–9, 117–18, and 121–7.

22 Marshall not only reflected Mill's optimism about the moral benefits of abundance but embraced the traditional philosophical distinction between activity and appetite: Alfred Marshall, *Principles of Economics* (London, 1920), pp. 87–9 and 689–90.

23 For an illuminating discussion, see Williams, *Dream Worlds*, pp. 48–9 and 247–59. Note also Gary Cross, *Quest for Time: The Reduction of Work in Britain and France, 1840–1940* (Berkeley CA, 1989), ch. 8.

24 Veblen, *Leisure Class*, ch. 13 and *Instinct of Workmanship*, pp. 318–20.

25 For a definitive analysis, see David Riesman, *Thorstein Veblen, A Critical Interpretation* (New York, 1953), pp. 170–208 especially.

26 Lorine Pruette, *Women and Leisure. A Study of Social Waste* (New York, 1924), Preface, pp. 1–16, and ch. 5; and Christine Frederick, *Household Engineering* (New York, 1920), p. 8.

27 Horowitz, 'Consumption', p. 307. See also Gilbert, *Work Without Salvation*, pp. 48 and 59.

28 Hobson, *Work and Wealth*, pp. 301, 237.

29 Alfred Marshall, *Future of the Working Class* (London, 1873), pp. 9–12; *Principles*, p. 694. Like his nineteenth-century predecessors, Marshall held hope only for the young who were as yet uncorrupted by 'mechanical toil' and who still had access to 'play as [can] strengthen and develop the character'. And, like other Victorians, Marshall saw a connection between 'good citizens' and the presence of parents in the home, free from long, if not necessarily exhausting, work. Marshall, *Principles*, pp. 720–1. See also Cross, *Quest*, ch. 2.

30 George Gunton, *Wealth and Progress* (New York, 1887), pp. 4–5, 11, 21–32, 84, 88, 212, 232–48, and 260–6; and *Principles of Social Economics* (New York, 1891), especially pp. 22–4 and 213–14.

31 Lujo Brentano, *Hours and Wages in Relation to Production* (London, 1894), especially ch. 1. For further analysis, see Daniel Horowitz, *The Morality of Spending: Attitudes Toward Consumer Society in America, 1875–1940* (Baltimore MD, 1985), ch. 3.

32 A good survey of marginalist economic theory is Alon Kadish, *The Oxford Economists in the Late Nineteenth Century* (Oxford, 1982).

33 Xenos, *Scarcity*, pp. 78–80 and Fred Hirsch, *Social Limits to Growth* (Cambridge MA, 1976), ch. 1. Note also the famous Ernest Engel, *Productions und Konsumptionsverhaltnesse des Koenigreichs Sachsen* (Berlin, 1857).

34 W. Stanley Jevons, *The Theory of Political Economy* (London, 1871), pp. 175–6. See also Chris Nyland, *Reduced Worktime and the Management of Production* (Cambridge, 1989), pp. 16–29. This notion, of course, conformed with pre-classical theory that work effort could be maintained only if wages were kept low. The classic discussion is Furniss, *System of Nationalism*, especially pp. 118, 120–54, and 233–335.

35 J. M. Keynes, *Essays in Persuasion* (London, 1931), pp. 365–73; Fred Hirsch, *Social Limits*, ch. 9 and p. 61.

36 Rogers, *Work Ethic* and Gilbert, *Work Without Salvation* discuss the dilemma of the work ethic in a secular, mechanised era.

37 For impressive surveys of the intellectual complexity of these movements, see Anson Rabinbach, *The Human Motor: Energy, Fatigue, and the Origins of Modernity* (New York, 1990); and James Kloppenberg, *Uncertain Victory: Social Democracy and Progressivism in European and American Thought, 1870–1920* (New York, 1986).

38 Among the many studies of scientific management are Samuel Haber, *Efficiency and Uplift: Scientific Management in the Progressive Era, 1890–1920* (Chicago, 1964); Sudhir Kakar, *Frederick Taylor: A Study in Personality and Innovation* (Cambridge MA, 1970); and Daniel Nelson, *Frederick W. Taylor and the Rise of Scientific Management* (Madison WI, 1980). See also David Montgomery, *The Fall of the House of Labor* (New York, 1987), ch. 5.

39 Samuel Gompers, 'Miracles of Efficiency', *American Federationist*

(April 1911), pp. 273–7. This debate with Taylor gave rise to several famous Congressional hearings regarding Taylorism in government arsenals. A good primary source is Robert Hoxie, *Scientific Management and Organized Labor* (New York, 1915). See also Milton Nadworny, *Scientific Management and the Unions 1900–1932* (Cambridge MA, 1955).

40 Emile Pouget, *L'Organisation du surmenage* (Paris, 1914), pp. 53–4. On British 'Taylorism', see Craig Littler, *The Development of the Labour Process in Capitalist Societies* (London, 1982), pp. 99–145; and Steven Wood, ed., *The Degradation of Work? Skill, Deskilling and the Labour Process* (London, 1982), especially pp. 19–42.

41 See especially, Rabinbach, *The Human Motor*, chs 8 and 10; Cross, *Quest*, ch. 5; and Jean. T. McKelvey, *AFL Attitudes toward Production 1900–1932* (Ithaca NY, 1952), ch. 3.

42 Frederick W. Taylor, *The Principles of Scientific Management* (New York, 1967), pp. 19–24 and Frederick Taylor, 'Testimony Before the Special House Committee', in his *Scientific Management* (New York, 1947), pp. 24–30.

43 A fine analysis of the confluence of work science and labour in Europe before the war is in Rabinbach, *The Human Motor*, ch. 8.

44 Edwin Layton, *The Revolt of the Engineers* (Cleveland OH, 1971), ch. 7. Technocracy Inc was a curious amalgam of a consulting firm and political sect which advocated a sidestepping of the market and electoral politics for a planned economy built around the efficient use of energy. The result would be general prosperity and a four-hour/four-day work week distributed on around-the-clock shifts. Henry Elsner, *The Technocrats: Prophets of Automation* (Syracuse NY, 1967), chs 1, 2 and 7. For a summary of Scott's ideas see Frank Arkright, *The ABC of Technocracy Based on Authorized Material* (New York, 1933).

45 Many visited the Soviet Union for inspiration in what they saw as a technocratic revolution of rational production and distribution. Stuart Chase and Rexford Tugwell, eds, *Soviet Russia in the Second Decade: A Joint Survey by the Technical Staff of the First American Trade Union Delegation* (New York, 1928). For more background see, Arthur Schlesinger, *The Crisis of the Old Order* (Boston MA, 1957), pp. 94, 131–42; Richard Pells, *Radical Visions and American Dreams* (New York, 1973), pp. 61–9; Hunnicutt, *Work Without End*, ch. 9; and Peter Kuznick, *Beyond the Laboratory: Scientists as Political Activists in 1930s America* (Chicago, 1987), pp. 47–51 and 106–43.

46 Morris Cooke, 'Editors' Preface', in Morris Cooke, Samuel Gompers, and Fred Miller, eds, *Labor, Management, Productivity, Annals of the American Academy of Political and Social Science*, no. 91 (New York, 1920); *Bulletin, Taylor Society* (December 1925), p. 245, cited in McKelvey, *AFL Attitudes*, p. 70. See also Samuel Gompers, 'Organized Labor and Industrial Engineers', *American Federationist* 28 (January 1920), pp. 1–2. Excellent analysis of the 'new unionism' led by Sidney Hillman of the textile union and its connections to an emerging political and business elite of Fordists is in Steve Fraser, 'The "Labor Question" ', in S. Fraser and Gary Gerstle, eds, *The Rise and Fall of the New Deal Order, 1930–1980*, (Princeton NJ, 1989), pp. 55–84.

47 Rexford Tugwell, *Industry's Coming of Age* (New York, 1927), pp. 223–4.

48 Paul Douglas, 'Modern Technique of Mass Production and Its Relation to Wages', *Proceedings of the Academy of Political Science* 12, 3 (1927), pp. 18–42, data on p. 20; and Evan Claugh, 'Index of Productivity of Labor in the Steel, Automobile, Shoe and Paper Industries', *Monthly Labor Review* 23 (July 1926), pp. 1–19. See Nadworny, *Scientific Management*, pp. 130–2; Federated Engineering Societies, *Waste in Industry* (New York, 1921), pp. 8–9; and Nyland, *Reduced Worktime*, ch. 4 for a fuller discussion.

49 Edwin Layton stresses that the 'revolt of the engineers' was prompted not by hostility to business as such but to fear of status loss in the bureaucratisation of American industry. The hero of most American engineers was not Veblen's technocrats but Herbert Hoover. Layton, *Revolt*, pp. 1 and 53.

50 McKelvey, *AFL Attitudes*, chs 1–4 and 8; and Judith Merkle, *Management and Ideology: The Legacy of the International Scientific Management Movement* (Berkeley CA, 1980), ch. 2.

51 See Cross, *Quest*, chs 7 and 9.

52 Whiting Williams, *Mainsprings of Men* (New York, 1925), pp. 83, 282.

53 See various articles on output restriction in the *American Federationist* (October 1919), pp. 940–1, (November 1919), p. 1026, (February 1920), pp. 157–8, and (September 1920), pp. 846–7. For examples of the idea of reducing hours to impede technological unemployment, see William Green, 'The Five-Day Week to Balance Production and Consumption', *American Federationist*, 33 (October 1926), pp. 1299–1300; and American Federation of Labor, *Report of the Proceedings of the 46th Annual Convention* (Washington DC, 1926), pp. 195–207.

54 AFL, *Report of the Proceedings of the 45th Annual Convention* (Washington DC, 1925), pp. 231–3 and 271; E. Gluck, 'Wage Theories', *American Federationist* 32 (December 1925), pp. 1163–6, quotation, p. 1166; John Frey, 'A Sound Basis for Wages', *American Federationist* 33 (January 1926), p. 34; and AFL, *Organized Labor's Modern Wage Policy* (Washington DC, 1927), p. 1. McKelvey, *AFL Attitudes*, pp. 91–9 stresses the controversial reception to the productivity theory of wages in 1925 but also that it was widely embraced in the labour movement from 1920. See also Irving Bernstein, *The Lean Years* (New York, 1966), pp. 97–108 and 338.

55 Lord Leverhuhme, *The Six Hour Day* (London, 1918), pp. 5–8, 12, and 28–9. See also Charles Myers, *Mind and Work* (London, 1920), pp. 162–74; and B. Seebohm Rowntree, *The Human Factor in Business*, 3rd edn (London, 1937), pp. 16 and 91.

56 Arthur Gleason, *What the Workers Want?* (London, 1920), interviews with Robin Williams, pp. 40–59 and Tom Mann, pp. 104–11.

57 George Skelly, ed., *The General Strike* (London, 1976) p. 412; and TUC, *Proceedings* (London, 1929), pp. 66–8 and 198–9, and (1931), pp. 220–2. See also TUC, 'Memorandum on Technological Unemployment', (London School of Economics and Political Science Pamphlet Collection, London, 1928).

58 William Oualid, *Salaires et tarifs* (Paris, 1929), pp. 90 and 97. For

background on Thomas see Martin Fine, 'Albert Thomas: A Reformer's Vision of Modernization', *Journal of Contemporary History* 12 (July 1977), pp. 545–64.

59 CGT, *Congrès national corporatif, compte rendu* (Paris, 1918), pp. 234, 184–92 and *Information ouvrière et sociale* (11 January 1920). Good recent analyses are Rabinbach, *The Human Motor*, ch. 9; and Richard Kuisel, *Capitalism and the State in Modern France* (New York, 1981), pp. 59–69. For an analysis of French labour language as a critique of an unproductive bourgeoisie, see Robert Frost, 'Mechanical Dreams: Democracy and Progress Talk in Twentieth Century France', in Paul Durbin, ed., *Philosophy and Technology*, (London, 1991).

60 Georges Bricard, *L'Organisation scientifique du travail* (Paris, 1927), pp. 130–1 and 197–201; and Paul Devinat, *Scientific Management in Europe*, International Labor Office, *Studies and Reports*, Series B, No. 17 (Geneva, 1927). For summaries of the international productivity movement in the 1920s, see Thomas P. Hughes, *American Genesis. A Century of Invention and Technological Enthusiasm* (New York, 1989), ch. 6; and Nyland, *Reduced Worktime*, ch. 5. Note also Cross, *Quest*, chs 7 and 9; and Merkle, *Management and Ideology*, pp. 148–71.

61 *Le Peuple* (30 October 1926) for the CGT's 'Manifesto on Productivity'. Also important is *Le Peuple* (15 November 1927), 'Le Programme de la CGT'. See Raymond Manevy *La Défense de 8 heures* (Paris, 1922) for summary of CGT articles.

62 CGTU, *Congrès national ordinaire, compte rendu des débats* (September 1927), p. 508 and (September 1929), pp. 527–9.

63 In the US, while the workweek in industry dropped by seven hours between 1906 and 1919, it fell by just 1.3 hours in the 1920s; 49 per cent had a 48-hour week in 1919. One notable exception was in the steel industry which partially reduced the shift from twelve to eight hours in 1923. In western Europe, this contrast was even sharper with the standard of the 48-hour industrial workweek becoming nearly universal by the end of 1919 with practically no change in the 1920s. See John Owen, *The Price of Leisure* (Montreal, 1970), pp. 61–2; David Roediger and Philip Foner, *Our Own Time: A History of American Labor and the Working Day* (Westport CT, 1989), ch. 10; and Cross, *Quest*, ch. 7.

64 See, for example, McKelvey, *AFL Attitudes*, chs 1–4 and 8; Merkle, *Management and Ideology*, ch. 2; and Martin Fine, 'Toward Corporatism: The Movement for Capital-Labor Collaboration in France, 1914–1936' (Ph.D. dissertation, University of Wisconsin-Madison, 1971).

65 This was a key to the Soviet experiment with a 'seven-hour day' in the mid-1920s, a reform that met with major rank-and-file resistance. William Chase and Lewis Siegelbaum, 'Worktime and Industrialization in the U.S.S.R., 1917–1941', in Gary Cross, ed., *Worktime and Industrialization, An International History*, (Philadelphia, 1988), pp. 183–216; and Eviatar Zerubavel, *The Seven Day Circle. The History and Meaning of the Week* (New York, 1985), pp. 35–43.

66 In this book written in the depths of the Depression, Chase predicted that the economic crisis would create a new generation of technical

leaders from the ranks of management, not ownership, who would take control from the speculators. The result would be a balance of high wages and short hours replacing poverty and unemployment. Stuart Chase, *A New Deal* (New York, 1932), pp. 18–19, 23–4, 186–91, and 230–2. See also Stuart Chase, *The Economy of Abundance* (New York, 1934); George Soule, *A Planned Society* (New York, 1931), especially pp. 146–8; and George Soule, *The Coming American Revolution* (New York, 1934).

67 Dahlberg directed his proposal to managers and technicians as well as academics in the hopes of saving capitalism. Arthur Dahlberg, *Jobs, Machines, and Capitalism* (New York, 1932), pp. 21, 27, and 35.

68 Dahlberg, *Jobs*, pp. 76 and 224. For an influential analysis of the waste of 'forced' consumption, see Stuart Chase, *The Tragedy of Waste* (New York, 1925). A Depression-era update is Harold Loeb, *The Chart of Plenty* (New York, 1935).

69 Lewis Mumford, *Technics and Civilization* (New York, 1934), pp. 378–9 and 385–416.

70 A good example of the call for traditional skills and decentralised production is Arthur Penty, *Guilds and the Social Crisis* (London, 1919) and his attempt to place traditional craft values in a modern context, *Old Worlds for New. A Study of the Post-Industrial State* (London, 1917). For British and French labour resistance to economic rationalization see Cross, *Quest*, pp. 204–7.

71 Tugwell, *Industry's Coming of Age*, pp. 258–9, 261.

72 *Bulletin, Taylor Society* (December 1925), p. 245 cited in McKelvey, *AFL Attitudes*, p. 70.

73 F. J. Maynard, 'Fordism vs. Individuality', *Labour Magazine* (Febuary 1927), p. 474–5.

74 For background on Dubreuil, see Fine, 'Toward Corporatism', pp. 279–83; H. Dubreuil, *La République industrielle* (Paris, 1924); and *Information sociale* (4 September and 3 October 1924, 3 January and 28 May 1925, and 29 July 1926).

75 Dubreuil, *Standards*, pp. 48, 200, 172. Dubreuil had lost his interest in the crafts: 'all the hand trades are starvation trades, and that is enough to make me hold their poetry cheap'. Dubreuil, *Standards*, p. 248. A new ruling class was emerging which consisted not of the wealthy privileged but of an alliance of technocrats and modern skilled workers. Dubreuil, *Standards*, and Dubreuil, *Nouveaux Standards* (Paris, 1931).

76 See, for example, treatment of fatigue or work science as part of the scientific management movement by Devinat, *Scientific Management*, pp. 201–8.

77 ILO, *Social Aspects of Rationalization* (Geneva, 1931), in ILO, *Studies and Reports*, Series B, No. 17, p. 152. See also Devinat, *Scientific Management*, p. 30 and a series of articles by Charles Spinasse in *Le Peuple* describing model US factories (e.g., *Le Peuple* (12 December 1927)). Even Léon Blum shared a similar perspective; see *Le Populaire* (4 and 5 May 1927).

78 ILO, *Social Aspects*, pp. 279–80 and ch. 5.

79 Henry Ford, *My Life and My Work* (New York, 1922), p. 103.

80 H. de Man, *Joy in Work* (New York, 1929), pp. 13 and 67 especially;

and H. de Man, *The Psychology of Socialism* (London, 1927), pp. 65 and 56–7; quotations from de Man, *Joy in Work*. See also Joan Campbell, *Joy in Work, German Work* (Princeton NJ, 1989), chs 9 and 10.

81 For example, see Nyland, *Reduced Worktime*, pp. 139–46 and André Gorz, *Critique of Economic Reason* (London, 1989), pp. 63–72.

82 See Edmund Byrne, *Work Inc* (Philadelphia, 1990), ch. 3 for an interesting analysis of the persistence of the work ethic in an age of automation.

83 David Roediger, 'The Limits of Corporate Reform: Fordism, Taylorism, and the Working Week in the United States, 1914–1929', in Cross, *Worktime and Industrialization*, pp. 144–7.

84 For the French example, see Patrick Fridenson, 'Un Tournant taylorien de la société française (1914–1918)', *Annales: economies, sociétés, civilisations*, 42 (September-October 1987), pp. 1037–46; Aimée Moutet, 'Introduction de la production à la chaine en France du debut du XXe siècle à la grande crise en 1930', *Histoire, économie, société* (January-March 1983), pp. 63–82; and Cecil Smith, 'The Longest Run: Public Engineers and Planning in France', *American Historical Review*, 95 (June 1990), pp. 657–95. For Britain, see Littler, *Labour Process*, pp. 99–145.

85 Christopher Forman, *The General Strike, May 1926* (London, 1972); and Gerard Noel, *The Great Lock-Out of 1926* (London, 1976).

86 André Francois-Poncet, *La France et les huit heures* (Paris, 1922), pp. 10–14 and France, Chambre des députés, *Débats parlementaires* (7 July 1922), p. 810.

87 *New York Times* (8 January 1921), p. 18 cited in Hunnicutt, *Work without End*, p. 38. See also John Hobson, 'The Limited Market', *Nation* 120 (11 April 1925), pp. 350–2; J. Hobson, *Economics of Unemployment* (London, 1923), ch. 1; and F. J. Boland, *Wage-Rates and Industrial Depressions: A Study of the Business Cycle* (New York, 1924), pp. 4–7.

88 William Grimes, 'The Curse of Leisure', *Atlantic Monthly* 142 (April 1928), pp. 355–60.

89 Technocrats like Veblen and Henry Gantt had a simple solution: the industrial efficiency that led to gluts should be complemented by a rationalisation of distribution. This alone would eliminate wasteful competition for scarce markets and the creation of false wants to stimulate sales. Thorstein Veblen, *The Theory of Business Enterprise* (1906, repr. New York, 1920), p. 253. Background is provided in Layton, *Revolt*, chs 1, 3 and 10 especially.

90 Henry Ford, 'Why I Favor Five Days' Work with Six Days' Pay', *World's Work* 52 (October 1926), pp. 613–14 and *My Work and My Life* (New York, 1922), p. 116. See also Henry S. Dennison, 'Would the Five-Day Week Decrease Unemployment?' *Magazine of Business* 54 (November 1928), pp. 508–10.

91 National Association of Manufacturers, 'The Five Day Week: Can it Become Universal', *Pocket Bulletin* 27 (October 1926), pp. 2–12 cited in Roediger, 'Corporate Reform', pp. 143–5.

92 High-wage theory was not taken seriously by most American employers. Between 1925 and 1929, when so much lip service was given to this

idea, business scarcely raised real wages. This hypocrisy was evident even in Ford whose 1926 book, *Today and Tomorrow* popularised the theory of high wages even though he failed to raise wages between 1919 and 1929. See Bernstein, *Lean Years*, p. 180 and Hunnicutt, *Work Without End*, pp. 37–9.

93 Walter Pitkin, *The Consumer. His Nature and Changing Habits* (New York, 1932), pp. 341–5; quotations from pp. 341–2 and 345.

94 To be sure, Pitkin argued also that income security along with compulsory consumer education and social insurance was to be part of this suburban dream of personal happiness and mass markets. Pitkin, *Consumer*, pp. 387–402; quotation from pp. 387–8.

95 While Kyrk recognised, as did advertisers, that consumers had 'defenses', she also assumed the need for consumer education. Hazel Kyrk, *A Theory of Consumption* (New York, 1923), ch. 5 especially pp. 99 and 106–15; and Paul Nystrom, *Economic Principles of Consumption* (New York, 1929), ch. 1. Even more aggressive stances against manipulative advertising were taken by Elizabeth Hoyt, *The Consumption of Wealth* (New York, 1932), ch. 10; Chase, *Waste*, ch. 7; and Stuart Chase and F. J. Schlink, *Your Money's Worth* (New York, 1927).

96 Kyrk, *Consumption*, pp. 135–71 and 242; and Nystrom, *Principles of Consumption*, pp. 40–1 and 262–4. A recent update of a similar attempt to use psychology to better understand consumption is Tibor Scitovsky, *The Joyless Economy* (New York, 1977).

97 Kyrk, *Consumption*, pp. 220, 227, 229; quotations from pp. 252 and 255.

98 John Dewey, *Human Nature and Conduct* (New York, 1922), p. 66.

99 Kyrk, *Consumption*, pp. 258 and 289; quotations from pp. 291–2.

100 Frederick, *Household Engineering*, pp. 8–10 and 317, and Christine Frederick, *Selling Mrs. Consumer* (New York, 1929). See also, Glenna Matthews, *Just a Housewife: The Rise and Fall of Domesticity in America* (New York, 1987), chs 6 and 7; and Susan Strasser, *Never Done. A History of Housework in America* (New York, 1980), ch. 10.

101 Committee on Recent Economic Changes, *Recent Economic Changes*, vol. 1 (New York, 1929), p. xv; and Edward Cowdrick, 'The New Economic Gospel of Consumption', *Industrial Management* 74 (October 1927). p. 208.

102 Lionel Robbins, 'On the Elasticity of Incomes in Terms of Effort', *Economicia* 10 (June 1930), 123–9, quotation on p. 129. Still Robbins did not presume that consumption was unlimited, only that demand for goods could not be determined. See also Lionel Robbins, 'The Economic Effects of Variations of Hours of Labour', *Economic Journal* 39 (1929), pp. 25–40. While Paul Douglas felt that he had proven the backward-sloping labour supply curve by finding negative correlations between hourly earnings and hours of work based on historical data, he did not address directly the 'indeterminate' factor of demand for income: Paul Douglas, *The Theory of Wages* (New York, 1934), pp. 302–12.

103 This thesis was repeated many times in works by William Foster and W. Catchings including *Money* (Boston MA, 1923); *Profits* (Boston MA, 1925), quotation on p. 285; *Business Without A Buyer*

(Boston MA, 1928); and *The Road to Plenty* (Boston, 1928). In defence of 'thrift', Hansen argued that saving stimulated business borrowing leading to competition for economic factors and, with that, higher wages (and consumer spending): Alvin Hansen, *Business Cycle Theory* (New York, 1927), chs 3 and 7. For positive reception of Foster and Catchings, see John Frey, 'A Sound Basis for Wages', *The Federationist* 33 (January 1926), pp. 26–34.

104 Foster and Catchings, *Road to Plenty*, pp. 46, 62, and 65; and *Profits*, p. 239.

105 R. Sheldon and E. Arens, *Consumer Engineering, A New Technique for Prosperity* (New York, 1932), p. 64. See also Paul Mazur, *American Prosperity* (New York, 1928), pp. 224–5.

106 Austin and Lloyd, *Secret of High Wages*, chs 1–4, 13, and p. 104. For positive French reviews of this book, see *L'Information sociale* (15 April 1926) and *Le Peuple* (20 and 30 March 1926). See also H. Abbati, *The Unclaimed Wealth. How Money Stops Production* (London, 1924).

107 Sylvie Schweitzer, *Des Engrenages à la chaine. Les Usines Citroën, 1915–1935* (Lyon, 1982), pp. 11–16. When Ford's agents visited Europe, French employers strongly objected to their claim that he could provide the equivalent wage to European automobile workers: *Information sociale* (20 June 1929). See also Paul Gagnon, 'French Views of the Second American Revolution', *French Historical Studies* 2 (February 1962), pp. 430–49; and Victoria de Grazia, 'Mass Culture and Sovereignty: The American Challenge to European Cinemas, 1920–1960', *Journal of Modern History* 61 (March 1989), pp. 53–87. For the relative lack of consumerist modernisation in France, consult Frost, 'Mechanical Dreams' and Robert Frost, 'Assembly Lines and Vacuum Cleaners', (unpublished paper, Department of History, State University of New York at Albany, 1990).

108 Colin Clark, *Conditions of Economic Progress* (London, 1940), pp. 6–7, 438, and 446. The same analysis is in Wesley Mitchell, 'A Review', in Committee on Recent Economic Changes, eds, *Recent Economic Changes* (New York, 1929), pp. 841–910, especially p. 877.

109 Rexford Tugwell, *The Industrial Discipline and the Governmental Arts* (New York, 1933), pp. 25–8, 37–64, and 91–4.

110 Clark, *Economic Progress*, pp. 6–7. For an interesting exposition on this question, André Gorz, *Critique of Economic Reason* (London, 1989), pp. 1–3.

3 BARRIERS AND BRIDGES: CULTURAL ELITES AND THE DEMOCRATISATION OF TIME AND MONEY

1 Hannah Arendt, *The Human Condition* (Chicago, 1958), ch. 3; Sebastian de Grazia, *Of Time, Work, and Leisure* (New York, 1967), ch. 1 and pp. 65–87; and Patrick Brantlinger, *Bread and Circuses. Theories of Mass Culture as Social Decay* (Ithaca NY, 1983), ch. 2.

2 Key American studies of the rational recreation tradition include Paul Boyer, *Urban Masses and Moral Order in America, 1820–1920* (Cambridge MA, 1978); and Roy Rosenzweig, *Eight Hours for What We Will: Workers and Leisure in an Industrial City, 1870–1920* (New York,

1983). Two English sources are Peter Bailey, *Leisure and Class in Victorian England: Rational Recreation and the Contest for Control, 1830–1885* (London, 1978); and Hugh Cunningham, *Leisure in the Industrial Revolution* (New York, 1980).

3 Matthew Arnold, *Culture and Anarchy* (1869; London, 1957), pp. 44–6, 72, 99–107, and 204. See also Joseph Carroll, *The Cultural Theory of Matthew Arnold* (Berkeley, 1982); and Ben Knight, *The Idea of the Clerisy in the Nineteenth Century* (Cambridge, 1978).

4 Brantlinger, *Bread and Circuses*, ch. 1, pp. 186–99; and José Ortega y Gasset, *The Revolt of the Masses* (1930, repr. New York, 1957), ch. 3 and p. 88; Oswald Spengler, *The Decline of the West* (1926–8; repr. New York, 1980); and Leonard Woolf, *Barbarianism Within and Without* (New York, 1939).

5 Ortega, *Revolt*, pp. 7–8, 10–11, and 48–9.

6 Gustave Le Bon, *The Crowd* (New York, 1969). English disciples include: Wilfred Totter, *Instinct of the Herd in Peace and War* (London, 1916); William McDougall, *The Group Mind* (London, 1920); and Wyndham Lewis, *The Art of Being Ruled* (London, 1916). Note also Robert A. Nye, *The Origins of Crowd Psychology: Gustave Le Bon and the Crisis of Mass Democracy in the Third Republic* (London, 1975); and Susanna Barrows, *Distorting Mirrors: Visions of the Crowd in Late Nineteenth-Century France* (New Haven CT, 1981).

7 Brantlinger, *Bread and Circuses*, pp. 210–16; Leo Gerko, *Heroes, Highbrows, and the Popular Mind* (Indianapolis IN, 1953), chs 8–11; and Peter Miles and Malcolm Smith, *Cinema, Literature, and Society* (London, 1987), pp. 82–8.

8 F. R. Leavis, *Mass Civilisation and Minority Culture* (Cambridge, 1930). See also Q. D. Leavis, *Fiction and the Reading Public* (London, 1932); and Clive Bell, *Civilisation* (London, 1928). Historian Martin Wiener found this attitude to be a typically English rejection of business life, a result of an 'incomplete' industrial revolution where aristocratic values survived in the intellectual middle class. Martin Wiener, *English Culture and the Decline of the Industrial Spirit, 1850–1980* (Cambridge, 1981), especially chs 2 and 3. But this self-assumed mission of intellectuals was nearly universal in the industrialising world. Note, for example, the Americans, Van Wyck Brooks, 'America's Coming-of-Age', in *Van Wyck Brooks: The Early Years*, ed. Claire Sprague (New York, 1968), pp. 79–158; and Lewis Mumford, *Sticks and Stones* (New York, 1924), *The Golden Day* (New York, 1926), and *The Brown Decades* (New York, 1931).

9 An interesting discussion is in Andrew Ross, *No Respect: Intellectuals and Popular Culture* (London, 1989).

10 Emile Durkheim, *The Division of Labor in Society* (1893; repr. New York, 1964), pp. 10, 240–1. See Emile Durkheim, *Elementary Forms of Religious Life* (1912; repr. New York, 1965), especially p. 475 for discussion of the integrating quasi-religious function of secular leisure festivals.

11 Sigmund Freud, *Group Psychology* (1922; repr. New York, 1951), pp. 5–22, 82, and 99–100.

12 This general perspective prevailed in Wilhelm Reich's (1933) *The Mass*

Psychology of Fascism, trans. Vincent Carfagno (New York, 1970); and Erich Fromm's *Escape from Freedom* (New York, 1941). Leo Loewenthal's famous dictum, 'Mass Culture is psycho-analysis in reverse', shares this basic identification of the crowd with suggestibility and submerged neuroses. See also Brantlinger, *Bread and Circuses*, p. 172.

13 Sigmund Freud, *Civilization and its Discontents* (1929) repr. in *The Standard Edition of the Complete Psychological Works of Sigmund Freud*, vol. 21, ed. James Strachey (London, 1961), pp. 97 and 103; and *Future of an Illusion* (1927), repr. in *The Standard Edition*, vol. 21, ed. Strachey, pp. 7–8, 10, and 12.

14 Chris Rojek, *Capitalism and Leisure Theory* (London, 1985), p. 78. See also Philip Rieff, *Freud: The Mind of the Moralist* (New York, 1961), chs 6 and 7.

15 S. Freud, *Beyond the Pleasure Principle* (1920, repr. New York, 1950), pp. 4–5, 47, and 68; S. Ferenczi, 'The Sunday Neurosis', in his *Further Contributions to the Theory and Technique of Psycho-Analysis* (London, 1926), pp. 174–7.

16 C. G. Jung shared this dread of the release of instinctual forces in the 'play instinct'. It was a 'catastrophe when the barbarian side of the European comes uppermost, for who can guarantee that such a man, when he begins to play, shall forthwith take the aesthetic motive and the enjoyment of pure beauty as his goal?' (C. G. Jung, *Psychological Types* (New York, 1926), p. 135). Erich Fromm may have been more optimistic than Freud; but he too found modern freedom from necessity and social constraint led to an anxiety so frightening that 'we are ready to get rid of our individual self either by submission to new forms of authority or by compulsive comforming to accepted patterns' (*Escape from Freedom* (New York, 1941) p. 135). See also Rojek, *Leisure Theory*, pp. 74–82.

17 Theodor Adorno and Max Horkheimer, *Dialectic of Enlightenment* (1944; repr. New York, 1974), pp. 133–4, 131, 137, 144, 121. See also T. Adorno, 'The Culture Industry Reconsidered', *New German Critique* 6 (Fall 1975), pp. 12–19.

18 Theodor Adorno, 'On Popular Music', *Studies in Philosophy and Social Science* 9 (1941), pp. 17–48, especially pp. 37, 39.

19 Members of the Frankfurt School were largely exiled to commercialised America after the rise of Hitler, and isolated from the democratic optimism of western Europe during the Popular Front period. This may help explain why most members defended high European culture against the onslaught of mass consumption. For additional analysis of the Frankfurt School's views on popular culture, see, for example, Martin Jay, *The Dialectical Imagination* (New York, 1973), ch. 6; and M. Jay, *Fin de Siècle Socialism* (London, 1988) pp. 84–93; George Friedman, *The Political Philosophy of the Frankfurt School* (Ithaca NY, 1981), ch. 2; Philip Slater, *Origins and Significance of the Frankfurt School* (London, 1971), chs 1 and 4 especially; and David Held, *Introduction to Critical Theory* (Berkeley CA, 1980), chs 2–3.

20 G. Stanley Hall, *Youth: Its Education, Regimen, and Hygiene* (New York, 1909), p. 75. See also T. J. Jackson Lears, *No Place of Grace:*

Antimodernism and the Transformation of American Culture, 1880–1920 (New York, 1981), introduction and pp. 26–7.

21 For background on the American recreation movement, see Curtis Rainwater, *The Play Movement in the United States* (Chicago, 1927); and Henry Curtis, *The Play Movement and Its Significance* (New York, 1917). For the shift to adult play, see G. Stanley Hall, *Recreations of a Psychologist* (New York, 1920), ch. 8; J. Lees, *Play in Education* (New York, 1920), pp. 95–101; and Luther Gulick, *A Philosophy of Play* (New York, 1920), pp. 23–54.

22 William James, 'The Gospel of Relaxation', in his *Talks to Teachers on Psychology* (New York, 1900), p. 112. See also Annie P. Call, *How to Live Quietly* (Boston MA, 1914).

23 G. T. W. Patrick, *Psychology of Relaxation* (Boston MA, 1916), p. 270. See also Benjamin Hunnicutt, *Work Without End: Abandoning Shorter Hours for the Right to Work* (Philadelphia, 1988), pp. 130–4. For an analysis using critical theory see Robert Goldman, 'Meanings of Leisure in Corporate America, 1890–1930', (unpublished Ph.D. dissertation, Duke University, Durham NC, 1977).

24 Hall, *Youth*, pp. 78, 57. Other examples of this vitalist tradition in the US are Luther Gulick, *The Efficient Life* (New York, 1907) and his *The Philosophy of Play* (New York, 1920), pp. 23–54 especially. See also Dorothy Ross, *G. Stanley Hall: The Psychologist as Prophet* (Chicago, 1972).

25 William Ogburn, *Social Change with Respect to Culture and Original Nature* (New York, 1922), pp. 200–4, 259–63, 287–312, and 363–5.

26 Ogburn, *Social Change*, pp. 354–5.

27 Charles Beard, 'Introduction', in Charles Beard, ed., *Whither Mankind* (New York, 1929), pp. 4–24. See also the essay by John Dewey, 'Philosophy', in this volume, pp. 313–31.

28 George Cutten, *The Threat of Leisure* (New Haven CT, 1926), pp. 73–7; Cyril Joad, *Diogenes or the Future of Leisure* (London, 1935), p. 9; and Stuart Chase, 'Play', in Beard, *Whither Mankind*, pp. 343–6. Note also the influential Johan Huizinga, *Homo Ludens, A Study of the Play Element in Culture* (1938; repr. Boston MA, 1950), ch. 12.

29 Cutten, *Threat of Leisure*, pp. 89, 99, 17; and F. R. Leavis and Denys Thompson, *Culture and Environment: The Training of Critical Awareness* (London, 1933), pp. 30–40, and 47.

30 R. G. Burnett and E. D. Martell, *The Devil's Camera: Menace of a Film-Ridden World* (London, 1932). More populist appeals are in Iris Barry, *Let's Go to the Pictures* (London, 1926). For American sources on moralist opposition to the movies see, for starters, T. Balio, *The American Film Industry* (Madison WI, 1976), pp. 103–18 and 213–28; M. Rosen, *Popcorn Venus* (New York, 1973), ch. 9; and H. J. Forman, *Our Movie Made Children* (New York, 1935).

31 J. B. Priestley, *English Journey* (1934, repr. London, 1937), p. 1.

32 George Orwell, *The Road to Wigan Pier* (London, 1937), p. 80.

33 Henry Durant, *The Problems of Leisure* (London, 1938), pp. 9–10; and Lewis Mumford, 'The Arts', in Beard, *Whither Mankind*, p. 280.

34 André Philip, *Le Problème ouvrier aux Etats-unis* (Paris, 1927),

pp. 147, 216, and 225. See also André Siegfried, *Les Etats-Unis d'au-jourd'hui* (Paris, 1927), translated as *America Comes of Age* (New York, 1927).

35 Ilya Ehrenburg, *The Life of the Automobile* (1929; New York, 1972), pp. 23 and 24–5.

36 Maurice Halbwachs, *La Classe ouvrière et les niveaux de vie* (Paris, 1913), pp. 125–35. Henri de Man, *Psychology of Socialism* (London, 1937), p. 269. Other examples are Jacques Valdour, *Ouvriers parisiens d'après-guerre* (Paris, 1921); J. Valdour, *Ateliers et taudis de les banlieux de Paris* (Paris, 1923); and Arnold Brémond, *Une Explication du monde ouvrier* (Paris, 1928), ch. 3. The socialist, Georges Lefranc also complained that joyless work along with a lack of domestic space led to 'exaggerated passions'; Georges Lefranc, *Une Expérience d'éducation ouvrière* (Paris, 1937), pp. 24–8. See also de Man, *Psychology of Socialism*, pp. 59–63 and 269.

37 Durant, *Problem of Leisure*, pp. 31 and 66; Constance Harris, *The Use of Leisure in Bethnal Green*, preface by L. P. Jacks (London, 1927), pp. 60–2, 52–4, and 66–7; and Halbwachs, *Les Niveaux de vie*, pp. 125–35 and 442–5. A similar source is J. P. Sizer, *Commercialization of Leisure* (Boston MA, 1917).

38 Robert and Helen Lynd, *Middletown* (New York, 1929), pp. 251–7; and George Lundberg, Mirra Komarovsky, and Mary McInerny, eds, *Leisure, A Suburban Study* (New York, 1933), pp. 15–24, 59–72 and 142–60.

39 David Riesman, Nathan Glazer and Reuel Denny, *The Lonely Crowd* (Garden City NY, 1950). Durant, *Problem of Leisure*, pp. 60–1 and 68–70. Orwell found a similar trend 'away from creative communal amusements and towards solitary mechanical ones'; George Orwell, *Collected Essays, Journalism and Letters of George Orwell, Volume III As I Please, 1943–45*, ed. Sonia Orwell and Ian Angus (London, 1970), pp. 61–2.

40 George Lansbury, *My England* (London, 1934), p. 15. Other examples of this rural myth in the interwar years are George Bourne [George Sturt], *Change in the Village* (London, 1935) and *The Wheelwright's Shop* (Cambridge, 1923). See Wiener, *English Culture*, ch. 4, pp. 118–21 especially. Note also 'The Holiday Dream', in Gary Cross ed., *Worktowners at Blackpool: Mass-Observation and Popular Leisure in the 1930s* (London, 1990), ch. 3; and Ian Jeffrey, *The British Landscape 1920–1950* (London, 1984), ch. 1.

41 Leavis and Thompson, *Culture and Environment*, pp. 71, 89, and 97.

42 R. and H. Lynd, *Middletown*, pp. 251–7 and 498–500; and Joad, *Diogenes*, p. 65.

43 A French example is Georges Duhamel's *America the Menace. Scenes from the Life of the Future*, trans. Charles Thompson (Boston MA, 1931).

44 Showing the interaction between American and British popular music are Ronald Pearsall, *Edwardian Popular Music* (Rutherford NJ, 1975), pp. 19–25; D. L. LeMahieu, *Culture for Democracy: Mass Communications and the Cultivated Mind in Britain between the Wars* (New York, 1988), pp. 66–9 and 82–99; Jeffrey Richards and Anthony Ald-

gate, *British Cinema and Society, 1930–1970* (Totowa NJ, 1983); and Victoria de Grazia, 'Mass Culture and Sovereignty: The American Challenge to European Cinemas, 1920–1960', *Journal of Modern History* 61 (March 1989), pp. 53–87.

45 Edgar Mowrer, *This American World* (London, 1928), pp. 44, 100–2; Joad, *Diogenes*, p. 65; Leavis and Thompson, *Culture and Environment*, pp. 64–5; and F. R. Leavis, *For Continuity* (Freeport NY, 1968), pp. 36 and 91. See also Wiener, *English Culture*, ch. 5; David Richards, 'America Conquers Britain: Anglo-American Conflict in the Popular Media during the 1920s', *Journal of American Culture* 3 (1980), pp. 95–104; and George Harmon Knoles, *The Jazz Age Revisited: British Criticism of American Civilization during the 1920s* (Stanford CA, 1955).

46 Examples of this equation of mass culture and totalitarianism are in Emil Lederer, *State of the Masses: The Threat of the Classless Society* (New York, 1940); and Karl Mannheim, *Man and Society in an Age of Reconstruction* (New York, 1940). The Frankfurt School's association of mass culture and totalitarianism has often been noted.

47 See Karl Mannheim, 'The Democratization of Culture', in his *Essays on the Sociology of Culture* (London, 1956), pp. 171–246. See also the classic by Pierre Bourdieu, *Distinction: A Social Critique of the Judgement of Taste* (Cambridge MA, 1984).

48 A fine discussion is in LeMahieu, *Culture for Democracy*, ch. 3 and p. 132.

49 T. S. Eliot, 'Notes Towards a Definition of Culture' in *Christianity and Culture* (London, 1948), pp. 95, 107, 111 and 115; and Aldous Huxley, *Along the Road* (London, 1925), p. 238 cited in Miles and Smith, *Cinema*, p. 114. See also John Harrison, *The Reactionaries* (New York, 1966) pp. 157–68; R. T. S. Kojecky, *Eliot's Social Criticism* (London, 1971); and Allen Austin, *T. S. Eliot: The Literary and Social Criticism* (Bloomington IN, 1971).

50 Leavis and Thompson, *Culture and Environment*, pp. 1, 98–109; F. R. Leavis, *For Continuity*, pp. 34–8; and F. R. Leavis, *Lectures in America* (London, 1969), pp. 9–11. Good analyses of the social character of the Leavis movement are in Raymond Williams, *Culture and Society, 1780–1959* (London, 1958), pp. 252–63; I. Wright, 'F. R. Leavis, The *Scrutiny* Movement and the Crisis', in Jon Clark, Margot Heinemann, David Margolies, and Carole Snee, eds, *Culture and the Crisis in Britain in the Thirties* (London, 1979), pp. 37–66.

51 Durant, *Problem of Leisure*, p. 31. Reduced differences in income and status, Durant also hoped, would produce a less emulative consumption: 'The things counted valuable, the standards of behaviour, the modes of dress, will not, as now, be copied from the few who occupy the leading social positions, but will be created by the people taking charge of their own lives.' Durant, *Problem of Leisure*, p. 262.

52 Typical of this approach are William Pangburn, 'The Worker's Leisure and his Individuality', *American Journal of Sociology* 27 (January 1922), pp. 433–44; and C. Rainwater, 'Socialized Leisure', *Journal of Applied Sociology* 24 (January 1919), pp. 373–88.

53 Examples of self-training in leisure are the English Sidney Dark, *After*

Working Hours: The Enjoyment of Leisure (London, 1929); and Margorie B. Greenbie, *The Arts of Leisure* (London, 1938).

54 H. A. Overstreet, *A Guide to Civilized Loafing* (New York, 1933); repr. as *A Guide to Civilized Leisure* (New York, 1934), p. 246.

55 I am especially indebted to Hunnicutt, *Work Without End*, ch. 4. Revealing American sources include J. Lee, 'Play as an Antidote to Civilisation', *Playground* 5 (July 1921), pp. 110–26; and US Department of the Interior, Office of Education, *Cardinal Principles of Secondary Education* Bulletin 35 (Washington DC, 1918), p. 32. See also J. Rogers, 'Education for Leisure', *National Education Association: Addresses and Proceedings* (New York, 1926) p. 209. English equivalences are L. P. Jacks, *Ethical Factors of the Present Crisis* (Baltimore MD, 1934), ch. 4; and Ernest Barker, *Uses of Leisure* (London, 1936).

56 R. and H. Lynd, *Middletown*, pp. 222 and 176.

57 LeMahieu, *Culture for Democracy*, pp. 141–54; Mark Pegg, *Broadcasting and Society, 1918–1939* (London, 1983), ch. 2; and especially Asa Briggs, *The History of Broadcasting in the United Kingdom: Birth of Broadcasting* (London, 1961), pp. 4–114. For a recent treatment of the early years of radio advertising, see Roland Marchand, *Advertising the American Dream* (Berkeley CA, 1985), pp. 88–110; and especially Hugh Aitken, *The Continuous Wave: Technology and American Radio, 1900–1925* (Princeton NJ, 1985). See also Daniel Czitrom, *Media and the American Mind* (Chapel Hill NC, 1982), ch. 3.

58 Philip. *Le Problème*, pp. 216 and 225.

59 Cutten, *Threat of Leisure*, pp. 106–7 and 135–7; Durant, *Problem of Leisure*, p. 3.

60 American commentators in the 1920s lavished great attention on the promise of the new leisure. Articles and books concerned with leisure in the US increased from 51 in the 1910s to 410 in the 1920s. See Eric Larrabee and Rolf Meyerson, *Mass Leisure* (Glencoe IL, 1958), p. 389. Influential American sociologists William Ogburn and Howard Odum hired Jesse Steiner to undertake a systematic study of leisure for Herbert Hoover's Committee on Recent Social Changes. President's Committee on Recent Social Trends, *Social Trends* vol. 1, pp. xiii–xiv, li–liii and lxxi; and Jesse Steiner, 'Recreation and Leisure Time Activities', in *Recent Social Trends* vol. 2, pp. 912–57. See also Hunnicutt, *Work Without End*, pp. 138–42 and his excellent bibliography. Note Bertrand and Dora Russell, *Prospects of Industrial Civilization* (London, 1923), p. 158.

61 See especially Jean-Louis Loubet del Bayle, *Les Non-conformistes des années 30* (Paris, 1969); Paul Nizan, *Les Chiens de garde* (Paris, 1932) translated as *The Watchdogs*, trans. Paul Fittingoff (New York, 1972); and Julien Benda, *La Trahison des clercs* (Paris, 1927) translated as *The Treason of the Intellectuals*, trans. Richard Aldington (London, 1928). For more discussion see David Schalk, *The Spectrum of Political Engagement* (Princeton NJ, 1979), chs 2 and 3; and Nicole Racine-Furlaud, 'Le Comités de Vigilance des intellectuels antifascistes (1934–1939)', in Jean Bouvier, ed., *France en mouvement* (Paris, 1986), pp. 298–322.

62 For analysis of personalism, see John Hellman, *Emmanuel Mounier*

and the New Catholic Left 1930–1950 (Toronto, 1981), chs 1, 3, 4, and 5; and Michel Winock, *Histoire politique de la revue 'Esprit'* (Paris, 1976), especially pp. 112–16. For a brief analysis of the sociology of French intellectuals in the 1930s, see Martin Stanton, 'French Intellectual Groups and the Popular Front: Traditional and Innovative Uses of the Media', in Martin Alexander and Helen Graham, eds, *The French and Spanish Popular Fronts. Comparative Perspectives*. (Cambridge, 1989), pp. 254–70.

63 Betty Reid, 'The Left Book Club in the Thirties', in Jon Clark *et al.*, eds, *Culture and the Crisis*, pp. 193–207.

64 Priestley, *English Journey*, p. 22. For analysis of Priestley's role, see Susan Cooper, *J. B. Priestley: Portrait of an Author* (London, 1970); and John Braine, *J. B. Priestley* (New York, 1979).

65 Matthew Josephson, *Portrait of the Artist as American* (New York, 1930), pp. 306–7; cited in Richard Pells, *Radical Visions and American Dreams: Culture and Social Thought in the Depression Years* (New York, 1973), p. 40.

66 John Hilton, *Why I Go in For the Pools* (London, 1935).

67 In 1931, Collie Knox in the *Daily Express* offered a column, critical of the BBC's snobbery. More challenging were the English language commercial stations on the continent, especially Radio Luxembourg. In response, BBC programming committees subtly accommodated popular taste with a greater stress on dance music and variety; gradually they abandoned their Sabbatarianism. Peter Black, *The Biggest Aspidistra in the World* (London, 1972), pp. 48 and 55–66; Asa Briggs, *The Golden Age of the Wireless* (London, 1965), pp. 35 and 40; and Pegg, *Broadcasting and Society*, pp. 92–109 and 195–215. See especially LeMahieu, *A Culture for Democracy*, pp. 138–53, 178–96, and 273–92.

68 Denys Hardy, 'The Place of Entertainment in Social Life', *Sociological Review* 26 (October 1934), pp. 393–406; Ivor Brown, *The Heart of England* (London, 1935), pp. 69, 20; and John Common, *The Freedom of the Streets* (London, 1938), pp. 1–16, 28–9, and 69–75.

69 C. Delise Burns, *Leisure in the Modern World* (London, 1932), pp. 3, 17–21, 63, 72, 77, 83, 91, 255, and 234. See also John Hammond, *The Growth of the Common Enjoyment* (London, 1933).

70 Mumford, 'The Arts', p. 288 and Lewis Mumford, *Technics and Civilization* (New York, 1934), pp. 279, 281, 319, 323, 325, 363, and ch. 8.

71 Because 'our pioneering work is almost done', Furnas argued, 'it is becoming increasingly difficult to invent something that the public will desire to buy'. His futuristic blueprint included a life-long 'labor debt' which the individual could work off in any of a variety of ways in exchange for the material fruits of industrial productivity. The balance of life would be free of social obligations. C. C. Furnas, *America's Tomorrow: An Informal Excursion into the Era of the Two-Hour Working Day* (New York, 1931), pp. 11, 12, 14, 183, and 186.

72 Furnas, *America's Tomorrow*, p. 234. Furnas confidently claimed that 'leisurely reading probably will come back to its own after we have learned to take everything more calmly'. Furnas, *America's Tomorrow*, pp. 242–3.

73 Jacques Duboin, *La Grande Relève des hommes par la machine* (Paris, 1935), pp. 341–54.

74 Burns, *Leisure in Modern Society*, pp. 23, and 206, 253, and 274.

75 Russell, *Praise of Idleness*, pp. 26–7.

76 Burns, *Leisure in Modern Society*, pp. 23, 206, 253, and 274; and Russell, *In Praise of Idleness*, pp. 28–9.

77 George Orwell, *The Lion and the Unicorn* (1941; rep. London, 1962), pp. 74–5.

78 Burns, *Leisure in Modern Society*, pp. 74–114 and 217.

79 H. G. Wells, *The Shape of Things to Come* (London, 1933), pp. 409 and 413.

80 Howard Braucher, 'The Theory of the Economic Value of Waste', *Playground* 24 (December 1930), p. 473; and Henry F. Pratt, 'Exit the Gospel of Work', *Harper's Magazine* 161 (1931), pp. 641–52.

81 Tom Harrisson and Charles Madge, *Britain, A Mass-Observation Study* (Harmondsworth, 1939), Preface; and Tom Jeffrey, *Mass-Observation: A Short History* (Birmingham, 1978), pp. 3–4.

82 Against a growing nostalgia for the rural landscape, Bolton (called Worktown by the observers) was the nadir of the ideal. 'Bolton looked like the bottom of a pond with the water drained off. In here were the people who, if they could endure this, could endure anything.' William Gerharde, 'Climate and Character', *The English Genius* (London, 1939), cited in Ian Jeffrey, *The British Landscape* (London, 1984), pp. 11–13, quotation from p. 11.

83 Between Manchester and Bolton, Priestley declared, is an 'ugliness that is so complete that it is almost exhilarating'. Priestley, *English Journey*, pp. 263–5.

84 Sherwood Anderson, *Puzzled America* (New York, 1935). See also James Rorty, *Where Life Is Better* (New York, 1936); Edmund Wilson, *The American Jitters* (New York, 1932), p. xv; Louis Adamic, *My America* (New York, 1938); Nathan Asch, *The Road: In Search of America* (New York, 1936); Erskine Caldwell, *Some American People* (New York, 1935); and Theodore Dreiser, *Tragic America* (New York, 1932).

85 Anderson, *Puzzled America*, p. 57. Other examples of the populist theme are Caldwell, *Some American People*; and especially James Agee, *Let Us Now Praise Famous Men* (New York, 1941), a sympathetic description of southern sharecroppers, who nevertheless were portrayed as people who were so distorted and numbed by their exploitation as never to be able to live human lives. The simplicity and spontaneity of the poor would have to be combined with the 'civilization' of the advantaged. See p. 399 especially.

86 George Soule, *A Planned Society* (New York, 1932), p. 283.

87 *Combat Social* (20 July 1935) cited in Julian Jackson, *The Popular Front in France: Defending Democracy, 1934–38* (Cambridge, 1988), p. 116.

88 Charles Madge and Tom Harrisson, *Mass-Observation* (London, 1937), pp. 16–17.

89 Anderson, *Puzzled America*, pp. ix, 158, 161, 164; and Adamic, *My*

America, pp. 214, 219, and 298. This theme permeates Rorty's *Where Life is Better*. See also Wilson, *American Jitters*, p. 304.

90 Pells, *Radical Visions*, ch. 5.

91 Pells, *Radical Visions*, p. 199.

92 Archibald MacLeish, *A Time to Speak* (New York, 1940), pp. 13, 20, and 112. See also Max Lerner, *It is Later than You Think: The Need for a Militant Democracy* (New York, 1938), pp. 78, 84, 116; note also Granville Hicks, *I Like America* (New York, 1938).

93 Gilbert Seldes, *Mainland* (New York, 1936), pp. 6–7 65, 81, 412–13, 424–5, and 428.

94 See P. Ory, 'Le Front Populaire et la création artistique', *Bulletin de la Société d'histoire moderne* 8 (1974), p. 7.

95 *Le Musée vivant* (June 1937) cited in Jackson, *Popular Front*, p. 130.

96 See the homage to the French way of life and culture by the communist intellectual, Paul Vaillant-Couturier, *Vers des lendemains qui chantent* (Paris, 1962), pp. 263–85. See also E. Strebel, 'Renoir and the Popular Front', *Sight and Sound* 49 (Winter, 1979–80), pp. 36–41; G. Vincendeau and K. Reader, *La Vie est à nous: French Cinema of the Popular Front* (London, 1986); and Jackson, *Popular Front*, pp. 119–21, 138–45.

97 Lewis Mumford, *Faith for Living* (New York, 1940), pp. 72–92 especially. See also, Pells, *Radical Visions*, ch. 8.

98 Robert and Helen Lynd, *Middletown in Transition* (New York, 1937), especially pp. 7–20 and 453–5. Helen Lynd, though nominally an author, had moved on to other research by the mid-1930s, especially a very interesting study of Britain in the 1880s.

99 Carl Becker, *Progress and Power* (New York, 1936), pp. 91–6 cited in Robert Lynd, *Knowledge for What?* (Princeton NJ, 1939), pp. 107–8.

100 Lynd, *Knowledge for What?*, pp. 5, 49, 65, 90, and 105.

101 Harold Lasswell, *Politics: Who Gets What, When, How* (Cleveland OH, 1936), pp. 112–16; and Thurmon Arnold, *The Folklore of Capitalism* (New York, 1937), pp. 110–11, 178, and 390–3. See also Pells, *Radical Visions*, pp. 319–29.

102 Lynd, *Knowledge for What?*, p. 107 and chs 4–6. See the excellent article of Richard Wightman Fox, 'Epitaph for Middletown: Robert S. Lynd and the Analysis of Consumer Culture', in Richard Wightman Fox and T. J. Jackson Lears, *Culture of Consumption* (New York, 1983), pp. 103–41, quotations on pp. 104 and 140.

103 Clement Greenberg, 'Avant-Garde and Kitsch', *Partisan Review* 6 (Fall 1939), pp. 33–47; Dwight Macdonald, 'Kulturebolschewismus is Here', *Partisan Review* 8 (November-December 1941), pp. 441–8; William Phillips, 'The Intellectual's Tradition', *Partisan Review* 8 (November-December 1941), pp. 485–90; see also James Gilbert, *Writers and Partisans: A History of Literary Radicalism in America* (New York, 1968), especially pp. 155–233.

104 Priestley, *English Journey*, pp. 202, 52, 332–3, 109, 116, and 323; Orwell, *Lion*, pp. 77–8.

105 Priestley, *English Journey*, pp. 211–12.

4 TIME BECOMES MONEY: THE POLITICS OF DISTRIBUTION AND RECOVERY

1 From data collected for 1890–1900, workweeks varied from 42 for miners to up to 96 for tailors in Britain and from 51 for miners to 108 for railroad clerks in France. At roughly the same period, some American miners worked 48 hours; but streetcar workers were on duty 90 hours or more. Gary Cross, *A Quest for Time: The Reduction of Work in Britain and France, 1840–1940* (Berkeley CA, 1989), pp. 233–6; and David Roediger and Philip Foner, *Our Own Time. A History of American Labor and the Working Day* (Westport CT, 1989), pp. 156–7.

2 Some sources are Marion Cahill, *Shorter Hours: A Study of the Movement Since the Civil War* (New York, 1932), pp. 118–33; Josephine Goldmark, *Fatigue and Efficiency* (New York, 1912); and P. S. Florence, *Economics of Fatigue and Unrest* (London, 1924). See also J. Trepp McKelvey, *AFL Attitudes Toward Production 1900–1921* (Ithaca NY, 1952), pp. 2–11; Cross, *Quest*, ch. 5; Anson Rabinbach, *The Human Motor: Energy, Fatigue, and the Origins of Modernity* (New York, 1990), chs 9 and 10; and Roediger and Foner, *Our Own Time*, chs 9 and 10.

3 Victoria Yans-McLaughlin, 'Patterns of Work and Family Organization: Buffalo's Italians', *Journal of Interdisciplinary History* 2 (Autumn 1971), pp. 299–314; Alice Koesler-Harris, 'Organizing the Unorganized: Three Jewish Women and Their Incomes', *Labor History* 17 (Winter, 1976), pp. 5–15; and Benjamin Hunnicutt, 'The Jewish Sabbath Movement in the Early Twentieth Century', *American Jewish History* 69 (December 1979), pp. 196–225.

4 A summary is provided in Health of Munitions Workers' Committee, 'Final Report', *British Parliamentary Papers* 12 (1918), pp. 40–2. More documentation is offered in Cross, *Quest*, ch. 5; and John Horne, *Labour at War: France and Britain, 1914–1918* (Oxford, 1991), p. 178.

5 See Horne, *Labour at War*, pp. 333–9 and 359–64; Cross, *Quest*, ch. 6; and Roediger and Foner, *Our Own Time*, p. 212.

6 For example, New York clothing unions agitated for the two-day weekend because of declining job opportunities due to rationalisation and the desire of Jewish garment workers to win the right to a Saturday Sabbath. Hunnicutt, 'Sabbath Movement', pp. 196–225.

7 William Green, 'Shorter-Hours Cure for Overproduction', *Literary Digest* 90 (18 September 1926), p. 16 cited in Benjamin Hunnicutt, *Work Without End: The Abandonment of Shorter Hours for the Right to Work* (Philadelphia, 1988), p. 77. Representative sources also include William Green, 'The Five-Day Week to Balance Production and Consumption', *American Federationist* 33 (March 1926), p. 1299; and AFL, *Report of the Proceedings of the 46th Annual Convention* (Washington, DC, 1926), pp. 195–207.

8 William Green, 'Less Work is Logical', *American Labor World*, 3 (November 1926), p. 20. See also *American Federationist* 33 (January 1926) and 34 (April 1927). For additional discussion, see chapter 2 above.

9 Included in this rich literature are James Walvin, *Beside the Seaside* (London, 1978); Harriet Bridgeman and Elizabeth Drury, *Beside the*

Seaside (London, 1977); the novel by J. L. Hodson, *Carnival at Black-port* (Manchester, 1938); B. Turner and S. Palmer, *The Blackpool Story*, (Blackpool, 1976); John K. Walton, *The Blackpool Landlady, A Social History* (Manchester, 1978) and especially his *The English Seaside Resort: A Social History, 1750–1914* (London, 1984); and Sue Farant, 'London by the Sea: Resort Development on the South Coast of England, 1880–1939', *Journal of Contemporary History* 22 (1987), pp. 137–62.

10 The seaside habit was much less developed in France than in England. Note Patrice Boussel, *Histoire des vacances* (Paris, 1961); and R. Guerrand, *La Conquête des vacances* (Paris, 1963).

11 James Jakle, *The Tourist* (Lincoln NE, 1985), chs 3 and 4; and Warren Belasco, *Americans on the Road: From Autocamp to Motel* (Cambridge MA, 1979), especially pp. 111–15.

12 Charles Mills, *Vacations for Industrial Workers* (New York, 1927), pp. 149–50; Boussel, *Histoire des vacances*, pp. 27–161; and note 9, this chapter.

13 Mills, *Vacations*, pp. 24–5; and Donna Allen, *Fringe Benefits: Wages or Social Obligation, An Analysis with Historical Perspectives from Paid Vacations*, revised edn (Ithaca NY, 1969), ch. 3.

14 John Beard and A. Dalgleish, *Out-of-Work Pay, or Holidays with Pay Which?* (Birmingham, 1926), pp. 1–15; TUC, *Proceedings* (1926), p. 433; Industrial Relations Staff, 'Annual Paid Vacations for Workers in Countries Outside of the United States', (New York, 1925) (typed pamphlet in the TUC Archive), pp. i–iii and 5–8; Mills, *Vacations*, p. 308; and TUC Archive HD5106 for various union vacation with pay proposals and agreements, 1920–4. See also Stephen Jones, 'Trade-Union Policy between the Wars: The Case of Holidays With Pay in Britain', *International Review of Social History* 31 (1986), pp. 40–55.

15 Between 1919 and 1925, legislation extended paid vacations to various workers in six eastern and central European countries. Georges Bachelier, *Les Congés payés à l'étranger du point de vue internationale* (Zurich, 1937), pp. 197–8 and 'Congés payés aux ouvriers', *Bulletin du Ministère du Travail* (April-June 1929), pp. 121–9.

16 Mills, *Vacations*, p. 71, see also pp. 239–73. 'Do Factory Vacations Pay?', *Factory* 26 (1921), p. 1086 cited in Allen, *Fringe Benefits*, p. 46 and ch. 3.

17 National Industrial Conference Board, *Vacations with Pay for Wage Earners*, (New York, 1935), pp. 10, 4, and 9; Industrial Relations Staff, 'Annual Paid Vacations', p. 6; Mills, *Vacations*, pp. 70 and 76; and US Department of Labor, Bureau of Labor Statistics, *Vacations with Pay in Industry, 1937* (Washington DC, 1939), pp. 7–8.

18 Louis Walker, *Distributed Leisure* (New York, 1932), p. 34.

19 For a full analysis see Hunnicutt, *Work Without End*, chs 3 and 5. Other sources include Chris Nyland, *Reduced Worktime and the Management of Production* (Cambridge, 1989), pp. 146–55; Harry Millis, *Organized Labor* (New York, 1945), pp. 420–9; and Irving Bernstein, *A History of the American Worker 1933–1941. Turbulent Years* (New York, 1970), pp. 22–31.

20 Hunnicutt, *Work Without End*, p. 152. His chapter 5 has an excellent bibliography dealing with this theme.

21 John Frey, 'The Economics of Wages and Hours', *American Federationist* 38 (1931), pp. 290–1.

22 *New York Times* (17 February 1932), cited in Roediger and Foner, *Our Own Time*, p. 245.

23 Hunnicutt, *Work Without End*, pp. 173, 175, and 196. S. I. Rosenman, compiler, *The Public Papers and Addresses of Franklin D. Roosevelt, The Year of Crisis, 1933* 2 (New York, 1938), pp. 22 and 252; and Harold Ickes, 'Jobs Versus the Dole', *American City* 49 (December 1934), p. 43. Note also Irving Bernstein, *The Caring Society. The New Deal, the Worker, and the Great Depression* (Boston MA, 1985), pp. 116–19.

24 Hunnicutt, *Work Without End*, chs 7 and 8.

25 See especially George Paulsen, 'The Legislative History of the Fair Labor Standards Act', Ph.D. dissertation, Ohio State University, 1959, pp. 101, 104, 151, 162, and 238–57; and Paul Douglas and James Hackman, 'The Fair Labor Standards Act of 1938', *Political Science Quarterly* 53 (December 1938), pp. 502–31.

26 Bernstein, *The Caring Society*, pp. 126–31, 142; Rosenman, *Addresses of Franklin D. Roosevelt*, 6, pp. 209–10; and Paulsen, 'Fair Labor Standards Act', p. 248.

27 Roediger and Foner, *Our Own Time*, pp. 259–62.

28 Maurice Leven, Harold Moulton, and Clark Warburton, *America's Capacity to Consume* (Washington DC, 1934), pp. 127–32.

29 Brookings Institution, *The Recovery Problem in the United States* (Washington DC, 1936), pp. 25, 243–4, 256–9, and 541–3; and Harold Moulton and Maurice Leven, *The Thirty-Hour Week* (Washington DC, 1935), pp. 7, 13, and 20. Similar attitudes toward industrial recovery and the 30-hour week are in Mordecai Ezekiel, *Jobs for All Through Industrial Expansion* (New York, 1939), especially pp. 219–24.

30 See Steve Fraser, 'The "Labor Question" ', and Alan Brinkley, 'The New Deal and the Idea of the State', in S. Fraser and Gary Gerstle. eds, *The Rise and Fall of the New Deal Order* (Princeton NJ, 1989), pp. 55–84 and 85–121.

31 Walker, *Distributed Leisure*, pp. 222, 227, 234, and 240–1.

32 Harold Ickes, *Back to Work. The Story of PWA* (New York, 1935), p. 195.

33 Examples of the reformist French disillusionment with rationalisation include CGT, *Congrès national corporatif* (Paris, 1931), pp. 43–51; and *Le Peuple* (12 and 15 September 1931). Communist views are summarised in CGTU, *Congrès national ordinaire* (Paris, 1931), pp. 39–40, 128–9; 153–8, 450, and 458. British sentiments are expressed in the *Proceedings at a Meeting between Engineering and Allied Employers' National Federations and Various Trade Unions, 40 Hours Week* (London, 1934), pp. 1–5, 8–9, and 11–12; and International Association for Social Progress, *Inquiry into the Hours Problem* (London, 1933), pp. 48–51.

34 In France, for example, in 1930 only 5 per cent worked less than 48 hours. But by 1935, almost half worked under this standard (Statistics

from *La Voix du Peuple* (December 1934), p. 814). But the *International Labour Review* (December 1934), p. 876 reported that the hours of British textile workers were raised to 55 to take advantage of export opportunities made available with the abandonment of the gold standard. The French trade journal, *L'Usine* (2 November 1933), p. 23 similarly reported the widespread use of overtime to met seasonal job orders. See also Allen Hutt, *The Condition of the Working Class in Britain* (London, 1933), pp. 22–3, 30, 61–5, and 169–70; and Marie-Antoinette Boudet, *Le Semaine de 40 heures* (Paris, 1935), pp. 85–8 and 101–8.

35 Bertrand Russell, *In Praise of Idleness and Other Essays* (London, 1935), p. 17

36 TUC, *Proceedings* (London, 1933), pp. 71–2 and 214; Public Records Office LAB 2 1008 IL 113/1933, undated report on the TUC; and *Labour Magazine* (February 1933), pp. 438–42. See also, Stephen Jones, 'Trade Unions Movement and Work-Sharing Policies in Interwar Britain', *Industrial Relations Journal* 16 (Winter 1985); pp. 57–69.

37 International Association for Social Progress, *Hours Problem*, pp. 48–9; *Proceedings between Engineering Various Unions, 40 Hour Week*, pp. 8–9; William Sherwood, 'Shipbuilding Industry. Application for the 40 Hour Week, Without Reduction in Pay', (Edinburgh, 27 June 1934), pp. 1–26, TUC Archive, HD 9678.

38 See, for example, Charles Dukes of the General and Municipal Workers, *Labour Magazine* (January 1935), p. 112.

39 Bevin speech, TUC, *Proceedings* (London, 1936), p. 340 and Ernest Bevin, *My Plan for 2,000,000 Workless* (London, 1936), pp. 9–14 and 23–4. M. Steward (New Fabian Research Board), *The 40 Hours Week* (London, 1937), especially pp. 25–31; *Industrial Welfare* (October 1934), pp. 42–3; F. S. Hayburn, in *Daily Herald* (14 March 1933); and Harold Browden in *The Times* (27 October 1932).

40 Communist Party of Great Britain, 'Friday Night Till Monday Morning' (September 1937), TUC Archive, HD5106.

41 For Clark's views, see his speech in C. A. Macartney (League of Nations Union Conference), *Hours of Work and Employment* (London, 1934), pp. 40–5 and 51.

42 Modern Records Centre, Engineering Employers Federation (EEF) H 11/3, National Committee of Employers' Organisations, 'The Unemployment Situation, Report Submitted to the Ministry of Labour', 6 December 1933. See also the Engineering Employers' Federation's opinion in *The Times* (11 May 1934).

43 Jacques Duboin, *La Grande Relève des hommes par la machine* (Paris, 1935), pp. 10–23. A similar work is Maurice Lacoin, *Vers un équilibre nouveau* (Paris, 1933), ch. 6.

44 CGT, *Pourquoi la semaine de 40 heures* (Paris, 1933), pp. 7–15 and 22; CGT, *La Semaine de quarante heures* (Paris, 1932), pp. 22, 28, and 30; CGT, *Congrès Confédéral* (Paris, 1933), pp. 43–4; and *Voix du peuple* (January 1934), p. 36. For the communist view see Jacques Doriot, *Journée de sept heures avec salaire de huit heures* (Paris, 1932) and Confédération générale du Travail Unitaire, *Congrès* (Paris, 1931), p. 562.

45 CGT, *Pourquoi*, pp. 14–15; Jouhaux's speech at Lille, 26 Febuary 1933 cited in Boudet, *Semaine*, p. 162; and CGT, *La Semaine de quarante*, p. 4.

46 See CGT, *Affiche et Lutte* (Paris, 1978), pp. 98–9, and 105 for examples of this propaganda. On CGT priorities, see for example, *Voix du peuple* (January 1934), p. 36 and (December 1934), p. 778. See also Boudet, *Semaine*, pp. 211 and 213.

47 M. Lambert-Ribot, a metal-goods manufacturer, argued against all restrictions on overtime as 'about as reasonable as abolishing the safety valve in order to get up more steam' *L'Usine* (1 February 1934). See also Pierre Collet, *La Semaine de quarante heures* (Paris, 1934), pp. 10–15, 33–9, 54–5, and 150; Maurice Pinot, *La Semaine de 40 heures, le chômage et les prix* (Paris, 1933), pp. 2–65, 39–121, and 133; and Eugène Combaz, *La Semaine de travail de 40 heures* (Marseille, 1932).

48 Boudet, *Semaine*, pp. 112–13. *Industrial and Labor Information* (22 February 1934); pp. 111–13. The CGT cited Roosevelt and the 30-hour bill in the US Senate as models of their demand for the 40-hour week with no reduction in pay. CGT, *Congrès Confédéral* (Paris, 1935), pp. 79–80.

49 Since 1931, Mussolini had been encouraging 'short-time work' and regulated overtime hours. ILO *Yearbook* (Geneva, 1933), p. 95 and ILO, *Hours of Work and Unemployment. Report to the Preparatory Conference* (Geneva, 1933), pp. 1–2, 8–9, 17–19, 28–9, and 48–65.

50 ILO, *Hours of Work and Unemployment Report of the Preparatory Conference, January 20 to 25, 1933*, (Geneva, 1933), pp. 8–10, 12–13, and 22–3; and Public Records Office LAB 2 1008 IL 13/1933, reports on the ILO conference in January 1933 (7 February 1933).

51 In the summer of 1935, two new members of the ILO, the US and the Soviet Union, joined France in support of a draft 40-hour convention, but the British government allied with employers in opposition. The International Labour Conferences of 1933–8 are replete with hours matters as are British Cabinet and Labour Ministry papers at the Public Records Office. See also Charles Kindleberger, *World in Depression* (Berkeley CA, 1978).

52 TUC, *Proceedings* (1933), pp. 243–9, (1935), pp. 70–1, 138–42, 161–3, 171–4, and 314–16, and (1936), pp. 71, 171–3, and 341–4; and *Labour Magazine* (March 1935), p. 159 and (August 1937), p. 294.

53 Attempts of the Labour Party to introduce a 40-hour week in municipal and national government works also met with little success. *Labour Magazine* (November 1933), p. 70. See also Jones, 'Work-Sharing Policies', pp. 57–69. Bevin speech, TUC, *Proceedings* (London, 1936), p. 341.

54 *The Times* (23 January 1935).

55 Official material on the 40-hour week is in France, *Documents Parlementaires, Chambre des Députés*, (1936), pp. 853 and *Débats Parlementaires, Chambre des Députés* (12 June 1936), pp. 1412–43. Notable was the opposition of Paul Reynaud, later important in the dismantling of the 40-hour week. For Reynaud, like the American, Harold Moulton, shorter hours threatened economic recovery. A summary of the 40-

hour campaign is in CGT, *Congrès Confédéral* (1935) p. 74–84 and (1938), pp. 65–6.

56 Surveys of French business opposition are in *Industrial and Labor Information* 60 (2 and 16 November 1936); pp. 264–5 and 333; 62 (10 May 1937), pp. 199–200; and 66 (2 May 1938), pp. 134–5.

57 Details of these *de facto* extensions of the workweek are in *Industrial and Labor Information* 65 (24 and 31 January 1938), pp. 80–3, 114–15; 66 (6 June 1938), pp. 267–9; 68 (12 December 1938), pp. 352–7; 69 (16 January 1939), pp. 72–5; and 70 (22 May 1939), pp. 586–7. See also E. Du Reau, 'L'Aménagement de loi instituant la semaine de 40 heures', in René Rémond, ed., *Edouard Daladier, Chef du gouvernement, avril 1938–septembre 1939* (Paris, 1977), pp. 131–48.

58 The Iron and Steel Trade Conference, which had pushed for four shifts of six hours in the early 1930s and a 40-hour week (in five shifts) in 1937, accepted a continuous working week with a 48-hour schedule in 1946–7. See Modern Records Centre, Iron and Steel Trades Conference records, MS 36 30A/99.

59 See Karl Hinrichs, William Roche, and Carmen Sirianni, eds., *Working Time in Transition* (Philadelphia, 1991), pp. 15–19 for another explanation of the timing of worktime reductions.

60 A summary is in CGT, *Congrès Confédéral* (1935) p. 74–84 and (1938), pp. 65–6. See also *Voix du peuple* (June 1936), pp. 65 and 388. A fine recent analysis of the period is Julian Jackson, *The Politics of Depression in France* (New York, 1985).

61 See Léon Blum's defence in his *L'Histoire jugera* (Paris, 1945), pp. 283–91. Another version is his *Léon Blum Before his Judges at the Supreme Court of Riom, March 11 and 12, 1942* (London, 1943) pp. 39–100.

62 Pierre Cot admitted in the 1940s that the law had been 'too rigid' at first; but, he insisted, this was quickly remedied in defence industries. In any case there was no choice but a 40-hour law in the social upheaval of the Spring of 1936, a point stressed also by Blum. Cot denied that the 40-hour week decreased productivity claiming that it rose in 1936 and 1937 by comparison with the previous two years and declined again after the law was suspended in 1938–9. Pierre Cot, *Triumph of Treason* (Chicago, 1944), pp. 166–8.

63 For a moderate stance, consider the following by Jean-Charles Asselain, 'La Semaine de 40 heures, le chômage, et l'emploi', *Le Mouvement social* 54 (January-March 1966), pp. 184–204; 'Une Erreur de politique économie. La Loi de quarante heures de 1936', *Revue économique* 25 (1974), pp. 688–91; and 'La Loi des quarante heures de 1936', in J.-C. Asselain, ed., *La France en Mouvement, 1934–1938*, (Paris, 1986), pp. 164–92. For more negative assessments, see Alfred Sauvy, *Histoire économique de la France entre les deux guerres*, 2 (Paris, 1984), pp. 297–302. A more positive view is in Jacques Kergoat, *La France du Front Populaire* (Paris, 1986), pp. 348–53.

64 Seidman argues that French industrial workers used their increased power in nationalised defence plants to restrict production and to relax work rules. Whatever may have been the public ideology of trade union or Popular Front officials, the French rank-and-file resisted work and

did not embrace productivism; instead they insisted on only the leisure and wage benefits of Popular Front legislation. Michael Seidman, 'The Birth of the Weekend and The Revolts Against Work During The Popular Front, 1936–1938', *French Historical Studies* 12 (Fall 1982), pp. 249–76 and Michael Seidman, *Workers Against Work: Labor in Paris and Barcelona During The Popular Fronts* (Berkeley CA, 1991), ch. 11.

65 Herrick Chapman argues that aircraft workers 'bent over backwards to show that they, and not employers, were the champions of rearmament, and that hostile bureaucrats and bottlenecks in supplies, and not the forty-hour week, were blocking the way'. The 40-hour week meant not an escape from work, but 'represented shifts in political power – at the factory and in the country at large'. Herrick Chapman, 'Political Life of the Rank and File: French Aircraft Workers During The Popular Front, 1934–38', *International Labor and Working Class History* 30 (Fall, 1986), pp. 13–31, quotation from p. 21. See especially his *State, Capitalism and Working-Class Radicalism in the French Aircraft Industry* (Berkeley CA, 1991), pp. 178, 180, 183–5, and 189–90.

66 Even the sceptical Asselain stressed that the 40-hour week failed primarily because it became the flashpoint for political conflict which impeded necessary flexibility in its application and prevented Blum from having adequate time to make it work. Asselain, 'Loi des quarante heures', pp. 175–82.

67 Lionel Robbins, *Economic Planning and International Order* (London, 1937), pp. 178–82.

68 John Hobson, *The Economics of Unemployment*, revised edn (London, 1931), ch. 2 and *Rationalisation and Unemployment, An Economic Dilemma* (London, 1930), p. 123.

69 See, for example, Alvin Hansen, *Fiscal Policy and Business Cycles* (New York, 1941), chs 4, 12, and 14. Useful analysis is in Brinkley, 'The Idea of the State'; and Dean May, *From New Deal to New Economics: The American Liberal Response to the Recession of 1937* (New York, 1981).

70 US Department of Labor, *Vacations with Pay*, p. 8 and Allen, *Fringe Benefits*, p. 67–8.

71 'The American Vacation', *Fortune*, 14 (1936), pp. 161. By 1937, between 91 and 83 per cent of public utility, retail and wholesale trade workers enjoyed paid vacations compared to only 1 per cent of coal miners. Only 25 per cent of unionised workers had vacation agreements by 1940. 'Vacations With Pay in Union Agreements, 1940', *Monthly Labor Review* 51 (1940), pp. 1071. Donna Allen stresses, and probably exaggerates, the indifference of unions to vacations with pay, mistaking the disincentive of workers in seasonal industries to place vacations high on their bargaining agenda for general trade-union indifference. Allen, *Fringe Benefits*, pp. 72–83.

72 'Vacations and Defense Studied in Steel Mills', *Iron Age* 147 (1941), p. 87; and US Department of Labor, Bureau of Labor Statistics, *Vacations with Pay in American Industry 1943 and 1944* (Washington, 1945); National Industrial Conference Board, *Vacation and Holiday Practices* (New York, 1946), especially p. 4; and US Department of

Labor, Bureau of Labor Statistics, *Paid Vacations Provisions in Major Union Contracts, 1957* (Washington DC, 1958), pp. 28, 30. See also Allen, *Fringe Benefits*, chs 5–8; and Clyde Dankert, *Contemporary Unionism in the United States* (New York, 1948), pp. 332–4.

73 For background on vacation legislation in France, see Conseil supérieur du travail, *Compte rendu* (Paris 1935), pp. 129–40, 187–223, and 228–32; A. Lorch, *Les Congés payés en France* (Paris, 1938); and Nicole Odinet, *Les Congés annuels payés* (Paris, 1937). For British background, see Jones, 'Holidays With Pay', pp. 45–6.

74 Note for example the comments of employers in James Whittaker, *Holidays with Pay* (London, 1937), pp. 7–12.

75 J. Mensch, 'Urban Workers' Need for a Holiday', *Labour Magazine* (March 1932), pp. 502–3. See, for example, the following articles in *Industrial Welfare*: J. L. Hammond, 'Industry and Leisure', (May 1934), p. 27; 'Recreation Education', (May 1936), pp. 21–5; and 'Notes on Towns, Centres and Tours', (April 1937), pp. 27–31.

76 For details see ILO, 'Holidays with Pay, Report V', *International Labour Conference* (Geneva, 1935) and 'Holidays With Pay, Report II', *International Labour Conference* (1936).

77 Conseil supérieur du travail, *Compte rendu* (1935), pp. 226–7.

78 UK House of Commons, *Report on the Committee on Holidays with Pay* (London, April 1938), (Command Document 5724), pp. 5–7; and House of Commons, *Minutes of Evidence Taken Before The Committee on Holidays with Pay* (London, 1937), pp. 135–6, 142, 153, 165, 171–3, 178–80, 189–90, and 335–46. See also Jones, 'Holidays with Pay', pp. 45–55.

79 UK House of Commons, *Committee on Holidays with Pay*, pp. 21–23. Brunner, *Holiday Making*, pp. 3–4; UK Ministry of Labour, *Holidays with Pay, Collective Agreements Between Organisations of Employers and Workpeople* (London, 1939), pp. 7 and 10. See also Jones, 'Holidays With Pay', pp. 45–6.

80 A good summary is in Francis Horden, 'Genèse et vote de la loi du 20 juin 1936 sur les congés payés', *Mouvement social*, 150 (January-March 1990), pp. 19–34.

5 DEMOCRATIC LEISURE AND THE FAILURE OF CULTURAL POLITICS

1 Jean Viard, *Penser les vacances* (Paris, 1984), especially pp. 9–10, 87–97, 106–16, and 132–5.

2 John Bodnar, *Remaking America: Public Memory, Commemoration and Patriotism in the Twentieth Century* (Princeton NJ, 1991), ch. 7.

3 Some sources include Stephen Jones, *Workers at Play: A Social and Economic History of Leisure, 1919–1939* (London, 1986), pp. 170–7; Ralph Bond, 'Cinema in the Thirties, Documentary Film and Labour Movements', in Jon Clark, Margot Heinemann, David Margolies, and Carol Snee, eds, *Culture and Crisis in Britain in the 1930s*, (London, 1979), pp. 241–56; and Jeffrey Richards, *The Age of the Dream Palace* (London, 1984), pp. 34–42.

4 Léon Pasquier, *La Loi sur la journée de huit heures. Quelques*

conséquences économiques et sociales (Lyon, 1921), pp. 113–14; J. Borderel and M. R. Georges-Picot, *L'Utilisation des loisirs des travailleurs* (Paris, 1925), pp. 16–21; and Georges-Picot, 'Les Loisirs et l'éducation populaire' *Redressement français* 21 (1927), pp. 133. Comité national d'études sociales et politiques, *L'Organisation des loisirs ouvriers* (Paris, 1930), quotation of Lacoin, p. 44. See also L. Burdy, *Pour nos loisirs* (St Marie aux mines, 1924), pp. 1–70; A. P. Pacaud, *Essai sur l'organisation des loisirs ouvriers* (Nancy, 1929), pp. 18–51; Edouard Labbe, *Les Loisirs ouvriers* (Lille, 1929) pp. 18–19; Société d'Education Familiale de l'Aube, *Organisations des loisirs à la campagne* (Paris, 1932), pp. 8–9; and Madame Gaston Etienne, *L'Utilisation des loisirs des travailleurs* (St Cloud, 1935). On workers' gardens see Henri Robin, *Les Jardins ouvriers* (Paris, 1905); and Louis Rivière, *La Terre et l'atelier: jardins ouvriers* (Paris, 1904).

5 As historian André Rauch noted, camp leaders created a 'corporal practice' for city children. Camps offered, not only fresh air, discipline, and right thinking, but a cult of youthful spontaneity against family and school and a romantic rural image of a 'providential land offering healthful food'. The ideas were as influential in the Popular Front as they were among Vichyites. A. Rauch, *Vacances et pratiques corporelles* (Paris, 1988), pp. 111–14, 156–61, and 168. See also R. -P. Rey-Herme, *La Colonie de vacance, hier et aujourd'hui* (Paris, 1955), pp. 9 and 19.

6 Patrice Boussel, *Histoire des vacances* (Paris, 1961), pp. 83–4, and 92; and Jacques Guerin-Desjardins, *L'Adolescence ouvrière. Conférence de Service Social au Centre de Formation sociale des cadres de l'Industrie et du Commerce* (Paris, 1939), pp. 10–19, 37–42, 63–4, 273, 297, and 300–1.

7 Employer-provided workers' gardens increased from 77,000 in 1919 to 160,000 in 1922; yet, this was scarcely more than a gesture. And attempts of the General Confederation of French Employers in 1930 to establish a Commission on Leisure to spread paternalistic programmes to smaller firms, especially in the individualistic regions of the west and south, met with little success. See Czeslaw Kaczmarek, *L'Emigration polonaise en France après la guerre* (Paris, 1928), pp. 280–94; and Jean Beaudemoulin, *Enquête sur les loisirs d'ouvrier français* (Paris, 1924), Part 2; Yves Becquet, *L'Organisation des loisirs des travailleurs* (Paris, 1919), pp. 218–19 and 223–9; and Robert Pinot, *Les Oeuvres sociales des industries métallurgiques* (Paris, 1924), chs 1–3. See also Suzanne Trist, 'Le Patronat face à la question des loisirs ouvriers avant 1936 et après' *Mouvement social* 150 (January-March 1990), pp. 46 and 52.

8 Gaston Rives, *La Corvée de joie* (Paris, 1924), pp. 175–8, 189–90, and 207.

9 The English playground movement emerged in 1897 and by 1933 there were 41 centres in the London area. Only about 1 in 40 children (5 to 14 years old) used them in a 1933 survey. Herbert May and Dorothy Petgen, *Leisure and its Uses: Some International Observations* (New York, 1928), p. 174; and H. L. Smith *New Survey of London Life and Labour*, vol. 9 (London, 1935), pp. 72–3. See also *Industrial Welfare* (September 1938), pp. 350–3.

10 Private groups like the Footpaths Preservation Societies, and London

Playing Field Society conserved trails, football grounds, and cricket pitches. The National Playing Fields Association in 1925 advocated a national effort to democratise open spaces and to provide five acres per 1,000 people. This was far more than the one acre for 975 in Manchester, perhaps the 'greenest' town in Britain at the time. May and Petgen, *Leisure and its Uses*, pp. 155–74; and B. S. Rowntree, *Poverty and Progress* (London, 1941), pp. 333 and 387.

11 Eleanor Ells, *History of Organized Camping: The First 100 Years* (Martinsville IN, 1986), pp. 1–85.

12 Clarence Rainwater, *The Play Movement in the United States* (New York, 1922), pp. 100–5; and Henry Curtis, *The Play Movement and Its Significance* (New York, 1917), pp. 60–5. We still must ask how successful were these efforts. Historian Dom Cavallo doubts that more than 20 per cent of immigrant youth visited urban playgrounds in the period, 1900–20. And increasingly from the 1920s play programmes were integrated into the schools and recess. See D. Cavallo, *Muscles and Morals: Organized Playgrounds and Urban Reform, 1880–1920* (Philadelphia, 1981), pp. 46–8.

13 The Playground Association, 'The Playground Association of America: Purpose', *Playground* 4 (1910), p. 73, cited in Cavallo, *Muscles and Morals*, p. 37.

14 Jacques Donzelot, *The Policing of Families* (New York, 1979), pp. 3–96.

15 Robert Holt, *Sport and Society in Modern France* (New York, 1981), pp. 191–201; and Gerard Cholvy, ed., *Mouvements de jeunesse crétiens et juifs* (Paris, 1985), especially pp. 14–57, 83–123, and 233–46.

16 Victoria de Grazia, *Politics of Consent* (Cambridge, 1982), ch. 1; and Ernest Hamburger, 'Significance of the Nazi Leisure Time Program' *Social Research* 12 (1945), pp. 226–49.

17 See, for example, Lizabeth Cohen, *Making a New Deal: Industrial Workers in Chicago, 1919–1939* (Cambridge, 1990), pp. 162–83; and Jack Petrill, *After the Whistle Blows* (New York, 1949).

18 E. Plevant's article in *Le Réveil du Nord* (17 May 1922); or E. Antonelli in *Le Peuple* (28 June 1923).

19 As early as 1918, the dramatic composer Alfred Doyen joined trade unions and artists to create 'Fêtes du Peuple', popular choral and orchestral celebrations of democratic values. Doyen's composition 'The Triumph of Liberty', set to words by Romain Rolland, was to create a 'crowd that sings'. In response to the eight-hour day, the CGT in 1922 established a Commission for Education and Leisure in Paris to coordinate local cultural programmes. Jean Marguerite, *Les Fêtes du peuple. L'Oeuvre, les moyens, l'but* (Paris, 1921), pp. 1–20, 40–8, 55; and Georges Lefranc, *Une Expérience d'éducation ouvrière* (Paris, 1971), p. 20–2. See also Paul Crouzet, 'L'Education populaire et les 8 heures' *La Grande Revue* (October 1921), pp. 23–54; *Peuple* (30 July 1922); Bacquet, *Loisirs*, pp. 195–225; and Rives, *Corvée de joie*, pp. 60–97.

20 In a study of factories in the St Etienne region in 1935, 80 of 85 factories had sports clubs, mostly run by workers. The communist stronghold of Bobigny in suburban Paris in 1930 provided an inexpensive 42-day summer camp for up to 300 children by 1930 with the hope that 'fresh

air' would make militants. Holt, *Society and Sports*, p. 203; P. Marie, *Pour le sport ouvrier* (Paris, 1934), pp. 1–14, 24–9; Jean P. Depretto and V. Schweitzer, *Le Communisme à l'usine* (Paris, 1984), pp. 18–19; M. de Veth, 'La Politique culturelle des syndicats ouvriers pendant l'entre les deux guerres' (Thesis, Institut français d'Utrecht, 1981), pp. 116–21 and 150–88; Benoit Frachon, *Le rôle social des syndicats* (Paris, 1937), pp. 5–6; and Tyler Stovall, *The Rise of the Paris Red Belt* (Berkeley CA, 1990), pp. 138–40.

21 Bacquet, *Loisirs*, pp. 22–6; and Rives, *Corvée de joie*, pp. 80, 29–30, and 50.

22 Jones, *Workers at Play*, pp. 142–7. See also, David Clark, *Colne Valley: Radicalism to Socialism* (London, 1981); and Chris Waters, *British Socialists and the Politics of Popular Culture* (Manchester, 1990).

23 The communist-inspired British Workers' Sports Federation consciously tried to win wage-earners from commercial spectator sport. And, by July 1933, the TUC's monthly, *Labour Magazine*, began to devote a regular column to George Elvin's Workers' Sports Association. May and Petgen, *Uses of Leisure*, pp. 187–92; T. Kelly, *A History of Adult Education in Great Britain* (Liverpool, 1962), especially pp. 276–300; *Labour Magazine* (October 1933), p. 45; (December 1933), p. 94, etc. See also, Stephen Jones, 'Sport, Politics, and the Labour Movement: The Workers' Sports Federation, 1923–1935' *British Journal of Sports History* 2 (1985), pp. 154–78.

24 Marius Hansome, *World Workers' Educational Movements. Their Social Significance* (New York, 1931), pp. 284–92, 314–36; Margaret Hodgen, *Workers' Education in England and the United States* (London, 1925), chs 6 and 7; and T.W. Price, *Story of the WEA, 1903–1924* (London, 1924). H. L. Smith found that enrolment at various adult workers' classes attracted 75,000 in 1933 but mostly reached clerks seeking cultural enhancement rather than manual labourers studying social issues or vocations. Smith, *New London Lives and Labour* 9, pp. 108–9.

25 Despite the fact that pubs were usually owned by breweries, they were often bastions of working-class sociability. The number of working men's clubs rose from 1,558 in 1913 to 2,488 by 1926. Increasingly they were centres of sports and gambling rather than drunkenness. Other forms of respectable working-class pastimes included the 1.2 million allotments or gardens that were cultivated in 1934. Working Men's Clubs and Institute Union, *Annual Report* (1913), p. 71 and (1926), p. 46; Smith, *London Lives and Labour*, vol. 9, chs 2, 6–8, 10, and 13. S. B. Rowntree, *Progress*, pp. 333, 354, and 375. See also C. Forman, *Industrial Town: Self-Portrait of St. Helens in the 1920s* (St Albans, 1979), pp. 185–202. Two fine surveys with sources are Jones, *Workers at Play*; and John Lowerson and Alun Howkins, *Trends in Leisure, 1919–1939* (London, 1979), pp. 7–54.

26 Hansome, *Workers' Educational Movements*, pp. 229–40; Hodgen, *Workers' Education*, pp. 212–36, 240–55; Education Bureau of America, *Workers Education in the United States. Second National Conference* (New York, 1922); T. R. Adam, *The Worker's Road to Learning* (New York, 1940); James Maurer, 'Leisure and Labor' *Playground* 20

(1927), pp. 649–55; and Irving Bernstein, *The Lean Years* (Baltimore MD, 1960), pp. 104–6.

27 Cohen, *Making a New Deal*, pp. 340–9.

28 Comité national d'études sociales et politiques, *Loisirs ouvriers*, speech by Thomas, pp. 6–7. Note also Victoria de Grazia, 'La Politique sociale du loisir: 1900–1940', *Les Cahiers de la recherche architecturale* 15–17 (1985), pp. 24–35.

29 See ILO, *International Labour Conference, Report on the Development of Facilities for the Utilisation of Workers' Leisure* (Geneva 1924); Georges Mequet, 'Workers' Spare Time', *International Labour Review* 10 (November 1924), p. 555; and Raymond Unwin, 'The Influence of Housing Conditions on the Use of Leisure', *International Labour Review* 9 (June 1924), pp. 915–28. See also Leifur Magnusson, 'The ILO and the Leisure Movement', *Playground* 29 (March 1927), pp. 656–8.

30 Jean-Henri Adam shared Thomas' interest in physical fitness (rather than skilled sport) and non-partisan local athletic clubs in order to restore the health of the 'race'. J.-H. Adam, 'L'Education physique et les sports' *Redressement français* 21 (1927), p. 80.

31 Comité national d'études sociales et politiques, *Loisirs ouvriers*, pp. 2–8; International Association for Workers' Spare Time, *Official Bulletin* 1 (1938), pp. 4–19 and 48–9; May and Petgen, *Leisure*, pp. 15–16; and ILO, 'Les Loisirs du travailleur', *Etudes et documents*, Series G, 4 (Geneva, 1935).

32 International Central Bureau, 'Joy and Work', *Report. World Congress for Leisure Time and Recreation* (Berlin, 1937), pp. 35–8, 85, and 89.

33 A. Sternheim, 'Leisure in the Totalitarian State', *Sociological Review* 30 (June 1938), pp. 43–8. See also Theo Beckers, 'A. Sternheim and the Study of Leisure in Early Critical Theory', *Leisure Studies* 9 (1990), pp. 197–212.

34 ILO, 'Les loisirs du travailleur', pp. 135–47; and International Association for Workers' Spare Time, *Official Bulletin* 2 (1938), pp. 15 and 35–6. See also Lebert H. Wier, *Europe at Play. A Study of Recreation and Leisure Time Activities* (New York, 1937).

35 See, for example, Hugh Cunningham, *Leisure in the Industrial Revolution* (New York, 1980); Peter Bailey, *Leisure and Class in Victorian England: Rational Recreation and the Contest for Control, 1830–1885* (London, 1978); and Paul Boyer, *Urban Masses and Moral Order in America, 1820–1920* (Cambridge MA, 1978).

36 William Ogburn, *Social Change with Respect to Cultural and Original Nature* (New York, 1922), p. 141; Martin and Ester Neumeyer, *Leisure and Recreation. A Study of Leisure and their Sociological Aspects* (New York, 1936), pp. 198–207; and Edward Lindeman, *Leisure – a National Issue* (New York, 1929), pp. 215–18.

37 These Chicago studies include Frederic Trasher, *The Gang* (1927); Harvey Zorbaugh, *The Gold Coast and the Saloon* (1929); Paul Cressey, *Taxi Dance Hall* (1932); and Walter Rechless's *Vice in Chicago* (1933).

38 President's Research Committee on Social Trends, *Recent Social Trends in the United States*, vol. 1 (New York, 1933), p. liii. See also L. A. Thompson, 'Workers' Leisure: A Selected List of Reference', *Monthly Labor Review* 24 (March 1927), pp. 637–47.

39 Neumeyer, *Leisure and Recreation*, pp. 65–9. Eugene Lies, *New Leisure Challenges the Schools* (Washington DC, 1933), pp. 26–9. See also US Office of Education, Committee on Youth Problems, *Youth* (Washington DC, 1936); and Weaver W. Pangburn, *Adventures in Recreation* (New York, 1936).

40 C. G. and Harley Wrenn, *Time on Their Hands, A Report on Leisure, Recreation, and Young People* (Washington, 1941), p. xix. Or, as Newton Baker, the Secretary of War for Woodrow Wilson and public recreation advocate, put it: 'I think the whole idea of leisure is that people should be permitted to use it the way they want to use it', National Recovery Administration (NRA), *Report of the New York Committee on the Use of Leisure Time* (New York, 1934), p. 15. See also the editorial of Howard Braucher, *Recreation* 24 (January 1931), p. 539.

41 See Lies, *New Leisure*, pp. 22–4; and Ernest Calkins, *Care and Feeding of Hobby Horses* (New York, 1934). An excellent analysis and bibliography are in Steven Gelber, 'A Job You Can't Lose: Work and Hobbies in the Great Depression', *Journal of Social History* 24 (1990), pp. 741–66.

42 The New York Committee advocated everything from new teaching methods and 'frill courses' in order to encourage lifelong reading and interest in the arts to night-time and summer use of schools. It even suggested subtle techniques like offering both cultural and athletic programmes in the same facility. NRA, *New York Committee*, p. 11 and *passim*.

43 Lindeman, *Leisure – A National Issue*, pp. 13–14, 22–4, 54–5. See also J. B. Nash, *Spectatoritis* (New York, 1932); and Wrenn, *Time on their Hands*, pp. 25–7. Useful sketches of recreation leaders in this period are in George Butler, *Pioneers in Public Recreation* (Minneapolis, 1965).

44 The impact of declining personal income on free-time pursuits fascinated investigators. For example, sociologist Jesse Steiner wondered whether austerity would lead to the revival of the 'diversions of pioneer days', to increased conversation with neighbours, or to greater use of public libraries and parks. See, especially, Jesse Steiner, *Research Memorandum on Recreation in the Depression* (New York, 1937), pp. 33–6 and 40–6; Neumeyer, *Leisure and Recreation*, pp. 54 and 68–9; NRA, *New York Committee*, pp. 30–1; and National Recreation Association, *The Leisure Hours of 5,000 People* (New York, n.d.).

45 NRA, *New York Committee*, pp. 15–18.

46 Dorothy Hewitt, *Adult Education: A Dynamic for Democracy* (New York, 1937), chs 4, 5, and 6, and p. 148. T. R. Adam, *Road to Learning*, pp. 78–9 and 132–6. The professional orientation of adult education is amply illustrated by authorities like Lyman Bryson, a professor of education at Columbia University. L. Bryson, *Adult Education* (New York, 1936).

47 During the 1920s, enrolment in the Boy Scouts grew from 250,000 to 800,000; youth summer camps expanded from their early roots in the northeast throughout the US in the 1920s. The number of American museums increased from 94 in 1910 to 108 in 1920, and to 149 by 1930;

and capital invested rose by 386 per cent. The function of federal and state parks shifted from conservation toward recreational use. Even the laissez-faire president Calvin Coolidge advocated that cities set aside 10 per cent of public land for parks and community centres. As early as 1930, one acre of parks was provided for every 208 people in American towns with parks, high in comparison to England. The number of park and recreation departments in the US rose from 146 in 1921 to 428 by 1931. Finally, the number of recreation professionals employed by local governments rose from 10,218 in 1920 to 24,949 in 1930. Jesse Steiner, *Americans at Play* (New York, 1933), ch. 3 and p. 169; President's Committee on Recent Social Trends, *Recent Social Trends* 2 (New York, 1933), p. 995; and US Bureau of the Census, *The Statistical History of the United States* (New York, 1976), p. 399.

48 Wrenn, *Time on Their Hands*, pp. 52–4, 94–8, 195–8, and 222–32; Dorothy Cline, *Training for Recreation* (Washington DC, 1939), ch. 2; and Jesse Steiner, *Recreation during the Depression*, pp. 57–66 and 82–3. Note also that professional recreationists (employed by local governments) declined from 25,508 in 1931 to 18,496 in 1935, rising slowly only to 24,533 in 1940. US Bureau of the Census, *Statistical History*, p. 398.

49 Lindeman, *Leisure*, pp. 54–5.

50 For example, see *L'Humanité* (19 August 1937).

51 The metalworkers often simply took over organisations formerly controlled by the employers. Julian Jackson, 'Popular Tourism', in Martin Alexander and Helen Graham, eds, *The French and Spanish Popular Fronts. Comparative Perspectives* (Cambridge, 1989), p. 233; and Pascal Ory, 'La Politique culturelle du Front Populaire français, 1935–1939', 5 vols (Doctorat d'Etat thesis, University of Paris, 1990), vol. 4, pp. 1515–23.

52 Trist, 'La question des loisirs ouvriers', pp. 45–58. See also Igno Kolboom, *La Revanche des patrons* (Paris, 1986).

53 This organ of anti-communist labour leaders hoped that gardens, collectively cared for by trade unionists, would create lifelong friends among members. *Syndicats* (11 December 1936 and 29 July 1937).

54 de Veth, 'Politique culturelle des syndicats ouvriers', pp. 138–9. The pamphlet, 'Lire, Pourquoi? Comment? Quoi?', published in 1932 and distributed by the Confederal Centre of Workers' Education stressed that workers should read 'great works' in order to broaden their understanding across space and time. Not only should unions have their own library, but so should workers. The preferred list included both socialist authors such as Marx, Dolleans, and Georges Lefebvre and such bourgeois authors as Charles Gide, J. S. Mill, H. Spencer, and Bergson. And the Centre printed an extensive series of study guides in general and trade union education. For background on the French adult education movement see, Bénigno Cacérès, *Histoire de l'éducation populaire* (Paris, 1964); Antoine Léon, *Histoire de l'éducation populaire* (Paris, 1985); and Geneviève Poujol, *L'Education populaire: Histoires et pouvoirs* (Paris, 1981).

55 Georges Lefranc, *Education ouvrière*, pp. 40–5; Marc Deboin, *L'Aspiration ouvrière vers la culture et les loisirs des travailleurs* (Paris, 1937),

pp. 40–3; Emile and Georges Lefranc, 'Workers' Education in France' *International Labour Review* 37 (May 1937), pp. 618–43; and Rolande Trempé, 'Une Initiative d'éducation populaire en milieu ouvrier et Le Centre Confédéral d'Education Ouvrière de la CGT, 1932–1939', *Les Cahiers de l'animation* 32 (1981).

56 Institut Supérieur Ouvrier, *La Vie du Centre Confédéral d'Education Ouvrière et des Collèges du Travail* (Paris, 1938), pp. 5–6 and 9–18; Lefranc, *Education ouvrière*, pp. 227–42; *Syndicats* (4 December 1936); and Georges Lefranc, *Le Problème de la Culture* (Paris, 1931). See also Léon, *Education populaire*, pp. 168–76; and especially Ory, 'La Politique culturelle' 3, pp. 1323–44.

57 *Le Musée vivant* (June 1937) cited in Julian Jackson, *Popular Front in France* (Cambridge, 1988), p. 130, see also, pp. 119–21, 138–45; *Populaire* (1 August 1936); and *Intransigeant* (15 August 1937).

58 Claude Bellanger, *Le Foyer communal d'éducation et des loisirs* (Paris, 1938). Catholic activities and views can be found in Jeune ouvrière catholique, *Jeunesse forte. Manuel des loisirs*, (Paris, 1938), quotation on p. 75. Other volumes of the *Manuel des loisirs* include *Loisirs artisiques* and *Loisirs et culture* each with practical how-to-do-it advice. See also Auguste Waast, 'L'Organisation des loisirs', *Dossiers de l'Action Populaire* 24 (25 June 1937), pp. 1471–2.

59 E. B. Castles (New Education Foundation), *The Coming of Leisure* (London, 1935), pp. 18–19 and 35; and Lancelot Hogben, *Education for an Age of Plenty*, (London, 1937), p. 10–14.

60 W. E. Williams and A. E. Heath, *Learn and Live: The Consumers' View of Adult Education* (London, 1936), pp. 5, 11, 31–44; Jones, *Workers at Play*, p. 168; 'Leisure of the Adult Student: A Sample Investigation in London', *Adult Education* (March 1937); and Mass-Observation Archive, Topical File Collection, 36, *Adult Education* (1937).

61 *The Listener* (18 January, 10 May, and 14 June 1933), pp. 85, 738, and 932; and National Council of Social Services, *Village Halls* (London, 1938).

62 Kate Liepmann, *The Journey to Work: Its Significance for Industrial and Community Life* (London, 1944), pp. 74–5, 169.

63 Emile Brunner, *Holiday Making and the Holiday Trades* (London, 1945), pp. 5–10; John Pimlott, *The Englishman's Holiday* (London, 1947), p. 240; James Walvin, *Beside the Sea* (London, 1978), p. 117; Lowerson and Howkins, *Trends in Leisure, 1919–1939*, pp. 56–60.

64 Rowntree, *Progress*, pp. 396–8. See also Howkins and Lowerson, *Trends in Leisure*, pp. 50–4; Ann Holt, 'Hikers and Ramblers: Surviving a Thirties' Fashion' *International Journal of Sports History* 4, (May 1987), pp. 157–67; and Helen Walter, 'The Popularisation of the Outdoor Movement' *British Journal of Sports History* 2 (September 1985), pp. 140–53.

65 Holiday Fellowship pamphlets (British Library WP15115) and T. A. Leonard (founder of Holiday Fellowship), *Adventures in Holiday Making* (London, 1934). See also Philippa Bassett, 'A List of Historical Records of the Holiday Fellowship' (Birmingham, 1981), pp. ii-iii.

66 John Lowerson, 'Battles for the Countryside', in Frank Gloversmith,

ed., *Class, Culture, and Social Change; A New View of the 1930s* (Brighton, 1980), pp. 251–71; Brunner, *Holiday Making*, p. 5; Pimlott, *Englishman's Holiday*, pp. 237–40; Ian Jeffrey, *The British Landscape 1920–1950* (London 1984), ch. 1; Mass-Observation Archive, 'Worktown Project,' Box 51, September 1937. See also Gary Cross, ed., *Worktowners at Blackpool: Mass-Observation and Popular Leisure in the 1930s* (London, 1990), ch. 3.

67 *Labour Yearbook* (London, 1924), p. 305.

68 Cross, *Blackpool*, pp. 48–9, 137. Mass-Observation Archive, Topical File Collection, 2509, 'Holiday Report, 1947', pp. 12 and 44. For an analysis and sources of the holiday camp, see Colin Ward and Denis Hardy, *Goodnight Campers* (London, 1986); and Jill Drower, *Good Clean Fun: The Story of Britain's First Holiday Camp* (London, 1983).

69 The vacation with pay was not even included in the common programme of the communists and socialists in September 1935; and on a list of demands of Renault workers it ranked eleventh immediately after a request for garages for workers' bicycles. *L'Etincelle* (13 March 1935) cited in Patrick Fridensen, 'Ideologie des grands constructeurs dans l'entre-deux-guerres', *Mouvement social* 72 (October–December 1972), p. 65. See also Jean-Claude Richez and Léon Strauss, 'Généalogie des vacances ouvrières', *Mouvement social* 150 (January–March 1990), pp. 3–18.

70 Ramond de Flocourt, *Le Camping au point de vue sociale et juridique* (Toulouse 1937), pp. 2–27; Michel Damay, *Les Loisirs de l'adolescent* (Paris, 1939), pp. 39–40 and 204–10; Jean Parant, *Le Problème du tourisme populaire* (Paris 1939), pp. 93–119; Jean-Henri Adam, *L'Education populaire* (Paris, 1927), pp. 3–40; and Becquet, *Organisation des loisirs*, pp. 211–12. See also Henri Noguères, *La Vie quotidienne en France au temps du Front populaire* (Paris 1977), pp. 173–8; and Bénigno Cacérès, *'Allons au-devant de la vie' La Naissance du temps des loisirs en 1936* (Paris, 1981), ch. 2.

71 Holiday Fellowship Pamphlets, British Library and Industrial Welfare Society, *Report on the Conference on Workers' Holidays* (London, 1938), pp. 21–2.

72 Marie Butts speech in William Boyd, ed., *The Challenge of Leisure* (London, 1935), p. 66; 'Billy Butlin', brochure and report, Mass-Observation Archive, Worktown Project Box 2/G; and *Le Musée social* (May 1938). For background on the Butlin camps, see Rex North, *The Butlin Story* (London, 1962), chs 5–7.

73 Boyd, *Challenge of Leisure*, pp. 70–1, 50; C. Northcott Greene, *Time to Spare* (London, 1933), pp. 119–33, 13–25, and 116; and Lefranc, *L'Expérience d'éducation*, pp. 7 and 16.

74 Pierre Tissier, *The Riom Trial* (London, 1942), p. 91.

75 Of 1,947 wage-earners surveyed in 1962 who had been at least 24 years old in 1936, only 211 had taken a vacation in 1936. This number rose to merely 640 in 1946, but increased to 1,348 by 1962. Richez and Strauss, 'Vacances ouvrières', pp. 3–18; Michel Verret, *La Culture ouvrière* (Paris, 1988), pp. 45–9, 74–5. Marc Boyer, '1936 et les vacances des Français', *Mouvement social* 150 (January–March 1990), pp. 35–44. See also P. Bovier, *Travail et expression ouvrière* (Paris,

1980); and especially F. Cribier, *La Grande migration de l'été des citadins en France* (Paris, 1969), pp. 44–6 and 248–52.

76 *Le Populaire* (12 August 1937); and *Vu* (17 June 1936).

77 *Regards* (1 and 7 July, 5 August, and 2 September 1937); *Le Populaire* (4 September 1937); *L'Humanité* (1 August 1936, 9 September 1936, and 25 August 1936); and *Syndicats* (8 April 1937). For a conservative view of this Parisian flood of vacationers, see *Figaro* (5 August 1936 and 14 August 1937); and *Je suis partout* (29 August 1936). Compare with *Syndicats* (12 August 1937) and *Vendredi* (18 June 1937) for the Left's response to conservatives' disquiet over the mass holiday. See also Lydia Elhadad and Olivier Querouil, 'L'Apparition des congés payés', *Temps libre* 1 (1981), pp. 83–91.

78 *Le Populaire* (4 September 1937) and *Vendredi* (13 August 1937).

79 Jackson, 'Popular Tourism', p. 235; Jean Parant, *Le Problème du tourisme populaire* (Paris, 1939), pp. 79–180; Becquet, *Organisation des loisirs*, pp. 227–8; and *Peuple* (11, 19, 23, 24 April, 5, 7, 11 May, 13 July, and especially 1 August 1937). The best documented source on this and related themes is Ory, 'Politique culturelle', see especially vol. 4, pp. 1413–662.

80 See Gilbert Proteau and Eugène Raude, *Le Message de Léo Lagrange* (Lyon 1950); and Jean-Louis Chappat, *Les Chemins de l'espoir ou les combats de Léo Lagrange* (Paris, 1983) for sympathetic accounts of Lagrange's life and work. Note also Pascal Ory, 'La Politique culturelle du premier gouvernement Blum', *Nouvelle Revue socialiste* 10–12 (1975), pp. 84–5; and his 'Politique culturelle', vol. 3, pp. 1274–97 and 4, pp. 1600–46.

81 *Vendredi* (9 July 1937); *Le Populaire* (26 July and 25 December 1936 and 9 August 1937); *Regards* (5 August, 1937); Georges Lefranc, *Juin '36: Archives* (Paris 1971), pp. 309–19; Louis Bodin and Jean Touchard, *Front populaire 1936* (Paris, 1961), pp. 144–61; Henri Noguères, *La Vie quotidienne en France au temps du Front populaire* (Paris, 1977), pp. 152–66 and 173–88; Jacques Kergoat, *La France du Front populaire* (Paris, 1986), pp. 335–6, 362; Holt, *Sport*, pp. 207–8; and especially Ory 'Politique culturelle', vol. 4, pp. 1532–60.

82 *Vendredi* (12 June 1936); and *Le Populaire* (26 July 1936). See also Jackson, 'Popular Tourism', pp. 231–2.

83 Proteau and Raude, *Léo Lagrange*, pp. 37–9, 43, and 131–2. On the linkage between Lagrange and the youth hostel movement see Chappat, *Combats de Léo Lagrange*, p. 204; M. Chavardés, *Eté 1936. La Victoire du Front populaire* (Paris, 1986) pp. 255–61; and *Cris des auberges de la Jeunesse* (July 1937). Jouenne quotation in *Peuple* (4 August 1937). Again see Ory, 'Politique culturelle', vol. 4, pp. 1415–30.

84 Proteau and Raude, *Léo Lagrange*, pp. 37–9.

85 The noted authority, Pascal Ory, shares a similar conclusion. He adds, however, that this policy was a positive model and 'the fragility of this form of pleasure says nothing against it'. Ory, 'Politique culturelle', vol. 4, p. 1657.

86 Brunner, *Holiday Making*, pp. 3–10; *Labour* (June 1939), pp. 34–8; Industrial Welfare Society, 'Conference on Workers' Holidays', (London, 30 November 1938); and National Saving Holiday Clubs,

'Holidays with Pay', (London, 1939) in the Trade Union Congress Archive, HD5106; Modern Records Centre, Engineering Employers Federation, H12/39, 'Memo on National Savings Committee', 17 September 1937; and Trade Union Congress, *Proceedings* (1936), pp. 118–19.

87 George Lansbury, 'Playing Fields Make for Prosperity', *Labour Magazine* (August 1931), pp. 146–9; *The New Leader* (18 July 1930); and *Labour's Immediate Programme* (London 1937), p. 6.; *Labour Magazine* (August 1937), p. 279. See also Jones, *Workers at Play*, pp. 135, 144, 168, 189. Sources on later labour policy include, R. C. Davison, *How to Tackle the Post War Holidays Problem* (London, 1944); and National Council of Social Services, *Holidays, A Study of the Post War Problem and the Field of Non-Commercial Enterprise* (London, 1945).

88 These groups, including the TUC and Labourites like Ernest Bevin, made concrete proposals in 1938 and after the war to extend the holiday season over a six-month period. Still the short summer school vacation and the understandable reluctance of many to accept a cooler and perhaps damper vacation in September or June defeated these efforts. See the local newspaper clipping (Spring 1938) in Mass-Observation Archive, Worktown Project, Box 31/D; TUC, *Proceedings* (1938), p. 440; and pamphlets concerning holidays in the TUC Archive, HD 5106.

89 Workers' Travel Association, 'Holidays with Pay Mean Hard Work for Somebody', *Labour Magazine* (August 1937), p. 282; and 'The National Committee to Provide Holidays for Unemployed Workers in Distressed Areas' (London, 1938), in TUC Archive HD 5106.

90 International Association for Workers' Spare Time, *Official Bulletin* 2 (1938), pp. 15 and 35–6.

91 Miners' Federation of Great Britain, *Annual Volume* (1938), pp. 18–22. Mass-Observation Archive, Worktown Project, Box 51, 'James Whittaker's essay contest entrants, September 1937'.

92 Mass-Observation Archive, Worktown Project, Box 2/G, 'Billy Butlin', and untitled report, 22 July 1947.

93 This pattern can be illustrated among the black urban poor in the US. Store-front churches provided nightly friendship as well as emotional outlets in singing and demonstrative religion for many 'respectable' black families. The church was an alternative to the informal card and dancing party which dominated the leisure hours of many working-class blacks of the 1930s. St Clare Drake and Horace Cayton, *Black Metropolis* 2 (New York, 1945), ch. 21.

94 Richard Hoggart, *Use of Literacy* (London, 1957), pp. 119–23.

95 Office of Community War Services, Division of Recreation, *Recreation – A National Economic Asset* (Washington, 1946?), pp. 20–1.

96 L. Hogben, *Education for an Age of Plenty* (London, 1937), p. 14.

97 Jackson, 'Popular Tourism', p. 237; and Michael Seidman, *Workers against Work: Labor in Paris and Barcelona during the Popular Fronts* (Berkeley, 1991), ch. 11.

98 See George and E. Lefranc, *Le Syndicalisme devant le problème des loisirs* (Paris, 1937), pp. 38–9; and Jackson, 'Popular Tourism', pp. 238–9.

6 TRAUMAS OF TIME AND MONEY IN PROSPERITY AND DEPRESSION

1 See, for example, John Owen, *The Price of Leisure: An Economic Analysis of the Demand for Leisure Time* (Rotterdam, 1969), chs 1 and 2. See also notes for ch. 2 of this volume.

2 M. A. Bienefeld, *Working Hours in British History, An Economic History* (London, 1972), pp. 145–48. John Owen finds that American demand for free time was linked to cheaper leisure goods early in this century. Owen, *Price of Leisure*, chs 1 and 5.

3 It also begs the question somewhat by identifying leisure as 'consumption time' and so measures the demand for leisure as cash spent on consumer goods. Moreover this analysis rejects any significant impact of labour or state intervention in the determination of worktime and instead assumes the marginalist theory that hours reflect employee preference, a theory that I attempt to refute below. Owen, *Price of Leisure*, ch. 1.

4 Chris Nyland, *Reduced Worktime and the Management of Production* (Cambridge, 1989).

5 For a full discussion for Britain and France, see Gary Cross, *Quest for Time: Reduction of Work in Britain and France, 1840–1940* (Berkeley CA, 1989), ch. 8. A similar analysis on the US in the same period is in David Roediger and Philip Foner, *Our Own Time. A History of American Labor and the Working Day* (Westport CT, 1989), pp. 213–31; and Selig Perlman and Philip Taft, in John R. Commons, ed., *History of Labor in the United States*, vol. 4 (New York, 1935), pp. 435–88.

6 Factory workers in France insisted on long lunches at home and it was not uncommon in Britain. Seamstresses continued to be tardy because of early morning family duties; and periods of 'playing' survived in seasonal trades like dockwork in Europe. So did traditional 'wakes' and patronal fêtes especially in rural areas; and British miners still took off on sunny summer days to enjoy cock fighting and free-for-all wrestling. See, for example, Ken Howarth, *Dark Days, Memoirs and Reminiscences of the Lancashire and Cheshire Coalmining Industry up to Nationalisation* (Manchester, 1978), pp. 1–3 and 48–53; International Association of Social Progress, *Inquiry into the Hours Problem* (London, 1933), pp. 29–30; and Paul Crouzet, 'L'Education populaire et les 8 heures', *Grande revue* (October 1921), p. 37.

7 International Association for Social Progress, *Hours Problem*, pp. 13–14, 31–3 and 186; Mother Jones, *Autobiography* (Chicago, 1925), p. 212, cited in Roediger and Foner, *Our Own Time*, p. 224; and David Brody, *Steelworkers in America. The Nonunion Era* (New York, 1960), pp. 235–6.

8 The average workyear in 1920 was only 220 days for soft coal miners in the US and conditions got worse in the 1920s as international competition and overproduction reduced prices and wages. Don Lescohier, in John R. Commons, ed., *History of Labor in the United States, 1896–1933*, vol 3 (New York, 1935), p. 53

9 For the best historical discussion of this see, Bienefeld, *Working Hours*, pp. 145–8, 162–78, 193, and 197. A very interesting analysis by an

economist who is similarly critical of neo-classical explanations of time/money 'choice', see Juliet Schor, *The Overworked American: The Unexpected Decline of Leisure in America* (New York, 1991), pp. 60–78 and 128–32.

10 Cross, *Quest*, ch. 6; and David Brody, *Steelworkers*, chs 7 and 8.

11 UK, Department of Employment and Productivity, *British Labour Statistics. Historical Abstract 1886–1968* (London, 1971), p. 306. There remains much dispute about the calculations of jobless rates. See Sean Glynn and John Oxborrow, *Interwar Britain. A Social and Economic History* (London, 1976), pp. 145–9. For American data, see, for example, Lescohier, *History of Labor*, pp. 79–80; and Lance Davis, *et al.*, *American Economic Growth* (New York, 1972), p. 213.

12 E. H. Phelps Brown, *A Century of Pay* (London, 1968), pp. 258–9.

13 Paul Rives, *La Corvée de joie* (Paris, 1924), pp. 49–50. Again, see Cross, *Quest*, pp. 186–90 for details.

14 Phelps Brown, *Pay*, p. 257; Cross, *Quest*, pp. 188–9.

15 Brody, *Steelworkers*, p. 94.

16 Cross, *Quest*, pp. 186–90; H. and R. Lynd, *Middletown* (New York, 1929), pp. 57–61; and Leila Houghteling, *The Income and Standard of Living of Unskilled Laborers in Chicago* (Chicago, 1927), pp. 29–32.

17 Roediger and Foner, *Our Own Time*, pp. 227–42.

18 Irving Bernstein, *The Lean Years. A History of the American Worker, 1920–1933* (Baltimore MD, 1960), pp. 84–7, 126–42, and 170–9. See also Glynn and Oxborrow, *Interwar Britain*, p. 168.

19 Note, for example, Whiting Williams, *Mainsprings of Men* (New York, 1925), p. 83; Susan P. Benson, *Counter-Cultures, Saleswomen, Managers and Customers in American Department Stores* (Urban IL, 1986); Patrice Fridenson, 'Automobile Workers in France and their Work, 1914–1983', in Steven Kaplan and Cynthia Koepp, eds, *Work in France* (Ithaca NY, 1986), pp. 71 and 80–2; and Liz Cohen, *Making a New Deal: Industrial Workers in Chicago, 1919–1939* (Cambridge, 1990), pp. 199–204.

20 R. and H. Lynd, *Middletown*, pp. 306–7. Lex Heerma van Voss, 'The Use of Leisure Time by Male Workers After the Introduction of the Eight Hour Day', in Lex Heerma van Voss and Frits van Holthoon, eds, *Working Class and Popular Culture* (Amsterdam, 1988), pp. 173–94.

21 'Weekly Expenditure of Working-Class Households', *Ministry of Labour Gazette* (December. 1940) cited in Glynn and Oxborrow, *Interwar Britain*, p. 40. See also Phelps Brown, *Pay*, p. 263.

22 *Information ouvrière et sociale* (9 October 1919).

23 Alfred Sauvy calculates, however, a rise in purchasing power in the 1930s up to 50 per cent by 1937 following the deflation of the early 1930s and the wage increases during the Popular Front, only to decline after 1936. These figures (based on hourly wages) are distorted by the fact of joblessness and short-time work in the 1930s. A. Sauvy, *Histoire économique de la France entre les deux guerres* vol. 3 (Paris, 1984), p. 378; see also vol. 2, pp. 214–34 and 302–3.

24 Phelps Brown, *Pay*, p. 258. The (American) National Bureau of Economic Research estimated that as early as 1914 British per capita income was only 73 per cent of the American and the French only 55 per cent.

National Bureau of Economic Research, *Income in the United States*, vol. 1 (Washington DC, 1914), p. 85.

25 Lewis Lorwin, *The American Federation of Labor* (Washington, 1933), p. 239. See also, Paul Douglas, *Real Wages in the United States, 1890–1926* (Boston MA, 1930), pp. 572; Bernstein, *Lean Years*, pp. 80–2; and John Cumbler, *Working-Class Community in Industrial America* (Westport CT, 1979), pp. 97–8.

26 For example, American construction workers in 1919–20 gained 35 per cent higher wages, double the inflation rate; and cost of living dropped 14 per cent in 1921. National Bureau of Economic Research, *Recent Economic Changes in the United States*, vol. 2 (New York, 1929), pp. 625–6, and vol. 2, p. 104; Lescohier, *History of Labor*, pp. 60, 76–85; and Davis, *American Economic Growth*, p. 213. See also Winifred Wandersee, *Women's Work and Family Values, 1920–1940* (Cambridge MA, 1981), ch. 1.

27 Owen, *Price of Leisure*, p. 86.

28 National Bureau of Economic Research, *Recent Economic Changes*, vol. 1, ch. 1; and Owen, *Price of Leisure*, pp. 84 and 92.

29 Improvement in both decades was mostly due to price decreases rather than wage increases. D. H. Aldcroft, *The Inter-War Economy: Britain, 1919–1939* (London, 1970), pp. 352 and 364. See also Phelps Brown, *Pay*, p. 263.

30 Wandersee, *Women's Work*, pp. 16–17 and ch. 1. This interpretation relies heavily on Robert Lynd's 'The People as Consumers', in President's Research Committee on Social Trends, *Recent Social Trends in the United States*, vol. 2 (New York, 1933), pp. 857–911, as well as a large number of social surveys cited in Wandersee, *Women's Work*. See also Martha Olney, *Buy Now, Pay Later: Advertising, Credit, and Consumer Durables in the 1920s* (Chapel Hill NC, 1991), ch. 3.

31 Cohen, *Making a New Deal*, pp. 101–4 for sources concerning working-class consumption in Chicago in the 1920s.

32 The survival of a large peasantry, slow population growth, a foreign labour force that was partially repatriated, wide use of short-time work, and 'hidden' unemployment may explain this phenomenon in France. S. Salais, 'Why Was Unemployment So Low in France During the 1930s?', in Barry Eichengreen and T. J. Halton, eds, *Interwar Unemployment in International Perspective*, (London, 1988), pp. 247–88. See also Nicolas Baverez, 'Chômage des années 1930, chômage des années 1980', *Mouvement Social* 154 (January-March 1991), pp. 102–30; J. -J. Carré, P. Dubois, and E. Malinvaud, *French Economic Growth* (Stanford CT, 1975), p. 231; G. Noiriel, *Les Ouvriers dans la société française* (Paris, 1986), pp. 159–62 and 170–3; and Marc Bamberger, Gabrielle Letellier, and Robert Marjolin, *Enquête sur le chômage* (Paris, 1942), pp. 113–39

33 US Bureau of the Census, *Historical Statistics of the United States* (Washington, 1960), p. 73. Glynn and Oxborrow, *Interwar Britain*, p. 154.

34 J. C. Asselain, *Histoire économique de la France*, vol. 2 (Paris, 1984), pp. 40–53.

35 Of course, French sources abound with observations of the social isolation and degradation of poor Parisian suburbs and of factory work

conditions. But none focuses on the psychology of joblessness or *relative* poverty. The participant observation and ethnographic methods so common in Anglo-American sociology emerged only after World War II in France. See, for example, Pierre Lhande, *Le Christ dans la banlieu* (Paris, 1927); Eugène Dabit, *Faubourgs de Paris* (Paris, 1933); Robert Garric, *Belleville. Scènes de la vie populaire* (Paris, 1928); Arnold Brémond, *Une Explication du monde ouvrier* (Alençon, 1927); and Jacques Valdour's, *Ouvriers parisiens d'après-guerre* (Paris, 1921) and *Le Désordre ouvrier* (Paris, 1937).

36 Colin Clark, *The Conditions of Economic Progress* (London, 1951), p. 470. Especially hard hit were shipbuilders (62 per cent) and pig-iron workers (43.8 per cent), while tram and bus workers experienced only 5.9 per cent unemployment, and distributive trades, 12.6 per cent. Glynn and Oxborrow, *Interwar Britain*, pp. 152–4. For American data see R.G. Gregory, 'The Australian and US Labour Markets in the 1930s', in Eichengreen and Halton, *Interwar*, pp. 399, 414.

37 George Orwell, *Road to Wigan Pier* (London, 1937), p. 77.

38 Following the encouragement of the Prince of Wales and the BBC broadcasts of S. P. B. Mais in 1932, local volunteers created some 1,405 occupational and 757 recreational centres by the end of 1934. Clubs were divided by sex: in 1937, there were 900 clubs for men (120,000 members) and 500 for women (40,000 members). One quarter of all members were employed but 40 per cent were over 45 years old. Eighty per cent of women members were married, often with husbands in a parallel club. These groups served as outlets for socialising. For additional details see, A. C. Richmond, 'The Action of Voluntary Organisations to Provide for Unemployed Workers in Great Britain', *International Labour Review* 37 (May 1938), pp. 644–51; National Council of Social Services (NCSS), *Work with the Unemployed* (London, 1932); NCSS, *Unemployment and Opportunity. Some Practical Suggestions* (London, 1933), with a supporting foreword by Labour Party leader, George Lansbury; NCSS, *Out of Adversity. A Survey of the Clubs for Men and Women* (London, 1939); Elizabeth Parry and Harold King, *New Leisure and Old Learning* (London, 1934); and especially S. P. B. Mais, *SOS. Talks on Unemployment* (London, 1933).

39 Certainly the Trades Union Congress and the communist-led unemployment movement saw the clubs as a threat both to the employed (for they provided cheap goods and services that competed with waged work) and to autonomous labour organisations. Richard Flanagan, *Parish-Fed Bastards: A History of the Politics of the Unemployed, 1884–1939* (New York, 1991), pp. 199–223; and Richard Croucher, *We Refuse to Starve in Silence: A History of the National Unemployed Workers' Movement, 1920–46* (London, 1987), pp. 153 and 163–7. For a study of British labour camps for unskilled youth, see David Colledge, *Labour Camps. The British Experience* (Sheffield, 1989). For a more positive interpretation see Ralph Hayburn, 'The Voluntary Occupational Centre Movement, 1932–1939', *Journal of Contemporary History* 39 (1971), pp. 156–71.

40 Investigators calculated that the jobless Marienthaler's day lasted only 13.5 hours compared to the fully-employed average of 17 hours. Maria

Jahoda, Paul Lazarsfeld, and P. Zeizel, *Marienthal. The Sociography of an Unemployed Community* (1931, repr. and translated Chicago, 1971), pp. 66–8, and ch. 5, 'A Weary Community'.

41 Examples of the psychologising approach include P. Eisenberg and P. F. Lazarsfeld, 'The Psychological Effects of Unemployment', *Psychological Bulletin* 35 (June 1936); D. Caradog Jones *et al.*, *The Social Survey of Merseyside* (London, 1934), pp. 276–300; Hugh Beales and R. S. Lambert, *Memoirs of the Unemployed* (London, 1934), introduction and pp. 1–49; E. Wight Bakke, *The Unemployed Man* (London, 1933), ch. 1; Henry Durant, *The Problem of Leisure* (London, 1937), pp. 103–10; and Pilgrim Trust, *Men Without Work* (London, 1938), pp. 152–8. American studies similarly stressed these psychological effects of joblessness. See, for example, Marian Elderton, *Case Studies of Unemployment* (Philadelphia, 1931), especially pp. 17–25; and Clinch Calkins, *Some Folks Won't Work* (New York, 1930).

42 Orwell, *Road to Wigan Pier*, p. 10. Like Rowntree's study at the turn of the century, his study of York in the mid-1930s stressed that unstructured free time produced gambling and drinking – although he admitted that the latter had decreased since World War I. B. S. Rowntree, *Poverty and Progress* (London, 1941), pp. 333, 354–62, and 369–71; see also International Association for Social Progress, *Hours Problem*, pp. 7, 14, and 29–33; Constance Harris, *The Use of Leisure* (London, 1927), pp. 1–2, 33–8, 60–2, 64, and 66–7; and L. Hubert Smith, *The New Survey of London Life and Labour*, vol. 9 (London, 1934), p. 315.

43 For American concern with youth joblessness see, Charles Wrenn, *Time on Their Hands* (Washington, 1941), pp. v, 4–27, 67–8, and 70–1; and Martin and Ester Neumeyer, *Leisure and Recreation* (New York, 1936), p. 57. British sources include Durant, *Problem of Leisure*, pp. 101–5; August Aichhorn, *Wayward Youth* (London, 1936), p. 221; Valentine Bell, *Juvenile Instruction Centres* (Edinburgh, 1934), p. 103; and Save the Children International Union, *Children and Young People and Unemployment* (Geneva, 1933). See also Carnegie UK Trust, *Disinherited Youth: A Survey, 1936–1939* (Edinburgh, 1943).

44 Ross McKibbin, 'The "Social Psychology" of Unemployment in Interwar Britain', in his *The Ideologies of Class. Social Relations in Britain 1880–1950* (Oxford, 1990), pp. 228–58; and Philip Massey, *Portrait of a Mining Village* (London, 1937), pp. 26–7, 37, and 49. In at least one study, Americans without work read far more than they passively listened to the radio. George Lundberg, Mirra Komarovsky, and Mary McInerny, *Leisure, A Suburban Study* (New York, 1933), adapted by Owen, *Price of Leisure*, p. 82. Eli Ginzberg, *The Unemployed* (New York, 1943), pp. 97–8 made similar points about Americans out of work.

45 Bakke, *Unemployed Man*, pp. 192–4. See also Beales and Lambert, *Memoirs* p. 70 and Pilgrim Trust, *Without Work*, especially pp. 275–6.

46 S. P. B. Mais saw in these voluntary organisations an opportunity for a meeting of the classes: there the 'overhoused' could join with those 'simple nice friendly folk, who have retained all the instincts of the villages from which they originally came'. Together they could find 'how best to retain a stable sense of values in our unstable world'. Mais,

SOS, pp. 272, xix, and 47; and *The Listener* (2 August 1933), pp. 156, and 164.

47 Despite efforts of elites to control administration, few bourgeois 'volunteers' actually participated in the daily life of the occupational clubs. A. C. Richmond, 'The Unwanted Worker and His Time', *The Nineteenth Century and After* 731 (January 1938), pp. 11–20; Hayward, 'Centre', p. 157; Massey, *Mining Village*, pp. 26–27; and Flanagan, *Parish-Fed Bastards*, pp. 371 and 386–7.

48 Pilgrim Trust, *Without Work*, p. 150; and Bakke, *Unemployed Man* pp. 63 and 71.

49 Only an average of 260 jobless people in Greenwich were on the street during working hours while there were about 3,500 unemployed in town. Forty-five per cent of Bakke's observed group of loafers in Greenwich were young males recently turned out of apprenticeships and doing what young men normally did, watching 'the beauty parade'. Most of the rest were pensioners; and they congregated near the labour exchange where they had weekly to appear to maintain their benefits. Family men and especially artisans stayed at home. The old 'gang' had long since broken up for men with families. This, pattern, Bakke concluded, was no different for employed men. Bakke, *Unemployed Man*, pp. 183–8; and Gary Cross, ed., *Worktowners at Blackpool. Mass-Observation and Popular Leisure in the 1930s* (London, 1990), ch. 1.

50 Ginzberg, *Unemployed*, p. 75; and Marie Jahoda, 'Time: A Social Psychological Perspective', in Michael Young and Tom Schuller, eds, *Rhythms of Society* (New York, 1988), p. 157. See also M. Jahoda, 'The Impact of Unemployment in the 1930s and 1970s', *Bulletin of the British Psychological Society* 32 (1979), pp. 309–14; M. Jahoda and H. Rush, *Employment and Unemployment* (Brighton, 1981); Sue Glyptis, *Leisure and Unemployment* (Milton Keynes, 1989), ch. 7; and John Hayes and Peter Nutman, *Understanding the Unemployed: The Psychological Effects of Unemployment* (London, 1981).

51 Steven Gelber, 'A Job You Can't Lose: Work and Hobbies in the Great Depression', *Journal of Social History* 24, 4 (1990): 741–66.

52 Beales and Lambert, *Memoirs*, pp. 176–80, 245.

53 André Gorz, *Critique of Economic Reason* (London, 1988), p. 207.

54 Bakke, *Unemployed Man*, p. 65.

55 E. Wight Bakke, *Citizens without Work. A Study of the Effects of Unemployment Upon the Workers' Social Relations and Practices* (New Haven CT, 1940), pp. 5–7. See also, E. Wight Bakke, *The Unemployed Worker* (New Haven CT, 1940).

56 Cohen, *Making the New Deal*, pp. 218–38; Walter Brierley, *Means Test Man* (London, 1935), p. 95; and Ellen Wilkenson, *The Town that Was Murdered* (London, 1939), ch. 13.

57 Bakke, *Unemployed Man*, pp. 153–4; Kate Liepmann, *The Journey to Work* (London, 1944), pp. 74–5, 169. Ruth Durant, *Watling: A Social Survey* (London, 1939), pp. 88–90, and ch. 4. See also Diana Gittins, *Fair Sex. Family Size and Structure, 1900–1939* (London, 1982), pp. 138–40.

58 Pilgrim Trust, *Without Work*, pp. 276–8. Some evidence suggests that these clubs could be empowering. The adult education programme in

Rhondda inspired a jobless miner to write 'I certainly created a wider circle of friends, and became more confident in myself.' Beales and Lambert commented: 'It has become clear to [the miners] that the future means a shorter working day, more sharing of work and leisure, and they are adapting themselves accordingly and may never get work but must keep learning.' Beales and Lambert, *Memoirs*, pp. 145–6.

59 The Pilgrim Trust investigators concluded that the jobless could not form effective organisations because their 'free' time was 'too unsettling to be used constructively'. The only solution was to organise the leisure of the employed. Pilgrim Trust, *Without Work*, p. 276–8, 282–4, and 333–45.

60 C. Northcott Greene, *Time to Spare* (London, 1933), p. 116.

61 'Memoirs of the Unemployed', *The Listener* (2 August 1933), pp. 165–88; and Brierley, *Means Test Man*, p. 12.

62 Bakke, *Citizens without Work*, pp. 191, 198; and Pilgrim Trust, *Without Work*, p. 150.

63 Elderton, *Case Studies*, p. 171 and Mirra Komarovsky, *The Unemployed Man and his Family* (New York, 1940), p. 40. See also Lois Scharf, *To Work and To Wed: Female Employment, Feminism, and the Great Depression* (Westport CT, 1980); Ruth Milkman, 'Women's Work and The Economic Crisis', in Nancy Cott and Elizabeth Pleck, eds, *A Heritage of Her Own* (New York, 1979), pp. 507–41; Kate Mourby, 'The Wives and Children of the Teeside Unemployed, 1919–1929', *Oral History and Labour History* 11 (1983), p. 56; and Jahoda *et al.*, *Marienthal*, pp. 74–6.

64 Margery Spring Rice, *Working-Class Wives. Their Health and Conditions* (1939; repr. London, 1981), p. 94 and ch. 5.

65 Greene, *Time to Spare*, pp. 13–25. See also Smith, *New London Survey*, vol. 9, pp. 9, 271–2 and C. D. Burns, *Leisure in the Modern World* (London, 1932), ch. 3.

66 Jahoda *et al.*, *Marienthal*, p. 76. Butts' quotation in Richard Evans and Alison Boyd, *The Use of Leisure in Hull* (Hull, 1935), p. 50. Rowntree's description of time budgets reveal little father-child interaction except on Sunday afternoons. Other leisure-time opportunities for the employed father were spent in pubs, hobbies, listening to radio, or reading newspapers. Saturday afternoons were devoted to club or sports. The excess of time at home with family surely must have been disorienting for fathers and their families. Rowntree, *Progress and Poverty*, pp. 429–44. A similar impression is given in Phyllis Willmott, *Growing Up in a London Village: Family Life Between the Wars* (London, 1979), pp. 20–6 and 105–11.

67 Evans and Boyd, *Leisure in Hull*, p. 6 for quotation; see also, pp. 18–21, 47–9. Note also Ginzberg, *Unemployed*, p. 73; and Wilkenson, *Town That Was Murdered*, pp. 232–3.

68 Komarovsky, *Unemployed Man and His Family*, pp. 81–3.

69 Robert and Helen Lynd, *Middletown in Transition* (New York, 1937), p. 246. Not only Depression-era adults but their children, argues Elder, became especially work-oriented. But he tempers this thesis with a recognition of post-1945 influences as well as personal and family differences. Glen Elder, *Children of the Great Depression* (Chi-

cago, 1974), pp. 183–7 and 192. See also C. Cook, 'The Work Ethic in the 1930s', *History Today* 33 (July 1983).

70 Recent British studies on the 1930s are Aldcroft, *Interwar Economy*; John Stevenson and Chris Cook, *The Slump: Society and Politics of the Depression* (London, 1977); and Steven Constantine, *Unemployment in Britain Between the Wars* (London, 1980). A good survey of scholarly opinion is in Sean Glynn and Alan Booth, eds., *The Road to Full Employment* (London, 1987).

71 Lescohier, *History of Labor*, pp. 92–3. Of course, per capita disposable income of Americans dropped from $682 to $363 between 1929 and 1933, rising only to $576 by 1940. US Bureau of the Census, *Historical Statistics*, p. 139.

72 Glynn and Oxborrow, *Interwar Britain*, p. 43 and n. 70.

73 Elder, *Children of Depression*, pp. 26, 53, and 61.

74 Roland Vaile, *Research Memorandum on Consumption in the Depression* (Washington, 1937), pp. 19 and 28. See also Frederic Mishkin, 'The Household Balance Sheet and The Great Depression', *Journal of Economic History* 38 (December 1978), pp. 918–36; Jesse Steiner, 'Recreation and Leisure Time Activities', in Committee on Social Trends, *Recent Social Trends*, vol. 2, p. 896; Wandersee, *Women's Work*, p. 43.

75 Orwell, *Road to Wigan Pier*, p. 80; Pilgrim Trust, *Without Work*, pp. 244–5. Hilton cited in John Stevenson, *British Society 1914–45* (London, 1984), p. 127.

76 Stephen Jones, *Workers at Play A Social and Economic History of Leisure, 1918–1939* (London, 1986), p. 118; Charles Mowat, *Britain Between the Wars, 1918–1940* (London, 1955), p. 485; Wandersee, *Women's Work*, pp. 46–54; 'How We Live on $2,500 a Year', *Ladies' Home Journal* 47 (October 1930), p. 104; Deidre Beddoe, *Back to Home and Duty: Women Between the Wars, 1918–1939* (London, 1989), pp. 102–3; and Greene, *Time to Spare*, p. 89.

77 As J. S. Duesenberry pointed out, atomistic models of spending behaviour, mathematically correlated to income, are inadequate for they ignore the social pressures to consume. J. S. Duesenberry, *Income, Saving, and the Theory of Consumer Behavior* (Cambridge MA, 1949).

78 Jesse Steiner, *Research Memorandum on Recreation in the Depression* (New York, 1937), pp. 16, 40, 43, and 45–6; National Recreation Association, *The Leisure Hours of 5,000 People*, (New York, 1934), p. 15. See also Marion Flad, 'Leisure Time Activities of Four Hundred Persons', *Sociology and Social Research* 18 (January 1934), pp. 265–74.

79 C. Northcott Greene, 'Filling In the Workless Day', in Greene, *Time to Spare*, p. 119–21 and Orwell, *Road to Wigan Pier*, pp. 88–104.

80 Although often associated with professional sporting matches, most of it was off-site and many bettors had no real interest in the game itself. While an 1899 law prohibited street betting in Britain, bookies freely practised their trade in and around pubs, drawing bets of sixpence to two shillings on the horses. In one English survey, 90 per cent of male bettors on the greyhounds never visited the tracks despite the availability of dog tracks (23 greyhound tracks as compared to nine

horse racetracks in the London area in 1929). Perhaps 80 per cent of
the working-class families of London engaged in some form of gam-
bling in the interwar years. Mass-Observation, *The Pub and the People*
(London, 1943), pp. 262–6; Burns, *Leisure in the Modern World*,
p. 102; Durant, *Problem of Leisure*, pp. 158, 169, 185; Rowntree,
Progress and Poverty, 399–406; B.S. Rowntree, *English Life and Leis-
ure* (London, 1951), ch. 2; John Hilton, *Why I Go In For the Pools*
(London, 1935); and Bakke, *Unemployed Man*, p. 188. Note especially
Jones, *Workers at Play*, pp. 38–40; and Ross McKibbin's essay,
'Working-Class Gambling in Britain, 1880–1939', reprinted in McKib-
bin's *The Ideologies of Class. Social Relations in Britain 1880–1950*
(Oxford, 1990), pp. 101–39.

81 Note the classic St Clair Drake and Horace Cayton, *Black Metropolis*
(1945; repr. New York, 1962), vol. 2, pp. 470–94; and John Findlay,
A People of Chance (New York, 1986), chs 4 and 5.

82 Smith, *London Life and Labour*, 9, p. 271; Rowntree, *Life and Leisure*, pp. 133–4; Hilton, *Why I Go In For the Pools*; McKibbin,
'Working-Class Gambling', pp. 116–23; and Ross McKibbin, 'Work
and Hobbies in Britain, 1880–1950', in Jay Winter, ed., *The Working
Class in Modern British History* (Cambridge, 1983), p. 144.

83 McKibbin, 'Working-Class Gambling', p. 114–15.

84 Paul Johnson, 'Credit and Thrift in the British Working Class,
1870–1939', in Winter, *Working Class in British History*, pp. 169–70.

85 Jack Commons, *Seven Shifts* (London, 1937), p. 165; and Walter
Greenwood, *Love on the Dole* (1933; repr. Harmondsworth, 1987),
pp. 171 and 77.

86 Ferdynand Zweig, *Labour Life, and Poverty*, (London, 1948),
pp. 75–6, 44–7. A 'good marriage' depended upon fulfilling roles –
men providing money and women managing it. But, because of the
male's economic and sometimes physical dominance, the failure of
wives to manage, even with decreasing household income, forced many
women into a shadow economy of taking in laundry and sewing, petty
trade, and even borrowing to avoid domestic violence. See Jane Lewis,
'Marriage Relations, Money and Domestic Violence in Working-Class
Liverpool, 1919–39', in Jane Lewis, ed., *Labour and Love: Women's
Experience of Home and Family, 1850–1940* (London, 1986), pp. 195–219.

87 R. and H. Lynd, *Middletown*, p. 81.

88 Bakke, *Unemployed Man*, ch. 6.

89 Cross, *Blackpool*, chs. 3 and 4.

90 Instalment buying shifted spending toward consumer-durable goods
rather than an increase in total consumption. Comparisons of the
distribution of American wage-earner's income between 1929 and 1932
show decreases in food and clothing spending but an increased share
in miscellaneous consumption by 4.5 per cent. Vaile, *Research Memorandum on Consumption*, pp. 19, 28; Lynd, 'People as Consumers',
pp. 862–3, 892, and 896; and R. and H. Lynd, *Middletown in Transition*, pp. 11 and 26.

91 Bakke, *Unemployed Man*, p. 197.

92 Mass-Observation, *The Pub*, pp. 178–82; Max Cohen, *I Was One of
The Unemployed* (London, 1945), especially p. 103; Beales and Lam-

bert, *Memoirs*, p. 245; Bakke, *Citizens Without Work*, pp. 11 and 192; and Komarovsky, *Unemployed Man*, pp. 122–8, quotation from pp. 122–3.

93 Greenwood, *Love on the Dole*, p. 170.

94 See for example, Greene, *Time to Spare*, p. 122; Bakke, *Citizens Without Work*, p. 197; and Brierley, *Means Test Man*, pp. 41 and 226.

95 Ginzberg, *Unemployed*, p. 74; and Komarovsky, *Unemployed Man*, p. 37

96 Bakke, *Unemployed Man*, pp. 69–70; and Komarovsky, *Unemployed Man*, p. 77. See Gabriel Wells, *The Inwardness of Unemployment* (London, 1925), p. 12, where he advocates differential lay-offs for men and women because 'civilisation is a process of progressive polarisation, distinct sphere and mission, usually supplemental'. Of course, this ideal had little practical impact given the sexual division of the labour market.

97 Bakke, *Citizens Without Work*, p. 190.

98 Wandersee, *Women's Work*, p. 26; and Margaret Mead, 'The Pattern of Leisure in Contemporary American Culture', *Annals of American Academy of Political and Social Science* (September 1957), pp. 11–15.

99 Pilgrim Trust, *Without Work*, p. 189; and Bakke, *Unemployed Man*, pp. 158–9.

100 See, for example, Rowntree, *Progress and Poverty*, pp. 408 and 429–45; and Richard Hoggart, *Uses of Literacy* (London, 1957), p. 24.

101 Pilgrim Trust, *Without Work*, p. 184; and Cross, *Blackpool*, p. 40.

102 This theme can be easily exaggerated: for example, the percentage of married women in the American workforce rose only from 11.7 per cent in 1930 to 15.6 per cent in 1940 and never more than 12 per cent of British married women held paid jobs in the 1930s. Of course, these figures doubtless ignore much work done in the 'informal' economy. US Bureau of the Census, *Historical Statistics of the United States* Part 1, p. 133; and UK Department of Employment, *Historical Abstract of Statistics (1921–61)* (London, 1962), p. xxx. See also, for Britain, Jane Lewis, ed., *Labour and Love: Women's Experience in Home and Family* (London, 1986); and Deidre Beddoe, *Back to Home and Duty: Women between the Wars, 1918–1939* (London, 1989). For the US, the standard work is Ruth S. Cowan, *More Work for Mother. The Ironies of Household Technology* (New York, 1983), in addition to Wandersee, *Women's Work*.

103 National Extension Homemakers Council, 'Voices of American Homemakers Project', a 4-volume typescript of interviews with American homemakers, mostly from small towns and farms, who lived during the Depression. See, for example, the comments of Essie Summers, 'Arkansas', pp. 12–13, Masa Scheer, 'Indiana', pp. 28–33, and Mrs Meyers, 'Michigan', pp. 27–8.

104 Komarovsky, *Unemployed Man*, p. 42; and Wandersee, *Women's Work*, chs 3–6, quotation on pp. 112–13. On British women's wartime experience, see Gail Braybon and Penny Summerfield, *Out of the Cage: Women's Experience in Two World Wars* (London, 1988), chs 4, 5, and 14.

105 Wandersee, *Women's Work*, pp. 115–16; and Elder, *Children of Depression*, pp. 279–82 and 290–1.
106 Komarovsky, *Unemployed Man*, p. 128.
107 R. and H. Lynd, *Middletown*, pp. 81–3; and Richard W. Fox, 'Epitaph for Middletown', in Richard Wightman Fox and T. J. Jackson Lears, eds, *Culture of Consumption* (New York, 1983), p. 103.

7 THE CONSUMER'S COMFORT AND DREAM

1 Note the following by Maurice Halbwachs: *L'Evolution des besoins dans les classes ouvrières* (Paris, 1933), pp. 97, 107–10, 136–9, and 145–6; *La Class ouvrière et les niveaux de vie* (Paris, 1913), pp. x–xi and 129–30; and *The Psychology of Social Class* (1937, repr. Glencoe IL, 1958), pp. 78 and 92–100. See also François Simiand, *L'Evolution sociale de la monnaie* (Paris, 1932), pp. 478–80; and Henri de Man, *Psychology of Socialism* (London, 1929), pp. 56–65 and 260.
2 See Marie Busch, *La Sociologie du temps libre* (Paris, 1974), pp. 182–4; and Mary Douglas' introduction to the English edition of Maurice Halbwach's, *The Collective Memory* (New York, 1980), for a critical evaluation.
3 Pierre Bourdieu, *Distinction: A Social Critique of The Judgment of Taste* (1979), trans. Richard Nice (Cambridge MA, 1984).
4 See, for example, Stuart Chase, *The Tragedy of Waste* (New York, 1925), ch. 7; James Rorty, *His Master's Voice: Advertising* (New York, 1934), pp. 16–17. See also Max Radin, *The Lawful Pursuit of Gain* (Boston MA, 1931); and Ralph Borsodi, *The Distribution Age* (New York, 1927). More recent versions of this thesis are in James Duesenberry, *Income, Saving and The Theory of Consumer Behavior* (New York, 1949), pp 28–41; John Galbraith, *The New Industrial State* (Boston MA, 1967); Michel Aglietta, *A Theory of Capitalist Regulation* (London, 1979), pp. 52–61; and Robert Goldman, ' "We Make Weekends": Leisure and the Commodity Form', *Social Text* 8 (Winter 1983–4), pp. 84–103. For a particularly nuanced view see Daniel Pope, *The Making of Modern Advertising* (New York, 1983), chs 1 and 2.
5 For example, labour writer William Walling and business leader Edward Filene recognised this linkage when they argued that workers had to be understood as both producers and consumers. As Filene put it, American industry would have to 'Fordise' both industry and distribution. William Walling, *American Labor and American Democracy* (New York, 1926); and Edward Filene, *The Way Out: A Forecast of Coming Change in American Business and Industry* (New York, 1924), ch. 10.
6 'To keep America growing', wrote an automobile dealer in 1928, 'we must keep Americans working, and to keep Americans working we must keep them wanting, wanting more than the bare necessities; wanting the luxuries and frills that make life so much more worthwhile.' Walter Engard, 'The Blessing of Time Sales', *Motor* 49 (April 1928), p. 122, cited in James Flink, *The Car Culture* (Cambridge MA, 1975), p. 147. See also Edward Filene, *The Consumer's Dollar* (New York, 1934), pp. 29–30.
7 W. D. Scott, *The Psychology of Advertising* (Boston MA, 1912),

pp. 82–92; F. H. Allport, *Social Psychology* (New York, 1924), pp. 52–6. For a cynical approach to appeals to female 'instincts', see Carl Naether, *Advertising to Women* (New York, 1928). See also Stuart Ewen, *Captains of Consciousness: Advertising and the Social Roots of Consumer Culture* (New York, 1976), pp. 37, 81–102, and 159–84; and Loren Baritz, *The Servants of Power: A History of the Use of Social Science in American Industry* (Middletown CT, 1960), pp. 21–8.

8 As one psychologist of advertising wrote: 'the average person does not understand what he wants. The impulses which force him, in restless fashion, to seek this, that or the other, spring from his unconscious.' Donald Laird, *What Makes People Buy* (New York, 1935), p. 22. Note also standard works like D. B. Lucas and C. E. Benson, *Psychology for Advertisers* (New York, 1930); and A. T. Poffenberger, *Psychology in Advertising* (New York, 1926).

9 William Ogburn, 'The Family and Its Functions', in President's Commission on Social Trends, *Recent Social Trends in the United States*, vol. 2 (New York, 1933), pp. 661–708; and Christine Frederick, *Selling Mrs. Consumer* (New York, 1929), especially chs 2 and 5. See also Ewen, *Captains*, Part III.

10 Robert Lynd, 'The People as Consumers', in President's Commission on Social Trends, *Recent Social Trends in the United States*, vol. 2 (New York, 1933), pp. 868–71 and 866.

11 Paul Nostrum, *Economics of Fashion* (New York, 1928), pp. 67–8, cited in Ewen, *Captains*, p. 85.

12 See, for example, Jean Baudrillard, *For A Critique of the Political Economy of the Sign* (St Louis MO, 1981), or *Le Système des objets: La Consommation des signes* (Paris, 1968). See also Henri Lefebvre, *Everyday Life in the Modern World* (New York, 1971), pp. 110–23; Guy Debord, *Society of the Spectacle* (New York, 1967); and Thomas Richards, *The Commodity Culture of Victorian England. Advertising and Spectacle, 1851–1914* (Stanford CA, 1990), especially pp. 58–70 and 168–204.

13 Among other works see David Riesman, Nathan Glazer, and Reuel Denny, *The Lonely Crowd* (New York, 1950); Christopher Lasch, *The Culture of Narcissism* (New York, 1979); Warren Susman, ' "Personality" and the Making of Twentieth-Century Culture', in John Higham and Paul Conkin, eds, *New Directions in American Intellectual History*, (Baltimore MD, 1979), pp. 212–26; and T. J. Jackson Lears, 'From Salvation to Self Realization', in Richard Wightman Fox and T. J. Jackson Lears, eds, *The Culture of Consumption*, (New York, 1983), pp. 1–38. For an English analysis, see Raymond Williams, 'Advertising the Magic System', in his *Problems in Materialism and Culture* (London, 1980), pp. 90–5. See also Donald Meyer, *The Positive Thinkers* (New York, 1980); Philip Rieff, *The Triumph of the Therapeutic* (New York, 1966); and T. J. Jackson Lears, *No Place of Grace: Antimodernism and the Transformation of American Culture* (New York, 1981).

14 As Roland Marchand argues, advertisers did not always encourage a mindless consumption but rather they saw themselves as therapists in the 'adaptation of consumers to the intensities of a new, complex scale of life' even as they sold Camel cigarettes as a healthful way of soothing

frayed nerves and tried to convince people that in free time 'you can have it all'. Roland Marchand, *Advertising The American Dream. Making Way for Modernity, 1920–1940* (Berkeley CA, 1985), pp. 1, 18–22, and 158–60. See also Pope, *Advertising*, pp. 14–15; and Michael Schudson, *Advertising, The Uneasy Persuasion* (New York, 1984).

15 Thorstein Veblen, *The Theory of the Leisure Class* (New York, 1922), especially chs 3 and 4. R. and H. Lynd, *Middletown in Transition* (New York, 1937), pp. 147–8.

16 Georg Simmel, *Philosophy of Money* (London, 1978), pp. 285–354, 390–3, and 485–503, and 'The Metropolis and Mental Life', in D. Levine, ed., *On Individuality and Social Form* (Chicago, 1971). See also David Frisby, *Fragments of Modernity. Theories of Modernity in the Works of Simmel, Kracauer, and Benjamin* (Cambridge MA, 1986), pp. 94–108.

17 Simmel, *Money*, p. 448, and 'Fashion', *International Quarterly* (1904), repr. *American Journal of Sociology* 62 (1957), pp. 541–58.

18 E. Goblot, *La Barrière et le niveau* (1925; repr. Paris, 1967), especially pp. 9 and 39–49; and Ernest Fluegel, *The Psychology of Clothes* (London, 1930), pp. 20–2 and 139–41. See also American versions in Hazel Kyrk, *A Theory of Consumption* (Boston MA, 1923), especially ch. 9; and E. A. Ross, *Social Psychology* (New York, 1908), ch. 6.

19 R. and H. Lynd, *Middletown* (New York, 1929), p. 83.

20 Fred Hirsch, *The Social Limits of Growth* (Cambridge MA, 1976); and Jean-Christophe Agnew, 'The Consuming Vision of Henry James', in Fox and Lears, eds, *Culture of Consumption*, p. 73. See also Walter Benjamin, 'Paris, Capital of the Nineteenth Century' in his *Charles Baudelaire: A Lyric Poet in the Era of High Capitalism* (London, 1973), pp. 154–76.

21 Herbert Blumer, 'Fashion: From Class Differentiation to Collective Selection', *Sociological Quarterly* 10 (Summer 1969), especially pp. 287–90.

22 Mary Douglas and Baron Isherwood, *The World of Goods* (New York, 1979), pp. 59, 89–91, 95, and 123–5.

23 Dan Miller, *Material Culture and Mass Consumption* (Oxford, 1987), pp. 7–9 and 190–1.

24 See Juliet Schor, *The Overworked American: The Unexpected Decline of Leisure in America* (New York, 1991), pp. 60–6.

25 R. Lenoir, *Information ouvrière* (1 September 1918); and H. Dubreuil, *Nouveaux Standards* (Paris, 1931), p. 213.

26 William Reddy, *Money and Liberty in Modern Europe* (Cambridge, 1987), ch. 3 and p. 200.

27 Daniel Bell, *Work and Its Discontents* (New York, 1970), p. 31.

28 A recent study on the history of working-class hobbies is Ross McKibbin's, *The Ideologies of Class. Social Relations in Britain, 1880–1950* (Oxford, 1990). Steven Gelber's work in progress is also concerned with individualist uses of goods in free time.

29 Tobacco, snack food, cosmetics, the cinema, fashion clothing, and gambling absorbed a large and growing share of discretionary income in the interwar years. In Britain, for example, per capita food consumption increased by a third in the interwar years, much of it in new processed

foods, while beer consumption decreased sharply (falling to half the pre-war level in the 1930s). John Stevenson, *British Society 1914–45* (London, 1984), pp. 125–8 and 383–412, offers a good accessible survey of discretionary consumption. John Burnett's, *Plenty and Want: A Social History of Diet in England* (London, 1966), is useful. See also Jean and Françoise Fourastié, 'Le Genre de vie', in Alfred Sauvy, ed., *Histoire économique de la France entre les deux guerres*, vol. 3 (Paris, 1984), pp. 211–27; Letitia Brewster and Michael Jacobson, *The Changing American Diet* (Washington DC, 1978); and Claire Brown, 'Consumption Norms, Work Roles and Economic Growth, 1918–80', in Clair Brown and Joseph Pechman, eds, *Gender in the Workplace*, (Washington, 1987), pp. 13–58.

30 Claude Olchanski, *Le Logement des travailleurs français* (Paris, 1946), p. 68; and sources in Peggy Phillips, *Modern France: Theories and Realities of Urban Planning* (Lanham MD, 1987).

31 Gerard Noiriel, *Workers in French Society in the 19th and 20th Centuries* (London, 1990), pp. 136, 158, and 177; H. Delpech, *Recherches sur le niveau de vie et les habitudes de consommation* (Toulouse, 1938), pp. 160–9; R. S. Vaile and H. G. Canoyer, *Income and Consumption* (New York, 1938), p. 240; and National Resources Planning Board, *Family Expenditures in the United States* (Washington, 1941), p. 2. See also M. Lamy, *Bien acheter mieux vivre* (Paris, 1933), p. 13; and A. Siegfried, *Aspects du xxe siècle* (Paris, 1955), ch. 4.

32 Note Paulette Bernège, *De la mèthode ménagère* (Paris, 1928), a handbook on domestic engineering modelled after the work of Christine Frederick; and Paul Bréton, *L'Art Ménager français* (Paris, 1952), pp. 9–11. The impact of these consumerist domestic values was reflected in conservative Jacques Valdour's claim in 1937 that all manual labourers, even communists, wanted to be home-owners. J. Valdour, *Désordre ouvrier* (Paris, 1937), p. 15. See also Martine Martin, 'La Rationalisation de travail ménager en France dans l'entre-deux-guerres', *Technique et culture* 3 (1980), pp. 157–65; Françoise Werner, 'Du Ménage à l'art ménager: L'Evolution du travail ménager dans la presse féminine française de 1919 à 1939', *Mouvement social* (October-November 1982), pp. 61–87; and Ellen Furlough, 'Selling The American Way in Interwar France: Prix Uniques and the Salons des Arts Ménagers', unpublished paper.

33 Pierre Chombart de Lauwe, *La Vie quotidienne des familles ouvrières* (Paris, 1956), pp. 86–91. See also O. Schwartz who stresses the male worker's obsession with 'poetic goods' – the 'do it yourself' or bricolage of the 'tinkering' husband at home which allowed the masculine display of competence, festive abundance, or lost traditions. O. Schwartz, *Le Monde privé des ouvriers* (Paris, 1990), pp. 379–84 and 419–20. Consider also Luce Giard and Pierre Mayol, *Habiter, Cuisiner. L'Invention du quotidien* (Paris, 1980), pp. 65–81, 131; and J. Destray, *La Vie d'une famille ouvrière* (Paris, 1971), pp. 84 and 117.

34 Colleen McDannell, *The Christian Home in Victorian America* (Bloomington IN, 1986); Gwendolyn Wright, *Moralism and the Model Home: Domestic Architecture and Cultural Conflict in Chicago, 1873–1913* (Chicago, 1980); and Jonas Frykman and Orvar Loefgren, *Culture Builders:*

An Historical Anthropology of Middle Class Culture (New Brunswick NJ, 1990), pp. 127 and 140. See also Margaret Marsh, *Suburban Lives* (New Brunswick NJ, 1990), ch. 1 and pp. 41 and 83; and Stuart Blumin, *The Emergence of the Middle Class: Social Experience in the American City, 1760–1900* (Cambridge, 1989), ch. 5.

35 Paul Johnson, *Saving and Spending. The Working-Class Economy in Britain 1870–1939* (Oxford, 1985), pp. 7–47 and 151–83.

36 See, for example, N. Duncan, 'Home Ownership and Social Theory', in James Duncan, ed., *Housing and Identity*, (London, 1981), pp. 98–134; Dolores Hayden, *Redesigning the American Dream: The Future of Housing, Work, and Family Life* (New York, 1984), pp. 32–4; and Robert Fishman, *Bourgeois Utopias* (New York, 1987), ch. 6. American home-owners increased from 45.9 per cent to 47.8 per cent in the 1920s. US Bureau of the Census, *Historical Statistics of the United States* (Washington, 1960), p. 395.

37 Frykman and Loefgren, *Culture Builders*, pp. 148–9 for quotation and the summary; O. Loefgren, 'Deconstructing Swedishness: Culture and Class in Modern Sweden', in Anthony Jackson, ed., *Anthropology at Home* (London, 1987), pp. 74–93. Similar analyses appear in Richard Sennett and Jonathan Cobb, *The Hidden Injuries of Class* (New York, 1972).

38 Note the frustrations of the 'upper lower' class families in Yankee City trying to maintain 'respectability' with their neighbours. F. Lloyd Warner and Paul Lunt, *The Social Life of a Modern Community* (New Haven CT, 1941), pp. 178–86 and 188–9.

39 Department of Employment, *Historical Abstract of Statistics (1921–61)* (London, 1962), p. xxx.

40 Only 10.7 per cent of married American women reported outside employment in the 1930 census (rising to 15.6 per cent in 1940). US Bureau of the Census, *The Statistical History of the United States* (New York, 1976), p. 133. In the French case, the high percentage of married women who produced income, may be still another sign of the relatively slow development of domestic consumption in France. Joan Scott and Louise Tilly, *Women, Work, and Family* (New York, 1978), chs 8 and 9.

41 Marsh identifies this as 'masculine domesticity' and situates it in the American Progressivist era when men were beginning to have more time to devote to home activities. Of course, it has deeper roots in rural working-class traditions of self-provisioning. Marsh, *Suburban Lives*, ch. 3.

42 Hayden, *American Dream*, p. 34, see pp. 67–95 for alternative 'models of home' especially the strategy of 'material feminists' led by M. F. Pierce. See also Glenna Matthews, *'Just a Housewife': The Rise and Fall of Domesticity in America* (Oxford, 1987), ch. 7. For pioneering analyses, see Heidi Hartmann, 'The Family as the Locus of Gender, Class and Political Struggle: The Example of Housework', *Signs: Journal of Women in Culture and Society* 6 (Spring 1981), pp. 366–94; and Elaine Tyler May, *Great Expectations: Marriage and Divorce in Post-Victorian America* (Chicago, 1980). British sources include the theoretical studies by Rosemary Deem, *All Work and No Play: The Sociology*

of Women and Leisure (Milton Keynes, 1986), chs 1, 5, and 8; and Liz Stanley, *Essays on Women's Work* (Manchester, 1987); as well as the historical works by Jane Lewis, ed., *Labour and Love: Women's Experience in Home and Family* (London, 1986); Deidre Beddoe, *Back to Home and Duty: Women Between the Wars, 1918–1939* (London, 1989); and Juliet Mitchell and Ann Oakley, *The Rights and Wrongs of Women* (London, 1976).

43 Carmen Sirianni's analysis of 'gendered time' is very useful here. C. Sirianni, 'The Self-Management of Time in Postindustrial Society', in Karl Hinrichs, William Roche, and C. Sirianni, eds, *Worktime in Transition*, (Philadelphia, 1991), pp. 245–8. See also Arlie Hochschild, *The Second Shift* (New York, 1989).

44 Tibor Scitovsky, *The Joyless Economy* (Oxford, 1976), ch. 6.

45 Despite a housing law in 1919 that encouraged local British councils to build some 213,000 dwellings, not only did high rents place them out of reach of manual workers, but a conservative tilt toward markets in 1923 led to reduced subsidies and instead the encouragement of private construction. A new law in 1933 reduced size standards and opened up the building of high-rise modern housing. John Barnett, *A Social History of Housing* (London, 1978), pp. 215–21, 233–7, and 249; Karl Silex, *John Bull at Home* (London, 1931), pp. 39–45; and C. Hall, *Married Women at Home* (London, 1977), pp. 62–81.

46 See A. A. Jackson, *Semi-Detached London* (London, 1973), ch. 9 and 11; Arthur Edwards, *The Design of Suburbia* (London, 1981), ch. 3; Gordon Cherry, *Leisure and the Home* (London, 1982), pp. 22–7; Ivor Brown, *The Heart of England* (London, 1935), p. 100; and Hall, *Women at Home*, pp. 78–81.

47 Improved plumbing and electric wiring made possible a revolution in household appliances; and more open living space accommodated smaller, more intimate, families. In the 1930s, builders transformed the bungalow into the one-story ranch home and spread out on even larger, more private lots. One typical advocate of more open interior spaces was Ernest Pickering, *Shelter for Living* (New York, 1941). See also Fishman, *Bourgeois Utopias*, ch. 6; Anthony King, *The Bungalow* (London, 1984), chs 2–4; Clifford Clark, *The American Family Home, 1800–1960* (Chapel Hill NC, 1986), chs 6–7; and Cliff May, *Western Ranch Houses* (Menlo Park CA, 1958). Marsh, *Suburban Lives*, pp. 30, 85, and 141 contains very revealing tables detailing changes in space use in American houses built between the 1860s and 1920s; see also Marsh, *Suburban Lives*, ch. 5.

48 Gertrude Fish, ed., *The Story of Housing* (New York, 1979), pp. 136 and 183–241; *The President's Conference on Home Building and Home Ownership* (Washington, 1932); Hayden, *American Dream*, pp. 32–4; Kenneth Jackson, *Crabgrass Frontier* (New York, 1985); pp. 172–87, and 204–18; Mark Foster, *From Streetcar to Superhighway* (Philadelphia, 1981), pp. 65–70; and Marsh, *Suburban Lives*, pp. 146–55.

49 Stuart Chapin, 'A Quantitative Scale for Rating the Home and Social Environment of Middle-Class Families in an Urban Community', *Journal of Educational Psychology* 19 (February 1928); Stuart Chapin, *Contemporary American Institutions* (New York, 1935), pp. 373–97; and

Dennis Chapman, *The Family, the Home and Social Status* (London, 1955), pp. 24–42. 50–1, 102, and 170–3. Since the 1970s, stress has shifted from linear status hierarchies to identifying more complex social styles based on gender, age, and ethnic culture revealed through home design and furnishings. See, for example, Duncan, *Housing and Identity* and the popular update Joan Kron, *Home-Psych. The Social Psychology of Home and Decoration* (New York, 1983).

50 Erving Goffman, *The Presentation of Self in Everyday Life* (New York, 1959), ch. 2.

51 George Lundberg, Mirra Komarovsky, and Mary McInerny, *Leisure, A Suburban Study* (New York, 1934), p. 155.

52 R. and H. Lynd, *Middletown*, p. 95.

53 Mass-Observation Archive, File Report 2084, 'Report on Hire-Purchase in Chester, 16 May 1944'; and Jackson, *Semi-Detached London*, pp. 168–9.

54 For an interesting analysis of the dynamics of the psychological pressure to upgrade goods to match a new luxury, see Grant McCracken's essay, 'Diderot Unities and the Diderot Effect', *Culture and Consumption* (Bloomington IN, 1988), pp. 118–29.

55 Michael Young and Peter Willmott, *Family and Kinship in East London* (London, 1957), pp. 107–8, 142–6, and 154–64. See also Alan Tomlinson, 'Home Fixtures', in his *Consumption, Identity and Style* (London, 1989), p. 70.

56 Brown, *British Life*, p. 104 and Mass-Observation Archive, File Report 2441A, 'Britain Can Make It', November 1946. Other interviews in the 1940s revealed that people longed mostly for modest amenities like an upstairs bath, a hot water heater, an extra cupboard and gas range, and 'kitchens' large enough to eat and 'live' in (and thus allowing the front room to be used as a formal parlour). And, even at that, seventy-two per cent surveyed in 1943 claimed to be content with their homes, often simply because of its lived-in comfort. Mass-Observation, *An Enquiry into People's Homes* (London, 1943), pp. ix, 99, 104, 112, 141, 149, 160, and 53–4.

57 R. Gamble, *Chelsea Child* (London, 1979), p. 20; and Phyllis Willmott, *Growing Up in a London Village: Family Life between the Wars* (London, 1974), pp. 1–28 and 133. See also Jerry White, *Rothschild Buildings: Life in an East End Tenement Block, 1887–1920* (London, 1980); Grace Foakes, *Between High Walls. A London Childhood* (London, 1972); and for a scholarly treatment, S. Muthesius, *The English Terraced House* (New Haven CT, 1982).

58 An obvious example is R. and H. Lynd, *Middletown*, pp. 250–7. That tradition survives in much of the history of the suburb. Note especially, Jackson, *Crabgrass Frontier*, p. 281.

59 See, for example, Elizabeth Roberts, *A Women's Place: An Oral History of Working-Class Women* (Oxford, 1984), ch. 4; and Charles Forman, *Industrial Town: A Self-Portrait of St. Helens in the 1930s* (St Albans, 1979), pp. 127–42.

60 Osburt Lancaster, *Here, Of All Places* (London, 1959), p. 152; Lewis Mumford, *Sticks and Stones: A Study in American Architecture and Culture* (New York, 1924), especially pp. 186–7. Examples of modernist

critiques of suburbia are Clarence Perry, *Housing for the Machine Age* (New York, 1939); Catherine Bauer, *Modern Housing* (New York, 1934); and Elizabeth Denby, *Europe Re-housed* (London, 1938). For an American attempt at a modern planned suburb see Daniel Shaffer, *Garden Cities of America: The Radburn Experience* (Philadelphia, 1982). For background for Britain, see Cherry, *Leisure and Home*, pp. 19–23; and for the US see John Stilgoe, *Borderland: Origins of the American Suburb* (New Haven CT, 1988), ch. 23.

61 Paul Oliver, ed., *Dunroamin: The Suburban Semi and its Enemies* (London, 1981), pp. 46–7 and 21–2.

62 I. Davis, 'A Celebration of Ambiguity', in Oliver, ed., *Dunroamin*, pp. 77–102.

63 See, for example, Marcia Mead, *Homes of Character* (New York, 1926); and *American Home*, a popular magazine reflecting the builder's perspective. Marsh, *Suburban Lives*, pp. 140–2 and Stilgoe, *Borderlands*, pp. 290–300 are good on this point.

64 Raymond Unwin, 'The Value of Good Design in Dwellings', in Ernest Betham, ed., *House Building, 1934* (London, 1934), pp. 17–22 and 126.

65 John Richards, *Castles on the Ground* (London, 1946), p. 35; and Brown, *Heart of England*, pp. 69–70. See also the revealing essays written by British Legion members concerning their 'Post War Hopes' for housing with gardens and privacy. Mass-Observation Archive, Topical Collection 40, '1944'.

66 See, for example, Robert Sommer, *Personal Space: The Behavioral Basis of Design* (Englewood Cliffs NJ, 1969), chs 3 and 4; and I. Altman and M. M. Chomers *Culture and Environment* (Monterey CA, 1980), chs 4–6.

67 Lawrence Veiler was prominent in attacks on the 'lodger evil' in urban tenements and for supporting home ownership as a means of conservative Americanisation. Lawrence Veiler, *Housing Reform: A Handbook for Practical Use in American Cities* (New York, 1910), pp. 6–35. See also Leslie Tentler, *Wage-Earning Women: Industrial Work and Family Life in the United States* (New York, 1979), pp. 115–19; and Carolyn Kirk and Gordon Kirk, 'The Impact of the City on Home Ownership', *Journal of Urban History* 7 (August 1981), pp. 474–6. For Britain, see Anthony Wohl, 'Sex and the Single Room: Incest among the Victorian Working Classes', in Anthony Wohl, ed., *The Victorian Family Structure and Stresses* (London, 1978), pp. 197–216.

68 *Daily Express* (22 November 1943); and Mass-Observation, *People's Homes* (London, 1943), pp. 121, 171–2, and 206.

69 Denis Chapman, *Home and Social Status* (London, 1955), pp. 42 and 170–3; and J. M. Mogley, *Family and Neighbourhood. Two Studies in Oxford* (Oxford, 1956), pp. 22 and 25. See also Richard Hoggart, *The Uses of Literacy* (London, 1957), ch. 2.

70 Warner and Lunt, *Modern Community*, pp. 81–91, 105–9, 141–4, 200, and 287–300, quotation on p. 107; F. Lloyd Warner, *The Living and the Dead. A Study of the Symbolic Life of Americans* (New Haven CT, 1959), pp. 45–50; R. and H. Lynd, *Middletown*, pp. 100–2.

71 Mihaly Csikszentmihalyi and Eugene Rochberg-Halton, *The Meaning of Things: Domestic Symbols of the Self* (New York, 1981); and Eugene

Rochberg-Halton, *Meaning and Modernity. Social Theory in Pragmatic Attitude* (Chicago, 1986), pp. 155–88, quotation on p. 168.

72 Ian Bentley, 'The Owner Makes His Mark', in Oliver, ed., *Dunroamin*, pp. 136–53. In an English survey, only 28 per cent admitted to never doing home decorating and almost half of the homes visited had male Do-It-Yourselfers compared to 27 per cent where wives alone did home improvements. Lyn Murfin, *Popular Leisure in the Lake Counties* (Manchester, 1990), ch. 1; Mass-Observation Archive, File Report 3131, 'Paint Colour and the Housewife' (June 1949); and Geoffrey Brown, *Patterns of English Life* (London, 1950), p. 32.

73 Examples of this literature are Virginia Robie, *The Quest for the Quaint* (Boston MA, 1917); Alice Van Leer Carrick, *The Next-to-Nothing House* (Boston, 1922); and the Stanley Rule and Level Plant publication, *How To Work With Tools and Wood: For the Home Workshop* (New Britain CT, 1927). See also Stilgoe, *Borderlands*, pp. 260–8.

74 As late as 1932, there were only about 500,000 French radios as compared with 5.2 million in Britain and about 17 million in the US. Mark Pegg, *Broadcasting and Society, 1918–1939* (London, 1983), p. 45; Jackson, *Semi-Detached London*, p. 183; and Hadley Cantril and Gordon Allport, *The Psychology of Radio* (New York, 1935), p. 37.

75 To be sure, the high-mindedness of the early BBC relented to mass-audience programming; and limited competition among the national networks in the US culminated in programming designed to deliver the largest market share to advertisers. But few historians find that this simply created a mass culture. Regional cultural and linguistic diversity survived in Britain; and far from creating a 'classless American culture', the radio, claims Liz Cohen, may well have contributed to 'an integrated working-class culture', built around ethnic groups who listened to the same radio programmes. Excellent analysis is in Daniel Czitrom, *Media and the American Mind from Morse to McLuhan* (Chapel Hill NC, 1982), pp. 80–3; and Cohen, *Making a New Deal*, pp. 327–30, quotation on p. 357.

76 See, for example, Paul Lazarsfeld, *Radio and the Printed Page* (New York, 1940).

77 Maurice Halbwachs, *La Mémoire collective* (Paris, 1950), p. 126; and Georges Gurvitch, *The Spectrum of Social Time* (Dordrecht, 1964), pp. 27–38, 58–63, and 71. See also Joseph McGrath, ed., *Time and Human Interaction: Toward a Social Psychology of Time* (New York, 1986), especially pp. 83–4; John Robinson, Vladmir Andreyenkov, and Vasilly Patrushev, *The Rhythm of Everyday Life* (Bolder CO, 1989). Also useful were Mogley, *Families and Neighbourhoods*, p. 55; and Michael Young and Tom Schuller, *Rhythms of Society* (London, 1988).

78 Frykman and Loefgren, *Culture Builders*, pp. 36–9; a French poster agitating for eight-hour day legislation in April 1919 shows a struggle between the bourgeoisie and workers with ropes lashed to the minute hand being pulled away and toward eight o'clock. See the cover to *Voix du peuple* (1 May 1919). Arnold Brémond quotes a common lament of factory workers in the 1920s: 'How will I be able to hold on until evening' and the complaint that factory clocks 'don't move'. Arnold Brémond, *Une Explication du monde ouvrier* (Alençon, 1927),

pp. 28–9. See also Gary Cross, ed., *Worktowners at Blackpool: Mass-Observation and Popular Leisure in the 1930s* (London, 1990), p. 21; and Daniel Bell, *Work and its Discontents* (New York, 1970), pp. 16–18. For discussion of public and private time see Anthony Giddens, *A Contemporary Critique of Historical Materialism* (Berkeley, 1981), pp. 130–5.

79 Willmott, *London Village*, pp. 26–7; Lancaster, *All Places*, p. 94; and Halbwachs, *Collective Memory*, p. 130. See also Rochberg-Halton, *Meaning and Modernity*, p. 173; David Harvey, *The Condition of Post-modernity* (Oxford, 1989), pp. 217 and 292; and G. Bachelard, *The Poetics of Space* (Boston MA, 1964), p. 173.

80 An interesting survey of Saturday-night activities is in Mass-Observation Archive, File Report 2467, (April 1947).

81 Mass-Observation, *Meet Yourself On Sunday* (London, 1949), pp. 10–11, 13, 30–1, and 14–15; and Mass-Observation Archive, File Report 2467, (April 1947).

82 E. R. Leach, 'Time and False Noses', in E. R. Leach, ed., *Rethinking Anthropology*, (London School of Economics Monographs in Social Anthropology, no. 22, 1961), pp. 132–6; and E. Zerubavel, *The Seven-Day Circle: The History and Meaning of the Week* (New York, 1985), ch. 5 and pp. 112–29. E. Durkheim makes similar points in *Elementary Forms of Religious Life* (New York, 1965), pp. 54 and 347. See also Pitirim Sorokin and Robert Merton, 'Social Time: A Methodological and Functional Analysis', *American Journal of Sociology* 42 (1937), pp. 615–29. For a popular treatment, see Witold Rybczynski, *Waiting for the Weekend* (New York, 1991).

83 Eviatar Zerubavel, 'Private-Time and Public-Time', in John Hassard, ed., *The Sociology of Time*, (London, 1990), pp. 168–87.

84 Examples of this point for the nineteenth century are Bonnie Smith, *Women of the Bourgeoisie* (Princeton NJ, 1981); and Leonore Davidoff, 'Landscape with Figures: Home and Community in English Society', in Mitchell and Oakley, eds, *The Rights and Wrongs of Women*, pp. 139–75. Other works that include the twentieth-century homemaker are Susan Strasser, *Never Done, A History of Housework in America* (New York, 1980); and Ruth S. Cowan, *More Work For Mother: The Ironies of Household Technology From the Open Hearth to the Micro-wave* (New York, 1983).

85 Jo Anne Vanek, 'Time Spent in Housework', *Scientific American* (November 1974), pp. 116–20; and Hayden, *American Dream*, p. 81.

86 Nelson Graburn, 'Tourism: The Sacred Journey', in Valence Smith, ed., *Hosts and Guests. The Anthropology of Tourism*, (Philadelphia, 1977), pp. 17–32; Leach, 'Time and False Noses'; and Carol Werner, 'Temporal Qualities of Rituals and Celebrations', in McGrath, *Sociology of Time*, pp. 203–32; and Destray, *Famille ouvrière*, p. 135.

87 Richards, *Commodity Culture*, pp. 241–8, quotation on p. 235.

88 These reports were edited by me in Cross, ed., *Worktowners at Black-pool: Mass-Observation and Popular Leisure in the 1930s* (London, 1990), p. 19 for quotation. See chapter 3 for a fuller discussion of Mass-Observation.

89 Cross, *Blackpool*, pp. 24–6.

90 Cross, *Blackpool*, ch. 10, and pp. 72 and 161. See also ch. 12 and pp. 166–7.

91 Confirming this point was J. L. Hodson's *Carnival at Blackport* (London, 1938), pp. 18–19, an autobiographical novel which had the boarding house landlady's home town displayed on the door in an attempt to attract customers from that town.

92 Cross, *Blackpool*, ch. 4, pp. 47, 59–60, 66, 55, 152, and 223.

93 Cross, *Blackpool*, pp. 59, 61, and 90–4.

94 F. Zweig, *Labour, Life and Poverty* (London, 1948), pp. 80, 138, and 153–5.

95 Arthur Greenwood, *Love on the Dole* (London, 1933), pp. 130–1.

96 Cross, *Blackpool*, p. 37.

97 Cross, *Blackpool*, pp. 56, 48–9, chs 10 and 13.

98 Cross, *Blackpool*, p. 57, chs 6 and 20.

99 Ironically the committee charged to develop a theme for the New York World's Fair in its first year stressed the leisure and social potential of new technology and the need of society to anticipate technological change and to reduce 'cultural lag'. But the Fair's perception of the home, as displayed in exhibits, was essentially as a consumer unit. The key economic problem was to link technology to a distribution system based on increased purchasing power.

> An American way of life was conceived in terms of individual ability to consume larger and larger quantities of material objects, not simply because of the positive impact on economic conditions, but because this behavior was an expression of confidence in the very nature of machine civilisation, and because the products themselves represented a basic element of the American character.

The Fair's Theme Center painted an integrated picture of a future of active leisure and democratic consumption. Corporate exhibits attempted to make commodities magical. Joseph Cusker, 'The World of Tomorrow: Science, Culture, and Community at the New York World's Fair', in Helen A. Harrison, ed., *Dawn of a New Day: The New York World's Fair, 1939/40*, (New York, 1980), pp. 3–15.

100 Mass-Observers even noted the linkage between 'progress' and a shift away from 'nature' (i.e., the sea and the dirty stall-holder) for the self-contained environment of the 'Norbreck Hydro'. They noted plans to replace the seedy Central Beach amusement centre with a glass-enclosed sunken garden and fountains. Cross, *Blackpool*, pp. 101, 122, 101–6, and 139.

101 Gurvitch, *Spectrum of Social Time*, p. 58.

102 Richard Hoggart, *The Uses of Literacy* (London, 1957), pp. 119–23.

103 Cross, *Blackpool*, pp. 159–62.

104 John Urry, *The Tourist Gaze: Leisure and Travel in Contemporary Societies* (London, 1990).

105 Cross, *Blackpool*, chs 16–17; and Hodson, *Blackport*, pp. 243–9.

106 'Drama and Crowds: Direct Sources of and Materials for Design', *Architectural Record* (August 1940), cited in Warren Susman, 'The People's Fair: Cultural Contradictions of a Consumer Society', in Harri-

son, ed., *Dawn of a New Day* p. 22; and F. E. Tyng, *Making a World's Fair* (New York, 1958), ch. 6.

107 Savings-club members began with a half-penny contribution the week following the holiday which increased by a half-penny each week for 24 weeks. For each week in the second half of the year leading up to the holiday that contribution decreased by a half-penny. Immediately before the vacation week all drew off their savings for the holiday binge. Cross, *Blackpool*, pp. 37–8.

108 Cross, *Blackpool*, p. 40 and ch. 21.

109 Urry, *Tourist Gaze*, especially chs 2 and 5.

8 CONSUMERIST MODERNITY, AN END OF HISTORY?

1 G. Poujol and R. Labourie, *Les Cultures populaires* (Toulouse, 1979), pp. 109–12. For sources on postwar British leisure policy see chapter 5, above.

2 Good sources are the articles by Alan Brinkley, 'The New Deal and the Idea of the State', in Steve Fraser and Gary Gerstle, eds, *The Rise and Fall of the New Deal Order, 1930–1980* (Princeton NJ, 1989), pp. 85–121; and Nelson Lichtenstein, 'From Corporatism to Collective Bargaining: Organized Labor and the Eclipse of Social Democracy in the Postwar Era', in Fraser and Gerstle, *The Rise and Fall of the New Deal Order, 1930–1980*, pp. 122–52.

3 See, for example, Andrew Shonfield, *Modern Capitalism: The Changing Balance of Public and Private Power* (London, 1965); Pat Thane, *The Foundations of the Welfare State* (London, 1982), pp. 223–69; and Herrick Chapman, *State, Capitalism, and Working-Class Radicalism in the French Aircraft Industry* (Berkeley CA, 1990), chs 9 and 10.

4 For example, see 'Our Country and Our Culture, A Symposium', in *Partisan Review* 19 (1952). Andrew Ross, *No Respect: Intellectuals and Popular Culture* (London, 1989), ch. 1 and pp. 45–7 and 220; Donald Lazare, ed., *American Media and Mass Culture* (Berkeley CA, 1987), introduction; and, for valuable commentary, Richard Pells, *The Liberal Mind in a Conservative Age* (New York, 1985), pp. 121–30.

5 Dwight Macdonald, 'Masscult and Midcult' in his *Against the American Grain* (New York, 1962), pp. 8, 37, and 64. An earlier, less conservative view, is in Dwight MacDonald, 'A Theory of Mass Culture', *Diogenes* 3 (Summer 1953), pp. 1–17, repr. in Bernard Rosenberg and David M. White, eds, *Mass Culture. The Popular Arts in America* (New York, 1957), pp. 59–73.

6 Leslie Fielder, 'The Middle Against Both Ends', *Encounter* 5 (1955), pp. 16–23; and T. S. Eliot, *Christianity and Culture* (London, 1948). For commentary on Macdonald, see Pells, *Liberal Mind*, pp. 174–82 and 229–32. But these views were common among those who abhorred conservatism. See, for example, Irving Howe, 'Notes on Mass Culture', *Politics* 5 (1948), pp. 120–3. A good analysis of this literature is in Patrick Brantlinger, *Bread and Circuses: Theories of Mass Culture as Social Decay* (New York, 1983), ch. 15.

7 David Riesman, *Abundance for What?* (New York, 1964), pp. 114–15, 120. For discussion of Anglo-American reaction to youth consumption

in the 1950s in the US see James Gilbert, *The Cycle of Outrage: America's Reaction to Juvenile Delinquent in the 1950s* (New York, 1985), especially ch. 12; Stuart Hall and Tony Jefferson, eds., *Resistance through Rituals: Youth Subcultures in Post-War Britain* (London, 1975); and Angela McRobbie, 'Working Class Girls and the Culture of Femininity', in Women's Study Group, Centre for Contemporary Culture Studies, *Women Take Issue* (London, 1978), pp. 96–108. Classic critiques of the principle of the bad driving out the good in television are Macdonald, 'Theory of Mass Culture', and Gunther Anders, 'The Phantom World of TV', both in Rosenberg and White, eds, *Mass Culture*, pp. 61–2 and pp. 358–67.

8 Harold Wilensky, 'The Uneven Distribution of Leisure: The Impact of Economic Growth on Free Time', *Social Problems* 9 (Summer, 1961); and Herman Kahn and Anthony Weiner, *The Year 2000* (New York, 1967), pp. 200–1. See also Erwin Smigel, ed., *Work and Leisure. A Contemporary Social Problem* (New Haven CT, 1963), especially the essay by Robert Weis and David Riesman, 'Some Issues in the Future of Leisure', pp. 168–81. Later, Daniel Bell's *Cultural Contradictions of Capitalism* (1976), epitomised this rising anxiety. Bell lamented that the economic rationality (and restraint), engendered by capitalism, was being undermined by capitalism's other offspring, the quest for self-realisation. Intellectuals were to blame for this perversion which was undermining the work ethic and leading to self-destructive mass hedonism. Daniel Bell, *The Cultural Contradictions of Capitalism* (New York, 1976), pp. 19, 53–4, and 80–4.

9 Clement Greenberg, 'Work and Leisure under Industrialism', *Commentary* 16 (July 1953), pp. 57–61. This Aristotelian bias greatly informed Sabastian de Grazia's influential book, *Work, Leisure and Time* (New York, 1967). See also Johan Huizinga, *Homo Ludens* (Boston MA, 1955); and Joseph Pieper, *Leisure the Basis of Culture* (New York, 1952).

10 Georges Friedman, *Le Travail en miettes. Specialisation et loisirs* (Paris, 1956), pp. 185–6. See also his, *Où va le travail humain?* (Paris, 1953), chs 3 and 4; and Jacques Ellul, *La Technique et l'enjeu du siècle* (Paris, 1954), pp. 340–6 and 361–8.

11 Working families, Riesman noted, often lived for years in trailers while building themselves a ' "decent," if not inspiring, shelter . . . with little regard for the symbolic values real estate agents find or invent in dwellings'; working people often chose to live 'where middle-class people are conspicuous by their absence'. Riesman, *Abundance For What?*, pp. 150, 153, and pp. 226–69. For background on Riesman, see Pells, *Liberal Mind*, pp. 233–48. See also Eli Chinoy, *Automobile Workers and the American Dream* (Boston MA, 1955), for details on workers' attitudes toward work and the quest for autonomy in leisure. Vance Packard, *The Status Seekers* (New York, 1959), and William Whyte, *The Organization Man* (New York, 1956) are classics in Veblenian interpretations of the new mass suburbs.

12 Reuel Denney, *The Astonished Muse. Popular Culture in America* (Chicago, 1957), pp. 13–17; Paul Lazarsfeld and Robert Merton, *The Communication of Ideas* (New York, 1948), pp. 116–18; Paul Lazarsfeld

and Henry Field, *The People Look at Radio* (Chapel Hill NC, 1946); and Elihu Katz and P. Lazarsfeld, *Personal Influence: The Part Played by People in the Flow of Mass Communications* (Glencoe IL, 1955); Edward Shils, *Center and Periphery* (Chicago, 1975), pp. 91–111; and D. Riesman, *Individualism Reconsidered* (New York, 1954), pp. 24–5, 50–2, and 46–7. Consider also Russell Lynes, *The Taste Makers* (New York, 1954), and 'Uses of Leisure', a special issue of *American Journal of Sociology* 62 (May 1957), edited by D. Riesman and Rolf Meyersohn of the Center for the Study of Leisure at the University of Chicago.

13 Herbert Gans, *The Levittowners* (New York, 1967) and his *Popular Culture and High Culture* (New York, 1974).

14 Raymond Williams, *Culture and Society, 1780–1950* (London, 1961); and Richard Hoggart, *Uses of Literacy* (London, 1957). Brian Jackson, *Working-Class Community* (Huddersfield, 1968), pp. 1–10, provides an interesting review of challenges to mass-culture theory. See also Peter Willmott, *The Evolution of a Community* (London, 1964). Analysis is in Patrick Brantlinger, *Crusoe's Footprints: Cultural Studies in Britain and America* (London, 1990), ch. 2.

15 Note René Kaes (with Jacques Charpendreau), *La Culture populaire en France* (Paris, 1962); Paul Chombart de Lauwe, *Images de la Culture* (Paris, 1956); P. Chombart de Lauwe, *Pour une sociologie des aspirations* (Paris, 1969); and Pierre Bourdieu, *Distinction: A Social Critique of the Judgment of Taste* (Paris, 1979), trans. Richard Nice (Cambridge MA, 1984).

16 Examples are endless: Paul Goodman, *Growing Up Absurd* (New York, 1960); Herbert Marcuse, *One-Dimensional Man* (Boston MA, 1964); Guy Debord, *The Society of the Spectacle* (New York, 1967); Henri Lefebvre, *Everyday Life in the Modern World* (New York, 1958–61 and 1971); and Stanley Aronowitz, *False Promises*, (New York, 1973). See also Theodore Adorno, 'The Culture Industry Reconsidered', *New German Critique* (Fall 1975), pp. 12–19; and *Telos* 62 (Winter 1984–85), for a special issue on, 'Debates in Contemporary Culture'.

17 Riesman, *Abundance for What?*, pp. 160, 161, 164, 169, 170, and 183.

18 Ross, *No Respect*, p. 45.

19 See, for example, Frederick Hayek, *The Road to Serfdom* (New York, 1944); Joseph Schumpeter, *Capitalism, Socialism, and Democracy* (London, 1942); and the survey, Francis Sutton, S. Harris, C. Kaysen, and J. Tobin, *The American Business Creed* (Cambridge MA, 1956).

20 Chester Bowles, *Tomorrow without Fear* (New York, 1946), p. 49; Reuther speech to the Automotive Council (17 January 1945), and 'SEE IT NOW' (9 June 1957), both in Walter Reuther Collection, Boxes 59 and 45 respectively (Wayne State University), cited in 'Why Automation Didn't Shorten the Work Week: The Politics of Work Time in the Automobile Industry, 1926–1970', an unpublished paper that the author, Ronald Edsforth, kindly made available to me.

21 Editors of *Fortune*, *The Changing American Market* (Garden City NY, 1953), chs 3 and 11. Proponents of class convergence include Robert Nisbet, 'The Decline and Fall of Social Class', *Pacific Sociological Review* 2 (Spring 1959), pp. 11–17; and Harold Wilensky, 'Mass Society and Mass Culture: Interdependence or Independence?', *American*

Sociological Review 29 (April 1964), pp. 173–97. For an analysis of this literature see, Paul Blumberg, 'The Decline and Fall of the Status Symbol', *Social Problems* 21 (Spring 1974), pp. 480–94. For a French perspective see Raymond Aron, *Progress and Disillusion: The Dialectics of Modern Society* (New York, 1968). British studies of affluence include Eric Nordlinger, *The Working-Class Tories* (London, 1967). For a British historian's interpretation of class and affluence in the 1950s, see James Cronin, *Labour and Society in Britain 1918–1979* (London, 1986), pp. 157–72.

22 George Katona, *The Mass Consumption Society* (New York, 1964), pp. 50–3 and 65, quotation from p. 50.

23 W. W. Rostow, *The Stages of Economic Growth* (Cambridge, 1961), p. 81. See also Seymour Harris, ed., *Saving American Capitalism: A Liberal Economic Program* (New York, 1948).

24 Daniel Bell, *End of Ideology*, (Glencoe IL, 1960), ch. 1 and p. 38. John Rae's history of American automobility combined a similar effort to equate democracy with mass ownership of this mobile durable good and to condemn critics for elitism. J. Rae, *The Road and the Car in America* (Cambridge MA, 1971). Similar views are in Peter Passell and Leonard Ross, *The Retreat from Riches: Affluence and its Enemies* (New York, 1971).

25 See, for example, Carolyn Bell, *Consumer Choice in the American Economy* (New York, 1967), ch. 10. Note also J. K. Galbraith's critique of economists in *The Affluent Society* (New York, 1958), pp. 139–60.

26 J. -J. Servan-Schreiber, *The American Challenge* (New York, 1968), ch. 3 and p. 250; P. Yonnet, *Modes et Masses. La Société française et le moderne, 1945–1985* (Paris, 1985), pp. 7, 73, and 378. For historical background on French responses to American marketing practices, see Richard Kuisel, 'Coca-Cola and the Cold Wars: The French Face Americanization, 1948–1953', *French Historical Studies* 17 (Spring 1991), pp. 96–116.

27 See the tables in Martha Olney, *Buy Now Pay Later: Advertising, Credit, and Consumer Durables in the 1920s* (Chapel Hill NC, 1991), pp. 50, 299, and 300; Clair Brown, 'Consumption Norms, Work Roles and Economic Growth, 1918–80', in Clair Brown and Joseph Pechman, eds, *Gender in the Workplace* (Washington, 1987), p. 30; and US Bureau of the Census, *The Statistical History of the United States* (New York, 1976), p. 646. For good material on the suburban ranch-house culture, see C. May, *Western Ranch Houses* (Menlo Park CA, 1958), pp. 93–122; Edward Eichler and Marshall Kaplan, *The Community Builders* (Berkeley CA, 1967); Clifford Clark, *The American Family Home, 1800–1960* (Chapel Hill NC, 1986), pp. 218–30; and Gwendolyn Wright, *Building the Dream: A Social History of Housing in America* (New York, 1981), chs 12–13.

28 John Blum, *V Was for Victory* (New York, 1976), p. 101.

29 Thomas Hine, *Populuxe* (New York, 1986), pp. 4 and 15–58.

30 John Robinson, *How Americans Use Time: A Social-Psychological Analysis of Everyday Behavior* (New York, 1977), pp. 173–80. See also Thomas Juster and Frank Stafford, eds, *Time, Goods, and Well Being* (Ann Arbor MI, 1985), pp. 294 and 305; Joseph McGrath, *The Social*

Psychology of Time (Beverly Hills CA, 1988), pp. 134–40; and the encyclopaedic, Alexander Szalai, *The Use of Time* (The Hague, 1972). A recent survey found television watching in the US had increased to fifteen hours per week (ranging from 21.3 hours for those with only a grade school education to 11.3 hours for the college-educated). John Robinson, 'I Love My TV', *American Demographics* (September 1990), pp. 25–7.

31 Benjamin Hunnicutt, 'The Death of Kellogg's Six-Hour Day', an unpublished paper provided by the author; and David Roediger and Philip Foner, *Our Own Time: A History of American Labor and the Working Day* (Westport CT, 1988), pp. 262–72 for details.

32 E. T. May, *Homeward Bound* (New York, 1989). See also Clifford Clark, 'Ranch-House Suburbia: Ideals and Realities', in Lary May, ed., *Recasting America: Culture and Politics in the Age of Cold War*, (Chicago, 1989), pp. 171–91.

33 Juliet Schor, *The Overworked American: The Unexpected Decline of Leisure in America* (New York, 1991), p. 107 and ch. 5. See also John Robinson, Philip Converse, and Alexander Szalai, 'Everyday Life in Twelve Countries', in A. Szalai, ed., *The Use of Time: Daily Activities of Urban and Suburban Populations in Twelve Countries* (The Hague, 1972), p. 114.

34 UK Department of Employment and Productivity, *British Labour Statistics, Historical Abstract* (London, 1971), pp. 407, 382–3, and 394; and Pearl Jephcott, *Rising Twenty. Notes on Some Ordinary Girls* (London, 1948), pp. 42–6 and 65–7.

35 Gordon Cherry, *Leisure and the Home* (London, 1982), pp. 48–50; BBC, *The People's Activities and Use of Time* (London, 1978); and Henley Centre for Forecasting, *Leisure Futures* (London, 1982), p. 43. See also UK, Office of Population Censuses and Surveys, *General Household Survey* (London, 1977). A fine summary is in Cronin, *Labour and Society*, chs 8 and 9.

36 Perhaps because of relatively poor housing and the paucity of gardens, the French continued to prefer long vacations as opposed to shorter workdays (even if the decline of the two-hour lunch was making for a more compact workday). Still, as late as 1964, only 41 per cent took vacations away from home, by 1983 that figure had peaked at 54 per cent. France, Conseil économique et social, *L'Evolution et les perspectives des besoins des français et leur mode de vie* vol. 2 (Paris, 1989), pp. 21 and 78; Victor Scardigli, *La Consommation: Culture du quotidien* (Paris, 1983), pp. 52 and 136; Maurice Legelle, *La Consommation* (Paris, 1956), p. 139; Michel Verret, *L'Ouvrier français. L'Espace ouvrier* (Paris, 1979), pp. 56–77 and 146; Paul Chombart de Lauwe, *Famille et habitation* vol. 2 (Paris, 1960), p. 260; Phillipe Ariès and Georges Duby, *Histoire de la vie privée* vol. 5 (Paris, 1985), pp. 127–8; and Institut du commerce et de la consommation, *La Démographie et l'évolution de la consommation* (Paris, 1984), pp. 20–1. See also Nicolas Herpin and Daniel Verger, *La Consommation des français* (Paris, 1988), pp. 62–70; and John Ardagh, *The New French Revolution* (New York, 1968), pp. 212–30, 258–71 and 281–97.

37 'Reduction du temps de travail et aménagement des congés', *Sondages*

2 (1964), pp. 63–75. See also Joffre Dumazedier and Maurice Imbert, *Espace et loisir dans la société française d'hier et de demain* (Paris, 1967), pp. 42–4.

38 Whyte, *Organization Man*; Vance Packard, *Status Seekers*; Marcuse, *One Dimensional Man*; George Soule, *Time for Living* (New York, 1955); and Galbraith, *Affluent Society*.

39 Jean Fourastié, *Les 40,000 heures* (Paris, 1965), pp. 1–7 and 81. Fourastié earlier took a less optimistic line about worktime reductions in, *Machinisme et bien-être* (Paris, 1951), p. 164. Other examples of forecasting include Henley Centre, *Futures*, pp. 2 and 93–4; Kahn and Weiner, *2000*, pp. 195–201; and Alvin Toffler, *The Third Wave* (New York, 1980). Note also Robert Theobald, 'Toward Full Unemployment', in Howard Didsbury, ed., *The World of Work* (Bethesda MD, 1983); Tom Stonier, *The Wealth of Information: A Profile of Post-Industrial Economy* (London, 1983), p. 122; and Anthony Veal, *Leisure and the Future* (London, 1987), ch. 7. For a good French bibliography and discussion see Marie Busch, *La Sociologie du temps libre: problèmes et perspectives* (Paris, 1974).

40 Raymond Williams, *Toward 2000* (London, 1983), pp. 266–8; André Decouflé, *La France en l'an 2000* (Paris, 1980), ch. 3; and Maurice Rustant, *Vers la semaine de 30 heures* (Paris, 1975), p. 95.

41 Joffre Dumazedier, *Révolution culturelle du temps libre, 1968–1988* (Paris, 1988), pp. 5–19, 48–50, 220–36, and 22. See also the short-lived journal, *Temps libre* (1981–5) with frequent contributions by Dumazedier as well as by his colleagues, Nicole Samuel and Roger Sue.

42 William Gossin, *Le Temps de la vie quotidienne* (Paris, 1974) pp. 11–12, 377, and especially 388; note also Gossin's *Le Travail et le temps* (Paris, 1969). Stanley Parker, *The Future of Work and Leisure* (London, 1971), chs 5 and 8; and S. Parker, *Leisure and Work* (London, 1982). Mihaly Csikszentmihalyi, *Beyond Boredom and Anxiety* (San Francisco, 1975), pp. 185, 36, and 3.

43 By contrast, 57 per cent of professors who were also asked their ideal workweek preferred 25 hours or less. (That figures!) Only 30 per cent of clerks and 26 per cent of hourly factory workers would have found such a short workweek ideal. Gossin, *Temps de la vie* , pp. 306–7.

44 Gary Becker, 'A Theory of the Allocation of Time', *Economic Journal* (September 1965), pp. 493–517; and Staffan Linder, *The Harried Leisure Class* (New York, 1970).

45 Philippe Barou d'Iriburne, *La Politique du bonheur* (Paris, 1973), ch. 1, pp. 29, 89, 118, 129, 147, and 84–5. For a wide-ranging critique of consumer rationality from a psychologically-informed economist see, Tibor Scitovsky, *The Joyless Economy. An Inquiry into Human Satisfaction and Consumer Dissatisfaction* (Oxford, 1976).

46 Fred Hirsch, *The Social Limits to Growth* (Cambridge MA, 1976), especially pp. 1–11, 84, 91–2, 151–7, and 172.

47 Barou rejected 'sumptuary laws' against old common luxuries or 'defensive signs' of those merely trying to keep up with the Joneses. Barou d'Iriburne, *Bonheur*, pp. 225, 209 and ch. 6.

48 Ivan Illich, *Towards a History of Needs* (New York, 1978), ch. 1, p. 39; Ivan Illich, *Tools of Conviviality* (New York, 1973); Henri Lefebvre

'Toward A Leftist Cultural Politics', in Cary Nelson and Lawrence Greenberg, eds, *Marxism and the Interpretation of Culture*, (Urbana IL, 1988), pp. 75–88; and E. F. Schumacher, *Small is Beautiful* (New York, 1973). Note also the less known, E. J. Mishan, *The Gods of Growth* (Harmondsworth, 1967).

49 In addition to the journal, *Turning Point* (1976–87), examples of this school included James Robertson, *Future Wealth* (London, 1989); and James Robertson, *Future Work: Jobs, Self-Employment and Leisure after the Industrial Age* (London, 1985), especially pp. 6–13 and 44–5, as well as Paul Ekins, ed., *The Living Economy* (London, 1986); and Mark Lux and Kenneth Lux, *Humanistic Economics: The New Challenge* (New York, 1988).

50 Clive Jenkins and Berrie Sherman, *Collapse of Work* (London; 1979), pp. 1–6, 11–13 and chs 5–7, and their sequel, *Leisure Shock* (London, 1981); Ivor Clemitson and George Rodger, *A Life to Live. Beyond Full Employment* (London, 1981), with a preface by Neil Kinnock, ch. 2 and p. 136. The German sociologist, Claus Offe, makes similar arguments in, *Disorganized Capitalism* (London, 1985), pp. 85–7 and 132–48. See also Jonathan Gershuny, *Social Innovation and the Division of Labour* (Oxford, 1983), ch. 2; Barry Bluestone and Bennett Harrison, *The Deindustrialization of America* (New York, 1982); and Barry Jones, *Sleepers Wake! Technology and the Future of Work* (Melbourne, 1982).

51 Echanges et Projets, *La Révolution du temps choisi* (Paris, 1981), especially pp. 92–3 and 139–76. For an early American version, see Fred Best, 'Flexible Work Scheduling: Beyond the Forty-Hour Impasse', in Best, ed., *The Future of Work* (Englewood Cliffs NJ, 1973), pp. 93–9; and Carmen Sirianni, 'The Self-Management of Time in Postindustrial Society', in Karl Hinrichs, William Roche, and Carmen Sirianni, eds, *Working Time in Transition* (Philadelphia, 1991), pp. 231–74.

52 André Gorz, *Critique of Economic Reason* (London, 1989), p. 7.

53 Echanges et projets, *Temps choisi*, p. 55; Clemitson and Rodger, *Beyond Full Employment*, pp. 10–11, 14, and 19–20; Robertson, *Future Work*, pp. ix and 6–7. See also Charles Handy, *The Future of Work* (Oxford, 1985), p. 184.

54 André Gorz, *Farewell to the Working Class* (London, 1982), chs 3, 7, pp. 80 and 95. See also Alain Touraine, *L'Après socialisme* (Paris, 1980).

55 Jenkins and Sherman, *Collapse*, pp. 154, 151, and *Shock*, chs 1, 6–8, and p. 57; Gorz, *Farewell*, pp. 96, 101, and *Economic Reason*, pp. 199–212; and Echange et Projets, *Temps choisi*, pp. 211–19.

56 Galbraith, *Affluent Society*, pp. 334–48; and Theodore Roszak, *The Making of a Counterculture* (New York, 1971); and Ronald Inglehart, *Cultural Shift* (Princeton NJ, 1990), chs 2, 4, 8, 9 and 11. See also Claus Offe, 'Challenging the Boundaries of Institutional Politics: Social Movements since the 1960s'; Charles Maier, 'The Politics of Time: Changing Paradigms of Collective Time and Private Time in the Modern Era'; and Laura Balbo, 'Family, Women, and the State: Notes Toward a Topology of Family Roles and Public Intervention', in Charles Maier,

ed., *The Changing Boundaries of the Political* (Cambridge, 1987), chs 2, 4, and 6 respectively. Note also Robertson, *Future Work*, ch. 6.

57 For example, in the US, married women's participation in the labour force rose from 13.8 per cent in 1940 to 30.5 per cent in 1960, and to 50.1 by 1980, while male employment dropped from 82.6 per cent to 77.4 per cent between 1940 and 1980. Clair Brown, 'Consumption Norms, Work Roles', pp. 31 and 35–58. Stanley Lebergott's Comment to Brown's paper, pp. 54–8 attacks the widely embraced claim that housework did not decline between the 1920s and 1960s; instead he finds a decrease in housework from 94 to 50 hours weekly between 1900 and 1979 and he insists that the key to wives' entry into the workforce was domestic technology, reduced childbearing, and the disappearance of boarders. Compare with J. Vanek, 'Time Spent in Housework', *Scientific American* 231 (November 1974), p. 118; and Maxine Margolis, *Mothers and Such* (Berkeley, 1984).

58 Jan Pahl, *Money and Marriage* (Basingstoke, 1989), pp. 146–50; Young and Willmott, *Symmetrical Family*, chs 4, 6 and 9; and Gershuny, *Social Innovation*, pp. 145–56. See also Richard Berk and Sarah Berk, *Labor and Leisure at Home* (Beverly Hills CA, 1979), chs 8 and 9; Sarah Berk, *The Gender Factory* (New York, 1985); Joseph Pleck, *Working Wives, Working Husbands* (Beverly Hills CA, 1985); and Susan Christopherson, 'Trading Time for Consumption: The Failure of Working-Hours Reduction in the United States', in Hinrichs, Roche, and Sirianni, eds, *Time in Transition*, pp. 174–84. A recent American survey has found that women spend 7.5 hours less doing housework per week in 1985 as compared to 1965, while men spend 5.2 hours more. J. P. Robinson, 'Who's Doing The Housework', *American Demographics* (December 1988), pp. 26–8.

59 Gershuny, *Social Innovation*, chs 3, 4, and 8. R. Pahl, *Division of Labour* (*Self Provisioning*) (Oxford, 1983), pp. 312–17, 335 and ch. 4; and Offe, *Disorganized Capitalism*, pp. 71–9.

60 Inglehart, *Culture Shift*, ch. 11; Claus Offe, *Disorganized Capitalism*, pp. 60–2; and Ross, *No Respect*, pp. 225–32.

61 Anthony Veal, *Sport and Recreation in England and Wales* (London, 1979), pp. 20–3; P. Branham and I. Henry, 'Political Ideology and Leisure Policy in the United Kingdom', *Leisure Studies* 4, 1 (1985), pp. 1–19; and UK, Office of Population Censuses and Surveys, *Social Trends* (London, 1981), pp. 178–9. See also Martha Hill, 'Investments of Time in Houses and Durables', in Juster and Stafford, eds, *Time, Goods, and Well-Being*, pp. 205–43. John Hargreaves, *Sport, Power, and Culture* (London, 1985), chs 5 and 9, stresses the conservative functions of public sponsorship of sports. See also UK, Office of Population Censuses and Surveys, *General Household Survey* (London, 1988), pp. 56–7, 62, and 236–7.

62 Henley Centre, *Leisure Futures*, pp. 30–1.

63 Jeff Bishop and Paul Hoggett, *Organizing Around Enthusiasms: Mutual Aid in Leisure* (London, 1986), pp. 55, 122, and 3.

64 Between 1967 and 1981, the proportion of French visiting art exhibits increased from 14 to 21 per cent and admissions to other museums rose from 18 to 30 per cent. By contrast, attendance at sporting

events declined from 29 to 20 per cent over the same period. Joffre Dumazedier, *Révolution culturelle*, p. 199; Conseil économique et social, *L'Evolution des besoins*, pp. 70–3 and 7; and Poujol and Labourie, *Cultures populaires*, pp. 109–11. Traditional hobby activities continued as well. Note the ethnographic study of miners and their raising of pigeons: J. Frisch-Gauthier, *La Colombophilie chez les mineurs du Nord* (Paris, 1961).

65 Robert Lanquar and Yves Raynouard, *Le Tourisme social* (Paris, 1978), p. 23; Kaes and Charpendreau, *Culture populaire* pp. 43–7 and ch. 3; Raymond Labourie, *Les Institutions socio-culturelles. Les mots clés* (Paris, 1978), pp. 10, 20–30, and 40–1; Jean Dumas, 'Cenon', *Cahier de l'observation du changement social* 18 (1982), p. 237; Dumazedier, *Révolution culturelle*, pp. 26–31; and Henri Mendras, *Social Change in Modern France* (Cambridge, 1991) pp. 216–25. See also Poujol and Labourie, *Cultures populaires*, and, for interpretation of the animators as manipulative see, Jacques Ion, B. Miège, and A. -N. Roux, *L'Appareil d'action culturelle* (Paris, 1974).

66 Robert Stebbins, *Amateurs: On the Margin Between Work and Leisure* (Beverly Hills CA, 1979), and *Amateurs: Professionals, and Serious Leisure* (Montreal, 1992). The Americans' Use of Time Project at the University of Maryland shows ambiguous trends: American devotion to hobbies between 1965 and 1985 increased from 2.1 to 2.2 hours per week, while Americans experienced a rise from 0.9 to 2.2 hours for sports and outdoor activity, and an increase from 1.3 to 1.9 hours for adult education. But organisations took up only 0.7 hours in 1985 as compared to 1 hour in 1965 and reading has declined from 3.7 to 2.8 hours over the same period. The greatest change was the increase of television viewing. It rose 10.5 to 15.1 hours per week. Blayne Culter, 'Where Does the Free Time Go', *American Demographics* (November 1990), pp. 36–41.

67 Gorz, *Economic Reason*, pp. 199, 102, and 158; and Roger Sue, *Vers une société du temps libre* (Paris, 1982), pp. 63–4.

68 Conseil économique et social, *L'Evolution et les perspectives des besoins des français et leur mode de vie* 2 (Paris 1989), pp. 61–2; Paul Koepp, 'L'Evolution récente de la durée du travail', *Travail et Emploi* 4 (April 1980); Archibald Evans, *Hours of Work in Industrial Countries* (Geneva, 1975), pp. 23–4; F. Cribier, *Le Grande Migration de l'été* (Paris, 1969), p. 45; and Jean-Pierre Jallade, 'Working-Time Policies in France', in Hinrichs, Roche, and Sirianni, eds, *Time in Transition*, p. 66.

69 British men in manual trades were still working 44.3 hours per week in 1984 as compared to 38.5 hours for white-collar male employees (39.4 and 36.5 hours respectively for women blue- and white-collar groups). Because of part-time jobs, British women never actually worked up to the nominal weekly standard. In the 1980s, British workers enjoyed a two- to three week holiday as compared to the legal minimum of five in France and the male retirement age remained 65 years as compared to the voluntary 60-year level in France, won in 1982. Paul Blyton, *Changes in Working Time. An International Review* (New York, 1985), p. 24; Evans, *Hours of Work*, pp. 28 and 160; *British Labour Statistics*,

p. 160; and Labour Research Department, *Long Suffering British Workers. Working Time in Europe* (London, 1981), p. 14.

70 Weekly work may have declined 1.5 hours between 1947 and 1986, almost all of it before 1960. But little of this gain can be attributed to vacations. While, by 1988, Americans enjoyed 19.5 days off per year on average, many had far fewer days of continuous vacation. Even when small companies are excluded, the average company in the 1980s gave fewer than nine days of holiday after one year and only two weeks after three years. And the mean tenure at one job was scarcely three years. John Owen, *Reduced Working Hours: Cure For Unemployment or Economic Burden?* (Baltimore MD, 1989), pp. 8–11 and ch. 3. See also Christopherson, 'Trading Time', pp. 177–8; Robert Hart, *Working Time and Employment* (Boston MA, 1987), pp. 14–15; and Roland Cuvillier, *The Reduction of Working Time: Scope and Implications in Industrial Market Economies* (Geneva, 1984), p. 9. Workyear data is from the *Washington Post* (9 June 1991), p. A35.

71 Fifty-one as opposed to 45 per cent of British workers favoured time over income while 54 to 41 per cent of the French preferred leisure in a 1977 survey. When asked how they would like free time packaged, more favoured early retirement (43 per cent) rather than shorter workdays (37 per cent) in the French survey. The majority claimed that they would use newly liberated time for 'family life'. In a 1982 British survey only 18 per cent preferred shorter workdays as compared to a quarter wanting fewer workdays, 24 per cent more holidays, 23 per cent early retirement, and 6 per cent preferred sabbaticals. This data is accessible in Cuvillier, *Working Time*, pp. 52–3. Similar attitudes toward the income/leisure trade-off were found among American workers; see Fred Best, *Flexible Life Scheduling* (New York, 1980), pp. 133–5.

72 For American hours movements in the 1950s and 1960s, see Edsforth, 'Why Automation Didn't Shorten the Work Week', and Roediger and Foner, *Our Own Time*, pp. 270–1. Examples of early short-hour appeals are Robert Bendiner, 'Could You Stand a Four-day Week?', *Reporter* (8 August 1957), pp. 10–14; 'Sharing the Benefits of Technology', *International Labour Review* (July 1960), pp. 1–25; and Sar Levitan, *Reducing Worktime as A Means To Combat Unemployment* (Kalamazoo MI, 1964). For a description of US congressional investigations of automation and work sharing, see Eugene McCarthy and William McGaughey, *Nonfinancial Economics. The Case for Shorter Hours of Work* (New York, 1989), ch. 1.

73 W. W. Leontief, 'The Distribution of Work and Income', *Scientific American* 247 (1982), pp. 152–64; Everett Kassalow, 'Beyond Keynes: European Unions Formulate New Economic Program', *Monthly Labor Review* (February 1980), 36–40; Hart, *Working Time*, pp. 1–5; Cuvillier, *Working Time*, ch. 3; and Anne Lapping, *Working Time in Britain and West Germany* (Oxford, 1983).

74 Job sharing was argued in B. Olmsted, 'Job Sharing – A New Way to Work', *Personnel Journal* (February 1977), pp. 78–81; Pam Silverstein and H. S. Jazette, *Flexitime: Where, When and How?* (Ithaca NY, 1979); and Ann Harriman, *The Work/Leisure Trade Off* (New York,

1982). See also Fred Best, *Flexible Life Scheduling* (New York, 1980); and Hinrichs, Roche, and Sirianni, eds, *Time in Transition*.

75 While Europeans took the lead, American advocates of work sharing were plentiful especially after 1975 when the AFL-CIO agreed to follow local and state unions to support campaigns for a 35-hour week (while others like the steelworkers favoured 30 hours of work for 40 hours of pay). Institut Syndical Européen, *La Réduction du temps de travail en europe occidentale* (Brussels, 1980), and *Congressional Record* (18 October 1979), PP. E5232–E 5133. See also Cuvillier, *Working Time*, ch. 2; R. Todd, *1000 Hours by the Year 2000. Timely Reasons for a Labour Forum* (Nottingham, 1980), pp. 1–2; and Roediger and Foner, *Our Own Time*, pp. 272–7. For an American example of the 'collapse of work' thesis see McCarthy and McGaughey, *Nonfinancial Economics*. Note also other American sources including Martin Morand and Ramelle MacCoy, eds, *Short-Time Compensation: A Formula for Work Sharing* (New York, 1984); and W. McGaughey, *A Shorter Workweek in the 1980s* (White Bear Lake MN, 1981).

76 Todd, *1000 Hours*, pp. 4–5; Dominique Taddei, *Le Temps de l'emploi* (Paris, 1988), ch. 1; Linda Hantrais, 'Leisure Policy in France', *Leisure Studies* 3 (May 1984), pp. 129–46; and Gert Hautsch, *Zeil: 35 Studen. Kampf um Arbeitszeitverkuerzung* (Frankfurt, 1980).

77 Sophisticated programmes financing such reductions were tried. These included temporary Short-Time Working Compensation Schemes in Britain and in several American states, and early retirement programmes in France. Y. Barou and J. Rigaudial, *35 Heures et l'emploi* (Paris, 1983), pp. 8, 11, 149–53, and 193–6; and Fred Best, *Reducing Workweeks to Prevent Layoffs* (Philadelphia, 1988), ch. 6. For other schemes encouraging flexible life work schedules, see Fred Block, *Postindustrial Possibilities* (Berkeley CA, 1990) and Sirianni, 'Self-Management of Time', pp. 262–8.

78 David Metcalf, *Cutting Worktime as a Cure for Unemployment* (London, 1987), pp. 5–6 and 11–12; Pierre Boisard, *La Réduction des durées travaillées* (Paris, 1982); and Hart, *Working Time*, ch. 12. For management's viewpoint of the costs of vacations see, Theresa Gries, *The Decline of Annual Hours Worked in the United States Since 1947* (Philadelphia, 1984). For a balanced (if rather sceptical) review of economic evaluation of work sharing in the US and Europe, see Owen, *Reduced Working Hours*. Note also Blyton, *Changes in Working Time*, pp. 36–40 and 43–7.

79 Hinrichs, Roche, and Sirianni, eds, *Time in Transition*, pp. 1–9, 16–21 for summary, and p. 19 for quotation. Roche stresses this point in his essay 'The Chimera of Changing Employee Time Preferences: Working Hours in British Industrial Relations since World War II', pp. 87–128. These authors hedge their pessimism on the demand for leisure by suggesting that prolonged trade-union campaigns may increase this desire even if the union motivation has been primarily negative, i.e., to reduce joblessness. In the same collection see also Jallade, 'Time Policies in France', pp. 70–85; and Roche, 'Changing Employee Preferences', pp. 100–19.

80 See, for example, 'International Working Time Issues', *European Indus-*

trial Relations Review 193 (February 1990), pp. 19–20; and 'Impact of Shorter Working Hours', *European Industrial Relations Review* 212 (September 1991), p. 5. Ronald's Edsforth's unpublished paper 'The Case for Shorter Hours: Work Time Reduction in the United States and Western Europe since 1930', has been useful.

81 Cuvillier, *Working Time*, p. 33; and Lapping, *Working Time*, p. 59.

82 Particularly penetrating are works by the British Scott Lash and John Urry, *The End of Organized Capitalism* (Cambridge, 1987), ch. 9; J. Urry, *The Tourist Gaze: Leisure and Travel in Contemporary Societies* (London, 1990), ch. 5; and S. Lash, *Sociology of Postmodernity* (London, 1990).

83 Schor, *Overworked American*, p. 112.

84 Donald Horne, *The Public Culture. The Triumph of Industrialism* (London, 1986), pp. 234, 244.

85 Michael Ignatieff, *The Needs of Strangers: An Essay on Privacy, Solidarity and the Politics of Being Human* (New York, 1985), p. 139.

86 Robert Venturi, D. Scott-Brown, and S. Izenour, *Learning from Las Vegas* (Cambridge MA, 1972); and J. Lyotard, *The Postmodern Condition* (Manchester, 1984). For an analysis and critique, see David Harvey, *The Condition of Postmodernity* (Oxford, 1989), pp. 57–60.

87 Inglehart, *Cultural Shift*, pp. 332–4; and Offe, 'New Social Movements', pp. 95–102.

88 This is the theme of Jeremy Rifkin in his *Time Wars* (New York, 1987).

89 American women have five to six hours less time free from wage and domestic work than do men. These problems are addressed in Gershuny, *Social Innovations*, pp. 48 and 183; Sirianni, 'Self-Management of Time', quotation on p. 47; and Christopherson, 'Trading Time', p. 180–1. For British commentary, see Veronica Beechey and Tessa Perkins, *A Matter of Hours: Women, Part-Time Work, and the Labour Market* (Cambridge, 1987).

90 Pahl, *Division of Labour*, pp. 316–17; Sue Glyptis, *Leisure and Unemployment* (London, 1989), pp. 107–30; and Harvey, *Condition of Postmodernity*, ch. 9; Christopherson, 'Trading Time', pp. 177–84; and M. Talbot, *Women and Leisure. A State of the Art Review* (London, 1982).

91 See, for example, George Gallup, *The Gallup Poll: Public Opinion* (New York, 1989), pp. 55–8, cited in Juliet Schor, *The Overworked American* (New York, 1991), p. 126. On the willingness of Americans to forgo *future* income for additional time, see Schor's pp. 130–1.

92 Schor, *Overworked American*, ch. 6, discusses some of these economic options.

Index

affluence: and cultural improvement 20–2; and productivity 28, 30, 32, 32–4; and sated needs 185, 186, 195, 212; in the United States 15, 30, 133–5, 190–2; in Western Europe 15, 32, 33, 133, 134, 193; and the work incentives 15, 17–19, 23, 41; *see also* needs; consumption
Abundance for What? 189
Adamic, Louis 68, 69
Adorno, Theodor 50, 51, 194
adult education 110, 113, 116
advertising 46, 156, 157
Affluent Society 194
amateurism 194, 202, 203
American Federation of Labour (AFL) 29, 31–3, 42, 79, 83, 85, 95, 192, 205
Americanisation 57; *see also* consumption and Americanisation; mass culture and Americanisation
Anderson, Sherwood 68, 69
Agnew, Jean-Christophe 160
Arnold, Matthew 47, 58, 61
Aragon, Louis 71
Aristotelian bias 154
Aristotle 46, 47, 65
Arnold, Thurmon 72
automation 197, 198, 205

Bakke, E. Wight 146, 148, 150
Barou d'Iriburne, Philippe 195, 196
Barou, Yves 206
Battle of Production 98
Beard, Charles 53
Becker, Gary 195

Becker, Carl 72
Bell, Daniel 190
Bell, Clive 59
Bellamy, Edward 18
Benda, Julien 63
Bevin, Ernest 91, 154
Bishop, Jeff 202
Black, Hugo 83
Blackpool 64, 68, 69, 73, 74, 115, 123, 155, 177–83
Blumer, Harold 160
Bolton (England) 68
Le Bon, Gustave 48, 49
Bourdieu, Pierre 156, 189
Bowles, Chester 190
Boyd, Allison 142
Brantlinger, Patrick 48
Braucher, Howard 67
Brentano, Lujo 25
Bretonne, N.E. de la 17
Brierley, Walter 141
British Broadcasting Corporation 61, 64, 113
Brody, David 132
Brookings Institution 85
Browden, Harold 88
Brown, Ivor 64, 172
Burns, C. Delise 64, 66, 67, 69, 71, 154
Butlin, Billy 114, 116, 123
Butts, Marie 116

camps, holiday 101–3, 114–16; *see also* holidays
Carnegie Foundation 114
Castles, E.B. 113
Catchings, Waddill 42, 86, 190
Catholicism 63, 103, 113, 116, 120

Changing American Market 190
Chapin, Stuart 169
Chapman, Dennis 169
Chapman, Herrick 94
Chase, Stuart 30, 34, 54, 69, 70
Chombart de Lauwe, Paul 189
cinema 46, 54, 55, 67, 101
Citroën, André 43, 101
Clark, Colin 43–5, 89
Clemitson, Ivor 197
Club Med 203
Cohen, Lizabeth 105, 140
cold war 1, 4, 185, 207
Cole, G.D.H. 122
Common, Jack 147
communism 2, 71, 88, 99, 104, 208, 209
community centres 113, 155; *see also* occupational clubs
computers 197
Coney Island 51
Congress of Industrial Organizations (CIO) 105; *see also* American Federation of Labor
consumer education 20, 22, 61
consumer revolution 4
consumerism: critiques of 4, 5, 7, 9, 13, 171, 194–6, 209–12; and totalitarianism 58; theories of 155–62; *see also* consumer education; consumption; mass culture
consumerist consensus 184
consumption: American patterns 134, 135, 165, 166, 169, 173, 190–2; and Americanisation 156, 203; as artefacts 172, 173; British patterns 133, 135, 165, 166, 168, 170–2, 177–83, 193; and civilisation 20, 25, 161, 190; during the Depression 143–53; domestic 12, 40, 41, 57, 148–51, 153, 164, 167–76, 191–3; French patterns 133, 134, 165, 191, 193; gospel of 41; and male fraternity 148, 149, 150; manipulation of 50, 156–8, 160, 163, 201; and manufactured need 156–8; and marginalism 26, 195; after 1945 190, 193; in the 1920s 34, 35; and populism 67, 74, 75, 188, 191; psychology of 156–60, 185, 188, 189, 207–10; and public policy 185, 194, 196, 219, 212; and rising expectations 134; and scarcity 12, 13; as self-production 161, 162, 167, 172, 173, 188, 189; and social emulation 158–60, 163, 169–72, 179, 180, 188, 195–7, 209, 210; as social markers 161, 164, 195; and women 23, 41, 167–9, 172, 179, 185, 192, 193, 208, 211; and working-class luxury 145; and working-class respectability 147, 150, 151, 166, 171, 172; of youth 188; *see also* consumer education; consumerism; leisure as consumption; holidays, spending
Conyers, John 205
Cooke, Morris 29, 30
The Crowd, 48
Csikszentmihalyi, Mihaly 195
'culture industry' 48, 50
cultural lag 48, 52, 53, 60, 61, 194, 201
Cutten, George 54, 62, 154

Dahlberg, Arthur 24
'democratic leisure' 5, 10, 11, 46, 75, 100, 105–9, 111, 113–15, 120–2, 125, 185, 201; *see also* leisure; mass culture; rational recreation
Denney, Reuel 188
Depression, the Great 8, 9, 11, 12, 31, 44, 45, 62, 72, 77, 81, 82, 87, 96, 109, 114, 135, 138, 140
deskilling of labour 155, 156
Dewey, John 30, 40
Dialectic of Enlightenment 50
discipline: of work 9, 16, 17, 37, 39, 131, 132, 142, 162, 163
Disney, Walt 74
Disneyland 124
Dolleans, Edouard 112
'domestic speed up' 2
dopo lavoro 103
Douglas, Mary 161
Douglas, Paul 30
Duboin, Jacques 65, 89
Dubreuil, Hyacinthe 35, 36, 49
Dumazedier, Joffre 194, 195
Durant, Ruth 140
Durant, Henry 55–7, 60, 62
Durkheim, Emile 19, 21

Echanges et Projets 198
Edgerton, John 16
Educational Leagues (France) 106, 112
Ehrenburg, Ilya 55, 56, 59
eight-hour day 9, 10, 25, 32, 37, 76–8, 93, 99, 129, 130; *see also* forty-hour week
Elder, Glen 144, 151
Eliot, T.S. 58, 59, 73, 187
Engel, Ernst 26, 155, 156
Enlightenment 16, 17, 25
Esprit 63
EuroDisney 195
Ewen, Stuart 157

Fair Labor Standards Act 84
fascism 62, 70, 81, 99, 103, 106, 120, 121
fashion 157–61, 164, 168, 177; *see also* consumption and social emulation; social emulation
fatigue 28
Ferenczi, Sandor 50
Fiedler, Leslie 187
flexitime 198, 205
Fluegel, Ernest 159
Ford, Henry 43
Fordism 2, 3, 4, 5, 11, 35, 36, 37, 39, 54, 87, 128, 133, 154, 162, 163, 196, 208, 210, 211; *see also* productivity
Fortune 190
forty-hour week 8, 11, 37, 84, 85, 88–94, 98, 117, 129, 184, 192, 204; *see also* eight-hour day
Foster, William 42, 86, 190
Fourastié, Jean 194
Fox, Richard W. 73, 153
Franchon, Benoit 104
François-Poncet, André 38
Frankfurt School 50, 51
Franklin, Benjamin 17, 164
Frederick, Christine 23, 41, 157
Freud, Sigmund 49–52, 54
Fry, Roger 59
full-time employment 185, 197
Furnas, C.C. 65

Galbraith, John K. 194, 200
Gallup Poll 192
gambling 145–7
Gans, Herbert 188

Gantt, Henry 29
gardens 101, 102, 138, 173
Gelber, Steven 109, 139
gender roles 12, 100, 143, 150–2 167, 175, 185, 186, 200, 211; *see also* consumption, domestic; time and gender roles
General Confederation of Labour (France, CGT) 32, 33, 89, 91, 111, 112, 119
General Strike of 1926 (Britain) 37
Georges-Picot, M.R. 101
Gershuny, J. 201
Gide, Charles 20, 21
Goblet, G. 159, 160
Goffman, Erving 169
Gompers, Samuel 29, 30, 35
Gorz, André 36, 37, 198, 199, 203
Gossin, William 195
Green, William 35, 79, 83
Greenberg, Clement 73, 188
Greenwood, Walter 147, 149, 179
Gresham's Law 54
Guerin-Desjardins, Jacques 101, 103
Guinness Trust 116
Gunton, George 25, 42
Gurvitch, Georges 174, 181

Halbwachs, Maurice 56, 155, 162, 167, 174
Hall, G. Stanley 51, 52, 62
Hammond, John 15, 16, 64
Hansen, Alvin 95
Harris, Constance 56
Harrisson, Tom 69
Hayburn, F.S. 88
Hayday, Arthur 87
Hayden, Dolores 167
Hewitt, Dorothy 110
high culture 48–51, 128; *see also* mass culture
'high wages' 3, 15, 34, 39, 42, 43, 89, 162, 163
Hilton, John 145, 146
Hine, Thomas 12, 191
hire purchase 148, 169, 171
Hirsch, Fred 196
Hitler, Adolf 91
hobbies 109, 113, 136, 139, 167, 202, 204
Hobson, John 22–4, 45
Hoggart, Richard 124, 188

Hoggett, Paul 202
Holiday Fellowship 115, 116, 123, 124, 208
holidays: and employers 80–2; 95–8, 100; with pay 8, 11, 78, 80–2, 95–8, 118, 126, 204; and the Popular Front 100, 118–21; and politics 97–100; public provisions for 114–17, 119, 120, 122; spending 77, 80, 114, 177, 179–82; *see also* camps, holiday; consumption; leisure; working hours
homemakers 141, 151, 168, 172, 175, 180, 182, 192, 200
Hoover, Herbert 30
Horkheimer, Max 50, 51
Horne, Donald 210
Horowitz, Daniel 23
Hostels 114, 116, 120, 126; *see also* camps, holiday
housing 168–74, 193
L'Humanité 111, 118, 119
Hume, David 17, 18
Hunnicutt, Benjamin 83
Huxley, A. 58

Ickes, Harold 84, 87
Ignatieff, Michael 210
Illich, Ivan 197
Inglehart, Ronald 200, 201
instalment purchase 148, 169, 171
International Labour Organisation (ILO) 36, 77, 87, 90, 93, 105–7
international labour standard 76, 77
International Welfare Society 121
Isherwood, Baron 161

Jacks, L.P. 56
Jackson, Julian 125
Jahoda, Marie 139
James, William 51
Jenkins, Clive 197
Jevons, W. Stanley 25–7
Joad, Cyril 114, 154, 158
Johnson, Paul 147
Jones, G. Stedman 4
Jones, Stephen 104
Josephson, Matthew 63
Jouhaux, Léon 90

Kahn, Herman 187
Katona, George 190

Kellogg, W. W. 83, 192
Keynesianism 7, 9, 15, 27, 28, 45, 47, 85, 95, 163, 184, 185, 196, 205
Komarovsky, Mirra 142, 143, 151
Kraft durch Freude 81, 103, 107
Kyrk, Hazel 40–2

labour *see* consumption; deskilling of labour; productivity, labour attitudes toward; wages; working hours; time, cycles of; time, uses of; trade-union movement
Labour Magazine 122
Labour Party 88, 122, 123, 197
Lacoin, Maurice 101
Lafargue, Paul 18, 37
Lagrange, Léo 120–2, 126, 184
Lancaster, Osbert 171
Lansbury, George 57, 122
Lapping, Anne 207
Lasch, Christopher 157
Laski, Harold 122
Lasswell, Harold 72
Lazarsfeld, Paul 137, 188
Lears, T.J. Jackson 157
Leavis, F.R. 49, 54, 57, 58, 60
Lefebvre, Henri 197
Lefranc, Georges 112, 117
Left Book Club 63
Leger, Fernand 71
leisure: and American progressivism 102, 103, 124, 125; as consumption 6, 7, 12, 13, 86, 153, 192; declining value of 136–43; and the Depression 135–43; domestic 101, 106, 117, 119, 141, 193, 200, 201; as an entitlement 78, 82, 116; future prospects for 199–204, 207–12; and the Left (European) 99, 100, 103–5, 111, 112, 117–22, 125, 126; and the New Deal 110, 111, 125, 126; organised, 1920–1940 99, 101–6, 111–16, 123–5; organised, after 1945 194, 195, 201–4; popular forms 123, 124, 126; and religion 103, 104, 113; and the Right (European) 99–103, 105, 106, 113, 120, 121; threat of 7, 10, 23, 24, 54, 57, 62, 187, 188, 190; as therapy 108; and totalitarianism 106, 107, 120, 125;

and unemployment 116, 117; and
  voluntarism 184, 197–200, 202,
  203; and women 100, 116, 117;
  and youth 101–5, 116, 117; *see
  also* consumption; democratic
  leisure; holidays; mass culture
leisure class 19, 158
leisure society 194
leisure studies 195
Lemire, Abbé 101
Leroy-Beaulieu, Anatole 19
Leverhulme, Lord 32
liberal arts education 61
libraries 109, 110
Liepmann, Kate 140
Lies, Eugene 108
Linder, Staffan 195
The Listener 113
Lloyd-George, David 15, 168
The Lonely Crowd 56, 188
Love on the Dole 147
Lowerson, John 115
Lundberg, George 56, 58, 169
Lynd, Robert and Helen 56–8, 72,
  133, 143, 148, 157, 159, 169

Macdonald, Dwight 73, 187
MacLeish, Archibald 70
Mais, S.P.B. 142
Malraux, André 202
Mann, Tom 32
'machinery of amusement' 53, 60
Marcuse, Herbert 194
marginalism 25, 26, 40, 128, 129
Marie, Pierre 104
Marienthal 137, 142
Marshall, Alfred 22, 23, 26, 27, 48
Marxism 18, 161, 198, 199, 210
mass culture: and Americanisation
  57–9, 71, 72; impresarios of 46,
  47, 116, 124, 126; and the Left
  111, 112, 126, 127, 209, 210; and
  mechanisation 55, 56, 188; and
  populism 62–74, 188, 189; and
  the Popular Front 70, 71, 111,
  112; *see also* consumerism,
  critiques of; consumption; leisure
Mass-Observation 63, 64, 68, 74,
  123, 139, 150, 177, 178, 181, 182
May, Elaine 192
Maynard, F.J. 35
McKibbin, Ross 137, 138
Means Test Man 141

mechanisation 50, 55
Mendras, Henri 203
Middletown 132, 143, 148, 159
Mill, J.S. 17, 83
Miller, Dan 161
Mitchell, Wesley 43
modernity 10, 21
Mogley, J.M. 172, 173
money: as alternative to free time
  129–36, 192, 193, 205, 206, 212;
  and scarcity 143, 144, 150;
  definition of 5; *see also* affluence;
  consumption; needs; time
money culture 158
Mother Jones 130
Moulton, Harold 85, 86
Mounier, Emmanuel 63
Mowrer, Edgar 58
Mumford, Lewis 34, 55, 62, 65, 71,
  171
Museums 109, 110
Mussolini Benito 90, 91

National Association of
  Manufacturers 16, 38, 39
National Conference of Employers'
  Organisations 89
National Council of Social Services
  113, 136, 137
National Industrial Recovery Act 84
National Recreation Association
  64, 109
needs: and the 'educator' 18, 24, 45;
  and free time 16–18, 22, 83;
  'natural' 17, 18, 22, 24, 43, 45,
  83, 156, 157, 202; 'unlimited'
  16–18, 25, 26, 34, 40, 43–4, 156–8,
  160, 190, 195; *see also*
  consumption and social
  emulation; 'democratic leisure';
  mass culture
Neomalthusianism 101; *see also*
  productivity and
  Neomalthusianism; working
  hours
New Deal 11, 44, 84, 85, 110, 111,
  136
new social movements 98, 200
Nizan, Paul 62
Nostrum, Paul 157
Nyland, Chris 130
Nystrom, Paul 40

occupational clubs 136, 137, 141, 143; *see also* community centres
Offe, Claus 201
Ogburn, William 52, 53, 108
Olympic Games 106
Ortega y Gasset, José 48, 51, 53
Orwell, George 49, 50, 64, 66, 68, 73, 74, 136, 137, 145
overproduction 38, 39, 42, 43; *see also* productivity
Overstreet, Henry 61

Packard, Vance 188, 194
Pahl, R. 201
Parker, Stanley 195
Pasquier, Léon 101
Patten, Simon 20, 23, 45
Pells, Richard 70
Philip, André 55, 62
Pilgrim Trust 150
Pitkin, Walter 39
Platonic 47
Playground Movement 107, 108
Le Populaire 112, 118, 119
Le Peuple 118
Popular Front 62, 63, 69, 70, 71, 92–4, 100, 111, 116, 117, 120, 135
populism *see* mass culture and populism
postmaterialism 201
postmodernity 177
Pratt, Henry 67
President's Research Committee on Recent Economic Changes 41
President's Research Committee on Social Trends 108
Priestley, J.B. 49, 54, 63, 68, 73, 74
privacy 126, 138–41, 150, 152, 167, 171–3, 178, 192, 204, 208; *see also* consumption, domestic; time and private life
productivism 28–30, 32–4, 38, 199
productivity: labour attitudes toward 3, 29–36, 77; and Neomalthusianism 31, 76, 88; stated needs 7, 9, 16, 23, 24, 34, 40, 88; and 'high wages' 3, 28–34, 39, 77, 133, 134; and worktime 3, 15, 24, 28–39, 77, 79, 128; *see also* high wages; needs; working hours
progressivism 51, 61; *see also* leisure and American progressivism

prohibition 101
Pruette, Lorine 23

radio 145, 173
Ramblers' Association 115
rational recreation 47, 99, 100, 107, 108, 124; *see also* democratic leisure
Regards 119
Revolt of the Masses 48
Rice, M.S. 142
Richards, John 172
Richards, Thomas 177
Riesman, David 157, 187–9
Rives, Paul 132
Road to Wigan Pier 68, 145
Robbins, Lionel 41, 42
Robertson, James 197
Robinson, John 192
Rojek, Chris 50
Roosevelt, Franklin D. 83, 84, 91, 95, 110
Rorty, James 68, 70
Ross, Andrew 201
Rostow, W.W. 190
Rousseau, J.J. 17, 18
Ruskin, John 18
Russell, Bertrand 62, 66, 87, 212

sabbatarianism 47, 101
Sangnier, Marc 116
scarcity 1, 13, 15, 20; as a spur to luxury 144, 145, 147, 153, 156; *see also* needs
Schor, Juliet 1, 207, 209
Schumacher, E.F. 197
scientific management 28, 29, 32, 36
Scott, Walter Dell 157
Scrutiny 60
seaside resorts 80, 96, 114, 115, 118, 177; *see also* Blackpool; holidays
Seidman, Michael 94, 125
Seldes, Gilbert 70, 71, 73, 188
Servan-Schreiber, J.-J. 191
short-hours movements *see* eight-hour day; forty-hour week
Simmel, Georg 158, 160, 161
social democracy 38
social emulation 3, 19, 23, 153, 158–60, 162, 163, 166, 170, 172, 179; *see also* consumption and social emulation
socialism 2, 36, 104, 112, 162

Soule, George 30, 194
Soviet Union 37, 88
Spanish Civil War 119
sport 100, 102–4, 106, 110, 120,
    201–3; *see also* leisure
Steiner, Jesse 145
Sternheim, A. 107
Stilgoe, John 171
suburbs 65, 167, 169–74, 188, 192;
    see also consumption, domestic;
    housing
Susman, Warren 157
Syndicats 111

Tarde, Jean Gabriel 21, 22, 45
Tawney, R. H. 15
Taylor, Frederick 28, 29, 32
technocracy 29, 34–6, 38, 44, 53, 54,
    65, 66; *see also* productivity
Technocracy Inc. 29
television 191, 193
The Times 91
thirty-five hour week 192, 205, 206;
    see also working hours
thirty-hour week 8, 83–6, 192, 194,
    205; *see also* working hours
Thomas, Albert 32, 35, 36, 77,
    105–7, 109, 112, 120
time: as anticipation 181; in cycles
    138, 139, 141, 182, 183;
    definition of 5; and gender roles
    141–3, 152, 156, 210, 211;
    holiday expressions of 176–83;
    markers of 176; market 139, 174;
    as memory 171–4, 180; as money
    4, 5, 7, 77, 87, 164, 167, 180,
    183, 192; in private life 136–40,
    174, 175; as routine 137–9, 143,
    164, 175, 176, 181; self-
    management of 185, 198, 199–202,
    211, 212; uses of 138–43, 174–6,
    180–3, 192, 193; value of 136–43,
    192, 193; *see also* holidays;
    money; weekend; working hours
trade union movement *see*
    American Federation of Labour;
    General Confederation of
    Labour; Trades Union Congress
Trades Union Congress (TUC) 32,
    81, 87, 91, 93, 206
Tugwell, Rexford 30, 35, 44
two-income couples 1

unemployment 12, 31, 32, 42, 43,
    79, 82, 116, 117, 135, 136, 197,
    203; psychology of 135–9, 141;
    from technological change 43,
    44, 79, 82, 87, 88, 197, 198, 204;
    see also full employment; time,
    value of
United Auto Workers 190
Urry, John 181, 183

Veblen, Thorstein 19, 21, 22, 23,
    34, 35, 40, 45, 162, 194, 196
Vendredi 69, 120
Verret, Michel 118
Victorian culture 47, 51, 56, 117
vitalism 103
Vu 118

wages: motivations for increase of
    128–36; *see also* money
Wagner Act 84
Walker, Louis 82, 86
Wandersee, Winifred 145, 150, 151
Webb, Beatrice 105
Weber, Louis 19, 21
weekend 12, 77, 88, 114, 174, 175
Wells, H.G. 67
Werner, Carol 176
Whyte, William 188, 194
Williams, Raymond 60, 188
Williams, Whiting 31
Wilson, Edmund 68
women 5, 49, 99, 141, 142; *see also*
    consumption and women;
    gender roles; leisure and women;
    time in private life
Woolworth's 179
work ethic 16, 22, 26, 34–7, 44, 49,
    142, 143, 157, 198
work, collapse of 197, 198
work and spend culture 5, 194, 203,
    212
workers *see* consumption; deskilling
    of labour; productivity: labour
    attitudes toward; wages; working
    hours; time: cycles of; uses of;
    trade-union movement
Workers' Education Association 60
Workers' Travel Association 115,
    116
working hours: American patterns
    82–7, 129, 130, 132, 204, 206;
    British patterns 87–92, 130, 133;

employer attitudes toward 10, 15, 37, 38, 82, 85, 87, 89, 91, 92, 94, 95, 98, 131, 132, 207; determinants of 78, 128, 129; French patterns 89–91, 92–5, 129, 132; international aspects of 78, 87, 88, 90–2, 94, 98, 206, 207; and marginalism 25, 26, 128; motivation for the reduction of 128–36; since 1945 204–6; and Neomalthusianism 29, 31, 88; and policy making 82–6, 90–2, 94, 95, 98, 184, 185, 207, 212; and productivity 15, 24, 30–2, 37, 83, 88, 90, 197, 205; wage-earners' approach to 11, 76–9, 83, 87–9, 91–4, 190, 192, 193, 197; and work sharing 83, 84, 87, 130, 184, 185, 197, 198, 205, 212; *see also* productivity; short-hour movements; time, uses of; worktime

World War I 3, 6, 15, 26–9, 99, 129, 168, 184
World War II 6, 92, 126, 184
World's Fair (New York) 182

Xenos, Nicholas 26

Yonnet, P. 191

Zweig, F. 147, 179